John Dryden

FOUR COMEDIES

Curtain Playwrights

GENERAL EDITOR
R. C. Bald

John Dryden

FOUR COMEDIES

Edited by

L. A. Beaurline and Fredson Bowers

The University of Chicago Press

CHICAGO AND LONDON

Library of Congress Catalog Card Number: 66-30800

THE UNIVERSITY OF CHICAGO PRESS, CHICAGO & LONDON
The University of Toronto Press, Toronto 5, Canada

Preface

The purpose of this edition is to present as accurate a text as possible of some of Dryden's best comedies and tragicomedies, with the hope that they will receive more attention than they have in recent years. Dryden the poet has come to be justly esteemed, and his heroic plays seem to have a continuing fascination for a small number of readers. But, aside from *Marriage a-la-Mode*, his comedies are virtually ignored, and if they are read, in the old Scott and Saintsbury edition or in the eccentric edition by Montague Summers, they are frequently misunderstood. When L. C. Knights said that he found *Sir Martin Mar-All* the stupidest play he had ever read, we should wonder about the expectations that he brought to his reading and his basic capacity to enjoy farcical comedy. Therefore it has seemed necessary to include some introductory remarks and to supply some basic information as well as critical observations. The introductions, however, have been kept as brief as possible, especially since we do not wish to duplicate the elaborately annotated edition of Dryden in progress from the University of California Press.

Professor Bowers prepared the texts and the textual notes, although I made a few alterations and read the final page-proof. The introductions and the glosses are largely my work, but, of course, I am greatly indebted to other writers. Some of the general introduction is based on a draft by Mr. Bowers, especially the comments on Dryden's view of comedy; its final form, however, was my responsibility. The work of N. B. Allen on Dryden's sources has been very useful, even though I disagree with him about the closeness of the plays to their alleged sources. And I have freely drawn upon the insight of John Harrington Smith in his excellent study of the gay couple, perhaps the best book on Restoration comedy. In the commentary the definitions of words come from the Oxford English Dictionary unless otherwise specified.

The National Portrait Gallery kindly allowed the reproduction of the portrait of Nell Gwyn, and The Folger Shakespeare Library, The Newberry Library, and The University of Chicago Library permitted the duplication of title pages from their Dryden collections. I am especially grateful to my wife, who generously helped prepare the glosses, and to John Freehafer and Arthur Kirsch, for many excellent suggestions about the introductions.

L.A.B.

Contents

Abbreviations

Q   quarto

F   folio, *The Comedies Tragedies and Operas* written by John Dryden, 1701

Cibber   *An Apology for the Life of Mr. Colley Cibber*, edited by Robert W. Lowe, 1889

Downes   John Downes, *Roscius Anglicanus; or, An Historical Review of the Stage*, edited by Montague Summers, 1928

Essays   *Of Dramatic Poesy and Other Essays*, edited by George Watson, 1962

Farmer   John S. Farmer and W. E. Henley, *Slang and Its Analogues*, 1890–1904

Macd   Hugh Macdonald, *Dryden: a Bibliography*, 1939

Noyes   *Selected Dramas of John Dryden*, edited by George R. Noyes, 1910

OED   *The Oxford English Dictionary*, 1888–1928

S-S   *The Works of John Dryden*, edited by Sir Walter Scott, revised and corrected by George Saintsbury, 1882–93

Summers   *Dryden: The Dramatic Works*, edited by Montague Summers, 1931

Sutherland   *Marriage a la Mode*, edited by J. R. Sutherland, 1934

W & M   Gertrude L. Woodward and James G. McManaway, *A Check List of English Plays 1641–1700*, 1945

General Introduction

The ladies and gentlemen of the Restoration liked a disguise above all things. In assuming a masquerade, they felt themselves to have taken on another identity the more freely to commit those adventurous and sexually daring deeds that fulfilled their dreams of an ideal experience, within the forms of conventional society. They wanted to be very knowing, to penetrate the disguises of others, themselves remaining undetected. Disguise provided the perfect dramatic mode for the display of wit, which could exercise itself freely within the limits of social inhibitions, and could be at once bold and daring without arousing guilty feelings. In this way, a man and lady of genuine feeling could play the game of masquerade in earnest, using the social forms, affectations, manners, stylish talk, and stylish taste as a kind of stalking horse, a means of expressing some of their most personal emotions in this publicly licensed way. But in the same mode they could also mock others and, at times, even mock themselves, assured that they knew what was what and who was who, even though they chose to play this silly game. Occasionally they recognized that they were caught by the forms themselves or by forces greater than they could resist. The usual manner, however, expressed an exciting tension between knowledge and superficiality, between liberty and restraint, as two of the cavaliers see the masquerade in *Marriage a-la-Mode*.

> *Rhodophil.* I believe it was invented first by some jealous Lover, to discover the haunts of his Jilting Mistris; or, perhaps, by some distressed servant, to gain an opportunity with a jealous man's wife.
> *Palamede.* No, it must be the invention of a woman, it has so much of subtilty and love in it.
> *Rhodophil.* I am sure 'tis extremely pleasant; for to go unknown, is the next degree to going invisible.
> *Palamede.* What with our antique habits, and feign'd voices, do you know me? and I know you? methinks we move and talk just like so many over-grown Puppets. . . . Masquerade is Vizor-masque in debauch; and I like it the better for't: for, with a Vizor-masque, we fool our selves into courtship, for the sake of an eye that glanc'd; or a hand that stole it self out of the glove sometimes, to give us a sample of the skin: but in Masquerade there is nothing to be known, she's all *Terra incognita*, and the bold discoverer leaps ashoar, and takes his lot among the wild *Indians* and *Salvages*,

without the vile consideration of safety to his person,
or of beauty, or wholesomeness in his Mistris.

[IV.i.122–44.]

A much talked about escapade of the Earl of Rochester was
his pose as Alexander Bendo, an Italian mountebank, who
dispensed medicine, interpreted dreams, and cast horoscopes
on Tower Hill for several days in 1675–76. Dressed in an "old
overgrown Green Gown which he religiously wore in
Memory of Rabelais his Master . . . lyned through with
exotick furrs of divers colours, and Antique Cap, a great
Reverend Beared,"[1] Doctor Bendo played the role that may
very well have been suggested by Dryden's *Mock Astrologer*.
Ladies, wearing their masks and behaving like overgrown
puppets, came to the plays to see women acting their parts as
well as disguising as men, as Nell Gwyn did in the part of
Florimell. Pepys could not get over his delight in her maneuver
in Act V of *Secret Love*: "So great a performance of a comical
part was never, I believe, in the world before as Nell do this,
both as a mad girle, then most and best of all when she comes
in like a young gallant; and hath the motions and carriage of a
spark the most that ever I saw any man have. It makes me, I
confess, admire her."[2]

Restoration life imitated art as much as art imitated life,
and both art and life put a high value upon self-conscious,
extraordinary, or even outrageous behavior. The meaning of
this phenomenon is difficult to interpret; it is a curious combination of boldness and inhibition, secrecy and exhibitionism.
It was as if the traditional festivity of masking had become an
emblem of sophisticated life and of genteel comedy. Ulti-
mately, I suppose, it was the problem of combining artifice
with feeling. How could one live the urbane life and also
satisfy his inmost human needs? How could one combine
affectation with sincerity, or self-analysis with spontaneity?
Nowhere do we find these dilemmas more vigorously
expressed than in Dryden's comedies, and consequently, his
comedies provide the most instructive introduction to the
comic drama of his time.

II

Some of our puzzlement about Dryden and Restoration
comedy comes from Dryden's own casualness about his work.
He, like most of his genteel contemporaries, insisted that
comedy was beneath his full talent. Comedies were dashed off

[1] Quoted by Vivian de Sola Pinto, in his *Enthusiast of Wit* (1962),
p. 85.
[2] *Diary*, ed. Wheatley, March 2, 1666–67.

to satisfy public taste by men who had better things to do. So it pleased Dryden, throughout his literary career to deprecate his interest in comic writing. One of his plainest and most disarming statements appears in his *Defence of an Essay of Dramatic Poesy*:

> I confess my chief endeavours are to delight the age in which I live. If the humour of this be for low comedy, small accidents, and raillery, I will force my genius [i.e., his tutelary spirit] to obey it, though with more reputation I could write in verse. I know I am not so fitted by nature to write comedy: I want that gaiety of humour which is required to it. My conversation is slow and dull; my humour saturnine and reserved; in short, I am none of those who endeavour to break jests in company, or make repartees. So that those, who decry my comedies, do me no injury, except it be in point of profit: reputation in them is the last thing to which I shall pretend.[3]

The tone of the prologues and epilogues to his comedies betrays an offhand and jocular attitude toward himself and his plays. In complaisance to the audience, like a civil husband, he endeavors "To write in pain, and counterfeit a bliss Like the faint smackings of an after kiss."[4] This looks like the posing of a jaunty poet.

In the preface to *An Evening's Love* he wrote, "Neither, indeed, do I value a reputation gain'd from Comedy, so far as to concern my self about it any more than I needs must in my own defence: for I think it, in it's own nature, inferior to all sorts of Dramatick writing" (ll. 17–20). The distinction between the two forms of drama and his writing comedies merely to earn a living are again enforced in the *Defence*:

> The humour of the people is now for comedy; therefore, in hope to please them, I write comedies rather than serious plays: and so far their taste prescribes to me: but it does not follow from that reason, that comedy is to be preferred before tragedy in its own nature; for that which is so in its own nature cannot be otherwise, as a man cannot but be a rational creature: but the opinion of the people may alter, and in another age, or perhaps in this, serious plays may be set up above comedies. [I, 120.]

As a professional man of letters, then, Dryden openly followed public taste, even though he felt a certain tension between timeless literary value and contemporary taste, and he admitted that in modern as in ancient times tragedy was

[3] *Of Dramatic Poesy and Other Critical Essays*, ed. Watson (1962), I, 116.
[4] Prologue to *An Evening's Love*, ll. 9–10.

the superior literary form and the genre in which his talents could be best exhibited. The usual comparisons he made between tragedy and comedy give some hint about his reasons. As he remarks in the *Essay,* " 'tis comedy, where the persons are only of common rank, and their business private, not elevated by passions or high concernments, as in serious plays" (I, 74). In a serious play, "the plot, the characters, the wit, the passions, the descriptions, are all exalted above the level of common converse, as high as the imagination of the poet can carry them, with proportion to versimility," whereas comedy is "the imitation of common persons and oridnary speaking" (I, 87). Or in the *Defence,* "the action, character, and language of tragedy would still be great and high; that of comedy lower and more familiar; admiration [i.e., wonder] would be the delight of one, and satire of the other" (I, 119).

These statements associating tragedy with great characters, high sentiments, and noble actions, of chief appeal to the judicious, and comedy with ordinary life, of delight to the vulgar, derive from classical sources and were the common-places of the age. Dryden would normally have accepted the theory, no matter what his literary practice was. That he was himself "sullen" (meaning only not gay and light-spirited) in disposition and so not naturally suited to comedy, as he asserted, loses a little force when we find him acknowledging that his idol Ben Jonson's genius "was too sullen and saturnine" to portray love scenes or those of high passion. Moreover, it is noteworthy that throughout almost every discourse of dra-matic writing, although devoting much more time to the theory of tragedy, when he got down to particulars, he chose his practical examples from comedy. The Elizabethans whom he most admired—Shakespeare, Jonson, Beaumont and Fletcher—he almost invariably discussed in terms of comedy. In the preface to *An Evening's Love,* when he launches on an analysis of comedy that best speaks admiration, once the con-ventional protestations are over, Dryden the craftsman seems to be writing. (But even so, there is a curious contradiction between the theory of the preface and the practice of the play.) When his total pronouncements are surveyed and supplemented by his practice, the conclusion is hard to avoid that if comedy had been commonly esteemed an art form worthy of the most serious criticism, Dryden would have defended it and his own comedies with pleasure and candor.

Indeed, it seems evident that Dryden's reservations about comedy came from the low opinion of laughter he inherited from Ben Jonson. Writing for gentlemen as he was bound to do, with all the appeal to a discriminating audience that this implies, Dryden was contemptuous to find his spectators as easily moved to laughter by absurd extravagance as by nature satirized. Insofar as idle laughter triggered by farce was not admirable, the dramatist who catered to low comedy produced unworthy art and demeaned himself as a man of literature. Unfortunately, since it could be provoked by bad as easily as by good art, the laughter of the audience was no criterion of excellence and certainly not the most praiseworthy reaction that comedy could produce. This disparagement of laughter bulked large in Dryden's thinking and accounts for much of his self-criticism. To that extent Dryden's pride may be said to have produced his disclaimers.

Yet this attitude by no means implies that he thought his comedies were hackwork. Although in practice he often invented extravagant situations like the final scene of *An Evening's Love*, according to his own lights, he never forsook the theory of the naturalness of character. Character, in his view, was the foundation of dramatic art. Moreover, the evidence is clear that he devoted much thought to the art of comedy in constructing his plays and, indeed, in a highly original manner adapted the materials available to him with such power that he created something very close to the ideal forms that Restoration dramatists were to employ with the greatest success in farce, high comedy, and tragicomedy.

His own theory was founded on an admiration for Ben Jonson and the comic theory of humours; his practice on Fletcherean comedy and tragicomedy. Dryden prided himself on his management of plot, but he never assumed that plot was the focus of comic theory. In his criticism of classical comedy, he objected strenuously to the similarity of plots, especially in Roman comedy, and to the narrowness of the type characters who moved within these stories. On the other hand, in his own day he was moved to combat the popularity of the "Spanish Plot" comedy, like *The Adventures of Five Hours*, which depended on extreme complexity of plotting and on multiplicity of exciting incidents not necessarily placed in any coherent order. In both instances, it may seem, he objected when the nature of the plot was such that it interfered with the presentation of varied characters drawn from experience. It can be said quite firmly that Dryden's comic art recognized plot as the summation of actions appropriate for given characters, and not as an interest independent of character. Thus he always returned in his thinking and in his practice to character as a source of the comic wit that justified the form as literature.

One important element of character adapted from his great model Ben Jonson was the operation of the humours. Jonson defined a humour as a semimedical or psychological state that irresistibly seized on a man and forced all his "effects" (what Dryden called his "inclinations") into one channel. It usurped all other interests and colored all other concerns, so that this fixation, or strongly individualistic force in a character, was the source of all his thought and action. This theory of comic character freed Jonson from the narrow dependence on Roman stock characters whose dramatic usefulness had already been fully exploited.

Decorum is the moving principle of Roman comedy. According to this principle, characters always think and behave in accord with what is suitable for their condition and their place in society. An old man is supposed to be appreciative of the wisdom he has derived from experience and distrustful of youth; he should be suspicious, easily deceived, inclined to be loquacious, overcareful of family position and wealth, conservative and opposed to chance. A young man is supposed to be ardent, generous, brave, and ruled in his actions more by his emotions than by his reason. Such characteristics are universal, appearing in the cottage as well as in the manor house, and Horace, as interpreted by Renaissance critics, lent the weight of his authority to the whole theory. Decorum, moreover, was extended to various pursuits. A merchant was supposed to be prudent, cautious, peaceable; a soldier valiant, quarrelsome, honorable. Thus character of all trades and occupations became codified. It was as indecorous for a merchant to swagger like a bravo as for a swineherd to possess a refined sensibility. When an apparent opposite to the system was exhibited for satirical purposes, as in the person of the braggart soldier who was actually a coward, it was usually made clear that the person was, in fact, not a soldier at all. Thomas Rymer's criticism, which most fully developed the theory of decorum in English, is an unwitting caricature of the idea.

Since the actions of private men, the only suitable persons for comedy, were to concern common errors of ordinary life, with the intent by laughter to purge the audience of similar errors that it harbored, a considerable emphasis was put on the commonplace in character and in illustrative action. In order to put the fewest obstructions in the way of the audience's delight in complicated action full of sudden turns and surprises, the Romans relied exclusively on stock characters. These were established in their various types and temperaments by the principle of decorum, their underlying uniformity made palatable only by variations in the plot formula. The dramatist's observation of life went little deeper than this codification.

The Elizabethan love of variety was antagonistic to such formal consistency; and as the early drama grew more secularized, and the religious moral intent more ostensible than real, the degeneration of high seriousness in content was accompanied inevitably by degeneration in the consistency of word and action in the characters, if the entertainment of the audience was thereby served. In fact, one of the glories of the period was the constant pressure to break through the bland molds of type character and standardized plot. The danger lay in the disintegration of all form at the whim of the dramatist. Ben Jonson's humour comedy, therefore, was as much an attempt to seek out a new formula to prevent excesses of comic practice as it was an endeavor to found a new principle that would enlarge the tradition of decorum in the direction of needed variety.

Decorum and its type formulas are usually associated with an emphasis on manners, or a picture of ways of life, as represented in the adjustment of character to social position, or occupation, and customs. By focusing on and thus intensifying somewhat more general attributes found within the decorous characters of classical comedy, Jonson made a certain number of minor adaptations. In *Every Man in his Humour*, the elder Knowell is the overcareful father of Roman comedy, a figure of complete decorum for his age and station. The trace of humour in him stems chiefly from the fixation he has about the behavior of his son. Brainworm is a slightly modified clever slave. But in characters like Kitely or Justice Clement something new has been added. The irascibility of Clement is not necessarily associated with his position as justice of the peace, and his private amusement at the opportunities furnished by the powers of his office is very much an individual touch. Kitely is interesting because in type he is a merchant, peaceable, concerned with profit in trading and in upholding all the bourgeois virtues; but in humour he is an irrationally jealous man, an attribute that is by no means confined to the mercantile life. The shell of decorum, thus, is vitally expanded by packing into him personal attributes that have little or nothing to do with the attributes of his profession. His comic actions may be judged according to the ideas of what was suitable for a jealous man to do or say; but these have no connection with the more formal concept of decorous actions and words suitable for a merchant. Thus Jonson interchanges one concept for the other, back and forth; but only on a single occasion of deliberate tension, when Kitely's need to shadow his wife interferes with a profitable business deal, does Jonson make dramatic use of a conflict between them.

In *Epicoene*, critics are correct in taking Morose to be a creature of some social significance, and to that extent he is a figure of decorum in the character of a recluse. But the outrageousness of his humour about noise quite overshadows the general relationship of man and manners in society as reflected in his withdrawal from human intercourse. Jonson has, in effect, created a psychological and moral figure, more than a social one. Then he further complicated him by having Morose step out of his humour in order to marry; this brings on all his new troubles and becomes the mainspring of the plot.

In sum, although in various of their manifestations the humours that dominated Elizabethan comedy reinforced the theory of decorum in manners, as in the model comedy *Eastward Ho*, nevertheless the seeds of character interest that drove humours away from types and toward portraits of individualized fixations substituted another rationale to displace classical decorum: the rationale of inner faithfulness to a coherent psychology, encouraging an audience to treat a character as an individual on his own terms. Of course, dramatic characters are never fully developed or round characters such as we find in novels like *Middlemarch* or *Anna Karenina*, but they can present, through talented acting, an illusion of some inner dynamic, some unifying trait that seems to be the source of all their behavior. And it is natural that this should have happened in the seventeenth century, when religion was being internalized and philosophy was turning to psychology. Men began to keep diaries, so that they could examine themselves daily, in an effort to find signs of election. This self-scrutiny, a kind of inner time-and-motion study, lent itself nicely to the soliloquy and became a regular feature of Restoration drama.

The terrible picture of Harry Dampit in Middleton's *Trick to Catch the Old One* goes far beyond any contribution that the theory of decorum ever made to the type of a usurer. Correspondingly, the great dramatic character of Sir Giles Overreach in Massinger's *New Way to Pay Old Debts* suggests an internal rationale that transcends the usurer of stage tradition. The tendency of Elizabethan comedy, as it developed after Jonson, was therefore to free itself from the limitation of formal decorum as a dramatic principle and substitute the inner coherence in its own terms of observation, a rationale that places decorum on a raised level of truth to nature unknown in its classical antecedents except in the most general terms.

The line of development was clearly seen by Dryden, who rejected the French imitation of convention in classical plot and characterization and opted for the English love of variety. But going deeper than the professional playwright's desire to please an audience accustomed to varied experience was his own artistic recognition that decorum alone, without the assistance of some other principle, inhibited the development of dramatic characterization necessary to provide depth as well as richness to comedy, and that characterization alone separated comedy from low farce.

III

In the process of developing his critical views, Dryden redefined Jonson's idea of humour, identifying it as a "ridiculous extravagance of conversation, wherein one man differs from all others" (I, 72), and more pointedly, "by humour is meant some extravagant habit, passion, or affection, particular . . . to some one person, by oddness of which he is immediately distinguished from the rest of men; which being lively and naturally represented, most frequently begets that malicious pleasure in the audience which is testified by laughter" (I, 73). We do not have to look far in his plays for examples of extravagant habits, passions, and affections, or extravagances of conversation. But it should not be surprising that Dryden could not make his characters complete individuals, different from all others. In the task of making actable plays, he, like any other playwright, had to create recognizable characters in order to make them effective and intelligible to an audience. A true individual on the stage would not be sufficiently heightened; his speech would not be defined sharply enough, and his unpredictable behavior would confuse every scene.[5] It seems clear that individuals may be found approximated in novels, but drama does not have enough scope to include a fully round character. If a playwright makes a stage figure somewhat divided in his loyalties, somewhat driven by an inner need, and considerably vigorous in his speech, as Jonson did, he goes about as far as the comic stage will allow.

Dryden's Sir Martin Mar-All, for instance, imagines that he is clever; there is no doubt his fixation. But he seems to have other dimensions, other inclinations that are driven by his humour: a kind of grandiose feeling, "the heart of an Emperour and the brains of a Cobbler" (III.iii.17–18), which makes him more attractive and "good natured" than a mere lout would be. As an extension of his self-delusion, he has pretensions to honor and chivalry, for he will not tell a lie, he wishes to show his valor to his mistress, and he hates to see unfair combat. He would have Warner lie at his feet like a spaniel, in recognition of his knighthood. Although his honesty and great heart actually foil most of Warner's schemes, these are the traits that endear him to the audience and make him worthy of marrying happily. Such complications in Sir Martin are necessary for the play to hold together and help explain why Warner has not left his service even before the curtain opens.

The same kinds of mixed feelings are generated by Melan-

[5] See Harold Rosenberg, "Character Change and the Drama" in *The Tradition of the New* (1959), 135–50.

tha, in *Marriage a-la-Mode*, whose humour impels her to push herself forward into courtly society, which is beyond her birth. Because of the way Dryden presents her, with so much self-awareness and unaffected candor (as in III.i.108–15 and 268–92), we, along with Palamede, cannot fail to be sympathetic. Her compulsive behavior is so delightfully parodied, and she so frankly admits that Palamede has beat her at her own game, that we believe in her almost as in a real person. Although we recognize her as the female fop, we infer some extra dimensions to her character, some inner spirit, a divided soul, driven by desire but conscious of her folly. It is the illusion of her inner dynamic that has contributed to this effect.

The force of the part may be seen in Cibber's description of Mrs. Mountfort, acting in a revival.

> Melantha is as finish'd an impertinent as ever flutter'd in a drawing-room, and seems to contain the most compleat system of female foppery that could possibly be crowded into the tortured form of a fine lady. Her language, dress, motion, manners, soul, and body, are in a continual hurry to be something more than is necessary or commendable. And though I doubt it will be a vain labour to offer you a just likeness of Mrs. *Monfort*'s action, yet the fantastick impression is still strong in my memory that I cannot help saying something, tho' fantastically, about it. The first ridiculous airs that break from her are upon a gallant never seen before, who delivers her a letter from her father recommending him to her good graces as an honourable lover. Here now, one would think, she might naturally shew a little of the sexe's decent reserve, tho' never so slightly cover'd! No, sir; not a little of it; modesty is the virtue of a poor-soul'd country gentlewoman; she is too much a court lady to be under so vulgar a confusion; she reads the letter, therefore, with a careless, dropping lip and an erected brow, humming it hastily over as if she were impatient to outgo her father's commands by making a compleat conquest of him at once; and that the letter might not embarrass her attack, crack! she crumbles it at once into her palm and pours upon him her whole artillery of airs, eyes, and motion; down goes her dainty, divining body to the ground, as if she were sinking under the conscious load of her own attractions; then launches into a flood of fine language and compliment, still playing her chest forward in fifty falls and risings, like a swan upon waving water; and, to complete her impertinence, she is so rapidly fond of her own wit that she will not give her lover leave to praise it: silent assenting bows and vain endeavours to speak are all the share of the conversation he is admitted to, which at

last he is relieved from by her engagement to half a score visits, which she swims from him to make, with a promise to return in a twinkling.

[Cibber, *Apology*, I, 227–28.]

Dryden's most important contribution to comic characterization, however, went beyond the strict humour theory, but it seems to presuppose the inner dynamic of character that he learned from the humour tradition. In the epilogue to the second part of *The Conquest of Granada*, he speaks slightingly of the "mechanic humour" shown in Jonson's comedies, suited to that less gallant age, and in the "Defence of the Epilogue" (1672) he feels compelled to observe the "errors" of the poets of the last age. Although he admits his admiration for Elizabethan dramatists, he criticizes them "that poetry may not go backward, when all other arts and sciences are advancing" (I, 169). It is his part to make clear "that the language, wit, and conversation of our age are improved and refined above the last; and then it will not be difficult to infer that our plays have received some part of those advantages" (I, 170). Jonson's characters lack the "air and gaiety" of a Restoration gentleman; Truewit, the best of them, "was a scholar-like kind of man, a gentleman with an allay of pedantry, a man who seems mortified to the world by much reading. The best of his discourse is drawn not from the knowledge of the town, but books" (I, 180). Jonson's humours, good enough in themselves, seem to imitate "the meanness of . . . persons. Gentlemen will not be entertained with the follies of each other: and though they allow Cob and Tib to speak properly, yet they are not much pleased with their tankard or with their rags: and surely their conversation can be no jest to them on the theatre, when they would avoid it in the street" (I, 182). Therefore it has been generally accepted that Dryden endeavored in his comedies and tragicomedies to represent the "gallantry and civility" of his own age, displayed by wit; but the matter is not that simple.

As early as the *Essay of Dramatic Poesy* Dryden implied that not humour but wit was the distinguishing quality of Falstaff's character, although he was a "bundle of humours" nevertheless. This implies that Dryden thought both humour and wit could be present in a character, and, I think, such was his discovery about comic figures. The result was a combination of admirable wit and ridiculous folly in the same person, thus creating a delicate balance between an audience's sympathy and laughter. Few playwrights aside from Shakespeare had succeeded in this high art before Dryden, but he seems to have drawn upon what tradition there was. Shaping two almost original and vital characters, he set the pattern for the best comedy of the following thirty-three years. In the hands of lesser playwrights, they became rigid types as much as those under the ancient decorum, but from Dryden's hands the "gay couple", as they are now called, burst into life with all their exuberance, wit, and self-mockery. As John Harrington Smith has ably shown, railing and antagonistic lovers may be found in Shakespeare's Beatrice and Benedick or in Petrucio and Kate, as well as in a half dozen of Beaumont and Fletcher's and Shirley's plays. Sexual antagonism was a normal part of the enormously popular romances, such as D'Urfé's *L'Astrée*, and of the Cavalier drama. Dryden's *Wild Gallant* (1663) was an unsuccessful adaptation of the Fletcherean rake who was pursued by a clever woman. In James Howard's *The English Mounsieur* (*ca.* 1663), Wellbred and the teasing widow Lady Wealth maneuvered for advantage over each other through several acts. He impudently woos her, always avoiding a betrayal of his real feelings and always "keeping his humour" while he is irresistibly drawn into marriage. In Etherege's *The Comical Revenge* (1664) the same pair exhibited a more pronounced antiromantic bias, burlesquing romantic love, and playing tricks on each other. Dryden, however, changed the conventional merry widow into a pert young maiden, Florimell (in *Secret Love*, 1667), an intelligent and quick-witted, emancipated, and facetious woman; rigorously independent, endowed with strong feelings, and with a special admiration for a man of spirit. Unlike Beatrice, she knows what her true feelings are, but she masks them and mocks them.

Celadon, like Florimell, exudes self-confidence. His humour is that of a free spirit, and he is a man of enormous sexual appetite. "Constant to one!" he exclaims incredulously, "I have been a Courtier, a Souldier, and a Traveller, to good purpose, if I must be constant to one; give me some Twenty, some Forty, some a Hundred Mistresses; I have more Love than any one Woman can turn her to" (I.i.71–75). Thus Celadon immediately identifies himself as a libertine, one who is satisfied by variety alone.

The "witty" Marquis, in Madeleine de Scudéry's *Ibrahim*,[6] explains the philosophical view of the character and explicitly relates it to the theory of humours. All men, the Marquis says, should not be subordinated to one moral law, because the one true code of behavior is so "difficult to be known, as he who thinks he hath found it is oftentimes further from it than others, which without judging soveraignly of any thing simply, follow sense wherewith Nature hath inspired them."

---

[6] This volume is thought to be one of Dryden's sources for *Secret Love*, but so far as I know, the Marquis' comments have not hitherto been cited in connection with Dryden's gay couple. The first English edition was 1652; I quote from the 1674 edition, part II, Book I, pp. 104–5.

In truth, the inclinations of a man are the sources of much of his morality, and men differ so widely in their humours that no single standard applies to all. As a proof, we should observe the contrast of behavior of men of different humours. The melancholy lover may prefer to complain and sigh, but the same circumstances will make the merry lover laugh and write gallant verses. What causes the one to weep would cure the other of his passion. One would rave in conversing, wearying others and making his mistress hate him, while the other talks always of delights, to inspire her heart with joy, so he might introduce love into it, "to whom the painters do always give a bed of flowers, without ever laying him on thorns." Rather than urging his passion to her "by the langours" of his face, he would "show her so much satisfaction in [his] eyes, as she might very well perceive that her dominion would be pleasing." A man of an anxious humour would meditate murder if his mistress gave him cause for jealousy; a jolly man, on such an occasion, would "mock at his Mistress and his Rival." Therefore we see that "the diversity of humours of the body contributes much to our apprehensions; and that one and the same thing is seen after a quite different manner." Since Jupiter predominates the liberal lover, he must fulfill his destiny.[7] He must cultivate gracefulness, vivacity of spirit, fire which sparkles in the eye of a lover, respect, care, cajoleries, verses, music, and dancing; and although there may be one principle of good behavior, "yet we do oftentimes form many according to our fancy," and as we change temperament, we change our values. Therefore it is not surprising that a libertine loves whimsically, admiring one woman for her hair, another for her eyes, and a third for her lips. Perfect form, like perfect morals, cannot be found in this world, so the skeptics appear to settle for a fragmentary and momentary satisfaction.

Celadon clearly acts this part, with some additional complications, for he seems to be the careless rake who cannot be touched by loyalty or deep feeling; but beneath the stylish dress there is some inner force, some unpredictable power. When he is tempted to visit his lesser mistresses, Celadon admits, in an aside: "Now cannot I forbear and I should be damn'd, though I have scap'd a scouring so lately for it. Yet I love *Florimell* better then both of 'em together;—there's the Riddle o'nt: but onely for the sweet sake of variety" (III.i.425–28). Love is a mystery to him, a great riddle of definite heroic overtones, mixed with physical gratification, and reverberating with self-mockery. After Florimell reproaches him,

---

[7] It therefore seems appropriate that the amorous gallant, Jupiter, in Dryden's *Amphytrion* (1690) should enunciate libertine views. See Act I, scene i, Jupiter's opening speeches.

"Could you kiss [other women], though but once, and ne're think of me?" he half seriously replies, "Nay if I had thought of thee, I had kiss'd 'em over a thousand times, with the very force of imagination. . . . You are my Sultana Queen, the rest are but in the nature of your Slaves; I may take some slight excursion into the Enemies Country for forage or so, but I ever return to my head quarters" (III.i.404–14). And if Florimell were to rob him of his mistresses, he would grow "desperately constant" and all the tempest of his love would fall upon her head.

This talk may be interpreted as playful raillery; however, the serious implications of a mutual passion between Celadon and Florimell seem to grow with their later speeches. In spite of their fierce independence, like other gay couples, they feel impelled to take the great risk and to marry. Their greatest fear is that the "clashing and cloying", the "dullness and faintness" of marriage will kill their love, a passion too great for confinement in a conventional institution. Instead they will try to extend courtship into marriage, be married by the agreeable names of "Mistress and Gallant." A mixture of seriousness and self-parody comes out of Celadon's remark, "Well, if it be my fortune to be made a Cuckold, I had rather thou shoustld make me one then any one in Sicily: and for my comfort I shall have thee oftner then any of thy servants" (V.i.582–85). This is his high-spirited way of saying he loves her dearly, as dearly as Philocles loves his Asteria. For Celadon and Florimell, love is too whimsical, too evanescent, and too imaginative to be understood; it can only be cherished and heightened by constant variety, contrast, and difficulty. For that reason they feel they must perpetuate the love duel. The same interesting mixture of cynicism and belief, freedom and conscious control is found in the gay couples in *An Evening's Love* and *Marriage a-la-Mode*. Like most self-styled libertines, they maintain a naïve fidelity to an ideal love. Earthly women only approximate the perfect love, but the best to be found is a brilliant woman who conceals her feelings enough to tantalize imagination. As long as the lover is in doubt about what lies beneath her mask, he can still hope that she embodies perfection. This makes her an equal match of her cavalier.

It is conventional among critics to denounce these Restoration heroes and heroines as immoral, pursuing sex without love, not even adhering to the double standard. But in Dryden's plays as well as in Congreve's this is surely a misunderstanding. Modern readers are forgetting the code of the times—that one should never seem to be serious. And we forget that the heroines and heroes, often in asides, admit their genuine feelings. Florimell says, "Well if this is true may I die with my maidenhead," and Millamant admits, "Well, if

Mirabell should not make a good husband, I am a lost thing,—
for I find I love him violently." There can be no doubt that
they took their love seriously; else why would they have
bothered with one woman so long? In spite of their pretended
nonchalance and their principles of liberty, in spite of their
desperate desire to be skeptical and cynical, they fall hope-
lessly in love. Their high spirits are a sign that they are doubly
vulnerable to the mysterious darts of love; for they are
already predisposed to fall. They begin by being drunk with
the idea of love, as Sir John Suckling put it, in the language of
a gentleman,

> Make me but mad enough, give me good store
> Of Love, for her I Court,
>> I ask no more,
> 'Tis love in love that makes the sport.
>>>> ["Sonnet II," *Fragmenta Aurea*, 1646.]

But since love is an evanescent thing, a whimsical and precious
gift that comes by free grace and goes almost as quickly, the
state of being in love is a delicate condition of the imagination.
A man dreams of his ideal mistress, he hears her described, he
sees her masked or under a false identity. These "taking" suggestions are what excite the fancy and start the sport.

A true lover must use all of his wit to sustain his passion as
long as possible, by not seeming to spill it out all at once;
hence the need for a masquerade to supply the social form that
is inside conventional mores but is liberating enough to allow
spontaneity. The heroine is honest, but she must pretend to be
licentious enough to lure the hero; therefore marriage becomes a necessity, for fruition is, after all, a proper goal of
love. Genuinely loose women, like Mrs. Loveit in *The Man
of Mode*, Sylvia in *The Old Bachelor*, or Mrs. Marwood in *The
Way of the World*, are treated with great harshness in the plays
of the time. But the chaste woman in the gay couple is
respectable and daring, dancing on the brink of danger; her
wit is her salvation from disaster. If she wants a man,

> she must take him in marriage, not otherwise. This makes
> marriage preëminently the business of the woman; and
> occasionally she may be perceived in the act of steering
> the affair, behaving like a heroine in a play by Shaw. But
> it does not do to make too much of this difference
> [between her and the hero]. Since society has decreed the
> forms in accordance with which the family shall be
> established and perpetuated, it is the destiny of the
> Restoration gallant to marry, no less than the Restoration
> lady. Here lies, it seems to me, the rich point of the love
> game plays as a type. "Gay flirtations" indeed: but in
> what, pray, do these end? The youth of the time had
> thrown off the platonic love mode; gallant and lady, by

refusing to admit the power of love to engage their feelings, had defied each other; their mouths were full of scoffs at marriage. But it is their destiny, nevertheless, to love and marry. Marriage surprises Wildish and Olivia equally in [Sedley's] *The Mulberry-Garden.* And from Palamede and Doralice, in *Marriage a-la-Mode,* the conventions exact an equal sacrifice. The basic premise of this love game comedy is that however the individual may kick against the pricks, this revolt of his, since society and the conventions are stronger than he, can be productive only of fine comic effect. And it is no small part of the charm of the plays that hero and heroine are frequently permitted to savor this jest at their own expense.[8]

IV

Dryden's second great achievement was his comic dialogue, the proper language for his high spirited lovers. For this he built upon the foundation of Fletcher and the Cavalier poets, in order to form the *a-la-mode* style, surpassing his predecessors in exuberance, grace, and point, appearing to have the negligence of good prose. As Pope observed, in *The Art of Sinking in Poetry* (1727), the *a-la-mode* style is "fine by being new," and it draws its images from the "present Customs and best Fashions of our Metropolis." In other words, it is the urbane wit that Dryden, following Quintilian, admired.[9] In its most general sense, as applied to language, it was "propriety of thought in words,"[10] but in his comic wit, Dryden seems to have aimed for a special elegance, using terms and similitudes familiar to cultivated men: the law, hunting, soldiering, sailing, song, dance, gambling, and city life. Such easy language will not perplex the fair sex, and it is "most to be admired when a great thought comes dressed in words so commonly received that it is understood by the meanest apprehensions, as the best meat is the most easily digested" (I, 40). It has to be like Ovid's wit, which

> images more often the movements and affections of the mind, either combating between two contrary passions, or extremely discomposed by one. His words therefore are the least part of his care; for he pictures nature in disorder, with which the study and choice of words is

[8] John Harrington Smith, *The Gay Couple* (1948), pp. 77–78.
[9] See the preface to *An Evening's Love,* ll. 158–61. H. M. Richmond's *The School of Love* (1964) has some good observations on the relation between Cavalier poetry and Restoration comedy, as does Kathleen Lynch in her *Social Mode of Restoration Comedy* (1926).
[10] "The Author's Apology for Heroic Poetry," (1677), in *Essays,* I, 207.

inconsistent. This is the proper wit of dialogue or discourse, and consequently of the drama, where all that is said is to be supposed the effect of sudden thought; which, though it excludes not the quickness of wit in repartees, yet admits not a too curious election of words, too frequent allusions, or use of tropes or, in fine, anything that shows remoteness of thought or labour in the writer.   [I, 99.]

Repartee, the "soul of conversation" and the "greatest grace of comedy," is most appropriate to characters who pretend to be antagonistic. Although a wit begins the attack with an acute remark, a finer wit vanquishes by the quick reply.

Rhodophil. Prethee leave me to my own cogitations; I am thinking over all my sins, to find for which of them it was I marry'd thee.

Doralice. Whatever your sin was, mine's the punishment.

Rhodophil. My comfort is, thou art not immortal; and when that blessed, that divine day comes, of thy departure, I'm resolv'd I'll make one Holy-day more in the Almanack, for thy sake.

Doralice. Ay, you had need make a Holy-day for me, for I am sure you have made me a Martyr. [III.i.54–63.]

Such quick replies gain force when they take up the figure and turn it back in counterattack, doing credit to the invention and intelligence of the speaker. The effect is graceful when such wit helps one escape from an embarrassment, because the reply seems improvised, like Edmund Waller's celebrated reply to King Charles II, who pointed out that his poem on Oliver Cromwell was better than his ode on the return of the king. Waller answered, "Poets, Sire, succeed better in fiction than in truth."

The by-play especially suited to an ironic treatment, however, usually occurs at the end of the love duel, where the antagonists facetiously admit their sincerity. According to the social and comic conventions they must "unmask," and these lovers, without exactly saying so, move closer and closer to an open declaration of feeling. The subjunctive mood is their subterfuge. For example, in *An Evening's Love*, after Wildblood has "quite" broken off with Jacinta:

Wildblood. Well, since 'tis past, 'tis past; but a pox of all foolish quarrelling for my part.

Jacinta. And a mischief of all foolish disguisements for my part.

Wildblood. But if it were to do again with another Mistress, I would e'en plainly confess I had lost my money.

Jacinta. And if I had to deal with another Servant, I would learn more wit then to tempt him in disguises: for

that's to throw a Venice-glass to the ground, to try if
it would not break.

Wildblood. If it were not to please you, I see no necessity
of our parting.

Jacinta. I protest I do it only out of complaissance to you.

Wildblood. But if I should play the fool and ask you
pardon, you would refuse it.

Jacinta. No, never submit, for I should spoil you again
with pardoning you. [IV.i.839–55.]

This penchant for not meaning what one says leads naturally to the double entendre (another feature of the *a-la-mode* style), and as the quibble is to Shakespeare the double entendre is to Dryden; it is the golden apple for which he will always turn aside. And it scarcely ever fails him. Palamede wonders at Melantha's gibberish, " 'Tis true, in the day-time, 'tis tolerable, when a man has field-room to run from it; but, to be shut up in a bed with her, like two cocks in a pit; humanity cannot support it: I must kiss all night in my own defence, and hold her down, like a Boy at cuffs, nay, and give her the rising blow every time she begins to speak" (II.i.97–103). When a play becomes filled with such remarks, the audience has an impression that other speeches conceal naughty insinuations, more than are actually there. It is manifestly true, however, that the plays gain an extra dimension from their double meanings, and this is particularly obvious in Dryden's tragicomedies. Apparently the use of a double plot, combining romantic episodes with antiromantic ones, stimulates every kind of irony. In *Marriage a-la-Mode*, at first we hear only the clichés of compliment: "Such another word [that Doralice is virtuous] and I give up the ghost," "dispair and hang yourself," "jealousies, and duels, and death," and Melantha's incessant "Let me die." The romantic lovers foresee that they will actually die if they are separated. "And maidens, when I die, Upon my hearse white true-love-knots should tie," Palmyra says (II.i.519–20). In contrast, Doralice insists that she looks forward to her husband's death, "And I am resolv'd to marry the very same day thou dy'st, if it be but to show how little I'm concern'd for thee" (III.i.70–72). Leonidas would "die before" his beloved or "die with her" (III.i.348, 355). An audience rightly thinks little of these commonplaces until the masquerade (IV.ii–iii), where the well-known bawdy song intrudes upon the idealized world of Leonidas and Palmyra, immediately after she has agreed to come, in "strictest virtue," to Leonidas' house, for a secret meeting. With the sexual meaning of "Now die, my Alexis, and I will die too" before us, we can hardly avoid recalling how often the words had been innocently taken. The following scene reinforces the impression, when Melantha cries, "Let me die, if I enter into a pair of sheets with him that hate the French," and the meaning spreads to related activities in Palamede and Rhodophil's dialogue: fighting, crime, and warfare. They epitomize their attitude with the remark,

I'm sure we fight in a good quarrel:
Rogues may pretend Religion, and the Laws;
But a kind Mistris is the *Good Old Cause.*

[IV.iii.208–10.]

From this point on, Dryden encourages the audience to look at the action as tinged with this metaphor. Leonides must take his "love and crown by force" to "court Palmyra's bed" just as Palamede, in the antiromantic action, must "conquer" Melantha before he can marry her. He does so in a charming scene, masking his speech with Melantha's favorite French phrases, and he shoots her with a barrage of let-me-die's. Obviously the battle of the sexes is itself an image of sexual attraction, and Dryden has effectively supplied an appropriate subtext for the most emphatic theme in the play.

The subtext,[11] furthermore, seems to underlie the romantic as well as the antiromantic characters, suggesting that perhaps we err if we make an extreme contrast between idealized passion and the libertine sex duels represented in the double plots of *Secret Love* and *Marriage a-la-Mode.* Modern critics, under the influence of Coleridge and Hegel, who persist in thinking of plot as essentially conflict and of unity as a reconciliation of opposites, easily slip into the same habit when they discuss double plots. One part, they assume, must be the antithesis of the other or the foil to show up the other. On the other hand, Dryden seems at pains to suggest the complementary or at least alternate relevance of his double plots. Each exists for itself and each corresponds to and parodies the other. I use the term parody advisedly, derived from the medieval and renaissance practice, not in the modern use that involves ridicule or burlesque. The old use of parody grew out of periphrasis and euphemism, as a way of turning conventional phrases or proverbs, in order to extract a radically different meaning, and it was developed in larger forms such as the drama, into the use of corresponding pairs, such as the profane and sacred actions in *The Second Shepherd's Pageant.* On the Jacobean court stage Jonson experimented with the grotesque antimasque, preceding the solemn idealistic mask. Double plots in several Elizabethan plays work in a similar way, as the madhouse scenes of *The Changeling* seem to exist independently, and comment on the other action, without ridiculing it. In the same way, Dryden appears in his tragicomedies, to handle the high and low mimetic episodes,

---

[11] I use the term in the sense that Stanislavsky established.

making the low express more cynically and freely the concerns of the high mimetic action. William Empson explains their relations as if one plot is the *logos* and the other the *manna* of the same central mystery. Although Empson presses the analogy too far, I think, when he suggests that one plot has a covert causal influence on the other, he is probably right to insist that the two worlds of pastoral romance and urbane wit reflect each other.[12] Dryden himself seems to have recognized such a relationship, in his preface to the *Enchanted Island*, when he says that Davenant "designed the counterpart to Shakespeare's plot, namely that of a man who had never seen a woman, that by this means those two characters of innocence and love might the more illustrate and commend each other. . . . I confess that from the very first moment it so pleased me, that I never writ anything with more delight" (I, 135). It is little wonder Dryden was pleased, for he had already done essentially the same thing in the double plot of *Secret Love*.

V

Those of his comedies that do not combine high romantic or heroic plots with antiromantic plots are usually described as farces and comedies of manners. But it seems clear that they do not have a single consistent form, just as other Restoration comedies may not be profitably classified together as comedies of manners. Neither the best plays of Etherege, Wycherley, nor Congreve deserve such gross simplification, merely because they contain similar social themes as well as some similar characters. There is a world of difference between *Love for Love* and *The Country Wife*, as much as there is between *Mr. Limberham* and *An Evening's Love*. F. W. Bateson rightly observes that the comedies of the age used to be called high comedy (the seventeenth-century term) or genteel comedy (the early eighteenth-century term) with respect to the social class of the main characters, and the more recent appellation, comedy of manners, was first used by Charles Lamb, picked up by Meredith, and fixed by John Palmer in his influential book *Comedy of Manners* (1913).[13] Recent attempts to redefine the form as "comedy of wit" or "modern comedies" do not succeed much better. The one reduces them to a quality of their language, the other, put forth by Norman Holland in his interesting but disappointing book, reduces the plays to a commonplace theme: the opposition of appearance and nature.

[12] *Some Versions of Pastoral* (1935); I used the 1960 edition, pp. 25–84. For further comment see the introductions to *Secret Love* and *Marriage a-la-Mode* in the present edition.

[13] *Essays in Criticism*, I (1950), 89–93.

That opposition, it seems to me, may be found in any intrigue plot from *The Spanish Tragedy* to *The Importance of Being Earnest*. John Lyly's and Shakespeare's plays and Marston's tragicomedies repeatedly employ the theme. That universality of application ought to make us suspicious of the value of appearance versus nature (or "reality," as the more careless critics term it). Any concept so general as this is drained of most of its meaning; it explains too much and is as predictable as images of darkness and light in Milton's or Pope's poetry.

If we must have a descriptive label for *Sir Martin Mar-All* and *An Evening's Love*, the term "high farce" seems as good as any, but even that must be used provisionally, with the understanding that within the category a range of variation in form is still great. (*Mr. Limberham* is almost pure farce.) The conventional central action is a love-game, but it moves forward by means of intrigue more than in the tragicomedies. Romantic idealism is not so obviously parodied, and the esteemed values are more clearly money, beauty, and wit, in that order. The protagonists are beautiful, young, clever, and ardent; young, stupid, and ardent; old, rich, and gullible; and so on. The dichotomies are most firmly drawn between intelligence and stupidity, or between country and urban society. But there is no predictable connection between country folk and doltishness. Mistress Millicent, straight out of Kent, fresh in the city, loves true wit as much as anyone, although she may not be an experienced judge of it, and she seems naturally to scorn her blockheaded suitor, Sir John Swallow. Sir Martin, with strong city alliances and the best intentions, is more foolish than Sir John. Among the Englishmen traveling in Spain, the unimaginative Bellamy needs constant help from Wildblood, in order to bungle through his mock-astrologer's routine. The ideal seems to be a victorious union of lovers who, in at least one couple, combine all the cardinal virtues: an estate, good looks, and a gay spirit. The difficulties of the plot are mostly illusory. The conventional heavy father does his perfunctory duty, trying to marry his daughter to a rich, old, or otherwise obnoxious man, but these hinderances seldom offer much of a challenge to the true wits. The real barriers are in the minds of the principal lovers. How can a man force his mistress into a trustworthy declaration? How can a clever woman be sure that her suitor is really what he pretends to be? Can he pass the tests of fidelity, wit, and style worthy of a cavalier? Even with the help of clever servants, he fails, as Wildblood's infidelity is detected and Sir Martin's lumpishness is exposed. But a mistress who already has in her heart a secret inclination for him will, perversely, find herself more in love at the same time she becomes more suspicious.

The only way out of the dilemma is recourse to some

incredible sleight of hand, whereby the true wit charms everyone, the audience included, with some grand high-jinks. The fifth act, therefore, is devoted to an absurd and delightful assembly scene, stage-managed by Warner or Wildblood, where, by the spirit of fancy, sheer wish-fulfillment, and pure fun, all the difficulties are removed. Practical jokes are transformed into elaborate charades that isolate the blocking characters and liberate the gay lovers. Every man stays in his humour and is suitably matched; so it is significant for this kind of play that Warner the resourceful servant, rather than Sir Martin, should win the hand of Mistress Millicent. In traditional "lout comedy," such as Molière's *L'Etourdi* (one of Dryden's sources), the indiscreet or foolish fellow still wins the girl, but in Dryden's play the servant needs must outwit his master, and Warner's role is consequently more greatly developed. He is more honest and more proud than his French counterpart, Philipin. His reputation for wit is at stake; he is "resolved to bestow" Sir Martin on Millicent, "for the honour of my wit is engaged in it." With admirable economy, each scheme that is botched by Sir Martin enhances the wit of Warner, because he has to make extraordinary efforts, right on the brink of disaster, to save the situation. Like whips applied to a top (one of Dryden's happiest metaphors), his troubles make his brain work all the faster, "as the top spins the more you baste her." At the end, he can even make the "fool's plot," the double masked wedding, succeed, and Millicent sees to it that she marries the right man.

Although Dryden denounced farce as "forced humours" and "unnatural events," he seems to have recognized that in practice it could be mixed with regular comedy as long as one does not sink too low and write in the vulgar style. Along with most comic geniuses, like Aristophanes, Molière, and Shaw, Dryden found suitable moments in his comedies when a heap of coincidences and fanciful manipulation of events were absolutely necessary. For, in spite of Dryden's theory, we must admit that the best of comedy thrives on a certain amount of improbability and exaggerated humours. If modern audiences can be charmed by the high farce in the last scene of *Androcles and the Lion*, they ought to be able to see the appropriateness of the closing scenes of *Sir Martin Mar-All* and *An Evening's Love*. Therefore, it seems that Dryden rightly chose to break one of the "mechanick rules" of his theory in order to achieve the proper lively effect that a comedy must have.

The Text of This Edition

This edition presents a critical, old-spelling text of the plays, on the plan of *The Dramatic Works in the Beaumont and Fletcher Canon* (1966), with a few modifications for the sake of economy. The first edition in each case provides the copy-text, since it was the only one set from manuscript. The collation of all seventeenth-century quartos, as well as the folio of 1701, revealed no new authority, except in a few isolated readings, consequently there was no great difficulty in editing, and it did not seem necessary to print a complete historical collation. The apparatus is thus considerably reduced, to include only departures from copy. Substantive departures are noted at the foot of the page, above the commentary, and emendations of accidentals along with press variants are listed at the end of each play. Silent alterations are the same as in the Beaumont and Fletcher; notably modernized long *ſ*, *i*, and *j*, correction of turned letters, expanded abbreviations, normalization of spelling of proper names, capital letters at the beginning of sentences and lines of verse, full stops at the ends of speeches, and italicized proper names in the dialogue. In addition, apostrophes have been silently supplied before *s* in elisions of *is* and before *s* of genitive singular nouns, when no other orthographic change is required. Bracketed notations in stage directions are supplied by the editor. Prefaces, prologues, and epilogues as they appear in the first edition are included, but dedications and lists of actors have been regularly excluded. When these have significance, they are mentioned in the brief introductions or in the commentary.

For a detailed account of the method, the reader should consult *The Dramatic Works in the Beaumont and Fletcher Canon*, I, ix–xxv, along with Sir Walter Greg's "The Rationale of Copy-Text," *Studies in Bibliography*, III (1950–51), 19–36, Fredson Bowers' "Textual Criticism," in *The Aims and Methods of Scholarship in Modern Languages and Literature*, edited by James Thorpe (1964), and Bowers' "Current Theories of Copy-Text, with an illustration from Dryden," *Modern Philology*, XLVIII (1950), 12–20.

Dryden's Comedies and Tragicomedies

with dates of first performance
and publication

The Wild Gallant, 1663 (1669)

The Rival Ladies, 1664 (1664)

Secret Love, or the Maiden Queen, 1667 (1668)

Sir Martin Mar-All, or the Feign'd Innocence (with Newcastle), 1667 (1668)

The Tempest, or the Enchanted Island (with Davenant), 1667 (1670)

An Evening's Love, or the Mock Astrologer, 1668 (1671)

Marriage a-la-Mode, 1672 (1673)

The Assignation, or Love in a Nunnery, 1672 (1673)

The Kind Keeper, or Mr. Limberham, 1678 (1680)

The Spanish Friar, or the Double Discovery, 1680 (1681)

Amphitryon, or the Two Sosia's, 1690 (1690)

Love Triumphant, or Nature Will Prevail, 1694 (1694)

Secret Love

One indictment of criticism of Restoration drama is that *Secret Love, or The Maiden Queen* does not receive the attention it deserves. Absent from every anthology, even from selections of Dryden's plays, and scarcely mentioned in recent accounts of comedy of the era,[1] it is a stepsister lying among the cinders, neither a fit heroic play nor a proper comedy of manners. And to call it tragicomedy seems, for most critics, just another way of avoiding the issue: What holds the play together and what keeps it from being a mélange?

In *An Essay of Dramatic Poesy*, written at about the same time as *Secret Love* (1665–66), Lisideius attacks contemporary tragicomedy for much the same reasons: many scenes "carry on a design that is nothing of kin to the main plot"; we see "two plays, carried on together, to the confounding of the audience; who, before they are warm in their concernments for one part, are diverted to another; and by that means espouse the interest of neither. From hence . . . it arises, that the one half of our actions are not known to the other. They keep their distances, as if they were Montagues and Capulets, and seldom begin an acquaintance till the last scene of the fifth act, when they are to meet upon the stage." He dubs this English invention "absurd, . . . here a course of mirth, there another of sadness and passion, a third of honour, a fourth a duel."[2] Neander, defending tragicomedy, is not convinced that "compassion and mirth in the same subject destroy each other." He prefers the "variety and copiousness" of English plots, where, as in the scheme of the universe, contrary motions may be found to agree. French plots are single:

> they carry on one design which is pushed forward by all the actors, every scene in the play contributing and moving towards it: ours, besides the main design, have under-plots or by-concernments of less considerable persons and intrigues, which are carried on with the motion of the main plot; just as they say the orb of the fixed stars, and those of the planets, though they have motions of their own, are whirled about by the motion of the *primum mobile*, in which they are contained. That similitude expresses much of the English stage for if

[1] Norman Holland, *The First Modern Comedies* (1959) and Thomas Fujimura, *Restoration Comedy of Wit* (1952). The most sympathetic treatment of the play may be found in John Harrington Smith's *The Gay Couple* (1948), pp. 55–58.

[2] *Essays*, I, 45.

contrary motions may be found in nature to agree, if a planet can go east and west at the same time, one way by virtue of his own motion, the other by the force of the First Mover, it will not be difficult to imagine how the under-plot, which is only different, not contrary to the great design, may naturally be conducted along with it.

The English variety, "if well ordered, will afford a greater pleasure to the audience" (I, 58–59). The artistic values, then, implicit in the form are the baroque ideals of copiousness, variety, and contrast; the whole is supposed to reflect the plenum of God's Creation, and if we take a large enough view of the subject and if they are well ordered, the parts should be found to agree, even though their apparent tone be different.

The vagueness of this otherwise suggestive account lies in the word subject, which twentieth-century critics would interpret, equally vaguely, as "theme" or "motif." It is clear, nevertheless, that whatever unity we find in *Secret Love* will not lie so much in the explicit causal connections between the lesser and the greater actions as in the thematic analogies between them. Before the fifth act, there are incidental causal connections, and the final solution of the heroic plot is aided by characters from the other plot. But for our taste, we must see that the issues or the significance of the parts can be drawn together before we feel the proper pleasure.

Miss Lynch has pointed out that the "similitude debates" in Dryden's comedies burlesque the forms of *préciosité*, by praising inconstancy, unchastity, and irreverence toward love instead of their opposites.[3] Bonamy Dobrée makes a similar remark, although he thinks they are mocking the values of heroic drama.[4] Some critics have seen the union of two plots as a sign of Dryden's carelessness.[5] Mr. Allen, along with many others, sees the plots as deliberately contrasted, but he fails to follow the implications of the view; for a genuine contrast requires a basic similarity as well. We cannot significantly contrast apple pie and Spinoza's principle of sufficient reason. Therefore, I think we should not exaggerate the antithetical nature of the parts, because Dryden has encouraged us to look at events that may seem to go east, while they also go west.

First we must recognize that the language of Celadon and Florimell, when they are together, is calculated to mean something other than what it says. They have a secret love,

---

[3] *The Social Mode of Restoration Comedy* (1926), chap. IV.
[4] *Restoration Comedy* (1924), p. 20.
[5] B. J. Pendlebury, *Dryden's Heroic Plays* (1923), p. 104.

which, because of their humours, they dare not express seriously, so they adopt the mask of persiflage. Or, more accurately, they begin with mockery and end in earnest. Celadon exaggerates his ironic view of romance so extremely in the opening scenes, that at first we find it hard to believe him in love. Mocking the love-at-first-sight convention, Celadon professes his attachment upon the bare mention of Florimell: "A new Beauty, as wilde as you, and a vast Fortune." "I am for her before the world." On the first encounter, when Florimell is masked, he is drawn to her and she to him. "A rare Creature this!" he says, and she says, "A pretty odd kind of fellow this: he fits my humour rarely." Florimell claims that she wants a constant lover, and Celadon immediately obliges her, but he answers in such a way that it seems like a pose of constancy: "If you will needs fetter me to one, agree the matter between your selves; and the most handsome take me." Florimell takes him, and they shake hands, making a match, all within forty lines; and he has not yet seen her face. In effect, they have gotten over the silly preliminaries in order to clear the way for important matters. Their incredible romance continues with Celadon's description of his ideal beauty, the image that is drawn on his poetical heart, and except for the turned-up nose, it is the image of Nell Gwyn, who played Florimell. Since she still won't unmask, he threatens to be a constant "Maudlin" lover (the opposite of his humour).[6] She puts him off with a satiric quip, confessing to be more inconstant than he. That remark is enough for Celadon, apparently, and he pursues her offstage.

Any experienced theatergoer should know by this time that they are destined for each other, and that no matter how much they rail and joke about their feelings, their inner desires will draw them closer and closer. In real life the gay couple may, in fact, use badinage as a disguise for their hostility to each other, but on the stage, wit seems the vehicle of genuine passion. A woman cannot be too cautious; consequently, in the second act Florimell begins her investigation to see if Celadon means what he says; she will have "other proofs of love," according to the code of romance. The rest of their courtship involves his attempts to have his cake and eat it too and her jocular "disciplining" of Celadon for each infraction of the code. Nothing on the surface is sacred; she plays the tyrant and he the rebellious subject, to the very end. His fondest request to the queen, at the end of Act V, is "I beg, Madam, you will command Florimell never to be friends

---

[6] See the quotation from Madeleine de Scudéry's *Ibrahim* in the general introduction.

with me," which begins their most serious negotiation. In the first of the great proviso scenes in Restoration comedy, they agree to disagree about most marital matters. Theirs will be a truly modern marriage, never to show a moment of jealousy, and they will try to loosen the bonds just a little, for "there's some difference betwixt a Girdle and a Halter." The ultimate clue to their attitudes is given when they agree not to call each other husband and wife, but "will be married by the more agreeable names of Mistress and Gallant." Having discovered the form of insincere sincerity, whereby neither party will seem to have dominion over the other, they unite.

The romantic action has proceeded upon similar lines; for the queen's secret love is a tyrant, an irrational inclination, a passion that threatens to destroy her practical judgment. The heroic plot represents, therefore, the fundamental dilemmas of love, writ large. If the virgin is all-powerful, as Florimell has shown herself to be, supreme, imperial in her beauty, virtue, and control over her servant, then how can she perpetuate her power after marriage? The virgin queen, like Christiana of Sweden and Elizabeth of England, postpones as long as possible her decision to marry, just as the Millamants, Angelicas, and Florimells maneuver and delay an open declaration of love and a betrothal. On the man's side the romantic lover seeks to be worthy of his mistress, and he may aspire to love a queen, but he is driven to seize her power as well as her beauty. The interesting complications arise when the queen truly falls in love. How can she command as a queen when she must obey her passion? Secrecy is only a temporary solution, for she talks compulsively to Philocles about her love. She is a melancholy lover, "reserved, sad, and vex'd at little things." Although the undertone of the first interview between Philocles and the queen is insistently passionate, only Philocles fails to see it.

The second interview[7] between them increases this irony, when Philocles criticizes the queen's unknown beloved for his presumption, and to his amazement this angers the queen. And just as Celadon came closer to discovering Florimell, Philocles learns more and more of the queen's secret. Banished from court, he sees it is no good fleeing to some pastoral

[7] According to Allen, most of this scene (II.i) is not found in Dryden's source for the romantic action, Madeleine de Scudéry's *Artamène ou Le Grand Cyrus* (1658–53, English 1653–54), VII.ii. Nor is the first part of III.i, nor the rebellion in Act IV. The antiromantic story comes from the same work, IX.iii, and from Madeleine de Scudéry's *Ibrahim* (1641, English 1652), II.i; the sources do not emphasize the physical side of love, however, and the character of Florimell is not present. N. B. Allen, *The Sources of Dryden's Comedies* (1935), pp. 75–99, 249–60.

retreat, for even there a heroic lover will still "find Visions of Court will haunt [his] restless mind;/And glorious dreams stand ready to restore/The pleasing shapes of all [he] had before." Like Celadon's vision of ideal beauty, Philocles' vision of power and love of a princess has a controlling force over him, and his flight with Candiope is prevented by the queen's revenge (paralleling Florimell's revenge upon Celadon: she will marry him and cuckold him as he is trying to be inconstant to her).

After a series of maneuvers, in spite of their feelings, the queen and Philocles renounce each other, for the good of the state. Philocles submits to the tyranny of Candiope's eyes, and we are assured appropriately enough that the crown will eventually fall upon her head. Hence the romantic action, as well as the other action, explores the mysteries of secret love, of apparent male domination and real female power. In the lower action impudence and raillery express love; in the higher action rage and tenderness. In both love is a riddle.

The first performance may have been before February 5, 1666/67, the date of the epilogue to Buckingham's *The Chances*, which seems to allude to the play.[8] On March 2, at the King's House in Bridges Street, Drury Lane, Pepys saw the play, "mightily commended for the regularity of it, and the strain and wit."[9] The unusually large number of recorded performances and reprintings suggests that it was very popular. A prologue "*Spoken by Mrs.* Boutell *to the Maiden Queen, in mans Cloathes*" and an epilogue "*Spoken by Mrs.* Reeves *to the Maiden Queen, in mans Cloathes*" is found in *Covent Garden Drollery,* 1672 (edited by Thorn-Drury, 1928), written no doubt for a production with an all-female cast. As Professor Dearing notes, there are three manuscripts of the song from IV, ii, in B.M. MS. Harl. 3991, B.M. MS. Harl. 7332, and Bodleian MS. Rawl. poet. 65, none of whose readings seem authoritative.

The present edition is based on the Folger copy of Q1 1668 (Macd. 70a, W & M 445), entered at Stationers' Hall, August 7, 1667, bought by Pepys "newly printed" January 18. Comparison of the Folger copy (DFo) with copies from the Texas (TxU), Huntington (CSmH), and Clark (CLUC) libraries reveals one stop-press correction. In a cancel leaf, sig. B4, some changes appear to have been made to improve the meter. The original of leaf B4 may be found in the Bodleian

---

[8] John Harrington Smith, "Dryden and Buckingham: The Beginnings of the Feud," *MLN*, LXIX (1954), 242–45.

[9] See the general introduction for his remarks on Nell Gwyn in the role of Florimell.

copy of Q1. Subsequent editions, Q2 1669, Q3 1669, Q4 1679, Q5 1691, Q6 1698, and F 1701, introduce no new authority, except one reading in Q2 (I.i.380) that must be Dryden's revision. Q6 has a variant title page; W & M 451 is the official title and W & M 452 was the original title, differing in the imprint, which was never intended for a separate issue. Acts I–II, in Qq-F, contain scene divisions in the classical style, with a new scene at almost every entry, although Acts III–V are divided in the English fashion; consequently, the English convention has been used for the whole play, without specific notation.

"Nell Gwynn." Studio of Sir Peter Lely.
Courtesy of the National Portrait Gallery

SECRET-
LOVE,

OR THE

Maiden-Queen :

As it is Acted

By His Majesties Servants,

AT THE

THEATER-ROYAL.

Written by

JOHN DRYDEN Esq;

————*Vitiis nemo fine nafcitur ; optimus ille*
Qui minimis urgetur.　　　　　　HORACE,

LONDON,

Printed for *Henry Herringman,* at the Sign of the *Anchor,*
on the Lower-walk of the *New-Exchange,* 1668.

Title Page of the First Quarto, Folger Library Copy.

Vitiis . . . urgetur] No man is born without defects: he is the best who
is beset with least. Horace, *Satires,* I.iii.68–69.

31

Preface

It has been the ordinary practice of the *French* Poets, to dedicate their Works of this nature to their King, especially when they have had the least encouragement to it, by his approbation of them on the Stage. But I confess I want the confidence to follow their example, though perhaps I have as specious pretences to it for this Piece, as any they can boast of: it having been own'd in so particular a manner by His Majesty, that he has grac'd it with the Title of His Play, and thereby rescued it from the severity (that I may not say malice) of its Enemies. But, though a character so high and undeserv'd, has not rais'd in me the presumption to offer such a trifle to his more serious view, yet I will own the vanity to say, that after this glory which it has receiv'd from a Soveraign Prince, I could not send it to seek protection from any Subject. Be this Poem then sacred to him without the tedious form of a Dedication, and without presuming to interrupt those hours which he is daily giving to the peace and settlement of his people.

For what else concerns this Play, I would tell the Reader that it is regular, according to the strictest of Dramatick Laws, but it is a commendation which many of our Poets now despise, and a beauty which our common Audiences do not easily discern. Neither indeed do I value my self upon it, because with all that symmetry of parts, it may want an air and spirit (which consists in the writing) to set it off. 'Tis a question variously disputed, whether an Author may be allowed as a competent judg of his own works. As to the Fabrick and contrivance of them certainly he may, for that is properly the employment of the judgment; which, as a Master-builder may determine, and that without deception, whether the work be according to the exactness of the model; still granting him to have a perfect Idea of that pattern by which he works: and that he keeps himself always constant to the discourse of his judgment, without admitting self-love, which is the false surveigher of his Fancy, to intermeddle in it. These Qualifications granted (being such as all sound Poets are presupposed to have within them) I think all Writers, of what kind soever, may infallibly judg of the frame and con-texture of their Works. But for the ornament of Writing, which is greater, more various and bizarre in Poesie then in any other kind, as it is properly the Child of Fancy, so it can

---

21 but it is] but that it is Qq,F

8 *the Title of His Play*] i.e. his favorite play.

32

receive no measure, or at least but a very imperfect one, of its own excellencies or failures from the judgment. Self-love (which enters but rarely into the offices of the judgment) here predominates. And Fancy (if I may so speak) judging of it self, can be no more certain or demonstrative of its own effects, then two crooked lines can be the adæquate measure of each other. What I have said on this subject, may, perhaps, give me some credit with my Readers, in my opinion of this Play, which I have ever valued above the rest of my Follies of this kind: yet not thereby in the least dissenting from their judgment who have concluded the writing of this to be much inferior to my *Indian Emperour*. But the Argument of that was much more noble, not having the allay of Comedy to depress it: yet if this be more perfect, either in its kind, or in the general notion of a Play, 'tis as much as I desire to have granted for the vindication of my Opinion, and, what as nearly touches me, the sentence of a Royal Judg. Many have imagin'd the Character of *Philocles* to be faulty; some for not discovering the Queen's love, others for his joining in her restraint. But though I am not of their number, who obstinately defend what they have once said, I may with modesty take up those answers which have been made for me by my Friends; namely, that *Philocles*, who was but a Gentleman of ordinary birth, had no reason to guess so soon at the Queen's Passion, she being a person so much above him, and by the suffrages of all her people, already destin'd to *Lysimantes*: Besides, that he was prepossessed, (as the Queen somewhere hints it to him) with another inclination which rendred him less clear-sighted in it, since no man, at the same time, can distinctly view two different objects. And if this, with any shew of reason, may be defended, I leave my Masters the Criticks to determine whether it be not much more conducing to the beauty of my Plot, that *Philocles* should be long kept ignorant of the Queen's love, then that with one leap he should have entred into the knowledg of it, and thereby freed himself, to the disgust of the Audience, from that pleasing Labyrinth of errors which was prepar'd for him. As for that other objection of his joyning in the Queen's imprisonment, it is indisputably that which every man, if he examines himself, would have done on the like occasion. If they answer that it takes from the height of his Character to do it; I would enquire of my over-wise Censors, who told them I intended him a perfect Character, or indeed what necessity was there he should be so, the variety of Images, being one great beauty of a Play? It was as much as I design'd, to show one great and absolute pattern of honour in my Poem, which I did in the Person of the Queen: All the

defects of the other parts being set to show, the more to
recommend that one character of Vertue to the Audience.
But neither was the fault of *Philocles* so great, if the circumstances be consider'd, which, as moral Philosophy assures us,
make the essential differences of good and bad; He himself
best explaining his own intentions in his last Act, which was
the restauration of his Queen; and even before that, in the
honesty of his expressions when he was unavoidably led by
the impulsion of his love to do it. That which with more
reason was objected as an indecorum, is the management of
the last Scene of the Play, where *Celadon* and *Florimell* are
treating too lightly of their marriage in the presence of the
Queen, who likewise seems to stand idle while the great
action of the *Drama* is still depending. This I cannot otherwise defend, then by telling you I so design'd it on purpose
to make my Play go off more smartly; that Scene, being in
the opinion of the best judges, the most divertising of the
whole Comedy. But though the Artifice succeeded, I am
willing to acknowledg it as a fault, since it pleas'd His
Majesty, the best Judg, to think it so. I have onely to add,
that the Play is founded on a story in the *Cyrus*, which he
calls the Queen of *Corinth*; in whose Character, as it has been
affirm'd to me, he represents that of the famous *Christina*,
Queen of *Sweden*. This is what I thought convenient to
write by way of Preface, to the *Maiden-Queen*; in the reading
of which, I fear you will not meet with that satisfaction which
you have had in seeing it on the Stage; the chief parts of it
both serious and comick, being performed to that height of
excellence, that nothing but a command which I could not
handsomely disobey, could have given me the courage to
have made it publick.

109 *the Cyrus*] *Artamène, ou le Grand Cyrus*, by Mlle. de Scudéry,
published under her brother's name, Georges de Scudéry, 1649-53, in
English, 1653-54; see part VII, book ii.
111 *Christina*] Christina Alexandria, 1626-89, the famous Ama-
zonian queen, pupil of Descartes. She married her favorite, the Count
de la Gardie, to her cousin, whose brother succeeded her at her abdica-
tion in 1654 (Summers). She refused to marry, for fear of limiting her
freedom.

The Persons

Queen of *Sicily*.
Candiope, Princess of the Blood.
Asteria, the Queen's Confident.
Florimell, a Maid of Honour.
Flavia, another Maid of Honour.
Olinda, ⎫
Sabina, ⎬ Sisters.
Melissa, Mother to *Olinda* and *Sabina*.

Lysimantes, first Prince of the Blood.
Philocles, the Queen's favourite.
Celadon, a Courtier.
[*Phormio*, a Gentleman.
Three Friends to *Philocles*.
Followers of *Celadon*.
Three Deputies.
Musicians.]
Guards.
Pages of Honour.
Souldiers.

The Scene *Sicily*.

The Persons] The original cast, as listed in Q1: *Queen*, Rebecca
Marshall; *Candiope*, Anne Marshall Quin; *Asteria*, Mrs. Knepp; *Flori-
mell*, Nell Gwyn; *Flavia*, Francis Davenport; *Olinda*, Margaret Rutter;
Sabina, Elizabeth Davenport; *Melissa*, Katherine Corey; *Philocles*,
Michael Mohun; *Celadon*, Charles Hart; *Lysimantes*, Nicholas Burt.

Prologue

I.

He who writ this, not without pains and thought
From *French* and *English* Theaters has brought
Th'exactest Rules by which a Play is wrought.

II.

The Unities of Action, Place, and Time;
The Scenes unbroken; and a mingled chime
Of *Johnson's* humour, with *Corneille's* rhyme.

III.

But while dead colours he with care did lay,
He fears his Wit, or Plot he did not weigh,
Which are the living Beauties of a Play.

IV.

Plays are like Towns, which howe're fortifi'd
By Engineers, have still some weaker side
By the o'reseen Defendant unespy'd.

V.

And with that Art you make approaches now;
Such skilful fury in Assaults you show,
That every Poet without shame may bow.

VI.

Ours therefore humbly would attend your doom,
If Souldier-like, he may have termes to come
With flying colours, and with beat of Drum.

The Prologue *goes out, and stayes while a Tune is play'd,*
after which he returnes again.

Second Prologue

I had forgot one half I do protest,
And now am sent again to speak the rest.
He bowes to every great and noble Wit,
But to the little Hectors of the Pit
Our Poet's sturdy, and will not submit. 5
He'll be before-hand with 'em, and not stay
To see each peevish Critick stab his Play:
Each Puny Censor, who his skill to boast,
Is cheaply witty on the Poet's cost.
No Critick's verdict, should, of right, stand good, 10
They are excepted all as men of blood:
And the same Law should shield him from their fury
Which has excluded Butchers from a Jury.
You'd all be Wits ———
But writing's tedious, and that way may fail; 15
The most compendious method is to rail:
Which you so like, you think your selves ill us'd
When in smart Prologues you are not abus'd.
A civil Prologue is approv'd by no man;
You hate it as you do a Civil woman: 20
Your Fancy's pall'd, and liberally you pay
To have it quicken'd, e're you see a Play.
Just as old Sinners worn from their delight,
Give money to be whip'd to appetite.
But what a Pox keep I so much ado 25
To save our Poet? he is one of you;
A Brother Judgment, and as I hear say,
A cursed Critick as e're damn'd a Play.
Good salvage Gentlemen your own kind spare,
He is, like you, a very Wolf, or Bear; 30
Yet think not he'll your ancient rights invade,
Or stop the course of your free damning trade:
For he, (he vows) at no friend's Play can sit
But he must needs find fault to shew his Wit:
Then, for his sake, ne're stint your own delight; 35
Throw boldly, for he sets to all that write;
With such he ventures on an even lay,
For they bring ready money into Play.
Those who write not, and yet all Writers nick,
Are Bankrupt Gamesters, for they damn on Tick. 40

29 *salvage*] savage.
39 *nick*] criticize, censure.
40 *on Tick*] on credit.

Secret Love,
or the
Maiden-Queen

ACT I. Scene 1

The Scene is Walks, near the Court.

Enter Celadon, Asteria, *meeting each other: he in riding habit;
they embrace.*

Celadon. Dear *Asteria*!

Asteria. My dear Brother! welcome; a thousand welcomes:
Me thinks this year you have been absent has been so
tedious! I hope as you have made a pleasant Voyage,
5   so you have brought your good humour back again to
Court.

Celadon. I never yet knew any Company I could not be
merry in, except it were an old Woman's.

Asteria. Or at a Funeral.

10 *Celadon.* Nay, for that you shall excuse me; for I was never
merrier then I was at a Creditor's of mine, whose Book
perished with him. But what new Beauties have you at
Court? How do *Melissa's* two fair Daughters?

Asteria. When you tell me which of 'em you are in love
15   with, I'le answer you.

Celadon. Which of 'em, naughty sister, what a question's
there? With both of 'em, with each and singular of 'em.

Asteria. Bless me! you are not serious!

Celadon. You look as if it were a wonder to see a man in
20   love: are they not handsome?

Asteria. I, but both together ———

Celadon. I, and both asunder; why, I hope there are but
two of 'em, the tall Singing and Dancing one, and the
little Innocent one?

25 *Asteria.* But you cannot marry both?

Celadon. No, nor either of 'em I trust in Heaven; but I can
keep them company, I can sing and dance with 'em,
and treat 'em, and that, I take it, is somewhat better
then musty marrying them. Marriage is poor folk's
30   pleasure that cannot go to the cost of variety: but I am
out of danger of that with these two, for I love 'em so
equally I can never make choice between 'em. Had I
but one mistress, I might go to her to be merry, and
she, perhaps, be out of humour; there were a visit lost.

But here, if one of 'em frown upon me, the other will 35
be the more obliging, on purpose to recommend her
own gayety, besides a thousand things that I could name.
Asteria. And none of 'em to any purpose.
Celadon. Well, if you will not be cruel to a poor Lover,
you might oblige me by carrying me to their lodgings. 40
Asteria. You know I am always busie about the Queen.
Celadon. But once or twice onely, till I am a little flesh'd
in my acquaintance with other Ladies, and have learn'd
to prey for my self. I promise you I'le make all the haste
I can to end your trouble, by being in love somewhere 45
else.
Asteria. You would think it hard to be deny'd now.
Celadon. And reason good: many a man hangs himself for
the loss of one Mistris. How do you think then I should
bear the loss of two; especially in a Court where I think 50
Beauty is but thin sown.
Asteria. There's one *Florimell* the Queen's Ward, a new
Beauty, as wilde as you, and a vast Fortune.
Celadon. I am for her before the world: bring me to her,
and I'le release you of your promise for the other two. 55

Enter a Page.

Page. Madam, the Queen expects you.
Celadon. I see you hold her favour; Adieu Sister, you have
a little Emissary there, otherwise I would offer you my
service.
Asteria. Farwel Brother, think upon *Florimell*. 60
Celadon. You may trust my memory for an handsome
woman, I'le think upon her, and the rest too; I'le forget
none of 'em.   *Exit* Asteria [*and Page*].

*Enter a Gentleman walking over the Stage hastily:
after him,* Florimell, *and* Flavia *Masqued.*

Flavia. Phormio, Phormio, you will not leave us ———

---

42 flesh'd] flush'd Qq,F

42 *flesh'd*] The closest meaning of *flush'd* (Qq-F) that might apply
here is "to rush like birds on the wing, to flock or swarm." Its metaphorical use is illustrated by "whole flokes of interpreters flushed in"
(*OED*). Whereas *flesh'd* has a connection with the metaphorical con-
text, because a hawk or dog is fleshed in the game, with a taste of the
prey, in order to excite his eagerness for the chase. In Dryden's prologue
to *Circe*, ll. 6–10, he uses the metaphor: "The Sex that best does
pleasure understand, / Will always chuse to err on t'other hand. / They
check not him that's awkward in delight, / Thus heartn'd well, and
flesh't upon his Prey, / The Youth may prove a man another day."
Therefore, I emend (LAB).

65   *Gentleman.* In faith I have a little business ———

Exit Gentleman.

Celadon. Cannot I serve you in the Gentleman's room,
Ladies?

Flavia. Which of us would you serve?

Celadon. Either of you, or both of you.

70   *Flavia.* Why, could you not be constant to one?

Celadon. Constant to one! I have been a Courtier, a
Souldier, and a Traveller, to good purpose, if I must be
constant to one; give me some Twenty, some Forty,
some a Hundred Mistresses, I have more Love than any

75   one woman can turn her to.

Florimell. Bless us, let us be gone Cousin; we two are
nothing in his hands.

Celadon. Yet for my part, I can live with as few Mistresses
as any man: I desire no superfluities; onely for necessary

80   change or so; as I shift my Linnen.

Florimell (*aside*). A pretty odd kind of fellow this: he fits
my humour rarely.

Flavia. You are as unconstant as the Moon.

Florimell. You wrong him, he's as constant as the Sun; he

85   would see all the world round in twenty four hours.

Celadon. 'Tis very true, Madam, but, like him, I would
visit and away.

Florimell. For what an unreasonable thing it were to stay
long, be troublesome, and hinder a Lady of a fresh

90   Lover.

Celadon. A rare Creature this!—besides Madam, how like
a fool a man looks, when after all his eagerness of two
Minutes before, he shrinks into a faint kiss and a cold
complement.

95   Ladies both, into your hands I commit my selfe; share
me betwixt you.

Flavia. I'll have nothing to do with you, since you cannot
be constant to one.

Celadon. Nay, rather then loose either of you, I'll do more;

100   I'll be constant to an hundred of you: or, (if you will
needs fetter me to one,) agree the matter between your
selves; and the most handsome take me.

Florimell. Though I am not she, yet since my Masque's
down, and you cannot convince me, have a good faith

105   of my Beauty, and for once I take you for my servant.

Celadon. And for once, I'll make a blind bargain with you:
strike hands; is't a Match Mistriss?

Florimell. Done Servant.

105 *for once*] for the occasion.

40

Celadon. Now I am sure I have the worst on't: for you see
the worst of me, and that I do not of you till you shew
your face:——— 110
Yet now I think on't, you must be handsome.———
Florimell. What kind of Beauty do you like?
Celadon. Just such a one as yours.
Florimell. What's that? 115
Celadon. Such an Ovall face, clear skin, hazle eyes, thick
brown Eye-browes, and Hair as you have for all the
world.
Flavia. But I can assure you she has nothing of all this.
Celadon. Hold thy peace Envy; nay I can be constant an' 120
I set on't.
Florimell. 'Tis true she tells you.
Celadon. I, I, you may slander your self as you please; then
you have, ——— let me see.
Florimell. I'll swear you shan'not see. ——— 125
Celadon. A turn'd up Nose: that gives an air to your face:
Oh, I find I am more and more in love with you! a
full neather-lip, an out-mouth, that makes mine water
at it: the bottom of your cheeks a little blub, and two
dimples when you smile: for your stature 'tis well, and 130
for your wit 'twas given you by one that knew it had
been thrown away upon an ill face; come you are
handsome, there's no denying it.
Florimell. Can you settle your spirits to see an ugly face,
and not be frighted, I could find in my heart to lift up 135
my Masque and disabuse you.
Celadon. I defie your Masque, would you would try the
experiment.
Florimell. No, I won'not; for your ignorance is the Mother
of your devotion to me. 140
Celadon. Since you will not take the pains to convert me
I'll make bold to keep my faith: a miserable man I am
sure you have made me.
Flavia. This is pleasant.
Celadon. It may be so to you but it is not to me; for ought 145
I see, I am going to be the most constant *Maudlin.* ———

---

116 *Ovall face*] probably a description of Nell Gwyn. See the
illustration facing p. 31; one incongruous detail, the turned-up nose,
may have been included as a joke, like the ironic description of King
George in the person of the Emperor of Lilliput (*Gulliver's Travels*, I, ii).
128 *out-mouth*] i.e., having full lips.
129 *blub*] swelling.
134 *Can*] if you can.
146 *Maudlin*] melancholy lover. See the quotation from Scudéry's
Ibrahim in the general introduction.

Florimell. 'Tis very well, *Celadon,* you can be constant to one you have never seen; and have forsaken all you have seen.

150 *Celadon.* It seems you know me then: well, if thou shou'dst prove one of my cast Mistresses I would use thee most damnably, for offering to make me love thee twice.

Florimell. You are i'th'right: an old Mistriss or Servant is
155 an old Tune, the pleasure on't is past, when we have once learnt it.

Flavia. But what woman in the world would you wish her like?

Celadon. I have heard of one *Florimell* the Queen's Ward,
160 would she were as like her for Beauty, as she is for Humour.

Flavia. Do you hear that Cousin? *To* Florimell *aside.*

Florimell. *Florimell's* not handsome: besides she's unconstant; and only loves for some few days.

165 *Celadon.* If she loves for shorter time then I, she must love by Winter daies and Summer nights ifaith.

Florimell. When you see us together you shall judge: in the mean time adieu sweet servant.

Celadon. Why you won'not be so inhumane to carry away
170 my heart and not so much as tell me where I may hear news on't?

Florimell. I mean to keep it safe for you; for if you had it, you would bestow it worse: farwell, I must see a Lady.

Celadon. So must I too, if I can pull off your Masque ———
175 *Florimell.* You will not be so rude, I hope.

Celadon. By this light but I will.

Florimell. By this leg but you shan'not.

> *Exeunt* Florimell *and* Flavia *running.*

Enter Philocles, *and meets him going out.*

Celadon (aside). How! my Cousin the new Favourite!

Philocles. Dear *Celadon!* most happily arriv'd.
180 I hear y'have been an honour to your Country
In the *Calabrian* Wars, and I am glad
I have some interest in't.

Celadon.   But in you
I have a larger subject for my joyes:
To see so rare a thing as rising vertue,
185 And merit understood at Court.

Philocles. Perhaps it is the onely act that can
Accuse our Queen of weakness.

Enter Lysimantes *attended.*

Lysimantes. O, my Lord *Philocles,* well overtaken!
  I came to look you.
Philocles.   Had I known it sooner
  My swift attendance, Sir, had spar'd your trouble.   190
  Cousin, you see Prince *Lysimantes*   *To* Celadon.
  Is pleased to favour me with his Commands:
  I beg you'l be no stranger now at Court.
Celadon. So long as there be Ladies there, you need
  Not doubt me.   195
Philocles. Some of them will, I hope, make you a Convert.
                    Exit Celadon.
Lysimantes. My Lord *Philocles,* I am glad we are alone;
  There is a business that concerns me nearly,
  In which I beg your love.
Philocles.   Command my service.
Lysimantes. I know your Interest with the Queen is great;   200
  (I speak not this as envying your fortune,
  For frankly I confess you have deserv'd it.)
  Besides, my Birth, my Courage, and my Honour,
  Are all above so base a Vice. ——
Philocles. I know, my Lord, you are first Prince o'th' Blood;   205
  Your Countries second hope;
  And that the publick Vote, when the Queen weds,
  Designes you for her choice.
Lysimantes. I am not worthy, except Love makes desert:
  For doubtless she's the glory of her time;   210
  Of faultless Beauty, blooming as the Spring,
  In our *Sicilian* Groves; matchless in Vertue,
  And largely sould, where ere her bounty gives,
  As with each breath she could create new *Indies.*
Philocles. But jealous of her glory.   215
Lysimantes. You are a Courtier; and in other terms,
  Would say she is averse from marriage
  Least it might lessen her authority.
  But, whensoe're she does, I know the people
  Will scarcely suffer her to match   220
  With any neighb'ring Prince, whose power might bend
  Our free *Sicilians* to a foreign Yoke.
Philocles. I love too well my Country to desire it.
Lysimantes. Then to proceed, (as you well know, my Lord)
  The Provinces have sent their Deputies   225
  Humbly to move her she would choose at home:
  And, for she seems averse from speaking with them,
  By my appointment, have design'd these walks,

---

222 free] Q1 *cancel; omit* Q1 *original*

213 sould] i.e., souled.

43

230 Where well she cannot shun them. Now, if you
Assist their suit, by joyning yours to it,
And by your mediation I prove happy,
I freely promise you ———
Philocles. Without a Bribe command my utmost in it:——
And yet, there is a thing, which time may give me
The confidence to name.———
235 *Lysimantes.*   'Tis yours whatever.
But tell me true; does she not entertain
Some deep, and setled thoughts against my person?
Philocles. I hope not so; but she, of late, is froward;
Reserv'd, and sad, and vex'd at little things;
240 Which, her great soul asham'd of, straight shakes off,
And is compos'd again.
Lysimantes. You are still near the Queen, and all our Actions
Come to Princes eyes, as they are represented
By them that hold the mirour.
245 *Philocles.* Here she comes, and with her the Deputies; ———
I fear all is not right.

Enter Queen; *Deputies after her*; Asteria, *Guard*, Flavia,
Olinda, Sabina.
Queen *turns back to the Deputies, and speaks entring.*

Queen.   And I must tell you,
It is a sawcy boldness thus to press
On my retirements. ———
1. *Deputy.* Our business being of no less concern
250 Then is the peace and quiet of your Subjects ———
And that delay'd ———
2. *Deputy.*   We humbly took this time
To represent your people's fears to you.
Queen. My people's fears! who made them States-men?
They much mistake their business, if they think
255 It is to govern: ———
The Rights of Subjects and of Soveraigns
Are things distinct in Nature: theirs, is to
Enjoy Propriety, not Empire.
Lysimantes. If they have err'd, 'twas but an over-care;
An ill-tim'd Duty. ———

240–41 straight shakes off, / And is compos'd] Q1 *cancel*; shakes
them off, / And straight composes.——— Q1 *original*
247–48 Thus to press / On my retirements.] Q1 *cancel*; you assume / To press on my retirements. Q1 *original*
252 to you.] Q1 *cancel*; and dangers. Q1 *original*
258 *Propriety*] property.

Queen.   Cousin, I expect   260
    From your near Bloud, not to excuse, but check 'em;
    They would impose a Ruler upon their Lawful Queen:
    For what's an Husband else?
Lysimantes. Farr, Madam, be it from the thoughts
    Of any who pretends to that high Honour,   265
    To wish for more then to be reckoned
    As the most grac'd, and first of all your servants.
Queen. These are th'insinuating promises
    Of those who aim at pow'r: but tell me Cousin;
    (For you are unconcern'd and may be Judge)   270
    Should that aspiring man compass his ends,
    What pawn of his obedience could he give me,
    When Kingly pow'r were once invested in him?
Lysimantes. What greater pledge then Love? when those
        fair eyes
    Cast their commanding beams, he that cou'd be   275
    A Rebel to your birth, must pay them homage.
Queen. All eyes are fair
    That sparkle with the Jewels of a Crown:
    But now I see my Government is odious;
    My people find I am not fit to Reign,   280
    Else they would never ———
Lysimantes. So far from that, we all acknowledge you
    The bounty of the Gods to *Sicilie*:
    More than they are you cannot make our Joyes;
    Make them but lasting in a Successor.   285
Philocles. Your people seek not to impose a Prince;
    But humbly offer one to your free choice:
    And such an one he is, (may I have leave
    To speak some little of his great deserts) ———
Queen. I'le hear no more. ———   290
    For you, attend to morrow at the Council,
                                    To the Deputies.
    There you shall have my firm resolves; mean time
    My Cousin I am sure will welcome you.
Lysimantes [*aside*]. Still more and more mysterious: but I
        have gain'd
    One of her women that shall unriddle it: ———   295
    Come Gentlemen. ———
All Deputies.   Heav'n preserve your Majesty.
                                Exeunt Lysimantes *and Deputies.*
Queen. Philocles you may stay.
Philocles. I humbly wait your Majesties commands.
Queen. Yet, now I better think on't, you may go.

262 They] Q1 *cancel*; By all the Gods they Q1 *original*

300   *Philocles.* Madam!

       Queen. I have no commands, ——— or, what's all one,
         You no obedience.

       Philocles.   How, no obedience, Madam?
         I plead no other merit; 'tis the Charter
         By which I hold your favour, and my fortunes.

       Queen. My favours are cheap blessings, like Rain and Sun-
305   shine,
         For which we scarcely thank the Gods, because
         We daily have them.

       Philocles. Madam, your Breath which rais'd me from the
         dust
         May lay me there again:
310   But fate nor time can ever make me loose
         The sense of your indulgent bounties to me.

       Queen. You are above them now; grown popular:
         Ah *Philocles*, could I expect from you
         That usage I have found! no tongue but yours
315   To move me to a marriage? ———   *Weeps.*
         The factious Deputies might have some end in't,
         And my ambitious Cousin gain a Crown;
         But what advantage could there come to you?
         What could you hope from *Lysimantes* Reign
320   That you can want in mine?

       Philocles. You your self clear me, Madam, had I sought
         More pow'r, this Marriage sure was not the way.
         But, when your safety was in question,
         When all your people were unsatisfied,
325   Desir'd a King, nay more, design'd the Man,
         It was my duty then ———

       Queen. Let me be judge of my own safety;
         I am a woman,
         But danger from my Subjects cannot fright me.

330   *Philocles.* But *Lysimantes*, Madam, is a person ———

       Queen. I cannot love, ———
         Shall I, I who am born a Sovereign Queen,
         Be barr'd of that which God and Nature gives
         The meanest Slave, a freedom in my love?
335   ——— Leave me, good *Philocles*, to my own thoughts;
         When next I need your counsel I'le send for you. ———

       Philocles. I'm most unhappy in your high displeasure;
         But, since I must not speak, Madam, be pleas'd
         To peruse this, and therein, read my care.

          He plucks out a paper, and presents it to her. But drops,
            unknown to him a picture; Exit Philocles.

Queen reads. ⸻
    A Catalogue of such persons ⸻   340
    What's this he has let fall? *Asteria*?   *Spies the box.*
Asteria. Your Majesty ⸻
Queen. Take that up, it fell from *Philocles*.
                 She takes it up, looks on it, and smiles.
Queen. How now, what makes you merry?
Asteria. A small discovery I have made, Madam.   345
Queen. Of what?
Asteria. Since first your Majesty grac'd *Philocles*,
    I have not heard him nam'd for any Mistriss
    But now this picture has convinc'd me ⸻
Queen. Ha! Let me see it. ⸻   *Snatches it from her.*   350
    Candiope, Prince *Lysimantes* sister!
Asteria. Your favour, Madam, may encourage him ⸻
    And yet he loves in a high place for him:
    A Princess of the Blood, and what is more,
    Beyond comparison the fairest Lady   355
    Our Isle can boast. ⸻
Queen. How! she the fairest beyond comparison?
    'Tis false, you flatter her; she is not fair. ⸻
Asteria. I humbly beg forgiveness on my knees,
    If I offended you: But next yours, Madam,   360
    Which all must yield to ⸻
Queen.   I pretend to none.
Asteria. She passes for a beauty.
Queen. I, She may pass. ⸻ But why do I speak of her?
    Dear *Asteria* lead me, I am not well o'th sudden. ⸻
                        She faints.
Asteria. Who's near there? help the Queen.
                 The Guards are coming.
Queen.   Bid 'em away,   365
    'Twas but a qualm, and 'tis already going.⸻
Asteria. Dear Madam what's the matter!
    You are of late so alter'd I scarce know you.
    You were gay humour'd, and you now are pensive,
    Once calm, and now unquiet;   370
    Pardon my boldness that I press thus far
    Into your secret thoughts: I have at least
    A subject's share in you.
Queen.   Thou hast a greater,
    That of a friend; but am I froward, saist thou!
Asteria. It ill becomes me, Madam, to say that.   375

367–68 matter! You are] matter! y'are You are Q1 (*errata list orders deletion of* You are)

341 *the box*] a small case, perhaps containing a miniature portrait.
374 *froward*] hard to please.

Queen. I know I am: prithee forgive me for it.
I cannot help it, but thou hast not long
To suffer it.
Asteria. Alas!

380 *Queen.* I feel my strength each day and hour consume,
Like Lillies wasting in a Lymbeck's heat.
Yet a few dayes ———
And thou shalt see me lie all damp and cold,
Shrouded within some hollow Vault, among
My silent Ancestors.

385 *Asteria.*   O dearest Madam!
Speak not of death, or think not, if you die
That I will stay behind.
Queen. Thy love has mov'd me, I for once will have
The pleasure to be pitied; I'le unfold

390 A thing so strange, so horrid of my self ———
Asteria. Bless me, sweet Heaven!
         So horrid, said you, Madam?
Queen. That Sun, who with one look surveys the Globe,
Sees not a wretch like me: and could the world
Take a right measure of my state within,

395 Mankind must either pity me, or scorn me.
Asteria. Sure none could do the last.
Queen.   Thou long'st to know it:
And I to tell thee, but shame stops my mouth.
First promise me thou wilt excuse my folly,
And next be secret.
Asteria.   Can you doubt it Madam!

400 *Queen.* Yet you might spare my labour;
Can you not guess ———
Asteria.   Madam, please you, I'le try.
Queen. Hold: *Asteria:*
I would not have you guess, for should you find it
I should imagine, that some other might,

405 And then, I were most wretched.
Therefore, though you should know it, flatter me:
And say you could not guess it.———
Asteria. Madam, I need not flatter you, I cannot. ———
And yet,

410 Might not Ambition trouble your repose?
Queen My *Sicily* I thank the Gods, contents me.
But since I must reveal it, know 'tis love:
I who pretended so to glory, am
Become the slave of love. ———

415 *Asteria.* I thought your Majesty had fram'd designes

380 each day and hour] Q2; insensibly Q1

48

To subvert all your Laws; become a Tyrant,
Or vex your neighbours with injurious wars:
Is this all? Madam?
Queen.   Is not this enough?
Then, know, I love below my self; a Subject;
Love one who loves another, and who knows not   420
That I love him.
Asteria.   He must be told it, Madam.
Queen. Not for the world: *Asteria:*
When ere he knows it I shall die for shame.
Asteria. What is it then that would content you?
Queen. Nothing, but that I had not lov'd!   425
Asteria. May I not ask without offence who 'tis?
Queen. Ev'n that confirms me I have lov'd amiss;
Since thou canst know I love, and not imagine
It must be *Philocles.*
Asteria. My Cousin is indeed a most deserving person;   430
' Valiant and wise; and handsome; and well born, ———
Queen. But not of Royal bloud:
I know his fate unfit to be a King.
To be his wife I could forsake my Crown;
But not my glory: 435
Yet,—would he did not love *Candiope*;
Would he lov'd me,—but knew not of my love,
Or ere durst tell me his.
Asteria.   In all this Labyrinth,
I find one path conducing to your quiet, ———
Queen. O tell me quickly then.   440
Asteria. Candiope, as Princess of the Bloud,
Without your approbation cannot marry:
First break his match with her, by vertue of
Your Sovereign Authority.
Queen. I fear that were to make him hate me.   445
Or, what's as bad, to let him know I love him:
Could you not do it of your self?
Asteria. Ile not be wanting to my pow'r:
But if your Majesty appears not in it,
The love of *Philocles* will soon surmount   450
All other difficulties.
Queen. Then, as we walk, we'l think what means are best;
Effect but this, and thou shar'st halfe my breast.
                                        Exeunt.

ACT II. SCENE 1

The Queen's appartments.

[*Enter* Asteria.]

Asteria (*sola*). Nothing thrives that I have plotted:
For I have sounded *Philocles*, and find
He is too constant to *Candiope*:
Her too I have assaulted, but in vain,
5 Objecting want of quality in *Philocles*.
I'le to the Queen, and plainly tell her
She must make use of her Authority
To break the match.

Enter Celadon, *looking about him.*

Brother! what make you here

About the Queen's appartments?

10 Which of the Ladies are you watching for?

Celadon. Any of 'em that will do me the good turn to make me soundly in love.

Asteria. Then I'le bespeak you one; you will be desp'rately in love with *Florimell*: so soon as the Queen heard you
15 were return'd she gave you her for Mistriss.

Celadon. Thank her Majesty; but to confess the truth my fancy lies partly another way.

Asteria. That's strange: *Florimell* vows you are already in love with her.

20 *Celadon.* She wrongs me horribly if ever I saw or spoke with this *Florimell*.

Asteria. Well, take your fortune, I must leave you.

Exit Asteria.

Enter Florimell, *sees him, and is running back.*

Celadon. Nay 'faith I am got betwixt you and home, you are my pris'ner, Lady bright, till you resolve me one
25 question.   *She signs she is dumb.*
Pox; I think she's dumb: what a vengeance dost thou at Court, with such a rare face, without a tongue to answer to a kind question.
Art thou dumb indeed? then, thou canst tell no tales.

Goes to kiss her.

30 *Florimell.* Hold, hold, you are not mad!

Celadon. Oh, my miss in a Masque! have you found your tongue?

Florimell. 'Twas time, I think; what had become of me, if I had not?

35 *Celadon.* Methinks your lips had done as well.

Florimell. I, if my Masque had been over 'em, as it was
    when you met me in the walks.
Celadon. Well; will you believe me another time? did not
    I say you were infinitely handsome: they may talk of
    Florimell, if they will, but i'faith she must come short   40
    of you.
Florimell. Have you seen her, then?
Celadon. I look'd a little that way, but I had soon enough
    of her, she is not to be seen twice without a surfeit.
Florimell. However, you are beholding to her; they say   45
    she loves you.
Celadon. By fate she shan'not love me: I have told her a
    piece of my mind already: pox o' these coming women:
    they set a man to dinner before he has an appetite.

[*Enter*] Flavia *at the door.*

Flavia. *Florimell* you are call'd within. ——   *Exit.*   50
Celadon. I hope in the Lord you are not *Florimell*?
Florimell. Ev'n she at your service; the same kind and
    coming *Florimell* you have describ'd.
Celadon. Why then we are agreed already, I am as kind
    and coming as you for the heart of you: I knew at first   55
    we two were good for nothing but one another.
Florimell. But, without raillery, are you in Love?
Celadon. So horribly much, that contrary to my own
    Maxims, I think in my conscience I could marry you.
Florimell. No, no, 'tis not come to that yet: but if you are   60
    really in love you have done me the greatest pleasure
    in the world.
Celadon. That pleasure, and a better too I have in store for
    you.
Florimell. This Animal call'd a Lover I have long'd to see   65
    these two years.
Celadon. Sure you walk'd with your mask on all the while,
    for if you had been seen, you could not have been with-
    out your wish.
Florimell. I warrant you mean an ordinary whining Lover;   70
    but I must have other proofs of love ere I believe it.
Celadon. You shall have the best that I can give you.
Florimell. I would have a Lover, that if need be, should
    hang himself, drown himself, break his neck, and poyson
    himself for very despair: he that will scruple this is an   75
    impudent fellow if he sayes he is in love.

    74 and] Q2; or Q1
    ——
    36 *over 'em*] some masks covered the entire face, others only the
upper part.
    48 *coming*] inclined to make or meet advances.

Celadon. Pray, Madam, which of these four things would you have your Lover do? for a man's but a man, he cannot hang, and drown, and break his neck, and

80   poyson himself, all together.

Florimell. Well then, because you are but a beginner, and I would not discourage you, any one of these shall serve your turn in a fair way.

Celadon. I am much deceiv'd in those eyes of yours, if a

85   Treat, a Song, and the Fiddles, be not a more acceptable proof of love to you, then any of those Tragical ones you have mentioned.

Florimell. However you will grant it is but decent you should be pale, and lean, and melancholick to shew you

90   are in love: and that I shall require of you when I see you next.

Celadon. When you see me next? why you do not make a Rabbet of me, to be lean at twenty four hours warning? in the mean while we burn daylight, loose time and

95   love.

Florimell. Would you marry me without consideration?

Celadon. To choose, by heaven, for they that think on't, twenty to one would never do it; hang forecast, to make sure of one good night is as much in reason as a

100   man should expect from this ill world.

Florimell. Methinks a few more years and discretion would do well: I do not like this going to bed so early; it makes one so weary before morning.

Celadon. That's much as your pillow is laid before you go

105   to sleep.

Florimell. Shall I make a proposition to you? I will give you a whole year of probation to love me in; to grow reserv'd, discreet, sober and faithful, and to pay me all the services of a Lover. ———

110 *Celadon.* And at the end of it you'll marry me?

Florimell. If neither of us alter our minds before. ———

Celadon. By this light a necessary clause. ——— But if I pay in all the foresaid services before the day, you shall be obliged to take me sooner into mercy.

115 *Florimell.* Provided if you prove unfaithful, then your time of a Twelve-month to be prolong'd; so many services, I will bate you so many dayes or weeks; so many faults,

---

80 all together] Q4; altogether Q1–3,F

96 *consideration*] reflection upon one's interest.

97 *To choose*] by preference, as a thing to choose, somewhat arbitrarily.

98 *forecast*] foresight.

I will add to your 'Prentiship so much more: And of
all this I onely to be Judg.

      Enter Philocles *and* Lysimantes.

Lysimantes. Is the Queen this way, Madam?   120
Florimell. I'le see, so please your Highness: Follow me,
    Captive.   *She pulls him.*
Celadon. March on Conquerour. ———
               Exeunt Celadon, Florimell.
Lysimantes. You're sure her Majesty will not oppose it?
Philocles. Leave that to me my Lord.
Lysimantes.   Then, though perhaps   125
    My Sister's birth might challenge, an higher match,
    I'le weigh your merits on the other side
    To make the ballance even.
Philocles. I go my Lord this minute.
Lysimantes. My best wishes wait on you.   130
                   Exit Lysimantes.

      Enter the Queen *and* Asteria.

Queen. Yonder he is; have I no other way?
Asteria. O Madam, you must stand this brunt:
    Deny him now, and leave the rest to me:
    I'le to *Candiope's* Mother,
    And under the pretence of friendship, work   135
    On her Ambition to put off a match
    So mean as *Philocles.*
Queen (to Philocles).   You may approach, Sir,
    We two discourse no secrets.
Philocles. I come, Madam, to weary out your royal bounty.
Queen. Some suit I warrant for your Cousin *Celadon.*   140
    Leave his advancement to my care.
Philocles. Your goodness still prevents my wishes:
    ——— Yet I have one request,
    Might it not pass almost for madness, and
    Extream Ambition in me. ———   145
Queen. You know you have a favourable Judg,
    It lies in you not to ask any thing
    I cannot grant.
Philocles. Madam, perhaps you think me now too faulty:
    But Love alone inspires me with ambition,   150
    Though but to look on fair *Candiope,*
    Were an excuse for both.
Queen. Keep your Ambition, and let Love alone;

118 add to] Q1 *errata*; add more to Q1 *text*
151 on] Q1 *errata*; from Q1 *text*

That I can cloy, but this I cannot cure.
155　　I have some reasons (invincible to me)
　　　　Which must forbid your marriage with *Candiope*.
Philocles. I knew I was not worthy.
Queen. Not for that, *Philocles*; you deserve all things,
　　　　And to show I think it, my Admiral I hear is dead,
160　　His vacant place (the best in all my Kingdom,)
　　　　I here confer on you.
Philocles.　　　　　　　Rather take back
　　　　All you have giv'n before, then not give this.
　　　　For believe, Madam, nothing is so near
　　　　My soul, as the possession of *Candiope*.
165　*Queen*. Since that belief would be your disadvantage,
　　　　I will not entertain it.
Philocles. Why, Madam, can you be thus cruel to me?
　　　　To give me all things which I did not ask,
　　　　And yet deny that onely thing I beg:
170　　And so beg that I find I cannot live
　　　　Without the hope of it.
Queen.　　　　　　　　Hope greater things;
　　　　But hope not this.
　　　　Haste to o'recome your love, it is but putting
　　　　A short liv'd passion to a violent death.
175　*Philocles*. I cannot live without *Candiope*.
　　　　But I can die without a murmure,
　　　　Having my doom pronounced from your fair mouth.
Queen. If I am to pronounce it, live my *Philocles*,
　　　　But live without (I was about to say
180　　Without his love, but that I cannot do)　　　　*Aside*.
　　　　Live *Philocles* without *Candiope*.
Philocles. Ah, Madam, could you give my doom so
　　　　　　quickly
　　　　And knew it was irrevocable!
　　　　'Tis too apparent
185　　You who alone love glory, and whose soul
　　　　Is loosned from your senses, cannot judg
　　　　What torments mine, of grosser mould, endures.
Queen. I cannot suffer you
　　　　To give me praises which are not my own:
190　　I love like you, and am yet much more wretched
　　　　Then you can think your self.
Philocles. Weak barrs they needs must be that fortune puts
　　　　'Twixt Soveraign Power, and all it can desire.
　　　　When Princes love, they call themselves unhappy,

---

170 so] *errata*; to Q1 *text*

Onely because the word sounds handsome in a Lover's 195
  mouth.
But you can cease to be so when you please
By making *Lysimantes* fortunate.
Queen. Were he indeed the man, you had some reason;
  But 'tis another, more without my power,
  And yet a subject too. 200
Philocles. O, Madam, say not so,
  It cannot be a Subject if not he.
  It were to be injurious to your self
  To make another choice.
Queen. Yet *Lysimantes*, set by him I love, 205
  Is more obscur'd then Stars too near the Sun;
  He has a brightness of his own,
  Not borrow'd of his Fathers, but born with him.
Philocles. Pardon me if I say, who'ere he be,
  He has practis'd some ill Acts upon you, Madam; 210
  For he, whom you describe, I see is born
  But from the lees o'th people.
Queen. You offend me *Philocles*.
  Whence had you leave to use those insolent terms
  Of him I please to love: one I must tell you, 215
  (Since foolishly I have gone on thus far)
  Whom I esteem your equal,
  And far superiour to Prince *Lysimantes*;
  One who deserves to wear a Crown. ———
Philocles. Whirlwinds bear me hence before I live 220
  To that detested day. ——— That frown assures me
  I have offended, by my over freedom;
  But yet me thinks a heart so plain and honest
  And zealous of your glory, might hope your pardon
  for it.
Queen. I give it you; but when you know him better 225
  You'l alter your opinion;
  He's no ill friend of yours.
Philocles.   I well perceive
  He has supplanted me in your esteem;
  But that's the least of ills this fatal wretch
  Has practis'd. ——— Think, for Heaven's sake, Madam, 230
  think
  If you have drunk no Phylter.
Queen. Yes he has given me a Phylter; ———
  But I have drunk it onely from his eyes.
Philocles. Hot Irons thank 'em for't. ———

Softly or turning from her.

Queen.   What's that you mutter?

235   Hence from my sight: I know not whether
                I ever shall endure to see you more.
        Philocles. ——— But hear me, Madam: ———
        Queen. I say be gone. ——— See me no more this day.

                I will not hear one word in your excuse:
240   Now, Sir, be rude again; And give Laws to your Queen.
                                  Exit Philocles *bowing*.
        Asteria, come hither.
        Was ever boldness like to this of *Philocles*?
        Help me to reproach him; for I resolve
        Henceforth no more to love him.
245   *Asteria*. Truth is, I wondred at your patience, Madam:
                Did you not mark his words, his meen, his action,
                How full of haughtiness, how small respect?
        Queen. And he to use me thus, he whom I favour'd,
                Nay more, he whom I lov'd?
250   *Asteria*. A man, me thinks, of vulgar parts and presence!
        Queen. Or allow him something handsome, valiant, or
                so ———
        Yet this to me! ———
        Asteria. The workmanship of inconsiderate favour,
                The Creature of rash love; one of those Meteors
255   Which Monarchs raise from earth,
                And people wondring how they came so high,
                Fear, from their influence, Plagues, and Wars, and
                Famine.
        Queen. Ha!
        Asteria. One whom instead of banishing a day,
260   You should have plum'd of all his borrow'd honours:
                And let him see what abject things they are
                Whom Princes often love without desert.
        Queen. What has my *Philocles* deserv'd from thee
                That thou shouldst use him thus?
265   Were he the basest of Mankind thou could'st not
                Have given him ruder language.
        Asteria. Did not your Majesty command me,
                Did not your self begin?
        Queen. I grant I did, but I have right to do it;
270   I love him, and may rail; ——— in you 'tis malice;
                Malice in the most high degree; for never man
                Was more deserving then my *Philocles*.
                Or, do you love him, ha! and plead that title?

246 *meen*] mien.
254 *Meteors*] comets or shooting stars.

Confess, and I'le forgive you. ———
For none can look on him but needs must love.   275
Asteria. I love him, Madam! I beseech your Majesty
  Have better thoughts of me.
Queen. Dost thou not love him then!
  Good Heav'n, how stupid and how dull is she!
  How most invincibly insensible!   280
  No woman does deserve to live
  That loves not *Philocles*. ———
Asteria. Dear madam, recollect your self; alas
  How much distracted are your thoughts, and how
  Dis-jointed all your words; ———   285
  The Sybill's leaves more orderly were laid.
  Where is that harmony of mind, that prudence
  Which guided all you did! that sense of glory
  Which rais'd you, high above the rest of Kings
  As Kings are o're the level of mankind!   290
Queen. Gone, gone *Asteria*, all is gone,
  Or lost within me far from any use.
  Sometimes I struggle like the Sun in Clouds,
  But straight I am o'recast. ———
Asteria. I grieve to see it. ———
Queen.   Then thou hast yet the goodness   295
  To pardon what I said. ———
  Alas, I use my self much worse then thee.
  Love rages in great souls, ———
  For there his pow'r most opposition finds;
  High trees are shook, because they dare the winds.   300
                              Exeunt.

ACT III. [SCENE 1]

Scene of the Act, *The Court Gallery*.

[Enter] Philocles, *solus.*

Philocles. 'Tis true, she banish'd me but for a day;
  But Favourites, once declining, sink apace.
  Yet Fortune, stop,—this is the likeliest place
  To meet *Asteria*, and by her convey,
  My humble vows to my offended Queen.   5

---

286 *The ... laid*] "Whatever verses the [Sibyl] has traced on leaves
she arranges in order and stores away in a cave. These remain unmoved
in their places and quit not their rank; but when at the turn of the
hinge a light breeze has stirred them, and the open door scattered the
tender foliage, never does she thereafter care to catch them as they
flutter in the rocky cave." Virgil, *Aeneid*, III, 445–50 (Loeb translation).

Enter Queen *and* Asteria.

Ha! She comes her self; Unhappy man

Where shall I hide? ——— *Is going out.*

Queen. Is not that *Philocles*

Who makes such haste away? *Philocles, Philocles* ———

Philocles. I fear'd she saw me. *Coming back.*

10 Queen. How now Sir, am I such a Bugbear

That I scare people from me?

Philocles. 'Tis true, I should more carefully have shun'd

The place where you might be; as, when it thunders,

Men reverently quit the open Air

15 Because the angry Gods are then abroad.

Queen. What does he mean, *Asteria*?

I do not understand him.

Asteria. Your Majesty forgets you banish'd him,

Your presence for this day. *To her softly.*

20 Queen. Ha! banish'd him! 'tis true indeed;

But, as thou sayst, I had forgot it quite. *To her.*

Asteria. That's very strange, scarce half an hour ago.

Queen. But Love has drawn his pardon up so soon

That I forgot he e're offended me.

25 *Philocles.* Pardon me, that I could not thank you sooner:

Your sudden grace, like some swift flood pour'd in

On narrow bancks o'reflow'd my spirits.

Queen. No; 'tis for me to aske your pardon *Philocles*,

For the great injury I did you

30 In not remembring I was angry with you.

But I'le repair my fault,

And rowze my anger up against you yet.

Philocles. No, Madam, my forgiveness was your Act of

grace

And I lay hold of it.

35 Queen. Princes sometimes may pass,

Acts of Oblivion in their own wrong.

Philocles. 'Tis true; but not recall them.

Queen. But, *Philocles*,

Since I have told you there is one I love,

I will go on; and let you know

40 What passed this day betwixt us; be you judg

Whether my servant have dealt well with me.

Philocles. I beseech your Majesty excuse me:

Any thing more of him may make me

Relapse too soon, and forfeit my late pardon.

---

11 me] Q1 *errata*; *omit* Q1 *text*

36 *Acts of Oblivion*] as Charles II in 1660 declared his followers
forgiven for crimes done during the Civil War.

Queen. But you'l be glad to know it.
Philocles.   May I not hope then   45
   You have some quarrel to him?
Queen.   Yes, a great one.
   But first, to justifie my self,
   Know, *Philocles*, I have conceal'd my passion
   With such care from him, that he knows not yet
   I love, but onely that I much esteem him.   50
Philocles. O stupid wretch
   That by a thousand tokens could not guess it!
Queen. He loves elsewhere, and that has blinded him.
Philocles. He's blind indeed!
   So the dull Beasts in the first Paradise   55
   With levell'd eyes gaz'd each upon their kind;
   There fix'd their love: and ne're look'd up to view
   That glorious Creature Man, their soveraign Lord.
Queen. Y'are too severe, on little faults, but he has crimes,
      untold,
   Which will, I fear, move you much more against him.   60
   He fell this day into a passion with me,
   And boldly contradicted all I sed.
Philocles. And stands his head upon his Shoulders yet?
   How long shall this most insolent ———
Queen.   Take heed you rail not,
   You know you are but on your good behaviour.   65
Philocles. Why then I will not call him Traytor ———
   But onely rude, audacious and impertinent,
   To use his Soveraign so. ——— I beg your leave
   To wish you have, at least imprison'd him.
Queen. Some people may speak ill, and yet mean well: 70
   Remember you were not confin'd; and yet
   Your fault was great. In short, I love him
   And that excuses all; but be not jealous;
   His rising shall not be your overthrow,
   Nor will I ever marry him. ———   75
Philocles. That's some comfort yet,
   He shall not be a King.
Queen. He never shall. But you are discompos'd;
   Stay here a little; I have somewhat for you
   Shall shew you still are in my favour.   80
                    Exeunt Queen *and* Asteria.

         Enter to him Candiope *weeping.*

Philocles. How now, in tears, my fair *Candiope*?
   So through a watry Clowd
   The Sun at once seems both to weep and shine.

For what Forefather's sin do you afflict
85   Those precious eyes? for sure you have
None of your own to weep.
Candiope. My Crimes both great and many needs must show
Since Heav'n will punish them with loosing you.
Philocles. Afflictions sent from Heav'n without a cause
90   Make bold Mankind enquire into its Laws.
But Heav'n, which moulding beauty takes such care
Makes gentle fates on purpose for the fair:
And destiny that sees them so divine,
Spinn's all their fortunes in a silken twine:
95   No mortal hand so ignorant is found
To weave course work upon a precious ground.
Candiope. Go preach this doctrine in my Mother's ears.
Philocles. Has her severity produc'd these tears?
Candiope. She has recall'd those hopes she gave before,
100   And strictly bids me ne're to see you more.
Philocles. Changes in froward age are Natural;
Who hopes for constant weather in the fall?
'Tis in your pow'r your duty to transfer
And place that right in me which was in her.
105   *Candiope.* Reason, like foreign foes, would ne're o'recome,
But that I find I am betray'd at home.
You have a friend that fights for you within.
Philocles. Let Reason ever lose, so love may win.

Enter Queen *and* Asteria. Queen *with a Picture in her hand.*

Queen. See there, *Asteria*,
110   All we have done succeeds still to the worse;
We hindred him from seeing her at home,
Where I but onely heard they lov'd; and now
She comes to Court, and mads me with the sight on't.
Asteria. Dear Madam, overcome your self a little,
115   Or they'l perceive how much you are concern'd.
Queen. I struggle with my heart, —— but it will have some vent.
Cousin, you are a stranger at the Court.

                                   To Candiope.

Candiope. It was my duty I confess,
To attend oftner on your Majesty.
120   *Queen.* *Asteria*, Mend my Cousin's Handkerchief;
It sits too narrow there, and shows too much
The broadness of her Shoulders. —— Nay fie, *Asteria*,

114 *overcome*] control, get ahold.

Now you put it too much backward, and discover
The bigness of her breasts.
Candiope. I beseech your Majesty   125
Give not your self this trouble.
Queen. Sweet Cousin, you shall pardon me;
A beauty such as yours deserves a more
Then ordinary care, to set it out.
Come hither, *Philocles*, do but observe,   130
She has but one gross fault in all her shape,
That is, she bears up here too much,
And the malicious Workman has left it open to your
eye.
Philocles. Where, and 'please your Majesty, methinks 'tis
very well?
Queen. Do not you see it, Oh how blind is love!   135
Candiope (aside). And how quick-sighted malice! ———
Queen. But yet methinks, those knots of sky, do not
So well with the dead colour of her face.
Asteria. Your Majesty mistakes, she wants no red.
　　The Queen *here plucks out her Glass, and looks some-*
　　　　　　times on her self, sometimes on her Rival.
Queen. How do I look to day, *Asteria!*   140
Methinks not well.
Asteria. Pardon me, Madam, most victoriously.
Queen. What think you, *Philocles?* come do not flatter.
Philocles. Paris was a bold man who presum'd
To judg the beauty of a Goddess.   145
Candiope. Your Majesty has given the reason why
He cannot judge; his Love has blinded him.
Queen. Methinks a long patch here beneath her eye
Might hide that dismal hallowness, what think you
　　Philocles?
Candiope. Beseech you Madam, ask not his opinion;   150
What my faults are it is no matter;
He loves me with them all.
Queen. I, he may love, but when he marries you
Your Bridal shall be kept in some dark Dungeon.
Farwel, and think of that, too easie Maid,   155
I blush, thou shar'st my bloud.
　　　　　　　　　　　　Exeunt Queen, Asteria.
Candiope.　　　　　　　　Inhumane Queen!
Thou canst not be more willing to resign
Thy part in me, then I to give up mine.

---

137 *knots of sky*] bows of blue ribbon worn on the dress.
149 *dismal*] dark, somber.

Philocles. Love, how few Subjects do thy Laws fulfil,
160   And yet those few, like us, thou usest ill!
Candiope. The greatest slaves, in Monarchies, are they,
    Whom Birth sets nearest to Imperial sway.
    While jealous pow'r does sullenly o're spy,
    We play like Deer within the Lion's eye.
165   Would I for you some Shepherdess had been;
    And, but each May, ne're heard the name of Queen.
Philocles. If you were so, might I some Monarch be,
    Then, you should gain what now you loose by me:
    Then, you in all my glories should have part,
170   And rule my Empire, as you rule my heart.
Candiope. How much our golden wishes are in vain?
    When they are past we are our selves again.

       Enter Queen *and* Asteria *above.*

Queen. Look, look *Asteria*, yet they are not gone.
    Hence, we may hear what they discourse alone.
175 *Philocles.* My Love inspires me with a gen'rous thought
    Which you unknowing, in those wishes taught.
    Since happiness may out of Courts be found,
    Why stay we here on this enchanted ground?
    And choose not rather with content to dwell
180   (If Love and we can find it) in a Cell?
Candiope. Those who, like you, have once in Courts been
       great,
    May think they wish, but wish not to retreat:
    They seldom go but when they cannot stay;
    As loosing Gamesters throw the Dice away.
185   Ev'n in that Cell, where you repose would find,
    Visions of Court will haunt your restless mind;
    And glorious dreams stand ready to restore
    The pleasing shapes of all you had before.
Philocles. He, who with your possession once is blest,
190   On easie terms may part with all the rest.
    All my Ambition will in you be crown'd;
    And those white Arms shall all my wishes bound.
    Our life shall be but one long Nuptial day,
    And, like chaf't Odours, melt in Sweets away.
195   Soft as the Night our Minutes shall be worn,
    And chearful as the Birds that wake the Morn.
Candiope. Thus hope misleads it self in pleasant way;
    And takes more joyes on trust then Love can pay!

194 Sweets] Q1 *errata*; Sweats Q1 *text*
198 more] Q2; mores Q1

But Love, with long possession, once decay'd,
  That face which now you Court, you will upbraid.   200
Philocles. False Lovers broach these tenets, to remove
  The fault from them by placing it on Love. ———
Candiope. Yet grant in Youth you keep alive your Fire,
  Old age will come, and then it must expire:
  Youth but a while does at Love's Temple stay,   205
  As some fair Inn to lodge it on the way.
Philocles. Your doubts are kind; but to be satisfy'd,
  I can be true, I beg I may be try'd.
Candiope. Tryals of love too dear the making cost;
  For, if successless, the whole venture's lost.   210
  What you propose, brings wants and care along.
Philocles. Love can bear both.
Candiope.   But is your love so strong?
Philocles. They do not want, who wish not to have more;
  Who ever said an Anchoret was poor?
Candiope. To answer gen'rously as you have done,   215
  I should not by your arguments be wonn:
  I know I urge your ruine by consent;
  Yet love too well that ruine to prevent.
Philocles. Like water giv'n to those whom Feavers fry,
  You kill but him, who must without it die.   220
Candiope. Secure me I may love without a Crime;
  Then, for our flight, appoint both place and time.
Philocles. Th'ensuing hour my plighted vows shall be;
  The time's not long; or onely long to me.
Candiope. Then, let us go where we shall ne'r be seen   225
  By my hard Mother.
Philocles.   Or my cruel Queen.
                 Exeunt Philocles, Candiope.
Queen (above). O *Philocles* unkind to call me cruel!
  So false *Æneas* did from *Dido* fly;
  But never branded her with cruelty.
  How I despise my self for loving so!   230
Asteria. At once you hate your self and love him too.
Queen. No, his ingratitude has cur'd my wound:
  A painful cure indeed!
Asteria.   And yet not sound.
  His ignorance of your true thoughts
  Excuses this; you did seem cruel, Madam.   235
Queen. But much of kindness still was mix'd with it.
  Who could mistake so grosly not to know
  A *Cupid* frowning when he draws his Bowe?
Asteria. He's going now to smart for his offence.
Queen. Should he without my leave depart from hence?   240
Asteria. No matter; since you hate him, let him go.

Queen. But I my hate by my revenge will show:
　　Besides, his head's a forfeit to the State.
Asteria. When you take that I will believe you hate.

245　　Let him possess, and then he'll soon repent:
　　And so his Crime will prove his punishment.
Queen. He may repent; but he will first possess.
Asteria. O, Madam, now your hatred you confess:
　　If, his possessing her your rage does move,

250　　'Tis jealousie the avarice of love.
Queen. No more, *Asteria.* Seek *Lysimantes* out,
　　Bid him set Guards through all the Court and City.
　　Prevent their marriage first; then stop their flight.
　　Some fitting punishments I will ordain,

255　　But speak not you of *Philocles* again:
　　'Tis bold to search, and dangerous to find,
　　Too much of Heaven's, or of a Prince's mind.
　　　　　　　　　　　　　Queen descends and exit.
　　　　As the Queen *has done speaking,* Flavia *is going hastily*
　　　　　　　　　　　over the Stage; Asteria *sees her.*

Asteria. Flavia, Flavia, Whither so fast?
Flavia. Did you call, *Asteria?*

260　*Asteria.* The Queen has business with Prince *Lysimantes;*
　　Speak to any Gentleman that's next, to fetch him.
　　　　　　　　　　　　Exit Asteria *from above.*
Flavia. I suspect somewhat, but I'le watch you close;
　　Prince *Lysimantes* has not chose in me,
　　The worst Spy of the Court, ——

265　*Celadon!* what makes he here!

　　Enter Celadon, Olinda, Sabina; *they walk over the Stage*
　　　　　　together, he seeming to court them.

Olinda. Nay, sweet *Celadon.* ——
Sabina. Nay, dear *Celadon.* ——
Flavia. O-ho, I see his business now, 'tis with *Melissa's* two
　　Daughters: Look, look, how he peeps about to see if

270　the Coast be clear; like an Hawk that will not plume if
　　she be look'd on. ——
　　　　　　　　　　Exeunt Celadon, Olinda, Sabina.
　　So—at last he has truss'ed his quarry. ——

　　　　　　　　Enter Florimell.

Florimell. Did you see *Celadon* this way?
Flavia. If you had not ask'd the question, I should have

270 *plume*] pluck the feathers of its prey.
272 *truss'ed his quarry*] as a hawk seizes a bird in the air and comes
to the ground with it.

thought you had come from watching him; he's just 275
gone off with *Melissa's* Daughters.

Florimell. *Melissa's* Daughters! he did not Court 'em I
hope?

Flavia. So busily, he lost no time: while he was teaching
the one a tune, he was kissing the other's hand. 280

Florimell. O fine Gentleman!

Flavia. And they so greedy of him! Did you never see two
Fishes about a Bait, tugging it this way, and t'other
way; for my part, I look'd at least he should have lost
a Leg or Arm i'th service. ——— 285
Nay never vex your self, but e'en resolve to break with
him.

Florimell. No no, 'tis not come to that, yet; I'le correct
him first, and then hope the best from time.

Flavia. From time! Believe me, there's little good to be 290
expected from him. I never knew the old *Gentleman*
with the Scythe and Hour-glass bring any thing but
gray hair, thin cheeks, and loss of teeth: you see *Celadon*
loves others.

Florimell. There's the more hope he may love me among 295
the rest: hang't, I would not marry one of these solemn
Fops; they are good for nothing but to make Cuckolds:
Give me a servant that is an high Flier at all games, that
is bounteous of himself to many women; and yet
whenever I pleas'd to throw out the lure of Matrimony, 300
should come down with a swing, and fly the better at
his own quarry.

Flavia. But are you sure you can take him down when
you think good?

Florimell. Nothing more certain. 305

Flavia. What wager will you venture upon the Trial?

Florimell. Any thing.

Flavia. My Maydenhead to yours.

Florimell. That's a good one, who shall take the forfeit?

Flavia. I'le go and write a Letter as from these two Sisters, 310
to summon him immediately; it shall be deliver'd
before you. I warrant you see a strange combat betwixt
the Flesh and the Spirit: if he leaves you to go to them,
you'l grant he loves them better?

Florimell. Not a jot the more: a Bee may pick of many 315
Flowers, and yet like some one better then all the rest.

Flavia. But then your Bee must not leave his sting behind
him.

298 *high Flier*] a high-flying hawk is best.
300 *throw . . . lure*] call the hawk back.

320

Florimell. Well; make the experiment however: I hear him coming, and a whole noise of Fiddles at his heels. Heyday, what a mad Husband shall I have? ———

Enter Celadon.

Flavia. And what a mad wife will he have? Well, I must goe a little way, but I'le return immediately and write it: You'l keep him in discourse the while?

Exit Flavia.

325

Celadon. Where are you, Madam? what do you mean to run away thus? pray stand to't, that we may dispatch this business.

Florimell. I think you mean to watch me as they do Witches, to make me confess I love you. Lord, what-a

330

bustle have you kept this Afternoon? what with eating, singing and dancing, I am so wearied, that I shall not be in case to hear of any more love this fortnight.

Celadon. Nay, if you surfeit on't before Tryal, Lord have mercy upon you when I have married you.

335

Florimell. But what King's Revenue do you think will maintain this extravagant expence?

Celadon. I have a damnable Father, a rich old Rogue, if he would once die! Lord, how long does he mean to make it ere he dies!

340

Florimell. As long as ever he can, I'le pass my word for him.

Celadon. I think then we had best consider him as an obstinate old fellow that is deaf to the news of a better world; and ne're stay for him.

345

Florimell. But e'en marry; and get him Grandchildren in abundance, and great Grandchildren upon them, and so inch him and shove him out of the world by the very force of new Generations:—If that be the way, you must excuse me.

350

Celadon. But dost thou know what it is to be an old Maid?

Florimell. No, nor hope I sha'n't these twenty years.

Celadon. But when that time comes, in the first place thou wilt be condemned to tell Stories, how many men thou mightest have had; and none believe thee: Then thou

320 *noise of Fiddles*] band of musicians.
329 *Witches*] Those suspected of witchcraft were tied down and observed for twenty-four hours (usually in uncomfortable positions) to see if a familiar spirit would visit them (Summers).
332 *in case*] a form of procedure in Common Law, a legal suit for remedy in case (*OED*).
340 *pass*] pledge.

growest froward, and impudently weariest all thy   355
Friends to sollicite Man for thee.

Florimell. Away with your old Common-place wit: I am
resolved to grow fat and look young till forty, and then
slip out of the world with the first wrinckle, and the
reputation of five and twenty.   360

Celadon. Well, what think you now of a reckoning betwixt
us?

Florimell. How do you mean?

Celadon. To discount for so many dayes of my year's
service, as I have paid in since morning.   365

Florimell. With all my heart.

Celadon. Inprimis, For a Treat:
Item, For my Glass Coach:
Item, For sitting bare, and wagging your Fann:
And lastly, and principally, for my Fidelity to you this   370
long hour and half.

Florimell. For this I 'bate you three Weeks of your Service;
now hear your Bill of Faults; for your comfort 'tis a
short one.

Celadon. I know it.   375

Florimell. Inprimis, Item, and Sum totall, for keeping company with *Melissa's* Daughters.

Celadon (aside). How the Pox came you to know of that:
'Gad I believe the Devil plays booty against himself,
and tels you of my sins.   380

Florimell. The offence being so small the punishment shall
be but proportionable, I will set you back onely half a
year.

Celadon. You're most unconscionable: why then, do you
think we shall come together? there's none but the old   385
Patriarchs could live long enough to marry you at this
rate. What, do you take me for some Cousin of *Methusa-
lem's*, that I must stay an hundred years before I come to
beget Sons and Daughters?

Florimell. Here's an impudent Lover, he complains of me   390

367 *Inprimis*] in the first place, a formula for itemized lists in bills
and contracts. This is a "reckoning" he presents, asking that his bill be
reduced.

367 *Treat*] an entertainment, a dinner.

368 *Glass Coach*] a coach with glass windows, a great luxury.

369 *bare*] bare-headed.

372 *'bate*] rebate.

379 *plays booty*] plays falsely, as a gamester who plays badly, a
previous arrangement having been made with a confederate to share the
spoils, especially to encourage the victim by permitting him to win
small stakes (Farmer).

without ever off'ring to excuse himself; *Item*, a fortnight more for that.

Celadon. So, ther's another puff in my voyage has blown me back to the North of *Scotland*.

395 *Florimell.* All this is nothing to your excuse for the two Sisters.

Celadon. 'Faith if ever I did more then kiss 'em, and that but once ———

Florimell. What could you have done more to me?

400 *Celadon.* An hundred times more; as thou shalt know, dear Rogue, at time convenient.

Florimell. You talk, you talk; Could you kiss 'em, though but once, and ne're think of me?

Celadon. Nay if I had thought of thee, I had kiss'd 'em
405 over a thousand times, with the very force of imagination.

Florimell. The Gallants are mightily beholding to you, you have found 'em out a new way to kiss their Mistresses, upon other women's lips.

410 *Celadon.* What would you have? You are my Sultana Queen, the rest are but in the nature of your Slaves; I may make some slight excursion into the Enemies Country for forage or so, but I ever return to my head quarters.

Enter one with a Letter.

415 *Celadon.* To me?

Messenger. If your name be *Celadon*.

Celadon *reads softly.*

Florimell. He's swallowing the Pill; presently we shall see the operation.

Celadon (*to the Page*). Child, come hither Child; here's
420 money for thee: So, be gone quickly good Child, before any body examines thee: Thou art in a dangerous place, Child.——— *Thrusts him out.*
(*Aside*) Very good, the Sisters send me word they will have the Fiddles this Afternoon, and invite me to sup
425 there!—Now cannot I forbear and I should be damn'd, though I have scap'd a scouring so lately for it. Yet I love *Florimell* better then both of 'em together;—there's the Riddle o'nt: but onely for the sweet sake of variety. ——— Well, we must all sin, and we must all repent,
430 and there's an end on't.

Florimell. What is it that makes you fidg up and down so?

424 invite] Q1 errata; invites Q1 text

410–11 *Sultana Queen*] principal wife in a sultan's harem.
431 *fidg*] move about restlessly, to and fro.

Celadon. 'Faith I am sent for by a very dear friend, and
'tis upon a business of life and death.

Florimell. On my life, some woman!

Celadon. On my honour, some man; Do you think I   435
would lye to you?

Florimell. But you engag'd to sup with me!

Celadon. But I consider it may be scandalous to stay late
in your Lodgings.
Adieu dear Miss, if ever I am false to thee again ———   440
           Exit Celadon.

Florimell. See what constant metal you men are made of!
He begins to vex me in good earnest. Hang him, let
him go and take enough of 'em: and yet methinks I
can't endure he should neither. Lord, that such a Mad-
Cap as I should ever live to be jealous!   445
I must after him.
Some Ladies would discard him now, but I
A fitter way for my revenge will find,
I'le marry him, and serve him in his kind.
           Exit Florimell.

ACT IV. [SCENE 1]

Scene, *The Walks.*

[*Enter*] Melissa, *after her* Olinda *and* Sabina.

Melissa. I must take this business up in time: this wild
fellow begins to haunt my house again. Well, I'le be
bold to say it, 'tis as easie to bring up a young Lyon,
without mischief, as a Maidenhead of Fifteen, to make
it tame for an Husband's bed. Not but that the young   5
man is handsome, rich and young, and I could be content he should marry one of 'em; but to seduce 'em both
in this manner, ——— Well, I'le examine 'em apart,
and if I can find out which he loves, I'le offer him his
choice. ——— Olinda, Come hither Child. ———   10

Olinda. Your pleasure, Madam?

Melissa. Nothing but for your good *Olinda*, what think
you of *Celadon*?

Olinda. Why I think he's a very mad fellow; but yet I
have some obligements to him: he teaches me new   15
ayres on the Guitarre, and talks wildely to me, and I to
him.

Melissa. But tell me in earnest, do you think he loves you?

Olinda. Can you doubt it? There were never two so cut
out for one another; we both love Singing, Dancing,   20

Treats and Musick. In short, we are each other's counter-part.

Melissa. But does he love you seriously?

Olinda. Seriously! I know not that; if he did, perhaps I
25 should not love him: but we sit and talk, and wrangle,
and are friends; when we are together we never hold
our tongues; then we have always a noise of Fiddles at
our heels, he hunts me merrily as the Hound does the
Hare; and either this is Love, or I know it not.

30 *Melissa.* Well, go back, and call *Sabina* to me.

                                        Olinda *goes behind.*
This is a Riddle past my finding out: whether he loves
her or no is the question; but this I am sure of, she loves
him: ——   [Sabina *comes forward.*]
O my little Favourite, I must ask you a question con-
35 cerning *Celadon*: Is he in love with you?

Sabina. I think indeed he does not hate me, at least if a
man's word may be taken for it.

Melissa. But what expressions has he made you?

Sabina. Truly the man has done his part: he has spoken
40 civilly to me, and I was not so young but I understood
him.

Melissa. And you could be content to marry him?

Sabina. I have sworn never to marry; besides, he's a wild
young man; yet to obey you, Mother, I could be con-
45 tent to be sacrific'd.

Melissa. No, no, we wou'd but lead you to the Altar.

Sabina. Not to put off the Gentleman neither; for if I have
him not I am resolv'd to die a Maid, that's once,
Mother. ——

50 *Melissa.* Both my Daughters are in love with him, and I
cannot yet find he loves either of 'em.

Olinda. Mother, mother, yonder's *Celadon* in the walks.

Melissa. Peace wanton; you had best ring the Bells for joy.
Well, I'le not meet him, because I know not which to
55 offer him; yet he seems to like the youngest best: I'le
give him opportunity with her; *Olinda*, do you make
haste after me.

Olinda. This is something hard though.   *Exit* Melissa.

Enter Celadon.

Celadon. You see Ladies the least breath of yours brings
60 me to you: I have been seeking you at your Lodgings,
and from thence came hither after you.

27 *noise*] see III.1.320.
48 *that's once*] that's the whole of the matter, in short.

Sabina. 'Twas well you found us.

Celadon. Found you! Half this brightness betwixt you two was enough to have lighted me; I could never miss my way: Here's fair *Olinda* has beauty enough for one 65
Family; such a voice, such a wit, so noble a stature, so white a skin.

Olinda (aside). I thought he would be particular at last.

Celadon. And young *Sabina,* so sweet an innocence,
Such a Rose-bud newly blown. 70
This is my goodly Pallace of Love, and that my little withdrawing Room. (*To Sabina*) A word, Madam.

Olinda (aside). I like not this. —— Sir, if you are not too busie with my Sister, I would speak with you.

Celadon. I come, Madam. —— 75

Sabina. Time enough Sir; pray finish your Discourse,
—— and as you were a saying, Sir ——

Olinda. Sweet Sir ——

Sabina. Sister, you forget, my Mother bid you make haste.

Olinda. Well, go you and tell her I am coming.—— 80

Sabina. I can never endure to be the Messenger of ill news;
but if you please I'le send her word you won't come.—

Olinda. Minion, Minion, remember this. ——

Exit Olinda.

Sabina. She's horribly in love with you.

Celadon. Lord, who could love that walking Steeple: 85
She's so high that every time she sings to me, I am looking up for the Bell that tolls to Church. —— Ha!
Give me my little Fifth-rate! that lies so snug. ——
She, hang her, a Dutch built bottom: she's so tall, there's no boarding her. But we lose time—Madam, let 90
me seal my love upon your mouth.   *Kiss.*
Soft and sweet by Heaven! sure you wear Rose-leaves between your lips.

Sabina. Lord, Lord; What's the matter with me! my breath grows so short I can scarce speak to you. 95

Celadon. No matter, give me thy lips again and I'le speak for thee.

Sabina. You don't love me. ——

Celadon. I warrant thee; set down by me and kiss a-
gain. —— 100
(*Aside*) She warms faster than *Pygmalion's* Image. ——
(*Kiss*) —— I marry sir, this was the original use of lips; talking, eating, and drinking came in bith' by. —

88 *Fifth-rate*] warships were rated according to tonnage and the number of guns, into six classes, first-rate being the largest.
89 *Dutch built bottom*] with a very high and inaccessible main deck.

Sabina. Nay pray be civil; will you be at quiet?

105   *Celadon.* What, would you have me set still and look upon you like a little Puppy-dog that's taught to beg with his fore-leg up?

Enter Florimell.

Florimell. Celadon the faithful! in good time Sir. ———

Celadon. In very good time *Florimell*; for Heaven's sake
110   help me quickly.

Florimell. What's the matter?

Celadon. Do not you see! here's a poor Gentlewoman in a swoon! (swoon away!) I have been rubbing her this half hour, and cannot bring her to her senses.

115   *Florimell.* Alas, how came she so?

Celadon. Oh barbarous! do you stay to ask questions, run for charity.

Florimell. Help, help, alas poor Lady. ———

Exit Florimell.

Sabina. Is she gone?

120   *Celadon.* I, thanks to my wit that helpt me at a pinch;
I thank Heaven, I never pumpt for a lye in all my life yet.

Sabina. I am affraid you love her, *Celadon*!

Celadon. Onely as a civil acquaintance or so, but however
125   to avoid slander you had best be gone before she comes again.

Sabina. I can find a tongue as well as she. ———

Celadon. I, but the truth is, I am a kind of scandalous person, and for you to be seen in my company ———
130   Stay in the walks, by this kiss I'le be with you presently. ———   *Exit* Sabina.

Enter Florimell *running.*

Florimell. Help, help, I can find no body.

Celadon. 'Tis needless now my dear, she's recover'd, and gone off, but so wan and weakly. ———

135   *Florimell.* Umh! I begin to smell a ratt; what was your business here, *Celadon*?

Celadon. Charity, Christian charity; you saw I was labouring for life with her.

Florimell. But how came you hither; not that I care this,—
140   but onely to be satisfied ———   *Sings.*

Celadon. You are jealous, in my Conscience.

Florimell. Who I jealous! Then I wish this sigh may be the last that ever I may draw. ———   *Sighs.*

121 *pumpt*] labored, strained.

72

Celadon. But why do you sigh then?

Florimell. Nothing but a cold, I cannot fetch my breath 145
well. ———— But what will you say if I writ the Letter
you had, to try your faith?

Celadon. Hey-day! This is just the Devil and the Sinner;
you lay snares for me, and then punish me for being
taken; here's trying a man's Faith indeed: What, did 150
you think I had the faith of a Stock, or of a Stone?
Nay, and you go to tantalize a man,—'gad I love upon
the square, I can endure no tricks to be used to me.

Olinda and Sabina at the door Peeping.

Olinda & Sabina. Celadon, Celadon!

Florimell. What voices are those? 155

Celadon. Some Camerades of mine that call me to play;

———

(*Aside*) Pox on 'em, they'l spoil all. ————

Florimell. Pray let's see 'em.

Celadon. Hang 'em Tatterdemallions, they are not worth 160
your sight; 'pray Gentlemen be gone, I'le be with you
immediately.

Sabina. No, we'll stay here for you.

Florimell. Do your Gentlemen speak with Treble-voices?
I am resolv'd to see what company you keep. 165

Celadon. Nay, good my Dear. ————

He lays hold of her to pull her back; she lays hold of
Olinda, *by whom* Sabina *holds; so that he pulling,*
they all come in.

Florimell. Are these your Comerades?
(*Sings*) '*Tis* Strephon *calls, what would my love?*
Why do not you roar out like a great Bass-vyal, *Come*
follow to the Myrtle-grove. Pray Sir, which of these fair 170
Ladies is it, for whom you were to do the courtesie,
for it were unconscionable to leave you to 'em both;
What, a man's but a man you know.

Olinda. The Gentleman may find an owner.

Sabina. Though not of you. 175

Florimell. Pray agree whose the lost sheep is, and take him.

Celadon. 'Slife they'l cry me anon, and tell my marks.

Florimell. Troth I pity your Highness there, I perceive he
has left you for the little one: Me thinks he should have
been affraid to break his neck when he fell so high as 180
from you to her.

---

177 *marks*] distinguishing features, as those of a stray animal were
proclaimed by the crier in several marketplaces.

Sabina. Well my drolling Lady, I may be even with
you. ———

Florimell. Not this ten years by thy growth, yet.

185 *Sabina.* Can flesh and blood endure this! ———

Florimell. How now, my *Amazon in decimo sexto*! ———

Olinda. Do you affront my Sister? ———

Florimell. I, but thou art so tall, I think I shall never affront
thee. ———

190 *Sabina.* Come away Sister, we shall be jeer'd to Death else.
Exeunt Olinda, Sabina.

Florimell. Why do you look that way, you can'nt forbear
leering after the forbidden Fruit. ——— But when e're
I take a Wencher's word again! ———

Celadon. A Wencher's word! Why should you speak so
195 contemptibly of the better half of Mankind. I'le stand
up for the honour of my Vocation.

Florimell. You are in no fault I warrant;—'ware my
busk. ———

Celadon. Not to give a fair Lady the lye, I am in fault;—
200 but otherwise—Come let us be friends; and let me wait
you to your Lodgings.

Florimell. This impudence shall not save you from my
Table-book.

Item. A Month more for this fault. ———
They walk to the door.

205 *1. Souldier* (*within*). Stand.

2. Souldier [*within*]. Stand, give the word.

Celadon. Now, what's the meaning of this, trow? guards
set!

1. Souldier [*within*]. Give the word, or you cannot pass;
210 these are they brother; let's in, and seize em.

The two Souldiers enter.

1. Souldier. Down with him.

2. Souldier. Disarm him.

Celadon. How now Rascalls: ———
Draws and beats one off, and catches the other.
Ask your life you villain.

215 *2. Souldier.* Quarter, quarter.

Celadon. Was ever such an Insolence?

[*2.*] *Souldier.* We did but our duty; here we were set, to

186 *decimo sexto*] sixteenmo, a very small format of a printed
book, hence a diminutive person.

198 *busk*] stays, made of wood or whalebone, a weapon she
could draw to defend herself, when someone "gives her the lie."

203 *Table-book*] memorandum book.

take a Gentleman and Lady, that would steal a marriage
without the Queen's consent, and we thought you had
been they.   *Exit Souldiers.*   220

Florimell. Your Cousin *Philocles* and the Princess *Candiope*
on my life! for I heard the Queen give private Orders
to *Lysimantes,* and name them twice or thrice.

Celadon. I know a score or two of Madcaps here hard by,
whom I can pick up from Taverns and Gaming-houses,   225
and Bordells; those I'le bring to aid him: Now *Florimell,*
there's an argument for wenching; where would you
have had so many honest men together upon the sudden
for a brave employment?

Florimell. You'l leave me then to take my fortune?   230

Celadon. No; if you will, I'le have you into the places
aforesaid, and enter you into good company.

Florimell. 'Thank you Sir, here's a key will let me through
this back-door to my own Lodgings.

Celadon. If I come off with life, I'le see you this evening,   235
if not ——— Adieu *Florimell.* ———

Florimell. If you come not I shall conclude you are kill'd,
or taken; to be hang'd for a Rebel to morrow morning,—and then I'le honour your memory with a Lampoon instead of an Epitaph.   240

Celadon. No no, I trust better in my Fate: I know I am
reserv'd to do you a Courtesie.   *Exit* Celadon.

> *As* Florimell *is unlocking the door to go out,* Flavia *opens
> it against her, and enters to her, followed by a Page.*

Flavia. *Florimell,* do you hear the News?

Florimell. I guess they are in pursuit of *Philocles.*

Flavia. When *Lysimantes* came with the Queen's Orders,   245
He refused to render up *Candiope;*
And with some few brave friends he had about him
Is forcing of his way through all the Guards.

Florimell. A gallant fellow: I'le in, will you with me?
Hark, the noise comes this way!   250

Flavia. I have a message from the Queen to *Lysimantes,*
I hope I may be safe among the Souldiers.

Florimell. Oh very safe, perhaps some honest fellow in the
tumult may take pity of thy Maidenhead, or so—
Adiew.   255

Page. The noise comes nearer, Madam.   *Exit* Florimell.

Flavia. I am glad on't: this message gives me the opportunity of speaking privately with *Lysimantes.*

> *Enter* Philocles *and* Candiope, *with three friends; pursued by*
> Lysimantes *and Souldiers.*

75

Lysimantes. What is it renders you thus obstinate? you have
260   no hope of flight, and to resist is full as vain.
Philocles. I'le die, rather then yield her up.
Flavia. My Lord!
Lysimantes.   How now, some new message from the
    Queen?
    Retire a while to a convenient distance. *To Souldiers.*
           Lysimantes *and* Flavia *whisper.*
    Lysimantes. O *Flavia* 'tis impossible! the Queen in love
    with *Philocles*!
265 *Flavia.* I half suspected it before; but now,
    My ears and eyes are witnesses. ———
    This hour I over-heard her to *Asteria*
    Making such sad complaints of her hard fate!
    For my part I believe you lead him back
    But to his Coronation.
270 *Lysimantes.*   Hell take him first.
    Flavia. Presently after this she call'd for me,
    And bid me run, and with strict care command you
    On peril of your life he had no harm:
    But, Sir, she spoke it with so great concernment,
275 Me thought I saw love, anger and despair
    All combating at once upon her face.
    Lysimantes. Tell the Queen———
    I know not what, I am distracted so;———
    But go and leave me to my thoughts. ———
              Exit Flavia.
280 Was ever such amazing news
    Told in so strange and critical a moment!
    What shall I do!
    Does she love *Philocles*, who loves not her;
    And loves not *Lysimantes* who prefers her
285 Above his life! what rests but that I take
    This opportunity, which she her self
    Has given me, to kill this happy Rival!
    Assist me Souldiers.
    Philocles.   They shall buy me dearly.
    Candiope. Ah me, unhappy maid!

    Enter Celadon *with his Friends, unbutton'd and reeling.*

290 *Celadon.* Courage my noble Cousin, I have brought
    A band of Blades, the bravest youths of *Syracuse*:
    Some drunk, some sober, all resolv'd to run
    Your fortune to the utmost. Fall on mad Boyes. ———
    Lysimantes. Hold, a little; ———
295 I'm not secure of victory against these desperate ruffins.

Celadon. No, but I'le secure you; they shall cut your
throat for such another word of 'em. Ruffins quoth a!
call Gamesters, and Whoremasters, and Drunkards,
Ruffins! ———

Lysimantes. Pray Gentlemen fall back a little. ———   300

Celadon. O ho, are they Gentlemen now with you!
Speak first to your Gentlemen Souldiers to retire; and
then I'le speak to my Gentlemen Ruffians.
                    Celadon signs to his party.
There's your disciplin'd men now. ———
            They sign, and the Souldiers retire on both sides.
Come Gentlemen, let's lose no time; while they are   305
talking, let's have one merry mayn before we die—for
Mortality sake.

1 [Friend]. Agreed, here's my Cloak for a Table.

2 [Friend]. And my Hat for a Box. ———
                    They lie down and throw.

Lysimantes. Suppose I kill'd him!   310
'Twould but exasperate the Queen the more:
He loves not her, nor knows he she loves him:
A sudden thought is come into my head ———
So to contrive it, that this *Philocles,*
And these his friends shall bring to pass that for me   315
Which I could never compass. ——— True I strain
A point of honour; but then her usage to me ———
It shall be so. ———
Pray, *Philocles,* command your Souldiers off,
As I will mine: I've somewhat to propose   320
Which you perhaps may like.

Candiope. I will not leave him.

Lysimantes.   'Tis my desire you should not.

Philocles. Cousin, lead off your friends.

Celadon. One word in your ear Couz. Let me advise you;
either make your own conditions, or never agree with   325
him: his men are poor sober Rogues, they can never
stand before us.
        Exeunt omnes præter Lysimantes, Philocles, Candiope.

Lysimantes. Suppose some friend, e're night,
Should bring you to possess all you desire;
And not so onely, but secure for ever   330
The Nation's happiness ———

Philocles. I would think of him as of some God, or Angel.

Lysimantes. That God or Angel you and I

296 secure] Q1 *errata;* secur'd Q1 *text*
304 sign] Q6; *sing* Q1–5, F
306 mayn] game of hazard, somewhat like craps.

May be to one another. We have betwixt us
335   An hundred men; The Cittadel you govern:
What were it now to seize the Queen!
Philocles. O impiety! to seize the Queen!
To seize her, said you?
Lysimantes. The word might be too rough, I meant secure
her.
340 *Philocles.* Was this your proposition,
And had you none to make it to but me?
Lysimantes. Pray hear me out e're you condemn me:
I would not the least violence were offer'd
Her person; two small grants is all I ask,
345 To make me happy in her self, and you
In your *Candiope.*
Candiope. And will not you do this, my *Philocles?*
Nay now my Brother speaks but reason.
Philocles. Int'rest makes all seem reason that leads to it.
350 Int'rest that does the zeal of Sects create,
To purge a Church, and to reform a State.
Lysimantes. In short, the Queen hath sent to part you two;
What more she means to her, I know not.
Philocles. To her! alas! why, will not you protect her?
355 *Lysimantes.* With you I can; but where's my power alone?
Candiope. You know she loves me not: you lately heard
her
How she insulted over me: how she
Despis'd that beauty which you say I have;
I see she purposes my death.
360 *Philocles.* Why do you fright me with it?
'Tis in your Brother's pow'r to let us 'scape,
And then you run no danger.
Lysimantes.   True, I may;
But then my head must pay the forfeit of it.
Philocles. O wretched *Philocles,* whither would love
Hurry thee headlong!
365 *Lysimantes.*   Cease these exclamations.
Ther's no danger on your side: 'tis but
To live without my Sister, resolve that
And you have shot the gulf.
Philocles. To live without her! is that nothing think you?
370 The damn'd in Hell endure no greater pain
Then seeing Heaven from far with hopeless eyes.
Candiope. Candiope must die, and die for you;
See it not unreveng'd at least.

341 but me] Q4; but to me Q1–3

368 *shot the gulf*] succeeded in your dangerous enterprise, as
when a ship passes through perilous waters.

78

Philocles. Ha, unreveng'd! on whom should I revenge it?
  But yet she dies, and I may hinder it;   375
  'Tis I then murder my *Candiope*:
  And yet should I take armes against my Queen!
  That favour'd me, rais'd me to what I am!
  Alas, it must not be.
Lysimantes (*aside*). He cools again.——True; she once
    favour'd you;   380
  But now I am inform'd,
  She is besotted on an upstart wretch;
  So far, that she intends to make him Master,
  Both of her Crown and person.
Philocles (*aside*).   Knows he that!
  Then, what I dreaded most is come to pass. ——   385
  I am convinc'd of the necessity;
  Let us make haste to raze
  That action from the Annals of her Reign:
  No motive but her glory could have wrought me.
  I am a Traytor to her, to preserve her   390
  From Treason to her self; and yet Heav'n knows
  With what a heavy heart
  Philocles turns reformer: but have care
  This fault of her strange passion take no air.
  Let not the vulgar blow upon her fame.   395
Lysimantes. I will be careful, shall we go my Lord?
Philocles. Time wasts apace; Each first prepare his men.
  Come my *Candiope*. ——
               Exeunt Philocles, Candiope.
Lysimantes. This ruines him forever with the Queen;
  The odium's half his, the profit all my own.   400
  Those who, like me, by others help would climb,
  To make 'em sure, must dip 'em in their crime.
                   Exit Lysimantes.

[ACT IV.] Scene 2
The Queen's *appartments*.

Enter Queen *and* Asteria.

Queen. No more news yet from *Philocles*?
Asteria. None, Madam, since *Flavia's* return!
Queen. O my *Asteria*, if you lov'd me, sure
  You would say something to me of my *Philocles*;
  I could speak ever of him.   5

388 the] Q1 *errata; omit* Q1 *text*

79

Asteria. Madam, you commanded me no more to name
   him to you.

Queen. Then I command you now to speak of nothing else:
   I charge you here, on your allegiance, tell me
   What I should do with him.

10 *Asteria.* When you gave orders that he should be taken,
   You seem'd resolv'd how to dispose of him.

Queen. Dull *Asteria* not to know,
   Mad people never think the same thing twice.
   Alas, I'm hurried restless up and down,
15   I was in anger once, and then I thought
   I had put into shore!
   But now a gust of love blows hard against me,
   And bears me off again.

Asteria. Shall I sing the Song you made of *Philocles*,
20   And call'd it *Secret-love*.

Queen. Do, for that's all kindness: and while thou sing'st it,
   I can think nothing but what pleases me,

SONG

I feed a flame within which so torments me
That it both pains my heart, and yet contents me:
25 *'Tis such a pleasing smart, and I so love it,*
That I had rather die, then once remove it.

Yet he for whom I grieve shall never know it,
My tongue does not betray, nor my eyes show it:
Not a sigh nor a tear my pain discloses,
30 *But they fall silently like dew on Roses.*

Thus to prevent my love from being cruel,
My heart's the sacrifice as 'tis the fuel:
And while I suffer this to give him quiet,
My faith rewards my love, though he deny it.

35 *On his eyes will I gaze, and there delight me;*
While I conceal my love, no frown can fright me:
To be more happy I dare not aspire;
Nor can I fall more low, mounting no higher.

Queen. Peace: Me thinks I hear the noise
40   Of clashing Swords, and clatt'ring Armes, below.

Enter Flavia.

Now; what news that you press in so rudely?
Flavia. Madam, the worst that can be;

Your Guards upon the sudden are surpris'd,
Disarm'd, some slain, all scatter'd.
Queen. By whom?   45
Flavia. Prince *Lysimantes*, and Lord *Philocles*.
Queen. It cannot be; *Philocles* is a Prisoner.
Flavia. What my eyes saw ———
Queen. Pull 'em out, they are false Spectacles.
Asteria. O vertue, impotent and blind as Fortune!   50
  Who would be good, or pious, if this Queen
  Thy great Example suffers!
Queen. Peace, *Asteria*, accuse not vertue;
  She has but given me a great occasion
  Of showing what I am when Fortune leaves me.   55
Asteria. Philocles, to do this!
Queen. I, *Philocles*, I must confess 'twas hard!
  But there's a fate in kindness
  Still, to be least return'd where most 'tis given.
  Where's *Candiope*?   60
Flavia. Philocles was whispering to her.
Queen. Hence Screech-owl; call my Guards quickly there:
  Put 'em apart in several Prisons.
  Alas! I had forgot I have no Guards,
  But those which are my Jaylors.   65
  Never till now unhappy Queen:
  The use of pow'r, till lost, is seldom known;
  Now I would strike, I find my Thunder gone.
                          Exit Queen *and* Flavia.

Philocles *enters, and meets* Asteria *going out.*

Philocles. Asteria! Where's the Queen?
Asteria. Ah my Lord what have you done!   70
  I came to seek you.
Philocles.   Is it from her you come?
Asteria. No, but on her behalf: her heart's too great,
  In this low ebb of Fortune, to intreat.
Philocles. 'Tis but a short Ecclipse,
  Which past, a glorious day will soon ensue: 75
  But I would ask a favour too, from you.
Asteria. When Conquerors petition, they command:
  Those that can Captive Queens, who can withstand?
Philocles. She, with her happiness, might mine create;
  Yet seems indulgent to her own ill fate: 80
  But she, in secret, hates me sure; for why
  If not, should she *Candiope* deny?
Asteria. If you dare trust my knowledg of her mind,
  She has no thoughts of you that are unkind.

81

85   *Philocles.* I could my sorrows with some patience bear,
        Did they proceed from any one but her:
        But from the Queen! whose person I adore,
        By Duty much, by inclination more. ———
    Asteria (aside). He is inclin'd already, did he know
90   That she lov'd him, how would his passion grow!
    Philocles. That her fair hand with Destiny combines! ———
        Fate ne're strikes deep, but when unkindness joynes!
        For, to confess the secret of my mind,
        Something so tender for the Queen I find,
95   That ev'n *Candiope* can scarce remove,
        And, were she lower, I should call it love.
    Asteria (aside). She charg'd me not this secret to betray,
        But I best serve her if I disobey:
        For, if he loves, 'twas for her int'rest done;
100   If not, he'll keep it secret for his own. ———
    Philocles. Why are you in obliging me so slow?
    Asteria. The thing's of great importance you would know;
        And you must first swear secresie to all.
    Philocles. I swear.
    Asteria.   Yet hold; your oath's too general:
105   Swear that *Candiope* shall never know.
    Philocles. I swear.
    Asteria.   No not the Queen her self.
    Philocles.   I vow.
    Asteria. You wonder why I am so cautious grown
        In telling, what concerns your self alone:
        But spare my Vow, and guess what it may be
110   That makes the Queen deny *Candiope*:
        'Tis neither hate nor pride that moves her mind;
        Methinks the Riddle is not hard to find.
    Philocles. You seem so great a wonder to intend,
        As were, in me, a crime to apprehend.
115   *Asteria.* 'Tis not a crime, to know; but would be one
        To prove ungrateful when your Duty's known.
    Philocles. Why would you thus my easie faith abuse!
        I cannot think the Queen so ill would chuse.
        But stay, now your imposture will appear;
120   She has her self confess'd she lov'd elsewhere:
        On some ignoble choice has plac'd her heart,
        One who wants quality, and more, desert.
    Asteria. This, though unjust, you have most right to say,
        For if you'l rail against your self, you may.
125   *Philocles.* Dull that I was!
        A thousand things now crowd my memory

     121 On] Q1 *errata*; Or Q1 *text*

That make me know it could be none but I.
Her Rage was Love: and its tempestuous flame,
Like Lightning, show'd the Heaven from whence it
    came.
But in her kindness my own shame I see; 130
Have I dethron'd her then, for loving me?
I hate my self for that which I have done,
Much more, discover'd, then I did unknown.
How does she brook her strange imprisonment?
Asteria. As great souls should, that make their own con-
    tent. 135
The hardest term she for your act could find
Was onely this, O *Philocles*, unkind!
Then, setting free a sigh, from her fair eyes
She wip'd two pearls, the remnants of mild show'rs,
Which hung, like drops upon the bells of flowers: 140
And thank'd the Heav'ns,
Which better did, what she design'd, pursue,
Without her crime to give her pow'r to you.
Philocles. Hold, hold, you set my thoughts so near a Crown,
They mount above my reach to pull them down: 145
Here Constancy; Ambition there does move;
On each side Beauty, and on both sides Love.
Asteria. Me thinks the least you can is to receive
This love, with reverence, and your former leave.
Philocles. Think but what difficulties come between! 150
Asteria. 'Tis wond'rous difficult to love a Queen.
Philocles. For pity cease more reasons to provide,
I am but too much yielding to your side;
And, were my heart but at my own dispose,
I should not make a scruple where to choose. 155
Asteria. Then if the Queen will my advice approve,
Her hatred to you shall expel her love.
Philocles. Not to be lov'd by her, as hard would be
As to be hated by *Candiope*.
Asteria. I leave you to resolve while you have time; 160
You must be guilty, but may choose your crime.
                      Exit Asteria.
Philocles. One thing I have resolv'd; and that I'le do
Both for my love, and for my honour too.
But then, (Ingratitude and falshood weigh'd,)
I know not which would most my soul upbraid. 165
Fate shoves me headlong down, a rugged way;
Unsafe to run, and yet too steep to stay.
                      Exit Philocles.

160 *resolve*] remove the scruples from your conscience. A "resolved
soul" had as clean a conscience as the circumstances allow.

ACT V. [Scene 1]

Scene *The Court*.

[*Enter*] Florimell *in Man's Habit*.

Florimell. Twill be rare now if I can go through with it, to out-do this mad *Celadon* in all his tricks, and get both his Mistresses from him; then I shall revenge my self upon all three, and save my own stake into the bargain;
5   for I find I do love the Rogue in spight of all his infidelities. Yonder they are, and this way they must come.—
If cloathes and a *bon meen* will take 'em, I shall do't.
——— Save you *Monsieur Florimell*; Faith me thinks you are a very *janty* fellow, *poudré et ajusté* as well as the
10   best of 'em. I can manage the little Comb,—set my Hat, shake my Garniture, toss about my empty Noddle, walk with a courant slurr, and at every step peck down my Head:—if I should be mistaken for some Courtier now, pray where's the difference? ———

Enter to her Celadon, Olinda, Sabina.

15   *Olinda.* Never mince the matter!
Sabina. You have left your heart behind with *Florimell*; we know it.
Celadon. You know you wrong me; when I am with *Florimell* 'tis still your Prisoner, it onely draws a longer
20   chain after it.
Florimell (*aside*). Is it e'en so! then farwell poor *Florimell*, thy Maidenhead is condemned to die with thee. ———
Celadon. But let's leave the discourse; 'tis all digression that does not speak of your beauties. ———
25   *Florimell.* Now for me in the name of impudence! ———
Walks with them.
They are the greatest beauties I confess that ever I beheld. ———
Celadon. How now, what's the meaning of this, young fellow?
30   *Florimell.* And therefore I cannot wonder that this Gentleman who has the honour to be known to you should admire you,—since I that am a stranger ———

10 *Comb*] "To comb the wig. Fops affected to do this with grace and fashion" (Summers).
11 *Garniture*] ornaments.
11 *Noddle*] i.e., noodle.
12 *courant slurr*] a gliding movement, as in dancing the courant or coranto.

Celadon. And a very impudent one, as I take it, Sir. ———

Florimell. Am so extreamly surpriz'd, that I admire, love, am wounded, and am dying all in a moment.   35

Celadon. I have seen him somewhere, but where I know not! prithee my friend leave us, dost thou think we do not know our way in Court?

Florimell. I pretend not to instruct you in your way; you see I do not go before you! but you cannot possibly   40 deny me the happiness to wait upon these Ladies; ——— me, who ———

Celadon. Thee, who shalt be beaten most unmercifully if thou dost follow them! ———

Florimell. You will not draw in Court I hope! ———   45

Celadon. Pox on him, let's walk away faster, and be rid of him. ———

Florimell. O take no care for me, Sir, you shall not lose me, I'le rather mend my pace, then not wait on you.

Olinda. I begin to like this fellow. ———   50

Celadon. You make very bold here in my Seraglio, and I shall find a time to tell you so, Sir.

Florimell. When you find a time to tell me on't, I shall find a time to answer you: But pray what do you find in your self so extraordinary, that you should serve these Ladies   55 better then I; let me know what 'tis you value your self upon, and let them Judg betwixt us.

Celadon. I am somewhat more a man then you.

Florimell. That is, you are so much older then I: Do you like a man ever the better for his age, Ladies?   60

Sabina. Well said, young Gentleman.

Celadon. Pish, thee! a young raw Creature, thou hast ne're been under the Barber's hands yet.

Florimell. No, nor under the Surgeon's neither as you have been.   65

Celadon. 'Slife what wouldst thou be at? I am madder then thou art!

Florimell. The Devil you are; I'le Tope with you, I'le Sing with you, I'le Dance with you,—I'le Swagger with you. ———   70

Celadon. I'le fight with you.

Florimell. Out upon fighting; 'tis grown so common a fashion, that a Modish man contemns it; A man of Garniture and Feather is above the dispensation of the Sword.   75

45 *draw in Court*] a grave breach of etiquette, incurring heavy fines, because the presence of the king was supposed to reconcile disputes and calm disorder.

64 *under the Surgeon's*] treated for venereal disease.

[Enter Musicians.]

Olinda. Uds my life, here's the Queen's Musick just going
    to us; you shall decide your quarrel by a Dance.

Sabina. Who stops the Fiddles?

Celadon. Base and Trebble, by your leaves we arrest you
80   at these Ladies suits.

Florimell. Come on Sirs, play me a Jigg,
    You shall see how I'le baffle him.

Dance. [Exeunt Musicians.]

Florimell. Your judgment, Ladies.

Olinda. You sir, you sir: This is the rarest Gentleman: I
85   could live and die with him. ———

Sabina. Lord how he Sweats! please you Sir to make use
    of my Handkerchief?

Olinda. You and I are merry, and just of an humour Sir;
    therefore we two should love one another.

90 *Sabina.* And you and I are just of an age Sir, and therefore
    me thinks we should not hate one another.

Celadon. Then I perceive Ladies I am a Castaway, a
    Reprobate with you: why faith this is hard luck now,
    that I should be no less then one whole hour in getting
95   your affections, and now must lose 'em in a quarter of it.

Olinda. No matter, let him rail, does the loss afflict you
    Sir?

Celadon. No in faith does it not; for if you had not for-
    saken me, I had you: so the Willows may flourish for
100   any branches I shall rob 'em of.

Sabina. However we have the advantage to have left you;
    not you us.

Celadon. That's onely a certain nimbleness in Nature you
    women have to be first unconstant: but if you had not
105   made the more haste, the wind was veering too upon
    my Weathercock: the best on't is *Florimell* is worth both
    of you.

Florimell. 'Tis like she'll accept of their leavings.

Celadon. She will accept on't, and she shall accept on't;
110   I think I know more then you of her mind Sir.

Enter Melissa.

Melissa. Daughters there's a poor collation within that
    waits for you.

Florimell. Will you walk musty Sir?

Celadon. No merry Sir; I won'not; I have surfeited of that
115   old woman's face already.

Florimell. Begin some frolick then; what will you do for
    her?

Celadon. Faith I am no dog to show tricks for her; I cannot
come aloft for an old Woman.

Florimell. Dare you kiss her! 120

Celadon. I was never dar'd by any man,—by your leave
old Madam. ——— *He plucks off her Ruff.*

Melissa. Help, help, do you discover my nakedness?

Celadon. Peace Tiffany! no harm. *He puts on the Ruff.*
Now Sir here's *Florimell's* health to you. *Kisses her.* 125

Melissa. Away sir: ——— a sweet young man as you are to
abuse the gifts of Nature so.

Celadon. Good Mother do not commend me so; I am
flesh and blood; and you do not know what you may
pluck upon that reverend person of yours. ——— 130
Come on, follow your leader.

> *Gives* Florimell *the Ruff, she puts it on.*

Florimell. Stand fair Mother. ———

Celadon. What with your Hat on? lie thou there;—and
thou too. ———

> *Plucks off her Hat and Perruke, and discovers* Florimell.

Omnes. Florimell! 135

Florimell. My kind Mistresses how sorry I am I can do you
no further service! I think I had best resign you to
Celadon to make amends for me.

Celadon. Lord what a misfortune it was Ladies, that the
Gentleman could not hold forth to you. 140

Olinda. We have lost *Celadon* too.

Melissa. Come away; this is past enduring.

> *Exeunt* Melissa, Olinda.

Sabina. Well, if ever I believe a man to be a man for the
sake of a Perruke and Feather again. ——— *Exit.*

Florimell. Come *Celadon*, shall we make accounts even? 145
Lord what a hanging look was there: indeed if you had
been recreant to your Mistress, or had forsworn your
love, that sinner's face had been but decent, but for the
vertuous, the innocent, the constant *Celadon!* ———

Celadon. This is not very heroick in you now to insult 150
over a man in his misfortunes; but take heed, you have
robb'd me of my two Mistresses; I shall grow desperately constant, and all the tempest of my love will fall
upon your head: I shall so pay you.

---

122 *Ruff*] probably her neck cloth or collar. He is touzling and
mouzling her here; see J. H. Wilson's *All The King's Ladies* (1958), on
this popular stage business.

124 *Tiffany*] a wanton (Farmer). Tiffany is a transparent silk "which
instead of apparell to cover and hide shew[s] women naked through" it
(Holland's *Pliny*, 1601, xi, xxii).

155 *Florimell.* Who you, pay me! you are a banckrupt, cast
beyond all possibility of recovery.

Celadon. If I am a banckrupt I'le be a very honest one;
when I cannot pay my debts, at least I'le give you up
the possession of my body.

160 *Florimell.* No, I'le deal better with you; since you're unable to pay, I'le give in your bond.

Enter Philocles *with a Commander's Staff in his hand,*
Attended.

Philocles. Cousin I am sorry I must take you from your
company about an earnest business.

Florimell. There needs no excuse my Lord, we had dis-
165 patch'd our affairs, and were just parting. ———
Going.

Celadon. Will you be going Sir; sweet Sir, damn'd Sir,
I have but one word more to say to you.

Florimell. As I am a man of Honour, I'le wait on you
some other time. ———

170 *Celadon.* By these Breeches ———

Florimell. Which if I marry you I am resolv'd to wear; put
that into our Bargain, and so adieu Sir. ———
Exit Florimell.

Philocles. Hark you Cousin ———   *They whisper.*
You'll see it exactly executed; I rely upon you.

175 *Celadon.* I shall not fail, my Lord; may the conclusion of it
prove happy to you.   *Exit* Celadon.

Philocles (solus). Where're I cast about my wond'ring
eyes,
Greatness lies ready in some shape to tempt me.
The royal furniture in every room,
180 The Guards, and the huge waving crowds of people,
All waiting for a sight of that fair Queen
Who makes a present of her love to me:
Now tell me, Stoique! ———
If all these with a wish might be made thine,
185 Would'st thou not truck thy ragged vertue for 'em?
If Glory was a bait that Angels swallow'd,
How then should souls ally'd to sence, resist it!

Enter Candiope.

Ah poor *Candiope*! I pity her,
But that is all. ———
Candiope.   O my dear *Philocles*!
190 A thousand blessings wait on thee!

168 am] Q4; *omit* Q1–3
185 *truck*] barter.

88

The hope of being thine, I think will put
Me past my meat and sleep with extasie,
So I shall keep the fasts of Seraphim's,
And wake for joy like Nightingals in *May*.
Philocles (aside). Wake *Philocles*, wake from thy dream of
    glory,   195
'Tis all but shadow to *Candiope*:
Canst thou betray a love so innocent! ———
Candiope. What makes you melancholick? I doubt
    I have displeased you?
Philocles. No my love, I'am not displeas'd with you,   200
    But with my self, when I consider
    How little I deserve you.
Candiope. Say not so my *Philocles*, a love so true as yours
    That would have left a Court, and a Queen's favour
    To live in a poor Hermitage with me. ———   205
Philocles (aside). Ha! she has stung me to the quick!
    As if she knew the falshood I intended:
    But, I thank Heav'n, it has recal'd my vertue; ———
    (*To her*) O my dear, I love you, and you onely;
    Go in, I have some business for a while;   210
    But I think minutes ages till we meet.
Candiope. I knew you had; but yet I could not choose
    But come and look upon you. ———
                          Exit Candiope.
Philocles. What barbarous man could wrong so sweet a
    vertue!

    Enter the Queen *in black with* Asteria.

Madam, the States are straight to meet; but why   215
    In these dark ornaments will you be seen?
Queen. They fit the fortune of a Captive Queen.
Philocles. Deep shades are thus to heighten colours set;
    So Stars in Night, and Diamonds shine in Jet.
Queen. True friends should so, in dark afflictions shine,   220
    But I have no great cause to boast of mine.
Philocles. You may have too much prejudice for some,
    And think 'em false before their trial's come.
    But, Madam, what determine you to do?
Queen. I come not here to be advis'd by you: 225
    But charge you by that pow'r which once you own'd,
    And which is still my right, ev'n when unthron'd;
    That whatsoe're the States resolve of me,
    You never more think of *Candiope*.
Philocles. Not think of her! ah, how should I obey!   230
    Her tyrant eyes have forc'd my heart away.

Queen. By force retake it from those tyrant eyes,
　I'le grant you out my Letters of Reprize.

Philocles. She has, too well, prevented that design
235　　By giving me her heart in change for mine.

Queen. Thus foolish Indians Gold for Glass forgo,
　'Twas to your loss you priz'd your heart so low.
　I set its value when you were advanc'd.
　And as my favours grew, its rate inhanc'd.

240　*Philocles.* The rate of Subjects hearts by yours must go,
　And love in yours has set the value low.

Queen. I stand corrected, and my self reprove,
　You teach me to repent my low-plac'd love:
　Help me this passion from my heart to tear,
245　Now rail on him, and I will sit and hear.

Philocles. Madam, like you, I have repented too,
　And dare not rail on one I do not know.

Queen. This, *Philocles*, like strange perverseness shows,
　As if what e're I said, you would oppose;
250　How come you thus concern'd, for this unknown?

Philocles. I onely judg his actions by my own.

Queen. I've heard too much, and you too much have said.
　(*Aside*) O Heav'ns, the secret of my soul's betray'd!
　He knows my love, I read it in his face,
255　And blushes, conscious of his Queen's disgrace. ———
　(*To him*) Hence quickly, hence, or I shall die with shame.

Philocles. Now I love both, and both with equal flame.
　Wretched I came, more wretched I retire,
　When two winds blow it who can quench the fire!
　　　　　　　　　　　　　　　　Exit Philocles.

260　*Queen.* O my *Asteria*, I know not whom t'accuse;
　But either my own eyes or you, have told
　My love to *Philocles*.

Asteria. Is't possible that he should know it, Madam!

Queen. Me thinks you ask'd that question guiltily.
265　Confess, for I will know, what was the subject
　Of your long discourse i'th Antichamber with him.
　　　　　　　　　　　Her hand on Asteria's *shoulder.*

Asteria. It was my business to convince him, Madam,
　How ill he did, being so much oblig'd,
　To joyn in your imprisonment.

270　*Queen.* Nay, now I am confirm'd my thought was true;
　For you could give him no such reason
　Of his obligements as my love.

Asteria. Because I saw him much a Malecontent,
　I thought to win him to your int'rest, Madam,
275　By telling him it was no want of kindness

Made your refusal of *Candiope*.
  And he perhaps ———
Queen. What of him now!
Asteria. As men are apt, interpreted my words
  To all th'advantage he could wrest the sence,   280
  As if I meant you Lov'd him.
Queen. Have I deposited within thy breast
  The dearest treasure of my life, my glory,
  And hast thou thus betray'd me!
  But why do I accuse thy female weakness,   285
  And not my own for trusting thee!
  Unhappy Queen, *Philocles* knows thy fondness,
  And needs must think it done by thy Command.
Asteria. Dear Madam, think not so.
Queen. Peace, peace, thou should'st for ever hold thy
    tongue.   *To her.*   290
  For it has spoke too much for all thy life. ———
  Then *Philocles* has told *Candiope*,   [*To herself.*]
  And courts her kindness with his scorn of me.
  O whither am I fallen!
  But I must rouze my self, and give a stop   295
  To all these ills by headlong passion caus'd;
  In hearts resolv'd weak love is put to flight,
  And onely conquers when we dare not fight.
  But we indulge our harms, and while he gains
  An entrance, please our selves into our pains.   300

            Enter Lysimantes.

Asteria. Prince *Lysimantes*, Madam! ———
Queen. Come near you poor deluded criminal;
  See how ambition cheats you:
  You thought to find a Prisoner here,
  But you behold a Queen.   305
Lysimantes. And may you long be so: 'tis true this Act
  May cause some wonder in your Majesty.
Queen. None, Cousin, none; I ever thought you
  Ambitious, Proud, designing.
Lysimantes. Yet all my Pride, Designs, and my Ambition   310
  Were taught me by a Master
  With whom you are not unacquainted, Madam.
Queen. Explain your self; dark purposes, like yours,
  Need an Interpretation.
Lysimantes. 'Tis love I mean.
Queen.   Have my low fortunes giv'n thee   315
  This insolence, to name it to thy Queen?
Lysimantes. Yet you have heard love nam'd without
  offence.

As much below you as you think my passion,
I can look down on yours. ———

Queen (*aside*).   Does he know it too!
320   This is th'extreamest malice of my Stars! ———
Lysimantes. You see, that Princes faults,
      (How e're they think 'em safe from publick view)
      Fly out through the dark crannies of their Closets:
      We know what the Sun does,
325   Ev'n when we see him not in t'other world.
Queen. My actions, Cousin, never fear'd the light.
Lysimantes. Produce him then, your darling of the dark,
      For such an one you have.
Queen.   I know no such.
Lysimantes. You know, but will not own him.
330   Queen. Rebels ne're want pretence to blacken Kings,
      And this, it seems, is yours: do you produce him,
      Or ne're hereafter sully my Renown
      With this aspersion: ——— (*Aside*) Sure he dares not
      name him. ———
Lysimantes. I am too tender of your fame; or else ———
335   Nor are things brought to that extremity:
      Provided you accept my passion,
      I'le gladly yield to think I was deceiv'd.
Queen. Keep in your error still; I will not buy
      Your good opinion at so dear a rate,
340   As my own misery by being yours.
Lysimantes. Do not provoke my patience by such scornes,
      For fear I break through all, and name him to you.
Queen. Hope not to fright me with your mighty looks;
      Know I dare stem that tempest in your brow,
345   And dash it back upon you.
Lysimantes. Spight of prudence it will out: 'Tis *Philocles*.
      Now judge, when I was made a property
      To cheat my self by making him your Prisoner,
      Whether I had not right to take up armes?
350   Queen. Poor envious wretch!
      Was this the venome that swell'd up thy brest?
      My grace to *Philocles* mis-deem'd my love!
Lysimantes. 'Tis true, the Gentleman is innocent;
      He ne're sinn'd up so high, not in his wishes;
      You know he loves elsewhere.
355   Queen.   You mean your Sister.
Lysimantes. I wish some Sybil now would tell me
      Why you refus'd her to him?
Queen. Perhaps I did not think him worthy of her.
Lysimantes. Did you not think him too worthy, Madam?

This is too thin a vail to hinder your passion; 360
To prove you love him not, yet give her him,
And I'le engage my honour to lay down my Armes.
Queen (*aside*). He is arriv'd where I would wish. ———
    Call in the company, and you shall see what I will
    do. ———
Lysimantes. Who waits without there? ———
                         Exit Lysimantes. 365
Queen. Now hold, my heart, for this one act of honour,
    And I will never ask more courage of thee:
    Once more I have the means
    To reinstate my self into my glory;
    I feel my love to *Philocles* within me 370
    Shrink, and pull back my heart from this hard tryal,
    But it must be when glory says it must:
    As children wading from some River's bank
    First try the water with their tender feet;
    Then shuddring up with cold, step back again, 375
    And streight a little further venture on,
    Till at the last they plunge into the deep,
    And pass, at once, what they were doubting long:
    I'le make the same experiment; it shall be done in haste,
    Because I'le put it past my pow'r t'undo. 380

Enter at one door Lysimantes, *at the other* Philocles, Celadon,
    Candiope, Florimell, Flavia, Olinda, Sabina;
        the three Deputies, and Soldiers.

Lysimantes. In Armes! is all well, *Philocles*?
Philocles. No, but it shall be.
Queen.   He comes, and with him
    The fevour of my love returns to shake me.
    I see love is not banish'd from my soul,
    He is still there, but is chain'd up by glory. 385
Asteria. You've made a noble conquest, Madam.
Queen. Come hither, *Philocles*: I am first to tell you
    I and my Cousin are agreed, he has
    Engag'd to lay down Armes.
Philocles. 'Tis well for him he has; for all his party 390
    By my command already are surpriz'd,
    While I was talking with your Majesty.
Celadon. Yes 'faith I have done him that courtesie;
    I brought his followers, under pretence of guarding it,
    to a straight place where they are all coupt up without 395
    use of their Armes, and may be pelted to death by the
    small infantry o'the town.
Queen. 'Twas more then I expected, or could hope;
    Yet still I thought your meaning honest.

400   *Philocles.* My fault was rashness, but 'twas full of zeal:
        Nor had I e're been led to that attempt,
        Had I not seen it would be done without me:
        But by compliance I preserv'd the pow'r
        Which I have since made use of for your service.
405   *Queen.* And which I purpose so to recompence ———
    Lysimantes (*aside*). With her Crown she means; I knew
        'twould come to't.
    Philocles (*aside*). O Heav'ns, she'll own her love!
        Then I must lose *Candiope* for ever,
        And floating in a vast abyss of glory,
410   Seek and not find my self! ———
    Queen. Take your *Candiope*; and be as happy
        As love can make you both:———
        (*Aside*) How pleas'd I am that I can force my tongue,
        To speak words so far distant from my heart! ———
415   *Candiope.* My happiness is more then I can utter!
    Lysimantes. Methinks I could
        Do violence on my self for taking Armes
        Against a Queen so good, so bountiful:
        Give me leave, Madam, in my extasie
420   Of joy, to give you thanks for *Philocles*.
        You have preserv'd my friend, and now he owes not
        His fortunes onely to your favour; but
        What's more, his life, and more then that, his
        love. ———
        (*Aside*) I am convinc'd, she never lov'd him now;
425   Since by her free consent, all force remov'd,
        She gives him to my Sister.
        Flavia was an Impostor and deceiv'd me. ———
    Philocles. As for me, Madam, I can onely say
        That I beg respit for my thanks; for on the sudden,
430   The benefit's so great it overwhelmes me.
    Asteria. Mark but th' faintness of th'acknowledgment.
                                 To the Queen *aside.*
    Queen. I have observ'd it with you, and am pleas'd
                                  To Asteria.
        He seems not satisfi'd; for I still wish
        That he may love me.
435   *Philocles* (*aside*). I see *Asteria* deluded me
        With flattering hopes of the Queen's love
        Onely to draw me off from *Lysimantes*: ———
        But I will think no more on't.
        I'm going to possess *Candiope*,
440   And I am ravish'd with the joy on't! ha!
        Not ravish'd neither.

For what can be more charming then that Queen!
Behold how night sits lovely on her eye-brows,
While day breaks from her eyes! then, a Crown too:
Lost, lost, for ever lost, and now 'tis gone   445
'Tis beautifull. ———
Asteria. How he eyes you still! ———   *To the* Queen.
Philocles (*aside*). Sure I had one of the fallen Angels Dreams;
All Heav'n within this hour was mine! ———
Candiope. What is it that disturbs you Dear?   450
Philocles. Onely the greatness of my joy:
I've ta'ne too strong a Cordial, love,
And cannot yet digest it.
Queen. 'Tis done! but this pang more; and then a glorious
birth.   *Clapping her hand on* Asteria.
The Tumults of this day, my loyal Subjects,   455
Have setled in my heart a resolution,
Happy for you, and glorious too for me.
First for my Cousin, though attempting on my person,
He has incurr'd the danger of the Laws,
I will not punish him.   460
Lysimantes. You bind me ever to my loyalty.
Queen, Then, that I may oblige you more to it,
I here declare you rightful successor,
And heir immediate to my Crown: ———
This, Gentlemen,   *To the Deputies.*   465
I hope will still my subjects discontents,
When they behold succession firmly setled.
Deputies. Heav'n preserve your Majesty.
Queen. As for my self I have resolv'd
Still to continue as I am, unmarried: 470
The cares, observances, and all the duties
Which I should pay an Husband, I will place
Upon my people; and our mutual love
Shall make a blessing more then Conjugal,
And this the States shall ratifie.   475
Lysimantes. Heav'n bear me witness that I take no joy
In the succession of a Crown
Which must descend to me so sad a way.
Queen. Cousin, no more; my resolution's past,
Which fate shall never alter.   480
Philocles. Then, I am once more happy:
For since none can possess her, I am pleas'd
With my own choice, and will desire no more.
For multiplying wishes is a curse
That keep the mind still painfully awake.   485

478 a way] Q3; away Q1-2

>   *Queen. Celadon*!
>   Your care and loyalty have this day oblig'd me;
>   But how to be acknowledging I know not,
>   Unless you give the means.
> 490   *Celadon.* I was in hope your Majesty had forgot me;
>   therefore if you please, Madam, I onely beg a pardon
>   for having taken up armes once to day against you; for
>   I have a foolish kind of Conscience, which I wish many
>   of your Subjects had, that will not let me ask a recom-
> 495   pence for my loyalty, when I know I have been a Rebel.
>   *Queen.* Your modesty shall not serve the turn; Ask some-
>   thing.
>   *Celadon.* Then I beg, Madam, you will command *Florimell*
>   never to be friends with me.
> 500   *Florimell.* Ask again; I grant that without the Queen: But
>   why are you affraid on't?
>   *Celadon.* Because I am sure as soon as ever you are, you'l
>   marry me.
>   *Florimell.* Do you fear it?
> 505   *Celadon.* No, 'twill come with a fear.
>   *Florimell.* If you do, I will not stick with you for an Oath.
>   *Celadon.* I require no Oath till we come to Church; and
>   then after the Priest, I hope; for I find it will be my
>   destiny to marry thee.
> 510   *Florimell.* If ever I say word after the black Gentleman for
>   thee *Celadon* ———
>   *Celadon.* Then I hope you'l give me leave to bestow a
>   faithful heart elsewhere.
>   *Florimell.* I, but if you would have one you must bespeak
> 515   it, for I am sure you have none ready made.
>   *Celadon.* What say you, shall I marry *Flavia*?
>   *Florimell.* No, she'll be too cunning for you.
>   *Celadon.* What say you to *Olinda* then? she's tall, and fair,
>   and bonny.
> 520   *Florimell.* And foolish, and apish, and fickle.
>   *Celadon.* But *Sabina* there's pretty, and young, and loving,
>   and innocent.
>   *Florimell.* And dwarfish, and childish, and fond, and
>   flippant: if you marry her Sister you will get May-poles,
> 525   and if you marry her you will get Fayries to dance
>   about them.
>   *Celadon.* Nay then the case is clear, *Florimell*; if you take
>   'em all from me, 'tis because you reserve me for your
>   self.

---

487 your] Q2; you Q1
510 *black Gentleman*] clergyman.

Florimell. But this Marriage is such a Bugbear to me; 530
much might be if we could invent but any way to make
it easie.

Celadon. Some foolish people have made it uneasie, by
drawing the knot faster then they need; but we that
are wiser will loosen it a little. 535

Florimell. 'Tis true indeed, there's some difference betwixt
a Girdle and an Halter.

Celadon. As for the first year according to the laudable
custome of new married people, we shall follow one
another up into Chambers, and down into Gardens, 540
and think we shall never have enough of one another.
—— So far 'tis pleasant enough I hope.

Florimell. But after that, when we begin to live like
Husband and Wife, and never come near one another
—— what then Sir? 545

Celadon. Why then our onely happiness must be to have
one mind, and one will, *Florimell*.

Florimell. One mind if thou wilt, but prithee let us have
two wills; for I find one will be little enough for me
alone: But how if those wills should meet and clash, 550
Celadon?

Celadon. I warrant thee for that: Husbands and Wives
keep their wills far enough asunder for ever meeting:
one thing let us be sure to agree on, that is, never to be
jealous. 555

Florimell. No; but e'en love one another as long as we can;
and confess the truth when we can love no longer.

Celadon. When I have been at play, you shall never ask
me what money I have lost.

Florimell. When I have been abroad you shall never 560
enquire who treated me.

Celadon. *Item*, I will have the liberty to sleep all night,
without your interrupting my repose for any evil
design whatsoever.

Florimell. *Item*, Then you shall bid me good night before 565
you sleep.

Celadon. Provided always, that whatever liberties we take
with other people, we continue very honest to one
another.

Florimell. As far as will consist with a pleasant life. 570

Celadon. Lastly, Whereas the names of Husband and Wife
hold forth nothing, but clashing and cloying, and dulness and faintness in their signification; they shall be
abolish'd for ever betwixt us.

568 *honest*] chaste.

97

575   *Florimell.* And instead of those, we will be married by the more agreeable names of Mistress and Gallant.

        Celadon. None of my priviledges to be infring'd by thee *Florimell*, under the penalty of a month of Fasting-nights.

580   *Florimell.* None of my priviledges to be infring'd by thee *Celadon*, under the penalty of Cuckoldom.

        Celadon. Well, if it be my fortune to be made a Cuckold, I had rather thou shouldst make me one then any one in *Sicily*: and for my comfort I shall have thee oftner

585   then any of thy servants.

        Florimell. La ye now, is not such a marriage as good as wenching, *Celadon*?

        Celadon. This is very good, but not so good, *Florimell*,

        Queen. Now set me forward to th'Assembly.

590   You promise Cousin your consent?

        Lysimantes. But most unwillingly.

        Queen. Philocles, I must beg your voice too.

        Philocles. Most joyfully I give it.

        Lysimantes. Madam, but one word more; since you are so resolv'd,

595   That you may see, bold as my passion was,

        'Twas onely for your person, not your Crown;

        I swear no second love

        Shall violate the flame I had for you,

        But in strict imitation of your Oath

600   I vow a single life.

        Queen. Now, my *Asteria*, my joys are full;   *To* Asteria.

        The pow'rs above that see

        The innocent love I bear to *Philocles*,

        Have giv'n its due reward; for by this means

605   The right of *Lysimantes* will devolve

        Upon *Candiope*; and I shall have

        This great content, to think, when I am dead

        My Crown may fall on *Philocles* his head.

                                    Exeunt Omnes.

Epilogue

Written by a Person of Honour
[Spoken by *Florimell*.]

Our Poet something doubtful of his Fate
Made choice of me to be his Advocate,
Relying on my Knowledge in the Laws,
And I as boldly undertook the Cause.
I left my Client yonder in a rant   5
Against the envious, and the ignorant,
Who are, he sayes, his onely Enemies:
But he contemns their malice, and defies
The sharpest of his Censurers to say
Where there is one gross fault in all his Play.   10
The language is so fitted for each part,
The Plot according to the Rules of Art;
And twenty other things he bid me tell you,
But I cry'd, e'en go do't your self for *Nelly*.
Reason, with Judges, urg'd in the defence   15
Of those they would condemn, is insolence;
I therefore wave the merits of his Play,
And think it fit to plead this safer way.
If, when too many in the purchase share,
Robbing's not worth the danger nor the care;   20
The men of business must, in Policy,
Cherish a little harmless Poetry;
All wit wou'd else grow up to Knavery.
Wit is a Bird of Musick, or of Prey.
Mounting she strikes at all things in her way;   25
But if this Birdlime once but touch her wings,
On the next bush she sits her down, and sings.
I have but one word more; tell me I pray
What you will get by damning of our Play?
A whipt Fanatick who does not recant   30
Is by his Brethren call'd a suffring Saint;
And by your hands shou'd this poor Poet die
Before he does renounce his Poetry,
His death must needs confirm the Party more
Then all his scribling life could do before.   35
Where so much zeal does in a Sect appear,
'Tis to no purpose, 'faith, to be severe.
But 'tother day I heard this rhyming Fop
Say Criticks were the Whips, and he the Top;
For, as a Top spins best the more you baste her,   40
So every lash you give, he writes the faster.

14 *Nelly*] Nell Gwyn.

Preface 42 one,] ~ ⌃ 86 It] it
Persons 4 *Florimell,* a] *Florimell,* A
I.i.29 them.] ~ : 32 'em.] ~ : 34 lost.] ~ : 44 self.] ~ : 49
Mistris.] ~ ; 117 Eye- / browes 187 Accuse . . . Queen] *italic in* Q1
209 I . . . desert] Q1 *lines:* worthy. / Except 209 desert:] ~ ; 218
lessen] lesson 242–44 *prose in* Q1 255 govern:—] ~ : 261 'em;]
punctuation doubtful in Q1 262 They . . . Queen] Q1 *lines:* Ruler /
Upon 263 else?] ~ ; 266 reckoned] reckon'd 287 choice] chioce
289 deserts⌃)—] ~ .) ⌃ 294–96 *prose in* Q1 301 commands,
. . . one,] ~ . . . . ~ ⌃ 305 Sun- / shine] Sun-shine 309 again:]
~ ⌃ 319 Reign] *Reign* 323 question,] ~ . 357–58 Q1 *lines:*
How . . . fairest / Beyond . . . her; / She . . . fair.— 365–66 Q1
lines: Bid . . . qualm, / And . . . going.— 377–78 Q1 *lines:* I cannot
. . . hast / Not . . . it. 408–9 *one line in* Q1 425 lov'd!] ~ ? 431
born,—] ~ , ⌃ 434–35 *one line in* Q1 439 quiet,—] ~ , ⌃ 441
Bloud,] ~ ⌃ 445 I fear that] I fear. That 448 pow'r:] ~ ⌃ 449
it,] ~ ⌃ 452 best;] ~ ⌃
II.i.3 *Candiope:*] ~ ⌃ 25 She . . . dumb.] She signs. She is dumb. (*set
to left margin as speech*) 29 indeed?] ~ , 45 However, . . . her;]
~ ⌃ . . . ~ , 51 *Florimell?*] ~ ; 98 it; . . . forecast,] ~ , . . . ~ ;
99 one⌃] ~ , 116 services,] ~ ⌃ 117 faults,] ~ ⌃ 118 'Prenti-
ship⌃] ~ , 125–26 Q1 *lines* Then . . . challenge, / An . . . match
142–43 *one line in* Q1 151–52 *one line in* Q1 155–56 Q1 *lines:* I
. . . forbid / Your . . . 158 *Philocles;*] ~ , 159 dead,] ~ ⌃ 161–62
Q1 *lines:* Rather . . . before, / Then . . . 173–74 Q1 *lines:* But . . .
love, / It is . . . death. 225–27 Q1 *lines:* I give . . . but / When . . .
better / You'l . . . yours. 240 And . . . Queen.] *italic in* Q1
III.i.13 thunders,] ~ ⌃ 26–27 Q1 *lines:* Your . . . bancks / O'reflow'd
37–38 *one line in* Q1 38 love,] ~ . 47 self,] ~ ⌃ 58 Man] man
75 will] wil ! 76 yet,] ~ ⌃ 98 tears?] ~ : 108 lose,] ~ . 114
Madam,] ~ . 128–29 Q1 *lines:* A . . . yours / Deserves . . . care, /
To . . . 156 Inhumane] In humane 177 found,] ~ ⌃ 182 retreat:]
~ . 184 away.] ~ : 251–52 Q1 *lines:* No . . . Asteria. / Seek . . .
City. 264–65 *one line in* Q1 348 way,] ~ ⌃ 384 then,] ~ ⌃ 387
What,] ~ ⌃ 393 So,] ~ ⌃ 440 again—] ~ .
IV.i.7 'em;] ~ ⌃ 8 manner,] ~ . 9 I'le] 'Ile 21 counter- / part]
counterpart 89 Dutch] Duch 105 What,] ~ ⌃ 120 I,] ~ ⌃
135 ratt;] ~ , 141 jealous,] ~ ⌃ 146 writ] write 150 What,]
~ ⌃ 168 calls,] ~ ⌃ 173 What,] ~ ⌃ 207 trow?] ~ , 208 set !]
~ . 243 *Florimell,*] ~ . 249 more?] ~ : 256 *Page.*] Page 1 267
Asteria⌃] ~ . 277–78 *one line in* Q1 317–18 *one line in* Q1
332–34 Q1 *lines:* I . . . him / As . . . Angel. / That . . . another, / We
. . . us 354 why,] ~ ⌃ 376 'Tis] Tis 396 Lord?] ~ :
IV.ii.80 Yet] 'Yet
V.i.7 If] if 28 this,] ~ ⌃ 60 age,] ~ ⌃ 66 at?] ~ , 67 art !] ~ ?
121 man,] ~ . 144 Peruke] Perruks 186 swallo'd,] ~ ⌃ 265–66
Q1 *lines:* Confess . . . discourse / I'th . . . 294–95 *one line in* Q1
360 passion;] ~ , 363–64 *prose in* Q1 368–69 *one line in* Q1
416–17 *one line in* Q1 425 remov'd,] ~ ⌃ 455 Subjects,] ~ ⌃
462 it,] ~ . 514 I,] ~ ⌃ 521 *Sabina⌃*] ~ , 531 make] mak
578 *Florimell,*] ~ .
Epilogue 19 share,] ~ ⌃

Press Variant in Q1
Sheet a (inner forme)
Corrected: CLUC, DFo, TxU
Uncorrected: SCmH

Sig. a4
Second Prologue 12 him] *omit*

Sir Martin Mar-All

Sir Martin Mar-All, or the Feign'd Innocence stands as a warning to all who would generalize about Restoration taste for comedy. Here we have a very unsophisticated farce, lacking in verbal wit, that nevertheless became one of the most popular plays of the age. Almost all its appeal lies in its sure-fire comic situations, somewhat like Shakespeare's *Comedy of Errors*, except that Dryden's protagonist is a loveable lout, a sort of seventeenth-century Li'l Abner: a man with sterling ideals straight out of popular tradition. In order to reconcile the play with its contemporaries, we would have to rewrite the whole plot, turning Warner into a gallant and Millicent into an emancipated lady, at the expense of Martin's leading role.

At the beginning of the next century, John Downes, book-keeper for the Duke's Company, wrote:

> The Duke of *New-Castle*, giving Mr. *Dryden* a bare Translation out of a Comedy by the Famous *French* Poet *Monseur Moleire* [*L'Étourdi*]: He Adapted the Part purposely for the Mouth of Mr. *Nokes* [the leading comedian of the Company], and curiously Polishing the Whole. . . . This Comedy was Crown'd with an Excellent Entry: In the last Act at the Mask, by Mr. *Priest* [the landlord] and Madam Davies [Millicent]; This, and [Etherege's] *Love in a Tub*, got the Company more Money than any preceding Comedy.[1]

The play was first performed at the Duke's Theatre in Lincoln's Inn Fields, apparently on August 15, 1667. The next day Pepys remarked in his *Diary*: "A play made by my Lord Duke of Newcastle, but, as everybody says, corrected by Dryden. It is the most entire piece of mirth, a complete farce from one end to the other, that certainly was ever writ. I never laughed so in all my life. I laughed till my head [ached] all the evening and night with the laughing; and at very good wit therein, not fooling. The house full, and in all things a mighty content to me."[2] The play ran steadily, off and on, for the next two decades, as long as James Nokes played Martin, and was frequently revived in the early eighteenth century. It attracted more than the regular coterie audience; as Pepys noticed, January 1, 1668, there was an unusual "company of citizens, 'prentices, and others," who paid 2s. 6d. to go into the pit. Obviously others agreed with Pepys that

[1] Downes, p. 28.
[2] *Diary*, ed. Wheatley, August 16, 1667.

it was "undoubtedly the best comedy ever was wrote."[3]
Nokes' acting has been described vividly by Cibber:

> In the character of Sir Martin Marr-all, who is always
> committing blunders to the prejudice of his own interest,
> when he had brought himself to a dilemma in his affairs
> by vainly proceeding upon his own head, and was after-
> wards afraid to look his governing servant and counsellor
> in the face, what a copious and distressful harangue have
> I seen him make with his looks (while the house has been
> in one continued roar for several minutes) before he could
> prevail with his courage to speak a word to him! Then
> might you have at once read in his face vexation—that
> his own measures, which he had piqued himself upon,
> had fail'd. Envy—of his servant's superior wit—distress—
> to retrieve the occasion he had lost. Shame—to confess
> his folly, and yet a sullen desire to be reconciled and
> better advised for the future! What tragedy ever shew'd
> us such a tumult of passions rising at once in one bosom!
> or what buskin'd heroe standing under the load of them
> could have more effectually mov'd his spectators by the
> most pathetick speech than poor miserable Nokes did by
> this silent eloquence and piteous plight of his features?
>
> [Cibber, I, 203–4.]

The entry in the Stationers' Register for June 24, 1668,
bears the name of the Duke of Newcastle, but the title page
of the first edition does not mention an author. Nor do the
subsequent reprints give an author until Q4 1691, where it is
attributed to Dryden on a cancel title leaf. Q5 1697 and the
folio 1701 repeat the ascription with no mention of Newcastle, and most editors since have not doubted Dryden's
major part in the script.

We may question Downes's assertion that Newcastle gave
Dryden a bare translation of Molière's *L'Étourdi*, out of which
he made the play, because the closest source is Philippe
Quinault's *L'Amant indiscret* (acted 1654, printed 1664), for
episodes in the main plot of acts I, II, and III. Molière may
have suggested IV.i.1–185, 325–417, and V.i.305–532, although even these passages are much changed, particularized,
and made slightly more subtle in *Sir Martin*. Dryden increased
the contradictions in Sir Martin's character, making him more
doltish and causing him to affect cleverness; Martin begins to
sound like a would-be wit in III.i, and Warner becomes
cleverer, Millicent a fledging lover of wit. She overvalues Sir
Martin for some time, because she is rebelling from her father
and from Sir John's restraint, and she has been influenced by

[3] *Diary*, August 22, 1668.

Rose's persuasions. Hence she is "prepossessed . . . with another inclination which render[s her] less clear-sighted . . . since no man, at the same time, can distinctly view two different objects."[4] The jolly portrait of Mr. Moody is out of the English humour tradition, and the entire subplot is invented.[5]

Since there is a curious contradiction in time between the one day of the main plot and several weeks, perhaps months, in the subplot (enough time for Mistress Christian to meet Lord Dartmouth and become pregnant), Frank H. Moore has attributed the subplot to Newcastle. Dryden, he thinks, would not have been guilty of "such a discrepancy if he had been free to invent the subplot."[6] But until we have more objective evidence to distinguish the collaborators, the assignment of each man's work must remain undecided.

The play was written for the Duke's Theatre, the rival of the company with which Dryden is usually associated, and it ran in active competition with *Secret Love* at the King's Theatre. The choice of company may have been influenced by Newcastle's patronage of Davenant and his men, or it may have come as a result of a new friendship with Davenant himself, for in the same season Dryden helped him change Shakespeare's *Tempest* into *The Enchanted Island*.

When the first quarto of 1668 was in the press (Term Catalogue, November, 1668), or some time shortly thereafter, some difficulty arose concerning a scene in Act I between Mr. Moody and Sir John Swallow. Sheet C was printed, ending Act I on sig. C2 recto and beginning Act II on sig. C2 verso. At some later time, sigs. C1 and C2 were canceled and replaced by one leaf, sig. C1, making a C gathering of three leaves, numbered 9, 10, 13, 14, 15, and 16. In the unique copy (now Folger copy 3) once owned by Percy Dobell, and described by him in his *John Dryden, Bibliographical Memoranda* (1922), pp. 7–8, 30, there survives the original sig. C2, numbered pages 11 and 12. Sig. C2 verso contains the beginning

[4] Dryden's remark about Philocles, in the preface to *Secret Love*, ll. 68–71.
[5] A detailed account of the problem may be found in N. B. Allen's *The Sources of Dryden's Comedies*, pp. 211–25, although Allen exaggerates the fidelity to the sources and says that *Sir Martin* is an "avowed adaptation and did not pretend to be original." Summers, II, 76–77, says that the serenade of his mistress, V.i.129–252, and the Frolick of the Altitudes, V.ii, were devised with suggestions from two other sources. But the more sources that are cited, the more active we see Dryden's role in the original composition.
[6] *The Nobler Pleasure* (1963), pp. 57–58. Following Moore's suggested analogy between the subplot and Newcastle's *The Humerous Lovers*, John Loftis urges at length Newcastle's authorship of the subplot (*Works of John Dryden*, IX, 357–364).

of Act II, with identical text in another typesetting, as found on the replaced sig. C1 verso, but the sig. C2 recto preserves what must have been the original end of Act I, the last thirty-three lines. I estimate that the original form of Act I.i ended at line 353, and a second scene of about sixty lines followed, where Sir John and Moody had a disagreement about Sir John's language. An unnamed third character was possibly the mediator, but we cannot be sure, because his speech prefixes are blank. Dobell thought these were Sir John's speeches, but that does not seem likely, for Moody is addressing someone other than Sir John when he says, "Let the Gentleman express it so, and I am content." I quote the text from the Folger copy, verbatim, retaining the lineation and spacing as well.

(11)

Mood. But one blow at him, I will so Malchus his Ears.
        What do you mean by that Sir?
Mood. To have him by the Ears, and you too if you be prating.
Sir John. I beg of you to have a little patience.
Mood. So I may have a little patience, and yet knock him soundly: oh how my Fingers itch at him!
Sir John. Quiet your self I beseech you, and but hear me and believe me, for I will speak nothing but truth.
Mood. Well, speak, for I will both hear thee and believe thee, for I know thou art an honest man, speak!
Sir John. Sir, of my Soul I never meant you any injury, or the least affront, but all Civility and Service to you; for this expression of *Pardon me*, is the new fashion of speaking, *a la mode*, as much as to say *Excuse me*.
Mood. By Cox-nouns I hate Excuses; for they are but lyes, and I am all for truth.
        Sir, Pardon me is as much as Excuse me, or, By your Favour I am of another opinion.
Mood. By your Favour, is it no more? I understand that perfectly, 'tis civil, By your favour, though a man be never so ill-favour'd.
        Pray be friends Sir.
Mood. Let the Gentleman express it so, and I am content. Speak Sir for your self.
Sir John. Truly Sir, Pardon me, in King *Charles* the Seconds time, has no more offence or hurt in it, than, By your Favour, in *primo* of Queen *Elizabeth*.
Though your favour has been terrible to me.
Mood. Well! if it be so, then give me thy hand.
Sir John. I will lend it you Sir.
Mood. Well, and I'le pay thee agen presently, and there's an end of the business.
So, let's go then, and *Beati pacifici*.   [*Exeunt*.

104

The last line may also have been intended for the third speaker or for Sir John, since we should not expect Moody to use the phrase *"Beati pacifici."* At any rate, it seems clear that Moody was once supposed to appear in Act I, and even without the cancel leaf we might suspect that something had been disturbed, for Lady Dupe has formally prepared for his entrance, in her "character" of him in I.i.41–47. Possibly, as Allen speculates (p. 219), the linguistic pretensions of Sir John were thought inappropriate for him and diverting from Sir Martin's similar affectation. I believe that the omitted speech prefixes have something to do with the cancellation; possibly the printer was working from a draft of the scene where the author had not yet decided who was speaking certain lines. This opinion assumes that foul papers served as printer's copy and that, after printing, the scene was found to be too imperfect or too ineffective to remain.

The basis of the present text is the Folger (DFo⁴, Malone copy of Q1 1668 (Macd. 71a, W & M 453), which has been compared with three other Folger copies (DFo¹ Fitzgerald, DFo² Kendall, DFo³ Dobell) and a Clark Library (CLUC) copy, uncovering only minor press variants. A few obvious corrections, that need not be Dryden's, appear in later editions: Q2 1668 (Macd. 71b, W & M 455), Q3 1678, Q4 1691, Q5 1697, and F 1701. The supposed edition of 1669 (W & M 456) is another state of Q2. Many lines set as verse in Q1 have been silently altered to prose.

Sr Martin Mar-all,

OR THE

Feign'd Innocence:

A

COMEDY.

As it was Acted at

His HIGHNESSE the DUKE of *YORK'S*
THEATRE.

LONDON,

Printed for *H. Herringman*, at the Sign of the *Blew Anchor* in the
Lower walk of the *New Exchange.* 1668.

Title Page of the First Quarto, Folger Library Copy.

The Names of the Persons

Lord Dartmouth.	In love with Mrs. *Christian.*
Master Moody.	The Swash-buckler.
Sir Martin Mar-all.	A Fool.
Warner.	His Man.
Sir John Swallow.	A Kentish Knight.
Landlord.]	[Bribed by *Sir* Martin.]

Lady Dupe.	The old Lady.
Mistress Christian.	Her young Niece.
Mistress Millisent.	The Swash-buckler's Daughter.
Rose.	Her Maid.

Other Servants, Men and Women.
Bayliffs.

The Scene *Covent-Garden.*

Persons 10 *Rose* Her Maid.] *Rose* Her Maid / *Mrs. Preparation* Woman
    to the old Lady Qq,F
    11 Women.] Women. A Carrier. Qq,F

    The Names] the original cast: *Dartmouth,* John Young; *Moody,* Cave
Underhill; *Martin,* James Nokes; *Warner,* Henry Harris; *Swallow,*
William Smith; *Lady Dupe,* Mrs. Norris; *Christian,* ———; *Millisent,*
Moll Davis; *Rose,* ——— (Downes, p. 28). James Nokes "had a
shufflling shamble in his gait, with so contented an ignorance in his
aspect and an awkward absurdity in his gesture, that had you not
known him, you could not have believ'd that naturally he could have
had a grain of common sense"; he exuded a "plain and palpable
simplicity of nature." (Cibber's *Apology,* I, 201–4.)

    2 *Swash-buckler*] a noisy braggadocio, a swaggering bravo.

    10–11] *Mistress Preparation* (see textual note) may be a fossil of an
earlier draft, like the rejected scene with Moody at the end of Act I (see
the introduction to this play and the note on III.ii.76.1). The Carrier
was suggested by the Landlord "diguis'd like a Carrier" (II.ii.171.1).

Prologue

Fools, which each man meets in his Dish each day,
Are yet the great Regalios of a Play;
In which to Poets you but just appear,
To prize that highest which costs them so dear:
Fops in the Town more easily will pass;
One story makes a statutable Ass:
But such in Plays must be much thicker sown,
Like yolks of Eggs, a dozen beat to one.
Observing Poets all their walks invade,
As men watch Woodcocks gliding through a Glade:
And when they have enough for Comedy,
They stow their several Bodies in a Pye:
The Poet's but the Cook to fashion it,
For, Gallants, you your selves have found the wit.
To bid you welcome would your bounty wrong,
None welcome those who bring their chear along.

2 *Regalios*] objects of delight and entertainment, especially
fine food.

The Feign'd Innocence:
or
Sir Martin Marrall

ACT I. [SCENE I]

Enter Warner *solus.*

Warner. Where the Devil is this Master of mine? he is ever
out of the way when he should do himself good. This
'tis to serve a Coxcomb, one that has no more brains
than just those I carry for him. Well! of all Fopps commend me to him for the greatest; he's so opinion'd of   5
his own Abilities, that he is ever designing somewhat,
and yet he sows his Stratagems so shallow, that every
Daw can pick 'em up: from a plotting Fool the Lord
deliver me. Here he comes. O! it seems his Cousin's with
him, then it is not so bad as I imagin'd.   10

Enter Sir Martin Marrall, *Lady* Dupe.

Lady Dupe. I think 'twas well contriv'd for your access to
lodge her in the same house with you.
Sir Martin. 'Tis pretty well, I must confess.
Warner (aside). Had he plotted it himself, it had been
admirable.   15
Lady Dupe. For when her Father *Moody* writ to me to
take him lodgings, I so order'd it, the choice seem'd his,
not mine.
Sir Martin. I have hit of a thing my self sometimes, when
wiser heads have miss'd it. —— But that might be   20
meer luck.
Lady Dupe. Fortune does more than Wisdom.
Sir Martin. Nay, for that you shall excuse me; I will not
value any man's Fortune at a rush, except he have Wit
and Parts to bear him out. But when do you expect 'em?   25
Lady Dupe. This Tide will bring them from *Gravesend.*
You had best let your man go as from me, and wait
them at the Stairs in *Durham*-yard.
Sir Martin. Lord, Cousin, what a do is here with your
Counsel! As though I could not have thought of that   30
my self. I could find in my heart not to send him

24 *at a rush*] i.e., at a fig.
28 *Durham-yard*] one of the landing places from the Thames.

109

now—stay a little—I could soon find out some other
way.

Warner. A minute's stay may lose your business.

35 *Sir Martin.* Well, go then,—but you must grant, if he had
stay'd, I could have found a better way,—you grant it?
Exit Warner.

Lady Dupe. For once I will not stand with you.———
'Tis a sweet Gentlewoman this Mistress *Millisent*, if you
can get her.

40 *Sir Martin.* Let me alone for plotting.

Lady Dupe. But by your favour, Sir, 'tis not so easie: her
Father has already promis'd her, and the young Gentleman comes up with 'em: I partly know the man,—but
the old Squire is humoursome, he's stout, and plain in
45 speech and in behaviour; he loves none of the fine
Town-tricks of breeding, but stands up for the old
Elizabeth way in all things. This we must work upon.

Sir Martin. Sure! you think you have to deal with a Fool,
Cousin?

Enter Mistress Christian.

50 *Lady Dupe.* O my dear Neice, I have some business with
you.   *Whispers.*

Sir Martin. Well, Madam, I'le take one turn here i'th
Piazza's; a thousand things are hammering in this head;
'tis a fruitful Noddle, though I say it.
Exit Sir Martin.

55 *Lady Dupe.* Go thy ways for a most conceited Fool.———
But to our business, Cousin: you are young, but I am
old, and have had all the Love-experience that a discreet
Lady ought to have; and therefore let me instruct you
about the Love this rich Lord makes to you.

60 *Christian.* You know, Madam, he's married, so that we
cannot work upon that ground of Matrimony.

Lady Dupe. But there are advantages enough for you, if
you will be wise and follow my advice.

Christian. Madam, my Friends left me to your care, there-
65 fore I will wholly follow your Counsel with secrecy and
obedience.

Lady Dupe. Sweet-heart, it shall be the better for you
another day: well then, this Lord that pretends to you
is crafty and false, as most men are, especially in Love;—
70 therefore we must be subtle to meet with all his Plots,

---

37 *stand*] quarrel.
53 *Piazza's*] In Covent Garden the arcade built by Inigo Jones.
68 *pretends to*] tries to win.

and have Countermines against his Works to blow him
up.

Christian. As how, Madam?

Lady Dupe. Why, Girl, hee'l make fierce Love to you, but
you must not suffer him to ruffle you or steal a kiss: but   75
you must weep and sigh, and say you'l tell me on't,
and that you will not be us'd so; and play the innocent
just like a Child, and seem ignorant of all.

Christian. I warrant you I'le be very ignorant, Madam.

Lady Dupe. And be sure when he has tows'd you, not to   80
appear at Supper that night, that you may fright him.

Christian. No, Madam.

Lady Dupe. That he may think you have told me.

Christian. I, Madam.

Lady Dupe. And keep your Chamber, and say your head   85
akes.

Christian. O, most extreamly, Madam.

Lady Dupe. And lock the door, and admit of no night-
visits: at Supper I'le ask where's my Cousin, and being
told you are not well, I'le start from the Table to visit   90
you, desiring his Lordship not to incommode himself;
for I will presently wait on him agen.

Christian. But how, when you are return'd, Madam?

Lady Dupe. Then somewhat discompos'd, I'le say I doubt
the Meazles or Small-pox will seize on you, and then   95
the Girl is spoil'd; saying, Poor thing, her Portion is her
Beauty and her Vertue; and often send to see how you
do, by whispers in my Servants ears, and have those
whispers of your health return'd to mine: if his Lordship thereupon askes how you do, I will pretend it was   100
some other thing.

Christian. Right, Madam, for that will bring him further
in suspence.

Lady Dupe. A hopeful Girl! Then will I eat nothing that
night, feigning my grief for you; but keep his Lordship   105
Company at Meal, and seem to strive to put my passion
off, yet shew it still by small mistakes.

Christian. And broken Sentences.

Lady Dupe. A dainty Girl! And after Supper visit you
again, with promise to return strait to his Lordship: but   110
after I am gone send an Excuse, that I have given you a

75 *to ruffle*] to handle with rude familiarity, to touzle (see *Secret
Love*, V.i.122).
   80 *tows'd*] pulled about indelicately.
   94 *doubt*] fear.
   109 *dainty*] delightful.

Cordial, and mean to watch that night in person with you.

Christian. His Lordship then will find the Prologue of his trouble, doubting I have told you of his ruffling.

Lady Dupe. And more than that, fearing his Father should know of it, and his Wife, who is a Termagant Lady: but when he finds the Coast is clear, and his late ruffling known to none but you, he will be drunk with joy.

Christian. Finding my simple Innocence, which will inflame him more.

Lady Dupe. Then what the Lyon's skin has fail'd him in, the Fox's subtlety must next supply, and that is just, Sweet-heart, as I would have it; for crafty Folk's treaties are their advantage: especially when his passion must be satisfi'd at any rate, and you keep Shop to set the price of Love: so now you see the Market is your own.

Christian. Truly, Madam, this is very rational; and by the blessing of Heav'n upon my poor endeavours, I do not doubt to play my part.

Lady Dupe. My blessing and my pray'rs go along with thee.

Enter Sir John Swallow, *Mistress* Millisent, *and* Rose *her Maid.*

Christian. I believe, Madam, here is the young Heiress you expect, and with her he who is to marry her.

Lady Dupe. Howe're I am Sir *Martin's* Friend, I must not seem his Enemy.

Sir John. Madam, this fair young Lady begs the honour to be known to you.

Millisent. My Father made me hope it, Madam.

Lady Dupe. Sweet Lady, I believe you have brought all the Freshness of the Country up to Town with you.

They salute.

Millisent. I came up, Madam, as we Country-Gentlewomen use, at an *Easter*-Term, to the destruction of Tarts and Cheese-cakes, to see a New Play, buy a new Gown, take a Turn in the Park, and so down agen to sleep with my Fore-fathers.

Sir John. Rather, Madam, you are come up to the breaking of many a poor Heart, that like mine, will languish for you.

---

117 *Termagant*] tyrant.
122 *Lyon's skin*] a proverb.
137 *his*] i.e., Sir John's.

Christian. I doubt, Madam, you are indispos'd with your
Voyage; will you please to see the Lodgings your Father
has provided for you?

Millisent. To wait upon you, Madam.

Lady Dupe. This is the door,—there is a Gentleman will   155
wait you immediately in your Lodging, if he might
presume on your Commands.   *In whisper.*

Millisent. You mean Sir *Martin Marrall*: I am glad he has
intrusted his passion with so discreet a person.

                                        In whisper.

Sir *John*, let me intreat you to stay here, that my   160
Father may have intelligence where to find us.

Sir John. I shall obey you, Madam.

                                Exeunt Women.

            Enter Sir Martin.

Sir John. Sir *Martin Marrall*! most happily encounter'd!
how long have you been come to Town?

Sir Martin. Some three days since, or thereabouts: but I   165
thank God I am very weary on't already.

Sir John. Why, what's the matter, man?

Sir Martin. My villainous old luck still follows me in
gaming. I never throw the Dice out of my hand, but
my Gold goes after 'em: if I go to Picquet, though it be   170
but with a Novice in't, he will picque and repicque, and
Capot me twenty times together: and which most
mads me, I lose all my Sets, when I want but one of up.

Sir John. The pleasure of play is lost, when one loses at
that unreasonable rate.   175

Sir Martin. But I have sworn not to touch either Cards or
Dice this half year.

Sir John. The Oaths of losing Gamesters are most minded;
they foreswear play as an angry Servant does his Mistress, because he loves her but too well.   180

Sir Martin. But I am now taken up with thoughts of
another nature; I am in love, Sir.

Sir John. That's the worst Game you could have play'd at,

---

160 Sir] S–S; *Lady Dupe.* Sir Qq,F

154 *wait upon*] accompany.

160 *Sir John*] The assignment of this speech to Lady Dupe (Q1) is
clearly wrong, for she has no father who needs to have information on
her whereabouts. Millisent, however, has just arrived, and her father is
close behind.

170 *Picquet*] piquet, a card game in which *picque, repique,* and *capot*
are scoring plays (Cotton, *Compleat Gamester,* chap. vi, 1674).

173 *one of up*] within one point of winning.

178 *minded*] remembered, heeded, because they do not mean what
they say. Saintsbury suggests "least minded" instead of "most minded."

185 scarce one Woman in an hundred will play with you upon the Square: you venture at more uncertainty than at a Lottery: for you set your heart to a whole Sex of Blanks. But is your Mistress Widdow, Wife, or Maid?

Sir Martin. I can assure you, Sir, mine is a Maid; the Heiress of a wealthy Family, fair to a Miracle.

190 *Sir John.* Does she accept your service?

Sir Martin. I am the only person in her favour.

Enter Warner.

Sir John. Is she of Town or Country?

Warner (aside). How's this?

Sir Martin. She is of *Kent*, near *Canterbury*.

195 *Warner (aside).* What does he mean? this is his Rival———

Sir John. Near *Canterbury* say you? I have a small Estate lies thereabouts, and more concernments than one besides.

Sir Martin. I'le tell you then; being at *Canterbury*, it was
200 my Fortune once in the Cathedral Church ———

Warner. What do you mean, Sir, to intrust this man with your Affairs thus? ——— [*In whisper.*]

Sir Martin. Trust him? why, he's a friend of mine.

Warner. No matter for that; hark you a Word Sir.———

205 *Sir Martin.* Prethee leave fooling:—and as I was saying— I was in the Church when I first saw this fair one.

Sir John. Her Name, Sir, I beseech you.

Warner. For Heaven's sake, Sir, have a care.

Sir Martin. Thou art such a Coxcomb.—Her name's
210 *Millisent.*

Warner. Now, the Pox take you Sir, what do you mean?

Sir John. *Millisent* say you? that's the name of my Mistress.

Sir Martin. Lord! what luck is that now! well Sir, it happen'd, one of her Gloves fell down, I stoop'd to
215 take it up; And in the stooping made her a Complement.———

Warner [aside]. The Devil cannot hold him, now will this thick-skull'd Master of mine, tell the whole story to his Rival. ———

220 *Sir Martin.* You'l say, 'twas strange Sir; but at the first glance we cast on one another, both our hearts leap'd within us, our souls met at our Eyes, and with a tickling kind of pain slid to each other's breast, and in one moment settled as close and warm as if they long had
225 been acquainted with their lodging. I follow'd her

187 *Blanks*] lottery tickets which do not win a prize.

somewhat at a distance, because her Father was with
her.

Warner. Yet hold Sir ———

Sir Martin. Sawcy Rascal, avoid my sight; must you tutor
me?   230
So Sir, not to trouble you, I enquir'd out her Father's
House, without whose knowledge I did Court the
Daughter, and both then and often since, coming to
Canterbury, I receiv'd many proofs of her kindness to me.

Warner. You had best tell him too, that I am acquainted   235
with her Maid, and manage your love under-hand with
her.

Sir Martin. Well remember'd i'faith, I thank thee for that,
I had forgot it I protest! my *Valet de Chambre*, whom you
see here with me, grows me acquainted with her   240
Woman ———

Warner. O the Devil. ———

Sir Martin. In fine Sir, this Maid being much in her
Mistress's favour, so well sollicited my Cause, that in
fine I gain'd from fair Mistress *Millisent* an assurance of   245
her kindness, and an ingagement to marry none but
me.

Warner. 'Tis very well! you've made a fair discovery!—

Sir John. A most pleasant Relation I assure you: you are a
happy man Sir! but what occasion brought you now to   250
London?

Sir Martin. That was in expectation to meet my Mistress
here; she writ me word from *Canterbury*, she and her
Father shortly would be here.

Sir John. She and her Father, said you Sir?   255

Warner. Tell him Sir, for Heaven sake tell him all.———

Sir Martin. So I will Sir, without your bidding: her Father
and she are come up already, that's the truth on't, and
are to lodge by my Contrivance in yon House; the
Master of which is a cunning Rascal as any in Town—   260
him I have made my own, for I lodge there.

Warner. You do ill Sir to speak so scandalously of my
Landlord.

Sir Martin. Peace, or I'le break your Fool's head.—So that
by his means I shall have free egress and regress when I   265
please Sir—without her Father's knowledge.

Warner. I am out of patience to hear this.———

Sir John. Methinks you might do well, Sir, to speak
openly to her Father.

Sir Martin. Thank you for that i'faith, in speaking to old   270
Moody I may soon spoil all.

Warner. So, now he has told her Father's name, 'tis past recovery.

Sir John. Is her Father's name *Moody* say you?

275 *Sir Martin.* Is he of your acquaintance?

Sir John. Yes Sir, I know him for a man who is too wise for you to over-reach; I am certain he will never marry his Daughter to you.

Sir Martin. Why, there's the jest on't: he shall never know
280 it: 'tis but your keeping of my Counsel; I'le do as much for you mun. ———

Sir John. No Sir, I'le give you better; trouble not your self about this Lady; her affections are otherwise engag'd to my knowledge—hark in your Ear—her Father hates a
285 Gamester like the Devil: I'le keep your Counsel for that too.

Sir Martin. Nay but this is not all dear Sir *John.*

Sir John. This is all I assure you: only I will make bold to seek your Mistress out another Lodging.———

Exit Sir John.

290 *Warner.* Your Affairs are now put into an excellent posture, thank your incomparable discretion—this was a Stratagem my shallow wit could ner'e have reach'd, to make a Confident of my Rival.

Sir Martin. I hope thou art not in earnest man! is he my
295 Rival?

Warner. 'Slife he has not found it out all this while! well Sir for a quick apprehension let you alone.

Sir Martin. How the Devil cam'st thou to know on't? and why the Devil didst thou not tell me on't?

300 *Warner.* To the first of your Devil's I answer, her Maid *Rose* told me on't: to the second I wish a thousand Devils take him that would not hear me.

Sir Martin. O unparallell'd Misfortune!

Warner. O unparallell'd ignorance! why, he left her Father
305 at the water-side, while he lead the Daughter to her lodging, whither I directed him; so that if you had not laboured to the contrary, Fortune had plac'd you in the same House with your Mistress, without the least suspition of your Rival or of her Father. But 'tis well,
310 you have satisfi'd your talkative humour; I hope you have some new project of your own to set all right agen: for my part I confess all my designs for you are wholly ruin'd; the very foundations of 'em are blown up.

281 *mun*] a dialectal variant of *man*; usually implying contempt.
309 *Father*] The rewritten ending of Act I follows from this point, the beginning of leaf C1 (Q1). See the introduction for a fragment of the original ending.

Sir Martin. Prethee insult not over the Destiny of a poor undone Lover, I am punish'd enough for my indis- 315
cretion in my despair, and have nothing to hope for now but death.

Warner. Death is a Bug-word, things are not brought to that extremity, I'le cast about to save all yet.

Enter Lady Dupe.

Lady Dupe. O, Sir *Martin*! yonder has been such a stir 320
within. Sir *John*, I fear, smoaks your design, and by all means would have the old man remove his Lodging; pray God your man has not play'd false.

Warner. Like enough I have: I am Coxcomb sufficient to do it, my Master knows that none but such a great Calf 325
as I could have done it, such an over-grown Ass, a self-conceited Ideot as I.———

Sir Martin. Nay, *Warner*, ———

Warner. Pray, Sir, let me alone:—what is it to you if I rail upon my self? now could I break my own Loggar- 330
head.

Sir Martin. Nay, sweet *Warner*.

Warner. What a good Master have I, and I to ruine him: O Beast! ———

Lady Dupe. Not to discourage you wholly, Sir *Martin*, this 335
storm is partly over.

Sir Martin. As how? dear Cousin.

Lady Dupe. When I heard Sir *John* complain of the Land-lord, I took the first hint of it, and joyn'd with him, saying, if he were such an one, I would have nothing 340
to do with him: in short, I rattled him so well, that Sir *John* was the first who did desire they might be lodg'd with me, not knowing that I was your Kinswoman.

Sir Martin. Pox on't, now I think on't, I could have found out this my self. ——— 345

Warner. Are you there agen, Sir?—now as I have a Soul —

Sir Martin. Mum, good *Warner*, I did but forget my self a little, I leave my self wholly to you, and my Cousin; get but my Mistress for me, and claim what e're reward you can desire. 350

Warner. Hope of reward will diligence beget, Find you the money, and I'le find the wit.

Exeunt.

340 he] Q5; she Q1–4
318 *Bug-word*] a word that terrifies, a bug-a-boo or bogey.
321 *smoaks*] suspects.
330–31 *Loggarhead*] blockhead.
341 *rattled*] scolded.

ACT II. [Scene 1]

Enter Lady Dupe, *and Mistress* Christian.

Christian. It happen'd Madam, just as you said it would; but was he so concern'd for my feign'd sickness?

Lady Dupe. So much that *Moody* and his Daughter, our new Guests, took notice of the trouble, but the Cause was kept too close for Strangers to divine.

Christian. Heav'n grant he be but deep enough in love, and then ———

Lady Dupe. And then thou shalt distill him into Gold, my Girl.

Yonder he comes, I'le not be seen:—you know your Lesson, Child. *Exit.*

Christian. I warrant you.

Enter Lord Dartmouth.

Lord Dartmouth. Pretty Mistress *Christian*, how glad am I to meet you thus alone!

Christian. O the Father! what will become of me now?

Lord Dartmouth. No harm I warrant you, but why are you so 'fraid?

Christian. A poor weak innocent Creature as I am, Heav'n of his mercy, how I quake and tremble! I have not yet claw'd off your last ill usage, and now I feel my old fit come again, my Ears tingle already, and my back shuts and opens; I, just so it began before.

Lord Dartmouth. Nay, my sweet Mistress, be not so unjust to suspect any new attempt: I am too penitent for my last fault, so soon to sin agen, ——— I hope you did not tell it to your Aunt.

Christian. The more Fool I, I did not.

Lord Dartmouth. You never shall repent your goodness to me. But may not I presume there was some little kindness in it, which mov'd you to conceal my Crime?

Christian. Methought I would not have mine Aunt an angry with you for all this earthly good.
But yet I'le never be alone with you agen.

Lord Dartmouth. Pretty Innocence! let me sit nearer to you: you do not understand what love I bear you. I vow it is so pure—my Soul's not sully'd with one spot of sin:

---

15 *Father*] probably O God!
20 *claw'd off*] got free from, as of an itch by clawing the skin (Summers).
21–22 *my . . . opens*] possibly *I shudder.*

were you a Sister or a Daughter to me, with a more
holy Flame I could not burn.

Christian. Nay, now you speak high words—I cannot
understand you.   40

Lord Dartmouth. The business of my life shall be but how
to make your Fortune, and my care and study to advance
and see you settled in the World.

Christian. I humbly thank your Lordship.

Lord Dartmouth. Thus I would sacrifice my Life and For-   45
tunes, and in return you cruelly destroy me.

Christian. I never meant you any harm, not I.

Lord Dartmouth. Then what does this white Enemy so
near me?   *Touching her hand glov'd.*
Sure 'tis your Champion, and you arm it thus to bid   50
defiance to me.

Christian. Nay fye my Lord, in faith you are to blame.
                                   Pulling her hand away.

Lord Dartmouth. But I am for fair Wars, an Enemy must
first be search'd for privy Armour, e're we do ingage.
                                   Pulls at her glove.

Christian. What does your Lordship mean?   55

Lord Dartmouth. I fear you bear some Spells and Charms
about you, and, Madam, that's against the Laws of
Arms.

Christian. My Aunt charg'd me not to pull off my Glove
for fear of Sun-burning my hand.   60

Lord Dartmouth. She did well to keep it from your Eyes,
but I will thus preserve it.   *Hugging her bare hand.*

Christian. Why do you crush it so? nay now you hurt
me, nay—if you squeeze it ne're so hard—there's nothing
to come out on't—fye—is this loving one?—what   65
makes you take your breath so short?

Lord Dartmouth. The Devil take me if I can answer her a
word, all my Sences are quite imploy'd another way.

Christian. Ne're stir my Lord, I must cry out ———

Lord Dartmouth. Then I must stop your mouth—this Ruby   70
for a Kiss—that is but one Ruby for another.

Christian. This is worse and worse.

Lady Dupe (*within*). Why Neece, where are you Neece?

Lord Dartmouth. Pox of her old mouldy Chops.

Christian. Do you hear, my Aunt calls? I shall be hang'd   75
for staying with you ——— let me go my Lord.
                                   Gets from him.

61 *from your Eyes*] because they, like the sun, would burn your
hands.
74 *Chops*] jaws.

119

Enter Lady Dupe.

Lady Dupe. My Lord, Heaven bless me, what makes your
    Lordship here?

Lord Dartmouth. I was just wishing for you Madam, your

80   Neece and I have been so laughing at the blunt humour
    of your Country Gentleman, ——— I must go pass an
    hour with him.   *Exit Lord* Dartmouth.

Christian. You made a little too much haste; I was just
    exchanging a Kiss for a Ruby.

85   *Lady Dupe*. No harm done; it will make him come on the
    faster: never full-gorge an Hawk you mean to fly. The
    next will be a Neck-lace of Pearl I warrant you.

Christian. But what must I do next?

Lady Dupe. Tell him I grew suspitious, and examin'd you

90   whether he made not love; which you deny'd. Then
    tell him how my Maids and Daughters watch you; so
    that you tremble when you see his Lordship.

Christian. And that your Daughters are so envious, that
    they would raise a false report to ruine me.

95   *Lady Dupe*. Therefore you desire his Lordship, as he loves
    you, of which you are confident, hence-forward to
    forbear his Visits to you.

Christian. But how if he should take me at my word?

Lady Dupe. Why, if the worst come to the worst, he

100   leaves you an honest woman, and there's an end on't:
    but fear not that, hold out his messages, and then he'll
    write, and that is it my Bird which you must drive it
    to: then all his Letters will be such Extacies, such Vows
    and Promises, which you must answer short and simply,

105   yet still ply out of 'em your advantages.

Christian. But Madam! he's i'th' house, he will not write.

Lady Dupe. You Fool—he'll write from the next Chamber
    to you. And rather than fail, send his Page Post with it
    upon a Hobby-horse: ——— then grant a meeting,

110   but tell me of it, and I'le prevent him by my being
    there; hee'l curse me, but I care not. When you are
    alone, hee'l urge his lust, which answer you with scorn
    and anger. ———

Christian. As thus an't please you, Madam? What? does

115   he think I will be damn'd for him? Defame my Family,
    ruine my Name, to satisfie his pleasure?

Lady Dupe. Then he will be prophane in's Arguments,
    urge Nature's Laws to you.

---

86 *full-gorge*] allow him to stuff with food.
108 *Page Post*] delivery by a page.

Christian. By'r Lady, and those are shrewd Arguments.
But I am resolv'd I'le stop my Ears.   120
Lady Dupe. Then when he sees no other thing will move
you, hee'l sign a portion to you before hand. Take hold
of that, and then of what you will.

            Exeunt.

ACT II. [Scene 2]

Enter Sir John, *Mistress* Millisent, *and* Rose.

Sir John. Now fair Mistress *Millisent,* you see your
Chamber. Your Father will be busie a few minutes, and
in the mean time permits me the happiness to wait on
you. ———
Millisent. Methinks you might have chose us better   5
Lodgings. This house is full; the other we saw first, was
more convenient.
Sir John. For you perhaps, but not for me: You might
have met a Lover there, but I a Rival.
Millisent. What Rival?   10
Sir John. You know Sir *Martin,* I need not name him to
you.
Millisent. I know more men besides him.
Sir John. But you love none besides him, can you deny
your affection to him?   15
Millisent. You have vex'd me so, I will not satisfie you.
Sir John. Then I perceive I am not likely to be so much
oblig'd to you as I was to him.
Millisent. This is Romance,—I'le not believe a word on't.—
Sir John. That's as you please: however 'tis believ'd, his   20
wit will not much credit your choice. Madam, do
justice to us both; pay his ingratitude and folly with
your scorn; my service with your Love. By this time
your Father stays for me: I shall be discreet enough to
keep this fault of yours from him. The Lawyers wait   25
for us to draw your Joynture: and I would beg your
pardon for my absence, but that my Crime is punish'd
in it self.   *Exit.*
Millisent. Could I suspect this usage from a favour'd
Servant!   30
Rose. First hear Sir *Martin* ere you quite condemn him;
consider 'tis a Rival who accus'd him.
Millisent. Speak not a word in his behalf: ——— Methought too, Sir *John* call'd him Fool.
Rose. Indeed he has a rare way of acting a Fool, and does   35
it so naturally, it can be scarce distinguish'd.

Millisent. Nay, he has wit enough, that's certain.

Rose [*aside*]. How blind Love is!

Enter Warner.

40

Millisent. How now, what's his business? I wonder after such a Crime, if his Master has the face to send him to me.

Rose. How durst you venture hither? If either Sir *John* or my old Master see you ———

Warner. Pish! they are both gone out.

45

Rose. They went but to the next street; ten to one but they return and catch you here.

Warner. Twenty to one I am gone before, and save 'um a labour.

50

Millisent. What says that Fellow to you? what business can he have here?

Warner. Lord, that your Ladiship should ask that question, knowing whom I serve!

Millisent. I'le hear nothing from your Master.

55

Warner. Never breathe, but this anger becomes your Ladiship most admirably; but though you'l hear nothing from him, I hope I may speak a word or two to you from my self, Madam.

60

Rose. 'Twas a sweet Prank your Master play'd us: a Lady's well helpt up that trusts her Honour in such a person's hands: to tell all so,—and to his Rival too.

(*Aside*) Excuse him if thou canst.

Warner. How the Devil should I excuse him? thou knowest he is the greatest Fop in Nature. ———

Aside to Rose.

Rose. But my Lady does not know it; if she did———

65

Millisent. I'le have no Whispering.

Warner. Alas, Madam, I have not the confidence to speak out, unless you can take mercy on me.

Millisent. For what?

70

Warner. For telling Sir *John* you lov'd my Master, Madam. But sure I little thought he was his Rival.

Rose (*aside*). The witty Rogue has taken't on himself.

Millisent. Your Master then is innocent?

Warner. Why, could your Ladiship suspect him guilty? Pray tell me, do you think him ungrateful, or a Fool?

75

Millisent. I think him neither.

Warner. Take it from me, you see not the depth of him. But when he knows what thoughts you harbour of him, as I am faithful, and must tell him,—I wish he does not take some pet, and leave you.

79 *take some pet*] take offense at being slighted.

Millisent. Thou art not mad I hope, to tell him on't; if 80
  thou dost, I'le be sworn, I'le foreswear it to him.
Warner. Upon condition then you'l pardon me, I'le see
  what I can do to hold my tongue.
Millisent. This Evening in Saint *James's* Park I'le meet him.
                                          Knock within.
Warner. He shall not fail you, Madam. 85
Rose. Some body knocks,—Oh Madam, what shall we do!
  'Tis Sir *John*, I hear his voice.
Warner. What will become of me?
Millisent. Step quickly behind that Door.   *He goes out.*

          To them Sir John.

Millisent. You've made a quick dispatch, Sir. 90
Sir John. We have done nothing, Madam, our Man of
  Law was not within,—but I must look some Writings.
Millisent. Where are they laid?
Sir John. In the Portmanteau in the Drawing-room.
                                    Is going to the Door.
Millisent. Pray stay a little, Sir. ——— 95
Warner (at the Door). He must pass just by me; and if he
  sees me, I am but a dead man.
Sir John. Why are you thus concern'd? why do you hold
  me?
Millisent. Only a word or two I have to tell you. 'Tis of 100
  importance to you. ———
Sir John. Give me leave. ———
Millisent. I must not before I discover the Plot to you.
Sir John. What Plot?
Millisent. Sir *Martin's* Servant, like a Rogue comes hither 105
  to tempt me from his Master, to have met him.
Warner (at the Door). Now would I had a good Bag of
  Gun-powder at my Breech to ram me into some hole.
Millisent. For my part I was so startled at the Message,
  that I shall scarcely be my self these two days. 110
Sir John. Oh that I had the Rascal! I would teach him to
  come upon such Errands.
Warner. Oh for a gentle Composition now! An Arm or
  Leg I would give willingly.
Sir John. What Answer did you make the Villain? 115
Millisent. I over-reach'd him clearly, by a promise of an
  appointment of a place I nam'd, where I ne're meant to

  92 *look*] examine.
  113 *Composition*] agreement between warring armies, involving
surrender or sacrifice of something; compromise.
  116 *clearly*] entirely, cleanly (see *OED* adv. 8), although the com-
moner expression is "overreached cleanly," i.e., artfully.

          123

come: but would have had the pleasure first to tell you
how I serv'd him, and then to chide your mean sus-
120   picion of me.
Sir John. Indeed I wonder'd you should love a Fool. But
where did you appoint to meet him?
Millisent. In *Grayes-Inn* Walks.
Warner. By this light, she has put the change upon him!
125   O sweet Woman-kind, how I love thee for that heavenly
gift of lying!
Sir John. For this Evening I will be his Mistress; he shall
meet another *Penelope* then he suspects.
Millisent. But stay not long away.
130   *Sir John.* You over-joy me, Madam.   *Exit.*
Warner (entring). Is he gone, Madam?
Millisent. As far as *Grayes-Inn* Walks: now I have time to
walk the other way, and see thy Master.
Warner. Rather let him come hither: I have laid a Plot
135   shall send his Rival far enough from watching him e're
long.
Millisent. Art thou in earnest?
Warner. 'Tis so design'd, Fate cannot hinder it. Our Landlord where we lye, vex'd that his Lodgings should be
140   so left by Sir *John*, is resolv'd to be reveng'd, and I have
found the way. You'l see th'effect on't presently.
Rose. O Heavens! the door opens agen, and Sir *John* is
returned once more.

Enter Sir John.

Sir John. Half my business was forgot; you did not tell
145   me when you were to meet him. Ho! what makes this
Rascal here?
Warner. 'Tis well you're come, Sir, else I must have left
untold a Message I have for you.
Sir John. Well, what's your business, Sirrah?
150   *Warner.* We must be private first; 'tis only for your ear.
                                    [They walk apart.]
Rose. I shall admire his wit, if in this plunge he can get off.
Warner. I came hither, Sir, by my Master's order.———
Sir John. I'le reward you for it, Sirrah, immediately.
Warner. When you know all, I shall deserve it, Sir. I came
155   to sound the Vertue of your Mistress; which I have
done so cunningly, I have at last obtain'd the promise
of a meeting. But my good Master, whom I must con-

119–20 and then ... of me.] S-S *conjecture*; Qq,F *assign to* Sir John
128 *Penelope*] See III.11.76, *note.*
132 *Grayes-Inn Walks*] over a half mile away.

fess more generous than wise, knowing you had a
passion for her, is resolv'd to quit: And, Sir, that you
may see how much he loves you, sent me in private to   160
advise you still to have an eye upon her actions.

Sir John. Take this Diamond for thy good news; and give
thy Master my acknowledgments.

Warner (aside). Thus the world goes, my Masters, he that
will cozen you, commonly gets your good will into the   165
bargain.

Sir John. Madam, I am now satisfi'd of all sides; first of
your truth, then of Sir *Martin's* friendship. In short, I
find you two cheated each other, both to be true to me.

Millisent [aside]. *Warner* is got off as I would wish, and the   170
Knight over-reach'd.

Enter to them the Landlord *disguis'd like a Carrier.*

Rose. How now! what would this Carrier have?

Warner (aside to her). This is our Landlord whom I told you
of; but keep your Countenance.———

Landlord. I was looking here-away for one Sir *John Swallow*;   175
they told me I might hear news of him in this house.

Sir John. Friend, I am the man: what have you to say to
me?

Landlord. Nay, faith Sir, I am not so good a Schollard to
say much, but I have a Letter for you in my Pouch: 180
there's plaguy news in't, I can tell you that.

Sir John. From whom is your Letter?

Landlord. From your old Uncle *Anthony.*

Sir John. Give me your Letter quickly.

Landlord. Nay, soft and fair goes far.—Hold you, hold   185
you. It is not in this Pocket.

Sir John. Search in the other then; I stand on Thorns.

Landlord. I think I feel it now, this should be who.

Sir John. Pluck it out then.

Landlord. I'le pluck out my Spectacles and see first.   190

Reads.

To Master *Paul Grimbard*—Apprentice to—
No, that's not for you, Sir,—that's for the Son of the
Brother of the Nephew of the Cousin of my Gossip
Dobson.

Sir John. Prithee dispatch; dost thou not know the Con-   195
tents on't?

Landlord. Yes, as well as I do my *Pater noster.*

Sir John. Well, what's the business on't?

179 *Schollard*] scholar; vulgar speech.
188 *who*] the right one.

200   *Landlord.* Nay, no great business; 'tis but only that your
Worship's Father's dead.

Sir John. My loss is beyond expression! how dy'd he?

Landlord. He went to bed as well to see to as any man in
England, and when he awaken'd the next morning———

Sir John. What then?

205   *Landlord.* He found himself stark dead.

Sir John. Well, I must of necessity take orders for my
Father's Funeral, and my Estate; Heaven knows with
what regret I leave you, Madam.

Millisent. But are you in such haste, Sir? I see you take all
210   occasions to be from me.

Sir John. Dear Madam, say not so, a few days will, I hope,
return me to you.

          To them Sir Martin.

Noble Sir *Martin*, the welcomest man alive! Let me
embrace my Friend.

215   *Rose (aside).* How untowardly he returns the salute!
Warner will be found out.

Sir John. Well friend! you have oblig'd me to you eternally.

Sir Martin. How have I oblig'd you, Sir? I would have
220   you to know I scorn your words; and I would I were
hang'd, if it be not the farthest of my thoughts.

Millisent (aside). O cunning Youth, he acts the Fool most
naturally. Were we alone, how we would laugh
together?

225   *Sir John.* This is a double generosity, to do me favours and
conceal 'um from me. But honest *Warner* here has told
me all.

Sir Martin. What has the Rascal told you?

Sir John. Your plot to try my Mistress for me—you under-
230   stand me, concerning your appointment.

Warner. Sir, I desire to speak in private with you.

Sir Martin. This impertinent Rascal, when I am most
busie, I am ever troubled with him.

Warner. But it concerns you I should speak with you,
235   good Sir.

Sir Martin. That's a good one i'faith, thou knowst breeding
well, that I should whisper with a Serving-man before
company.

Warner. Remember, Sir, last time it had been better———

240   *Sir Martin.* Peace, or I'le make you feel my double Fists:

206 *take orders*] make arrangements.

If I don't fright him, the sawcy Rogue will call me Fool
before the Company.

Millisent (aside). That was acted most naturally again.

Sir John (to him). But what needs this dissembling, since
you are resolv'd to quit my Mistress to me? 245

Sir Martin. I quit my Mistress! that's a good one i'faith.

Millisent (aside). Tell him you have forsaken me.

Sir Martin. I understand you, Madam, you would save a
quarrel; but i'faith I'me not so base: I'le see him hang'd
first. 250

Warner. Madam, my Master is convinc'd, in prudence he
should say so: but Love o'remasters him; when you are
gone perhaps he may.

Millisent. I'le go then: Gentlemen, your Servant; I see my
presence brings constraint to the Company. 255

Exeunt Millisent, Rose.

Sir John. I'm glad she's gone; now we may talk more
freely; for if you have not quitted her, you must.

Warner. Pray, Sir, remember your self; did not you send
me of a message to Sir *John*, that for his friendship you
had left Mistress *Millisent*? 260

Sir Martin. Why, what an impudent lying Rogue art thou!

Sir John. How's this! has *Warner* cheated me?

Warner. Do not suspect it in the least: you know, Sir, it
was not generous before a Lady, to say he quitted her.

Sir John. O! was that it? 265

Warner. That was all: *(aside)* say, Yes good Sir *John*—or
I'le swindge you.

Sir Martin. Yes, good Sir *John*.

Warner. That's well, once in his life he has heard good
counsel. 270

Sir Martin. Heigh, Heigh, what makes my Landlord here?
he has put on a Fool's Coat I think to make us laugh.

Warner. The Devil's in him; he's at it again; his folly's like
a sore in a surfeited Horse; cure it in one place, and it
breaks out in another. 275

Sir Martin. Honest Landlord i'faith, and what make you
here?

Sir John. Are you acquainted with this honest man?

Landlord. Take heed what you say, Sir.

To Sir Martin *softly*.

Sir Martin. Take heed what I say, Sir, why? who should I 280
be afraid of? of you, Sir? I say, Sir, I know him, Sir;
and I have reason to know him, Sir, for I am sure I

267 *swindge*] beat.
274 *surfeited*] a disease of horses causing sores.

lodge in his House, Sir,—nay never think to terrifie me, Sir; 'tis my Landlord here in *Charles* Street, Sir.

285   *Landlord.* Now I expect to be paid for the News I brought him.

Sir John. Sirrah, did not you tell me that my Father ——

Landlord. Is in very good health, for ought I know, Sir; I beseech you trouble your self no farther concerning him.

290   *Sir John.* Who set you on to tell this lye?

Sir Martin. I, who set you on Sirrah? this was a Rogue that would cozen us both; he thought I did not know him: down on your marribones and confess the truth: have you no Tongue you Rascal?

295   *Sir John.* Sure 'tis some silenc'd Minister: he's grown so fat he cannot speak.

Landlord. Why, Sir, if you would know, 'twas for your sake I did it.

Warner. For my Master's sake! why, you impudent Varlet,

300   do you think to 'scape us with a lye?

Sir John. How was it for his sake?

Warner. 'Twas for his own, Sir; he heard you were th' occasion the Lady lodg'd not at his House, and so he invented this lye; partly to revenge himself of you; and

305   partly, I believe, in hope to get her once again when you were gone.

Sir John. Fetch me a Cudgel prithee.

Landlord. O good Sir! if you beat me I shall run into oyl immediately.

310   *Warner.* Hang him Rogue; he's below your anger: I'le maul him for you—the Rogue's so big, I think 'twill ask two days to beat him all over: *Beats him.*

Landlord. O Rogue, O Villain *Warner*! bid him hold and I'le confess, Sir.

315   *Warner.* Get you gone without replying: must such as you be prating?   *Beats him out.*

Enter Rose.

---

284 *Charles Street*] in Covent Garden, now named Wellington Street, "A very fashionable quarter for the lodgings of persons of quality" (Summers). Houses were designed by Inigo Jones.

293 *marribones*] knees, with a pun on Mary.

295 *silenc'd Minister*] silenced by the Act of Uniformity, May, 1662, "when every beneficed clergyman was ordered to use the services of the *Book of Common Prayer* . . ." (Summers). This meant that nonconformist ministers were silenced from preaching their usual longwinded sermons.

308 *run into oyl*] probably a reference to the method of obtaining oil from olives and other plants by beating in a mortar.

Rose. Sir, Dinner waits you on the Table.

Sir John. Friend will you go along, and take part of a bad
    Repast?

Sir Martin. Thank you; but I am just risen from Table.   320

Warner [*aside*]. Now he might sit with his Mistress, and
    has not the wit to find it out.

Sir John. You shall be very welcome.

Sir Martin. I have no stomack, Sir.

Warner. Get you in with a vengeance: you have a better   325
    stomack than you think you have.   *Pushes him.*

Sir Martin. This hungry *Diego* Rogue would shame me;
    he thinks a Gentleman can eat like a Servingman.

Sir John. If you will not, adieu dear Sir; in any thing
    command me.   *Exit.*   330

Sir Martin. Now we are alone; han't I carried matters
    bravely Sirrah?

Warner. O yes, yes, you deserve Sugar Plums; first for
    your quarrelling with Sir *John*; then for discovering
    your Landlord, and lastly for refusing to dine with your   335
    Mistress. All this is since the last reckoning was wip'd
    out.

Sir Martin. Then why did my Landlord disguise himself,
    to make a Fool of us?

Warner. You have so little Brains, that a Penn'orth of   340
    Butter melted under 'um, would set 'um afloat: he put
    on that disguise to rid you of your Rival.

Sir Martin. Why was not I worthy to keep your counsel
    then?

Warner. It had been much at one: you would but have   345
    drunk the secret down, and piss'd it out to the next
    company.

Sir Martin. Well I find I am a miserable man: I have lost
    my Mistress, and may thank my self for't.

Warner. You'l not confess you are a Fool, I warrant.   350

Sir Martin. Well I am a Fool, if that will satisfie you: but
    what, am I the neerer for being one?

Warner. O yes, much the neerer; for now Fortune's bound
    to provide for you; as Hospitals are built for lame
    people, because they cannot help themselves. Well; I   355
    have yet a project in my pate.

Sir Martin. Dear Rogue, what is't?

Warner. Excuse me for that: but while 'tis set a working
    you would do well to scrue your self into her Father's
    good opinion.   360

327 *Diego*] by analogy with the servant Diego "a great Coward and
a pleasant Droll" in Samuel Tuke's *The Adventures of Five Hours*, 1663
(Summers).

    Sir Martin. If you will not tell me, my mind gives me I
        shall discover it again.
    Warner. I'le lay it as far out of your reach as I can possible.
    ———— For secrets are edg'd Tools,
365   And must be kept from Children and from Fools.

                             Exeunt.

ACT III. [Scene 1]

Enter Rose *and* Warner *meeting.*

    Rose. Your Worship's most happily encounter'd.
    Warner. Your Ladiship's most fortunately met.
    Rose. I was going to your Lodging.
    Warner. My business was to yours.
5   *Rose.* I have something to say to you that————
    Warner. I have that to tell you————
    Rose. Understand then————
    Warner. If you'l hear me————
    Rose. I believe that————
10   *Warner.* I am of opinion that————
    Rose. Prithee hold thy peace a little till I have done.
    Warner. Cry you mercy, Mistress *Rose*, I'le not dispute
        your ancient priviledges of talking.
    Rose. My Mistress, knowing Sir *John* was to be abroad
15   upon business this Afternoon, has asked leave to see a
        Play: and Sir *John* has so great a confidence of your
        Master, that he will trust no body with her, but him.
    Warner. If my Master gets her out, I warrant her, he shall
        show her a better Play than any is at either of the
20   Houses—here they are: I'le run and prepare him to
        wait upon her.   *Exit.*

    Enter Old Moody, *Mistress* Millisent, *and Lady* Dupe.

    Millisent. My Hoods and Scarfs there, quickly.
    Lady Dupe. Send to call a Coach there.
    Moody. But what kind of man is this Sir *Martin*, with
25   whom you are to go?
    Lady Dupe. A plain downright Country Gentleman, I
        assure you.
    Moody. I like him much the better for't. For I hate one of
        those you call a man o'th' Town, one of those empty
30   fellows of meer outside: they've nothing of the true old
        English manliness.
    Rose. I confess, Sir, a Woman's in a sad condition, that has

    363 *possible*] i.e., possibly.

nothing to trust to, but a Perriwig above, and a well-trim'd shoe below.

To them Sir Martin.

Millisent. This, Sir, is Sir *John's* friend, he is for your 35
humour, Sir. He is no man o'th' Town, but bred up in
the old *Elizabeth* way of plainness.
Sir Martin. I, Madam, your Ladiship may say your pleasure
of me.

To them Warner.

Warner. How the Devil got he here before me! 'tis very 40
unlucky I could not see him first. ———
Sir Martin. But as for Painting, Musick, Poetry, and the
like, I'le say this of my self ———
Warner. I'le say that for him, my Master understands none
of 'um, I assure you, Sir. 45
Sir Martin. You impudent Rascal, hold your Tongue: I
must rid my hands of this fellow; the Rogue is ever
discrediting me before Company.
Moody. Never trouble your self about it, Sir, for I like a
man that ——— 50
Sir Martin. I know you do, Sir, and therefore I hope you'll
think never the worse of me for his prating: for though
I do not boast of my own good parts ———
Warner. He has none to boast of, upon my faith, Sir.
Sir Martin. Give him not the hearing, Sir; for, if I may 55
believe my friends, they have flatter'd me with an
opinion of more ———
Warner. Of more than their flattery can make good, Sir;—
'tis true he tells you, they have flatter'd him; but in
my Conscience he is the most downright simple natured 60
creature in the world.
Sir Martin. I shall consider you hereafter Sirrah; but I am
sure in all Companies I pass for a *Vertuoso.*
Moody. Vertuoso! what's that too? is not *Vertue* enough
without O *so*? 65
Sir Martin. You have Reason, Sir!
Moody. There he is again too; the Town Phrase, a great
Compliment I wiss; you have Reason, Sir; that is, you
are no beast, Sir.
Warner. A word in private, Sir; you mistake this old man; 70
he loves neither Painting, Musick, nor Poetry; yet
recover your self, if you have any brains.
Aside to him.
Sir Martin. Say you so? I'le bring all about again I warrant

66 *have Reason*] from French *avoir raison*, to be right.

131

75

you.—I beg your pardon a thousand times Sir; I vow
to Gad I am not Master of any of those perfections; for
in fine, Sir, I am wholly ignorant of Painting, Musick,
and Poetry; only some rude escapes—but, in fine, they
are such, that, in fine, Sir ———

Warner (*aside*). This is worse than all the rest.

80

Moody. By Coxbones one word more of all this Gibberish,
and old Madge shall fly about your ears: what is this
in fine he keeps such a coil with too?

Millisent. 'Tis a Phrase *a-la-mode*, Sir, and is us'd in conversation now, as a whiff of Tobacco was formerly, in

85

the midst of a discourse, for a thinking while.

Lady Dupe. In plain English, in fine, is in the end, Sir.

Moody. But by Coxbones there is no end on't me thinks:
if thou wilt have a foolish word to lard thy lean discourse with, take an English one when thou speakest

90

English; as So Sir, and Then Sir, and so forth; 'tis a more
manly kind of nonsense: and a Pox of In fine, for I'le
hear no more on't.

Warner (*aside*). He's gravell'd, and I must help him out.
Madam, there's a Coach at Door to carry you to the

95

Play.

Sir Martin. Which House do you mean to go to?

Millisent. The Duke's, I think.

Sir Martin. It is a damn'd Play, and has nothing in't.

Millisent. Then let us to the King's.

100

Sir Martin. That's e'ne as bad.

Warner (*aside*). This is past enduring.
There was an ill Play set up, Sir, on the Posts, but I can
assure you the Bills are altered since you saw 'um, and
now there are two admirable Comedies at both Houses.

105

Moody. But my Daughter loves serious Plays.

Warner. They are Tragi-Comedies, Sir, for both.

Sir Martin. I have heard her say she loves none but
Tragedies.

Moody. Where have you heard her say so, Sir?

110

Warner. Sir you forget your self, you never saw her in
your life before.

Sir Martin. What, not at *Canterbury*, in the Cathedral
Church there? this is the impudentest Rascal ———

---

77 *escapes*] unstudied or artless performances (this is the only example cited in *OED*). It may be derived from "escapes of wit," sallies.
80 *Coxbones*] a perversion of God's bones.
81 *old Madge*] his cudgel.
85 *thinking while*] duration of time to think.
93 *gravell'd*] nonplussed.

Warner. Mum, Sir ———

Sir Martin. Ah Lord, what have I done! as I hope to be   115
sav'd Sir, it was before I was aware; for if ever I set
Eyes on her before this day—I wish———

Moody. This fellow is not so much fool, as he makes one
believe he is.

Millisent (aside). I thought he would be discovered for a   120
wit: this 'tis to over-act one's part!

Moody. Come away Daughter, I will not trust you in his
hands; there's more in't than I imagin'd.

       Exeunt Moody, Millisent, *Lady* [Dupe], Rose.

Sir Martin. Why do you frown upon me so, when you
know your looks go to the heart of me; what have I   125
done besides a little *lapsus linguæ*?

Warner. Why, who says you have done any thing? you,
a meer Innocent.

Sir Martin. As the Child's that be born, in my intentions;
if I know how I have offended my self any more than   130
in one word. ———

Warner. But don't follow me however—I have nothing to
say to you.

Sir Martin. I'le follow you to the world's end, till you forgive me.   135

Warner. I am resolv'd to lead you a Dance then.

       Exit running.

Sir Martin. The Rogue has no mercy in him, but I must
mollifie him with money.

       Exit.

[ACT III. Scene 2]

Enter Lady Dupe.

Lady Dupe. Truly my little Cousin's the aptest Scholar,
and takes out love's lessons so exactly that I joy to see it:
she has got already the Bond of two thousand pounds
seal'd for her Portion, which I keep for her; a pretty
good beginning: 'tis true, I believe he has enjoy'd her,   5
and so let him; *Mark Anthony* wooed not at so dear a
price.

To her Christian.

Christian. O Madam, I fear I am a breeding!

Lady Dupe. A taking Wench! but 'tis no matter; have you
told any body?   10

116 *aware*] on my guard. Another slip of the tongue.

Christian. I have been venturing upon your foundations, a little to dissemble.

Lady Dupe. That's a good Child, I hope it will thrive with thee, as it has with me: Heaven has a blessing in store upon our endeavours.

Christian. I feign'd my self sick, and kept my bed; my Lord, he came to visit me, and in the end I disclos'd it to him in the saddest passion.

Lady Dupe. This frighted him, I hope, into a study how to cloak your disgrace, lest it should have vent to his Lady.

Christian. 'Tis true; but all the while I subt'ly drove it, that he should name you to me as the fittest instrument of the concealment; but how to break it to you, strangely does perplex him: he has been seeking you all o're the house; therefore I'le leave your Ladiship, for fear we should be seen together.   *Exit.*

Lady Dupe. Now I must play my part;
Nature, in Women, teaches more than Art.

Enter Lord [Dartmouth].

Lord Dartmouth. Madam, I have a Secret to impart, a sad one too, and have no Friend to trust but only you.

Lady Dupe. Your Lady or your Children sick?

Lord Dartmouth. Not that I know.

Lady Dupe. You seem to be in health.

Lord Dartmouth. In body, not in mind.

Lady Dupe. Some scruple of Conscience, I warrant; my Chaplain shall resolve you.

Lord Dartmouth. Madam, my Soul's tormented.

Lady Dupe. O take heed of despair, my Lord!

Lord Dartmouth. Madam, there is no Medicine for this sickness, but only you; your friendship's my safe Haven, else I am lost and shipwrack'd.

Lady Dupe. Pray tell me what it is.

Lord Dartmouth. Could I express it by sad sighs and groans, or drown it with my self in Seas of tears, I should be happy, ——— would, and would not tell.

Lady Dupe. Command whatever I can serve you in, I will be faithful still to all your ends, provided they be just and vertuous.

Lord Dartmouth. That word has stopt me.

Lady Dupe. Speak out, my Lord, and boldly tell what 'tis.

Lord Dartmouth. Then in obedience to your Commands; your Cousin is with Child.

Lady Dupe. Which Cousin?

15

20

25

30

35

40

45

50

45 *would and would not*] would and nould, whether or not.

Lord Dartmouth. Your Cousin *Christian* here ith' house.

Lady Dupe. Alas then she has stoln a Marriage, and undone   55
    her self: some young Fellow, on my Conscience, that's
    a Beggar; Youth will not be advis'd; well, I'le never
    meddle more with Girls; one is no more assur'd of 'um
    than Grooms of Mules, they'l strike when least one
    thinks on't: but pray your Lordship, what is her choice   60
    then for an Husband?

Lord Dartmouth. She is not married that I know of, Madam.

Lady Dupe. Not married! 'tis impossible, the Girl does
    sure abuse you. I know her Education has been such,
    the flesh could not prevail; therefore she does abuse   65
    you, it must be so.

Lord Dartmouth. Madam, not to abuse you longer, she is
    with Child, and I the unfortunate man who did this
    most unlucky act.

Lady Dupe. You! I'le never believe it.   70

Lord Dartmouth. Madam, 'tis too true; believe it, and be
    serious how to hide her shame; I beg it here upon my
    knees.

Lady Dupe. Oh, oh, oh. ——————   *She faints away.*

Lord Dartmouth. Who's there? who's there? help, help,   75
    help.

    Enter two Women, Rose, *Mistress* Millisent.

1 Woman. O merciful God, my Lady's gone!

2 Woman. Whither?

1 Woman. To Heaven, God knows, to Heaven.

Rose. Rub her, rub her; fetch warm Cloaths.   80

2 Woman. I say, run to the Cabinet of Quintessence;
    Gilbert's Water, *Gilbert's* Water.

1 Woman. Now all the good Folks of Heaven look down
    upon her.

Millisent. Set her in the Chair.   85

Rose. Open her mouth with a Dagger or a Key; pour,
    pour, where's the Spoon?

76.1 *Mistress* Millisent] S-S; Penelope Qq,F

76.1 *Mistress Millisent*] "Penelope," which stands in all the early
editions, must be another evidence of an earlier draft, like the character,
Mistress Preparation, mentioned in the dramatis personae. According
to the speech prefixes, Millisent is the fourth person on stage, suggesting
that the reviser, Dryden, eliminated a minor character and added a
small connection with the other plot. See II.ii.128.

81 *Cabinet of Quintessence*] medicine cabinet; quintessence was an
alcoholic solution.

82 *Gilbert's Water*] Gilbertus Anglicus employed distillation as a
means of purifying water (C. C. Mettler, *History of Medicine*, 1947,
p. 198), hence Gilbert's water probably was no cordial (as Summers
says), just distilled water.

2 Woman. She stirs, she revives, merciful to us all, what a thing was this! speak, Lady, speak.

90   *Lady Dupe.* So, so, so.

Millisent. Alas, my Lord, how came this fit?

Lord Dartmouth. With Sorrow, Madam.

Lady Dupe. Now I am better: *Bess*, you have not seen me thus.

95   *1 Woman.* Heav'n forefend that I should live to see you so agen.

Lady Dupe. Go, go, I'm pretty well; withdraw into the next Room, but be near I pray, for fear of the worst.

                        They go out.

—My Lord, sit down near me I pray, I'le strive to speak

100   a few words to you, and then to bed,—nearer,—my voice is faint.—My Lord, Heaven knows how I have ever lov'd you; and is this my reward? had you none to abuse but me in that unfortunate fond Girl that you know was dearer to me than my life? this was not

105   Love to her, but an inveterate malice to poor me. Oh, oh. ———   *Faints again.*

Lord Dartmouth. Help, help, help.

                       All the Women again.

1 Woman. This fit will carry her: alas it is a Lechery!

2 Woman. The Balsom, the Balsom!

110   *1 Woman.* No, no, the Chymistry Oyl of Rosemary: hold her up, and give her Air.

Millisent. Feel whether she breathes, with your hand before her Mouth.

Rose. No, Madam, 'tis Key-cold.

115   *1 Woman.* Look up, dear Madam, if you have any hope of Salvation!

2 Woman. Hold up your finger, Madam, if you have any hope of Fraternity. O the blessed Saints that hear me not, take her Mortality to them.

120   *Lady Dupe.* Enough, so, 'tis well,—withdraw, and let me rest a while; only my dear Lord remain.

1 Woman. Pray your Lordship keep her from swebbing.

                       Exeunt Women.

Lord Dartmouth. Here humbly once again, I beg your pardon and your help.

125   *Lady Dupe.* Heaven forgive you, and I do: stand up, my Lord, and sit close by me: O this naughty Girl! but did your Lordship win her soon?

---

95 forefend] Q2–5, F; foresend Q1

108 *Lechery*] S–S suggest a malapropism for Lethergy, a disorder characterized by unnatural sleep.

122 *swebbing*] swooning.

Lord Dartmouth. No, Madam, but with much difficulty.

Lady Dupe. I'm glad on't; it shew'd the Girl had some Religion in her, all my Precepts were not in vain: but you men are strange tempters; good my Lord, where was this wicked act then first committed? 130

Lord Dartmouth. In an out-room upon a Trunk.

Lady Dupe. Poor Heart, what shift Love makes! Oh she does love you dearly, though to her ruine! and then what place, my Lord? 135

Lord Dartmouth. An old waste Room, with a decay'd Bed in't.

Lady Dupe. Out upon that dark Room for deeds of darkness! and that rotten Bed! I wonder it did hold your Lordship's vigour: but you dealt gently with the Girl. Well, you shall see I love you: for I will manage this business to both your advantages, by the assistance of Heaven I will; good my Lord help, lead me out. 140

Exeunt.

[ACT III. SCENE 3]

[*Enter*] Warner, Rose.

Rose. A mischief upon all Fools! do you think your Master has not done wisely? first to mistake our old man's humour, then to dispraise the Plays; and lastly, to discover his Acquaintance with my Mistress: my old Master has taken such a Jealousie of him, that he will never admit him into his sight again. 5

Warner. Thou mak'st thy self a greater Fool than he, by being angry at what he cannot help.—I have been angry with him too; but these friends have taken up the quarrel.—(*Shews gold.*) Look you he has sent these Mediators to mitigate your wrath: here are twenty of 'um have made a long Voyage from *Guinny* to kiss your hands: and when the Match is made, there are an hundred more in readiness to be your humble Servants. 10

Rose. Rather then fall out with you, I'le take 'um; but I confess it troubles me to see so loyal a Lover have the heart of an Emperour, and yet scarce the brains of a Cobler. 15

Warner. Well, what device can we two beget betwixt us, to separate Sir *John Swallow* and thy Mistress? 20

---

133 *out-room*] an outlying room, perhaps what is now called a box-room.
12 *Guinny*] i.e., Guinea.

Rose. I cannot on the sudden tell; but I hate him worse than foul weather without a Coach.

Warner. Then I'le see if my project will be luckier than thine. Where are the Papers concerning the Joynture I have heard you speak of?

Rose. They lye within in three great Bags, some twenty Reams of Paper in each Bundle, with six lines in a sheet: but there is a little Paper where all the business lyes.

Warner. Where is it? canst thou help me to it?

Rose. By good chance he gave it to my custody before he set out for *London.* You came in good time, here it is, I was carrying it to him; just now he sent for ít.

Warner. So, this I will secure in my Pocket: when thou art ask'd for it, make two or three bad faces, and say, 'twas left behind: by this means he must of necessity leave the Town, to see for it in *Kent.*

Enter Sir John, *Sir* Martin, *Mistress* Millisent.

Sir John. 'Tis no matter, though the old man be suspicious; I knew the story all beforehand; and since then you have fully satisfi'd me of your true friendship to me.—Where are the Writings? *To* Rose.

Rose. Sir, I beg your pardon; I thought I had put 'um up amongst my Lady's things, and it seems in my haste I quite forgot 'um, and left 'um at *Canterbury.*

Sir John. This is horribly unlucky! where do you think you left 'um?

Rose. Upon the great Box in my Lady's Chamber; they are safe enough I'me sure.

Sir John. It must be so—I must take Post immediately: Madam, for some few days I must be absent; and to confirm you, friend, how much I trust you, I leave the dearest Pledge I have on Earth, my Mistress, to your care.

Millisent. If you lov'd me, you would not take all occasions to leave me thus!

Warner (aside). Do, go to *Kent,* and when you come again, here they are ready for you. *Shows the Paper.*

Sir Martin. What's that you have in your hand there, Sirrah?

Warner. Pox, what ill luck was this! what shall I say?

Sir Martin. Sometimes you've tongue enough; what, are you silent?

Warner. 'Tis an Accompt, Sir, of what Money you have lost since you came to Town.

Sir Martin. I'm very glad on't: now I'le make you all see 65
the severity of my Fortune,—give me the Paper.

Warner. Heaven! what does he mean to do, it is not fair
writ out, Sir!

Sir John. Besides, I am in haste, another time, Sir. ———

Sir Martin. Pray, oblige me, Sir,—'tis but one minute: all 70
people love to be pity'd in their Misfortunes, and so do
I: will you produce it, Sirrah?

Warner. Dear Master!

Sir Martin. Dear Rascal! am I Master or you? you Rogue!

Warner. Hold yet, Sir, and let me read it:—you cannot 75
read my hand.

Sir Martin. This is ever his way, to be disparaging me,—
but I'le let you see, Sirrah, that I can read your hand
better than you your self can.

Warner. You'l repent it, there's a trick in't, Sir. ——— 80

Sir Martin. Is there so, Sirrah? but I'le bring you out of all
your Tricks with a Vengeance to you. ——— *Reads.*
How now! what's this? A true particular of the Estate
of Sir *John Swallow* Knight, lying and scituate in, &c.

Sir John. This is the very Paper I had lost. (*Takes the Paper.*) 85
I'm very glad on't, it has sav'd me a most unwelcome
Journey,—but I will not thank you for the Courtesie,
which now I find you never did intend me—this is
Confederacy, I smoak it now.—Come, Madam, let me
wait on you to your Father. 90

Millisent. Well, of a witty man, this was the foolishest part
that ever I beheld.

        Exeunt Sir John, Millisent, *and* Rose.

Sir Martin. I am a Fool, I must confess it, and I am the
most miserable one without thy help,—but yet it was
such a mistake as any man might have made. 95

Warner. No doubt on't.

Sir Martin. Prethee chide me! this indifference of thine
wounds me to the heart.

Warner. I care not.

Sir Martin. Wilt thou not help me for this once? 100

Warner. Sir, I kiss your hands, I have other business.

Sir Martin. Dear *Warner*!

Warner. I am inflexible.

Sir Martin. Then I am resolv'd I'le kill my self.

Warner. You are Master of your own Body. 105

Sir Martin. Will you let me damn my Soul?

Warner. At your pleasure, as the Devil and you can agree
about it.

89 *smoak*] discover.

Sir Martin. D'ye see the point's ready? will you do nothing
110   to save my life?

Warner. Not in the least.

Sir Martin. Farewel, hard-hearted *Warner*.

Warner. Adieu soft-headed Sir *Martin*.

Sir Martin. Is it possible?

115 *Warner.* Why don't you dispatch, Sir? why all these
     Preambles?

Sir Martin. I'le see thee hang'd first: I know thou wou'dst
     have me kill'd, to get my Cloaths.

Warner. I knew it was but a Copy of your Countenance;
120   people in this Age are not so apt to kill themselves.

Sir Martin. Here are yet ten Pieces in my Pocket, take 'em,
     and let's be friends.

Warner. You know the Eas'ness of my Nature, and that
     makes you work upon it so. Well, Sir,—for this once I
125   cast an Eye of pity on you,—but I must have ten more
     in hand, before I can stir a foot.

Sir Martin. As I am a true Gamester, I have lost all but
     these,—but if thou'lt lend me them, I'le give 'em thee
     agen.

130 *Warner.* I'le rather trust you till to morrow.
     Once more look up, I bid you hope the best.
     Why should your folly make your Love miscarry,
     Since men first play the Fools, and then they marry?

                                 Exeunt.

ACT IV. [Scene 1]

Enter Sir Martin *and* Warner.

Sir Martin. But are they to be married this day in private,
     say you?

Warner. 'Tis so concluded, Sir, I dare assure you.

Sir Martin. But why so soon, and in private?

5 *Warner.* So soon, to prevent the designs upon her; and in
     private, to save the effusion of Christian Money.

Sir Martin. It strikes to my heart already; in fine, I am a
     dead man,———*Warner*.

Warner. Well, go your ways, I'le try what may be done.
10   Look if he will stir now; your Rival and the Old man
     will see us together, we are just below the Window.

Sir Martin. Thou can'st not do't.

Warner. On the peril of my twenty pieces be it.

---

119 *copy of your countenance*] your sham, humbug (Farmer).
  6 *Christian*] good, respectable.

Sir Martin. But I have found a way to help thee out, trust
to my wit but once.   15

Warner. Name your wit, or think you have the least grain
of wit once more, and I'le lay it down for ever.

Sir Martin. You are a sawcy masterly Companion, and so
I leave you.   *Exit.*

Warner. Help, help, good People, Murther, Murther!   20

Enter Sir John *and* Moody.

Sir John & Moody. How now, what's the matter?

Warner. I am abus'd, I am beaten, I am lam'd for ever.

Moody. Who has us'd thee so?

Warner. The Rogue my Master.

Sir John. What was the Offence?   25

Warner. A trifle, just nothing.

Sir John. That's very strange.

Warner. It was for telling him he lost too much at Play; I
meant him nothing but well, Heaven knows, and he in
a cursed damn'd humour would needs revenge his   30
losses upon me: A' kick'd me, took away my money,
and turn'd me off; but if I take it at his hands ———

Moody. By Cox nowns it was an ill-natur'd part, nay, I
thought no better could come on't, when I heard him
at his Vow to Gads, and in fines.   35

Warner. But if I live I'le cry quittance with him: he had
engag'd me to get Mistress *Millisent* your Daughter for
him; but if I do not all that ever I can to make her hate
him, a great Booby, an overgrown Oafe, a conceited
Bartlemew. ———   40

Sir John. Prethee leave off thy Choler, and hear me a
little: I have had a great mind to thee a long time; if
thou think'st my Service better than his, from this
minute I entertain thee.

Warner. With all my heart, Sir, and so much the rather,   45
that I may spight him with it. ——— This was the most
propitious Fate. ———

Moody. Propitious! and Fate! what a damn'd Scanderbag-
Rogue art thou to talk at this rate! hark you, Sirrah, one
word more of this Gibberish, and I'le set you packing   50
from your new Service; I'le have neither Propitious nor
Fate come within my doors. ———

33 *Cox nowns*] a perversion of *God's wounds*.

40 *Bartlemew*] Bartholmew Cokes, a term applied to a ninny. Cokes
means a fool, and the term became general owing to Squire Cokes, the
simpleton in *Bartholomew Fair* (Summers).

48 *Scanderbag*] brawling, a corruption of Iscander Bey, King
of Albania, who won twenty-two battles against the Turks.

Sir John. Nay, pray Father ———

55 *Warner.* Good old Sir be pacified: I was pouring out a little of the dregs that I had left in me of my former Service, and now they are gone, my stomach's clear of 'em.

Sir John. This Fellow is come in a happy hour; for now, Sir, you and I may go to prepare the Licence, and in the

60 mean time he may have an Eye upon your Daughter.

Warner. If you please I'le wait upon her till she's ready, and then bring her to what Church you shall appoint.

Moody. But, Friend, you'l find she'l hang an Arse, and be very loth to come along with you, and therefore I had

65 best stay behind, and bring her my self.

Warner. I warrant you I have a trick for that, Sir: she knows nothing of my being turn'd away: so I'le come to her as from Sir *Martin*, and under pretence of carrying her to him, conduct her to you.

70 *Sir John.* My better Angel ———

Moody. By th' mess 'twas well thought on; well Son, go you before, I'le speak but one word for a Dish or two at Dinner, and follow you to the Licence-Office. Sirrah—stay you here—till my return.

Exeunt Sir John *and* Moody.

75 *Warner* (*solus*). Was there ever such a lucky Rogue as I! I had always a good opinion of my wit, but could never think I had so much as now I find. I have now gained an opportunity to carry away Mistress *Millisent* for my Master, to get his Mistress by means of his Rival, to

80 receive all his happiness, where he could expect nothing but misery: after this exploit I will have *Lely* draw me in the habit of a Hero, with a Lawrel on my Temples, and an Inscription below it, *This is* Warner *the flower of Servingmen.*

Enter Messenger.

85 *Messenger.* Pray do me the favour to help me to the speech of Master *Moody.*

Warner. What's your business?

Messenger. I have a Letter to deliver to him.

[*Enter* Moody.]

---

81 Lely] S-S; Lilly Qq,F

63 *hang an Arse*] hang back.
71 *mess*] i.e., mass.
81 *Lely*] Sir Peter Lely (1618–80), the painter.
85 *speech*] opportunity of speaking with.

Warner. Here he comes, you may deliver it your self to him. 90

Messenger. Sir, a Gentleman met me at the corner of the next Street, and bid me give this into your own hands.

Moody. Stay friend, till I have read it.

Messenger. He told me, Sir, it required no Answer.

Exit Messenger.

 Moody reads. Sir, permit me, though a stranger, to give 95
you counsel; some young Gallants have had intelligence, that
this day you intend privately to marry your Daughter, the
rich Heiress; and in fine, above twenty of them have dis-
persed themselves to watch her going out: therefore put it off,
if you will avoid mischief, and be advised by 100
   Your unknown Servant.

Moody. By the Mackings, I thought there was no good in't, when I saw *in fine* there; there are some Papishes, I'le warrant, that lye in wait for my Daughter, or else they are no Englishmen, but some of your French 105 Outalion-Rogues; I owe him thanks however, this unknown Friend of mine, that told me on't.
Warner, no Wedding to day, *Warner.*

Warner. Why, what's the matter, Sir?

Moody. I say no more, but some wiser than some, I'le 110 keep my Daughter at home this Afternoon, and a fig for all these Outalians.   *Exit* Moody.

Warner. So, here's another Trick of Fortune as unexpected for bad, as the other was for good. Nothing vexes me, but that I had made my Game Cock-sure, and then to 115 be back-gammon'd: it must needs be the Devil that writ this Letter, he ow'd my Master a spight, and has paid him to the purpose: and here he comes as merry too, he little thinks what misfortune has befal'n him, and for my part I am asham'd to tell him. 120

   Enter Sir Martin *laughing.*

Sir Martin. Warner, such a jest, *Warner.*   *Laughs agen.*

Warner. What a Murrain is the matter, Sir? Where lyes this Jest that tickles you?

---

102 *By the Mackings*] a meaningless expression, probably suggested by either "by Mary" or "by the Mass."
103 *Papishes*] i.e., Papists, country dialect.
106 *Outalion*] foreign.
116 *back-gammon'd*] defeated by treachery, with a pun on back-gammon player, meaning a sodomist (see Farmer, *s.v.* back-door).
122 *Murrain*] plague, a common imprecation.

     Sir Martin. Let me laugh out my laugh, and I'le tell thee.
                                    Laughs agen.

125   *Warner.* I wish you may have cause for all this mirth.

     Sir Martin. Hereafter, *Warner*, be it known unto thee, I
       will endure no more to be thy May-game: thou shalt
       no more dare to tell me, I spoil thy projects, and dis-
       cover thy designs; for I have play'd such a Prize, without
130   thy help, of my own Mother-wit ('tis true I am hasty
       sometimes, and so do harm; but when I have a mind to
       shew my self, there's no man in *England*, though I say't,
       comes near me as to point of imagination). I'le make
       thee acknowledge I have laid a Plot that has a soul in't.

135   *Warner.* Pray, Sir, keep me no longer in ignorance of this
       rare Invention.

     Sir Martin. Know then, *Warner*, that when I left thee, I
       was possest with a terrible fear, that my Mistress should
       be married: well, thought I to my self, and mustring
140   up all the Forces of my Wit, I did produce such a
       Stratagem.

     Warner. But what was it?

     Sir Martin. I feign'd a Letter as from an unknown Friend
       to *Moody*, wherein I gave him to understand, that if his
145   Daughter went out this Afternoon, she would infallibly
       be snapt by some young Fellows that lay in wait for her.

     Warner. Very good.

     Sir Martin. That which follows is yet better; for he I sent
       assures me, that in that very nick of time my Letter
150   came, her Father was just sending her abroad with a very
       foolish rascally fellow that was with him,

     Warner. And did you perform all this a'god's name? could
       you do this wonderful miracle without giving your
       soul to the Devil for his help?

155   *Sir Martin.* I tell thee man I did it, and it was done by the
       help of no Devil, but this familiar of my own brain;
       how long would it have been e're thou couldest have
       thought of such a project? *Martin* said to his man, *Who's*
       the fool now?

160   *Warner.* Who's the fool? why, who uses to be the fool?
       he that ever was since I knew him, and ever will be so!

     Sir Martin. What a Pox? I think thou art grown envious,
       not one word in my commendations?

     127 shalt] Q2 (shal't); shall Q1
     153 giving] Q5; *omit* Q1–4
     160 uses] use Q1–3; us'd Q4–5

     127 *May-game*] tricks.
     156 *familiar*] a familiar devil, a demon, supposed to be in associa-
tion with or under the power of a man.

Warner. Faith Sir, my skill is too little to praise you as you
    deserve; but if you would have it according to my poor   165
    ability, you are one that had a knock in your Cradle,
    a conceited lack-wit, a designing Ass, a hair-brain'd
    Fop, a confounded busie brain, with an eternal Wind-
    mill in it; this in short, Sir, is the Contents of your
    Panegyrick.   170
Sir Martin. But what the Devil have I done, to set you
    thus against me?
Warner. Only this, Sir, I was the foolish rascally fellow
    that was with *Moody*, and your Worship was he to
    whom I was to bring his Daughter.   175
Sir Martin. But how could I know this? I am no Witch.
Warner. No, I'le be sworn for you, you are no conjurer.
    Will you go Sir?
Sir Martin. Will you hear my justifications?
Warner. Shall I see the back of you? speak not a word in   180
    your defence.   *Shoves him.*
Sir Martin. This is the strangest luck now ———   *Exit.*
Warner. I'm resolv'd this Devil of his shall never weary
    me, I will overcome him, I will invent something that
    shall stand good in spight of his folly. Let me see ———   185
        Enter Lord [Dartmouth].
Lord Dartmouth. Here he is—I must venture on him, for
    the tyranny of this old Lady is unsupportable; since I
    have made her my confident, there passes not an hour
    but she has a pull at my Purse-strings; I shall be ruin'd
    if I do not quit my self of her suddenly: I find now, by   190
    sad experience, that a Mistress is much more chargeable
    than a Wife, and after a little time too, grows full as
    dull and insignificant. Master *Warner*! have you a mind
    to do your self a courtesie, and me another?
Warner. I think, my Lord, the Question need not be   195
    much disputed, for I have always had a great service
    for your Lordship, and some little kindness for my self.
Lord Dartmouth. What if you should propose Mistress
    Christian as a Wife to your Master? you know he's
    never like to compass t'other.   200
Warner. I cannot tell that my Lord ———
Lord Dartmouth. Five hundred pounds are yours at the day
    of marriage.
Warner. Five hundred pounds! 'tis true, the temptation is
    very sweet, and powerful; the Devil I confess has done   205
    his part, and many a good Murder and Treason have
    been committed at a cheaper rate; but yet ———
Lord Dartmouth. What yet ———

   202 the] *omit* Qq,F

Warner. To confess the truth, I am resolv'd to bestow my
Master upon that other Lady (as difficultly as your Lordship thinks it) for the honour of my wit is ingag'd in it:
will it not be the same to your Lordship were she
married to any other?

Lord Dartmouth. The very same.

Warner. Come my Lord, not to dissemble with you any
longer, I know where it is that your Shoe wrings you:
I have observ'd something in the House, betwixt some
parties that shall be nameless: and know that you have
been taking up Linnen at a much dearer rate, than you
might have had it at any Draper's in Town.

Lord Dartmouth. I see I have not danc'd in a Net before you.

Warner. As for that old Lady, whom Hell confound, she
is the greatest Jilt in Nature, cheat is her study, all her
joy to cosen, she loves nothing but her self, and draws
all lines to that corrupted centre.

Lord Dartmouth. I have found her out, though late: first,
I'le undertake I n'ere enjoy'd her Neice under the rate
of five hundred pounds a time; never was woman's
flesh held up so high: every night I find out for a new
maidenhead, and she has sold it me as often as ever
mother *Temple, Bennet,* or *Gifford,* have put off boil'd
Capons for Quails and Partridges.

Warner. This is nothing to what Bills you'l have when
she's brought to bed, after her hard bargain, as they call
it; then cram'd Capons, Pea-hens, Chickens in the
grease, Pottages, and Frigacies. Wine from *Shatling,*
and *La-fronds,* with New River, dearer by six pence the

223 Jilt] Q4; Jill Q1-3
237 dearer] S-S; clearer Qq,F

210 *difficultly*] An emendation may not be necessary if the words
"thinks it may be done" are understood.

221 *danc'd in a Net*] acted with practically no disguise, while ex-
pecting to escape notice; the original use was to dance naked in a
net and go unseen.

223 *Jilt*] *Jill*, the reading in quartos 1-3 and folio, means wench,
but *jilt* was applied to a deceiving woman. "The jilt would not be
taken at her word," Dryden's translation of Ovid's *Art of Love*, 553.

229 *find out*] paid out, as a penalty (*fine with, fine for*, and *fine off*
are the only phrases recorded in *OED*).

231 *Temple . . . Gifford*] "Three most notorious maquerelles of
the day," whose activities are extensively described by Summers, II,
476-77.

232 *Quails*] girls, not domesticated by use.

236-37 *Shatling, and La-fronds*] Chatelin's, a French restaurant
in Covent Garden where Pepys frequently dined; La-fronds,
another fashionable ordinary mentioned throughout the literature
of the time (Summers).

237 *New River*] a canal for the supply of water to London, opened in 1613; hence pure water.

146

pound than ever God Almighty made it; then Mid-
wife—Dry-Nurse—Wet-Nurse—and all the rest of
their Accomplices, with Cradle, Baby-Clouts, and   240
Bearing-Cloaths—Possets, Cawdels, Broth, Jellies, and
Gravies; and behind all these, Glisters, Suppositers, and
a barbarous Pothecary's Bill, more inhumane than a
Taylor's.

Lord Dartmouth. I sweat to think on't.   245

Warner. Well my Lord! chear up! I have found a way to
rid you of it all, within a short time you shall know
more; yonder appears a young Lady whom I must
needs speak with, please you go in and prepare the old
Lady and your Mistress.   250

Lord Dartmouth. Good luck, and five hundred pounds
attend thee.   *Exit.*

Enter Millisent *and* Rose *above.*

Millisent. I am resolv'd I'le never marry him!

Rose. So far you are right, Madam.

Millisent. But how to hinder it, I cannot possibly tell! for   255
my Father presses me to it, and will take no denial:
wou'd I knew some way ———

Warner. Madam, I'le teach you the very nearest, for I have
just now found it out.

Rose. Are you there, Master Littleplot?   260

Warner. Studying to deserve thee, *Rose*, by my diligence
for thy Lady; I stand here, methinks, just like a wooden
Mercury, to point her out the way to Matrimony.

Rose. Or, Serving-man like, ready to carry up the hot meat
for your Master, and then to fall upon the cold your   265
self.

Warner. I know not what you call the cold, but I believe
I shall find warm work on't: in the first place then I
must acquaint you, that I have seemingly put off my
Master, and entred my self into Sir *John's* service.   270

Millisent. Most excellent!

Warner. And thereupon, but base ———

Enter Moody.

Millisent. Something he would tell us, but see what luck's
here!

Moody. How now, Sirrah? are you so great there already? 275

---

242 *Glisters, Suppositers*] Glisters may be connected with our word
glycerine. These were items used for purging.

262–63 *wooden Mercury*] a statue or image of Mercury, hence, a
signpost, and also a go-between in amorous affairs.

Millisent. I find my Father's jealous of him still!

Warner. Sir, I was only teaching my young Lady a new Song, and if you please you shall hear it.

SINGS

Make ready fair Lady to night,
> *And stand at the Door below,*
For I will be there
To receive you with care,
> *And to your true Love you shall go.*

Moody. Ods Bobs this is very pretty.

Millisent. I, so is the Lady's Answer too, if I could but hit on't.

SINGS

And when the Stars twinckle so bright,
Then down to the Door will I creep,
> *To my Love I will flye,*
> *E're the jealous can spye,*
And leave my old daddy asleep.

Moody. Bodikins I like not that so well, to cosen her old Father; it may be my own case another time.

Rose. Oh Madam! yonder's your Persecutor return'd.

Enter Sir John.

Millisent. I'le into my Chamber to avoid the sight of him as long as I can; Lord! that my old doting Father should throw me away upon such an Ignoramus, and deny me to such a Wit as Sir *Martin*.

> *Exeunt* Millisent *and* Rose *from above.*

Moody. O Son! here has been the most villainous Tragedy against you.

Sir John. What Tragedy? has there been any blood shed since I went?

Moody. No blood shed, but, as I told you, a most damnable Tragedy.

Warner. A Tragedy! I'le be hang'd if he does not mean a Stratagem.

Moody. Jack Sawce! if I say it is a Tragedy, it shall be a Tragedy in spight of you, teach your Grandham how to piss—what—I hope I am old enough to spought English with you Sir?

Sir John. But what was the reason you came not after me?

Moody. 'Twas well I did not, I'le promise you, there were

308–9 *teach . . . piss*] a variation on "teach your grannie to suck eggs," to instruct an expert in his own line of business (Farmer).

those would have made bold with Mistress Bride; an'
if she had stir'd out of doors, there were Whipsters   315
abroad i'faith, Padders of Maiden-heads, that would
have truss'd her up, and pick'd the lock of her affections,
e're a man could have said, what's this: but by good
luck I had warning of it by a friend's Letter.

                    [*Gives Letter to Sir* John.]

Sir John. The remedy for all such dangers is easie, you may   320
send for a Parson, and have the business dispatch'd at
home.

Moody. A match, i'faith, do you provide a *Domine*, and
I'le go tell her our resolutions, and hearten her up
against the day of battel.   *Exit.*   325

Sir John. Now I think on't, this Letter must needs come
from Sir *Martin*; a Plot of his, upon my life, to hinder
our marriage.

Warner. I see, Sir, you'l still mistake him for a Wit; but I
am much deceiv'd, if that Letter came not from another   330
hand.

Sir John. From whom I prithee?

Warner. Nay, for that you shall excuse me, Sir, I do not
love to make a breach betwixt persons that are to be so
near related.   335

Sir John. Thou seem'st to imply that my Mistress was in
the Plot.

Warner. Can you make a doubt on't? do you not know she
ever lov'd him, and can you hope she has so soon
forsaken him? you may make your self miserable, if   340
you please, by such a marriage.

Sir John. When she is once mine, her Vertue will secure
me.

Warner. Her Vertue!

Sir John. What, do you make a mock on't?   345

Warner. Not I, I assure you, Sir, I think it no such jesting
matter.

Sir John. Why, is she not honest?

Warner. Yes in my Conscience is she, for Sir *Martin's*
Tongue's no slander.   350

Sir John. But does he say to the contrary?

Warner. If one would believe him, which for my part I do
·not, he has in a manner confess'd it to me.

---

351 he] Q3; she Q1–2

315 *Whipsters*] debauchers.
316 *Padders*] robbers.
323 *Domine*] parson.
348 *honest*] chaste.

Sir John. Hell and Damnation! ———

355 *Warner.* Courage, Sir, never vex your self, I'le warrant you 'tis all a Lye.

Sir John. But how shall I be 'sur'd 'tis so?

Warner. When you are married you'l soon make tryal, whether she be a Maid or no.

360 *Sir John.* I do not love to make that Experiment at my own cost.

Warner. Then you must never marry.

Sir John. I, but they have so many tricks to cheat a man, which are entayl'd from Mother to Daughter through all

365 Generations, there's no keeping a Lock for that Door for which every one has a Key.

Warner. As for Example, their drawing up their breaths with Oh! you hurt me, can you be so cruel? then the next day she steals a Visit to her Lover, that did you the

370 Courtesie before-hand, and in private tells him how she cozened you; twenty to one but she takes out another Lesson with him to practise the next night.

Sir John. All this while miserable I must be their May-game.

375 *Warner.* 'Tis well if you escape so; for commonly he strikes in with you, and becomes your friend.

Sir John. Deliver me from such a friend that stays behind with my Wife, when I gird on my Sword to go abroad.

Warner. I, there's your man, Sir; besides he will be sure

380 to watch your haunts, and tell her of them, that if occasion be, she may have wherewithal to recriminate: at least she will seem to be jealous of you, and who would suspect a jealous Wife?

Sir John. All manner of ways I am most miserable.

385 *Warner.* But if she be not a Maid when you marry her, she may make a good Wife afterwards; 'tis but imagining you have taken such a man's Widow.

Sir John. If that were all; but the man will come and claim her again.

390 *Warner.* Examples have been frequent of those that have been wanton, and yet afterwards take up.

Sir John. I, the same thing they took up before.

Warner. The truth is, an honest simple Girl that's ignorant of all things, maketh the best Matrimony: There is such

395 pleasure in instructing her, the best is, there's not one Dunce in all the Sex; such a one with a good Fortune—

Sir John. I, but where is she, *Warner?*

Warner. Near enough, but that you are too far engag'd.

Sir John. Engag'd to one that hath given me the earnest of

400 Cuckoldom before-hand?

Warner. What think you then of Mistress *Christian* here in
the house? There's five thousand pounds and a better
penny.

Sir John. I, but is she Fool enough?

Warner. She's none of the wise Virgins, I can assure you.   405

Sir John. Dear *Warner*, step into the next Room, and
inveigle her out this way, that I may speak to her.

Warner. Remember above all things, you keep this
Wooing secret; if he takes the least wind, old *Moody*
will be sure to hinder it.   410

Sir John. Do'st thou think I shall get her Aunt's Consent?

Warner. Leave that to me.   *Exit* Warner.

Sir John. How happy a man shall I be, if I can but compass
this! and what a Precipice have I avoided! then the
revenge too is so sweet to steal a Wife under her Father's   415
nose, and leave 'um in the lurch who has abus'd me;
well, such a Servant as this *Warner* is a Jewel.

Enter Warner *and Mistress* Christian *to him.*

Warner. There she is, Sir, now I'le go to prepare her Aunt.
                                                           [*Exit.*]

Sir John. Sweet Mistress, I am come to wait upon you.

Christian. Truly you are too good to wait on me.   420

Sir John. And in the Condition of a Suitor.

Christian. As how, forsooth?

Sir John. To be so happy as to marry you.

Christian. O Lord, I would not marry for any thing!

Sir John. Why? 'tis the honest end of Woman-kind.   425

Christian. Twenty years hence, forsooth: I would not lye
in bed with a man for a world, their beards it will so
prickle one.

Sir John (aside). Pah,—what an innocent Girl it is, and very
child! I like a Colt that never yet was back'd; for so I   430
shall make her what I list, and mould her as I will:
Lord! her innocency makes me laugh my Cheeks all
wet.—Sweet Lady.———

Christian. I'm but a Gentlewoman, forsooth.

Sir John. Well then, sweet Mistress, if I get your Friend's   435
consent, shall I have yours?

Christian. My old Lady may do what she will, forsooth,
but by my truly, I hope she will have more care of me,
then to marry me yet; Lord bless me, what should I do
with a Husband?   440

---

409 he] Q2; it Q1

434 *Gentlewoman*] by understanding the old fashioned use of *lady* as
lady of rank, she makes herself appear the modest, well-bred gentlewoman.

Sir John. Well, Sweet-heart, then instead of wooing you,
I must wooe my old Lady.

Christian. Indeed, Gentleman, my old Lady is married
already: cry you mercy forsooth, I think you are a
445   Knight.

Sir John. Happy in that Title only to make you a Lady.

Christian. Believe me, Master Knight, I would not be a
Lady, it makes Folks proud, and so humerous, and so
ill Huswifes, forsooth.

450 *Sir John* [*aside*]. Pah,—she's a Baby, the simplest thing that
ever yet I knew; the happiest man I shall be in the
world; for should I have my wish, it should be to keep
School, and teach the bigger Girls, and here in one my
wish it is absolv'd.

Enter Lady Dupe.

455 *Lady Dupe.* By your leave, Sir: I hope this noble Knight
will make you happy, and you make him.

Christian. What should I make him?   *Sighing.*

Lady Dupe. Marry, you shall make him happy in a good
Wife.

460 *Christian.* I will not marry, Madam.

Lady Dupe. You Fool!

Sir John. Pray, Madam, let me speak with you, on my
Soul 'tis the pretti'st innocent'st thing in the world.

Lady Dupe. Indeed, Sir, she knows little besides her Work
465   and her Prayers; but I'le talk with the Fool.

Sir John. Deal gently with her, dear Madam.

Lady Dupe. Come, *Christian*, will not you marry this noble
Knight?

Christian. Yes, yes, yes. ———   *Sobbingly.*

470 *Lady Dupe.* Sir, it shall be to night.

Sir John. This innocence is a Dowry beyond all price.
             Exeunt Old Lady and Mistress Christian.

Enter Sir Martin *to Sir* John, *musing.*

Sir Martin. You are very melancholy methinks, Sir.

Sir John. You are mistaken, Sir.

Sir Martin. You may dissemble as you please, but Mistress
475   *Millisent* lyes at the bottom of your Heart.

Sir John. My Heart, I assure you, has no room for so poor
a Trifle.

471.2] *to* S-S; *and* Qq,F

448 *humerous*] fanciful, capricious.
454 *absolv'd*] accomplished, completed.

Sir Martin. Sure you think to wheadle me, would you
    have me imagine you do not love her?

Sir John. Love her! why should you think me such a Sot?   480
    love a Prostitute, and infamous person!

Sir Martin. Fair and soft, good Sir *John.*

Sir John. You see I am no very obstinate Rival, I leave the
    field free to you: go on, Sir, and pursue your good
    Fortune, and be as happy as such a common Creature   485
    can make thee.

Sir Martin. This is Hebrew-Greek to me; but I must tell
    you, Sir, I will not suffer my Divinity to be prophan'd
    by such a Tongue as yours.

Sir John. Believe it; whate're I say I can quote my Author   490
    for.

Sir Martin. Then, Sir, whoever told it you, ly'd in his
    Throat, d'you see, and deeper than that d'ye see, in his
    stomach and his guts d'ye see: tell me she's a common
    person! he's a Son of a Whore that said it, and I'le make   495
    him eat his words, though he spoke 'em in a privy
    house.

Sir John. What if *Warner* told me so? I hope you'l grant
    him to be a competent Judge in such a business.

Sir Martin. Did that precious Rascal say it?—Now I think   500
    on't I'le not believe you: in fine, Sir, I'le hold you an
    even Wager he denies it.

Sir John. I'le lay you ten to one, he justifies it to your face.

Sir Martin. I'le make him give up the Ghost under my
    fist, if he does not deny it.   505

Sir John. I'le cut off his Ears upon the Spot, if he does not
    stand to't.

            Enter Warner.

Sir Martin. Here he comes in Pudding-time to resolve the
    question: come hither, you lying Varlet, hold up your
    hand at the Bar of Justice, and answer me to what I   510
    shall demand.

Warner. What a Goodier is the matter, Sir?

Sir Martin. Thou Spawn of the old Serpent, fruitful in
    nothing but in Lyes!

Warner. A very fair beginning this.   515

Sir Martin. Didst thou dare to cast thy Venom upon such

---

  495 I'le] F; *omit* Qq

   508 *Pudding-time*] the time when puddings are to be had; hence, a
favorable time.

   512 *Goodier*] goodyear, the pox; possibly a corruption of *gougeer*,
from *gouge*, a soldier's trollop (Farmer).

a Saint as Mistress *Millisent*, to traduce her Vertue, and
say it was adulterate?

Warner. Not guilty, my Lord.

Sir Martin. I told you so.

520

Sir John. How, Master Rascal! have you forgot what you
said but now concerning Sir *Martin* and Mistress *Millisent*? I'le stop the Lye down your Throat, if you dare
deny't.

525

Sir Martin. Say you so! are you there agen i'faith?

Warner. Pray pacifie your self, Sir, 'twas a Plot of my own
devising.   [*In whisper.*]

Sir Martin. Leave off your winking and your pinking,
with a Horse-pox t'ye, I'le understand none of it; tell

530

me in plain English the truth of the business: for an'
you were my own Brother, you should pay for it:
belye my Mistress! what a Pox, d'ye think I have no
sense of Honour?

Warner. What the Devil's the matter w'ye? either be at

535

quiet, or I'le resolve to take my heels, and be gone.

Sir Martin. Stop Thief there! what, did you think to
scape the hand of Justice?   *Lays hold on him.*
The best on't is, Sirrah, your heels are not altogether so
nimble as your tongue.   *Beats him.*

540

Warner. Help! Murder! Murder!

Sir Martin. Confess, you Rogue, then.

Warner. Hold your hands, I think the Devil's in you,—I
tell you 'tis a device of mine.

Sir Martin. And have you no body to devise it on but my

545

Mistress, the very Map of Innocence?

Sir John. Moderate your anger, good Sir *Martin.*

Sir Martin. By your patience, Sir, I'le chastise him abundantly.

Sir John. That's a little too much, Sir, by your favour, to

550

beat him in my presence.

Sir Martin. That's a good one i'faith, your presence shall
hinder me from beating my own Servant?

Warner. O Traytor to all sense and reason! he's a going to
discover that too.

555

Sir Martin. An' I had a mind to beat him to Mummy, he's
my own, I hope.

Sir John. At present I must tell you he's mine, Sir.

Sir Martin. Hey-day! here's fine Jugling!

Warner. Stop yet, Sir, you are just upon the brink of a

560

Precipice.

Sir Martin. What is't thou meanest now?—(*aside*) a Lord!

528 *pinking*] looking with narrowed eyes, winking in a sly
manner.

my mind mis-gives me I have done some fault, but would
I were hang'd if I can find it out.

Warner. There's no making him understand me.

Sir Martin. Pox on't, come what will, I'le not be fac'd   565
down with a Lye; I say he is my man.

Sir John. Pray remember your self better; did not you turn
him away for some fault lately, and laid a Livery of
black and blew on his Back before he went?

Sir Martin. The Devil of any fault, or any black and blew   570
that I remember: either the Rascal put some Trick
upon you, or you would upon me.

Sir John. O, ho! then it seems the cudgelling and turning
away were pure invention; I am glad I understand it.

Sir Martin. In fine, it's all so damn'd a Lye ———   575

Warner. Alas! he has forgot it, Sir, good Wits, you know,
have bad Memories.

Sir John. No, no, Sir, that shall not serve your turn, you
may return when you please to your old Master, I give
you a fair discharge, and a glad man I am to be so rid of   580
you: were you thereabouts i'faith? what a Snake had
I entertain'd into my bosom? fare you well, Sir, and
lay your next Plot better between you, I advise you.
                    Exit Sir John.

Warner. Lord, Sir, how you stand! as you were nip'd
i'th' head: have you done any new piece of Folly, that   585
makes you look so like an Ass?

Sir Martin. Here's three pieces of Gold yet: if I had the
heart to offer it thee.
                    Holds the Gold afar off trembling.

Warner. Noble Sir, what have I done to deserve so great
a Liberality? I confess if you had beaten me for your   590
own fault, if you had utterly destroyed all my projects,
then it might ha' bin expected that ten or twenty
pieces should have been offer'd by way of recompence
and satisfaction. ———

Sir Martin. Nay, an' you be so full o' your Flowts, your   595
Friend and Servant; who the Devil could tell the
meaning of your signs and tokens, an' you go to that?

Warner. You are no Ass then?

Sir Martin. Well, Sir, to do you service, d'ye see, I am an
Ass in a fair way; will that satisfie you?   600

Warner. For this once produce those three pieces, I am
contented to receive that inconsiderable tribute, or make
'em six and I'le take the fault upon my self.

595 an'] Q4; ou' Q1; on' Q2-3

605

Sir Martin. Are we Friends then? if we are, let me advise
you ———
Warner. Yet advising ———
Sir Martin. For no harm, good *Warner*: but pray next
time make me of your Counsel, let me enter into the
business, instruct me in every point, and then if I dis-

610

cover all, I am resolv'd to give over affairs, and retire
from the world.
Warner. Agreed, it shall be so; but let us now take breath
a while, then on agen.
For though we had the worst, those heats were past,

615

Wee'l whip and spur, and fetch him up at last.

Exeunt.

ACT V. [SCENE 1]

Enter Lord [Dartmouth], *Lady* Dupe, *Mistress* Christian,
Rose, *and* Warner.

Lord Dartmouth. Your promise is admirably made good to
me, that Sir *John Swallow* should be this night married
to Mistress *Christian*; instead of that, he is more deeply
engag'd than ever with old *Moody*.

5

Warner. I cannot help these ebbs and flows of fortune.
Lady Dupe. I am sure my Neice suffers most in't, he's
come off to her with a cold Complement of a mistake
in his Mistress's Vertue, which he has now found out,
by your Master's folly, to be a Plot of yours to separate

10

them.
Christian. To be forsaken when a woman has given her
consent!
Lord Dartmouth. 'Tis the same scorn, as to have a Town
render'd up, and afterwards slighted.

15

Rose. You are a sweet youth, Sir, to use my Lady so, when
she depended on you; is this the faith of *Valet de Chambre*?
I would be asham'd to be such a dishonour to my
profession; it will reflect upon us in time, we shall be
ruin'd by your good example.

20

Warner. As how my dear Lady Embassadress?
Rose. Why, they say the women govern their Ladies, and
you govern us: so if you play fast and loose, not a
Gallant will bribe us for our good wills; the gentle
Guiny will now go to the Ordinary, which us'd as duly

24 *Ordinary*] a tavern that serves food. The sense seems to
be "Gentlemen who use to give us their guineas will spend
them at taverns instead."

156

to steal into our hands at the stair-foot as into Master 25
Doctor's at parting.
Lord Dartmouth. Night's come, and I expect your promise.
Lady Dupe. Fail with me if you think good, Sir.
Christian. I give no more time.
Rose. And if my Mistress go to bed a Maid to night —— 30
Warner. Hey-day! you are dealing with me, as they do
with the Banquers, call in all your debts together;
there's no possibility of payment at this rate, but I'le
coin for you all as fast as I can, I assure you.
Lady Dupe. But you must not think to pay us with false 35
Money, as you have done hitherto.
Rose. Leave off your Mountebank tricks with us, and fall
to your business in good earnest.
Warner. Faith, and I will *Rose*; for to confess the truth, I
am a kind of a Mountebank, I have but one Cure for 40
all your Diseases, that is, that my Master may marry
Mistress *Millisent*, for then Sir *John Swallow* will of
himself return to Mistress *Christian*.
Lord Dartmouth. He says true, and therefore we must all be
helping to that design. 45
Warner. I'le put you upon something, give me but a
thinking time. In the first place, get a Warrant and
Bailifs to arrest Sir *John Swallow* upon a promise of
marriage to Mistress *Christian*.
Lord Dartmouth. Very good. 50
Lady Dupe. We'll all swear it.
Warner. I never doubted your Ladiship in the least,
Madam—for the rest we will consider hereafter.
Lord Dartmouth. Leave this to us.
      Exeunt Lord [Dartmouth], *Lady* Dupe, Christian.
Warner. Rose, where's thy Lady? 55

      [*Enter* Millisent *above.*]

Millisent. What have you to say to her?
Warner. Only to tell you, Madam, I am going forward in
the great work of projection.
Millisent. I know not whether you will deserve my thanks
when the work's done. 60
Warner. Madam, I hope you are not become indifferent to
my Master.

54.1 Dupe, Christian] F; Dupe, Millisent, Christian Qq
  25–26 *Master Doctor's*] doctor whose advice was paid for, upon
parting, in guineas.
  28 *Fail with me*] default on me.
  28 *think good*] think it good; a veiled threat.
  58 *projection*] planning, scheming.

Millisent. If he should prove a fool after all your crying up his wit, I shall be a miserable woman.

65 *Warner.* A fool! that were a good jest i'faith: but how comes your Ladiship to suspect it?

Rose. I have heard, Madam, your greatest wits have ever a touch of madness and extravagance in them, so perhaps has he.

70 *Warner.* There's nothing more distant than wit and folly, yet like East and West, they may meet in a point, and produce actions that are but a hair's breadth from one another.

Rose. I'le undertake he has wit enough to make one laugh
75 at him a whole day together: He's a most Comical person.

Millisent. For all this I will not swear he is no fool; he has still discovered all your plots.

Warner. O Madam, that's the common fate of your
80 Machivilians, they draw their Designs so subtile, that their very fineness breaks them.

Millisent. However I'm resolv'd to be on the sure side, I will have certain proof of his wit before I marry him.

Warner. Madam, I'le give you one, he wears his cloaths
85 like a great sloven, and that's a sure sign of wit, he neglects his outward parts; besides, he speaks French, sings, dances, plays upon the Lute.

Millisent. Does he do all this, say you?

Warner. Most divinely, Madam.

90 *Millisent.* I ask no more, then let him give me a Serenade immediately; but let him stand in the view, I'le not be cheated.

Warner. He shall do't Madam: [*aside*] but how, the Devil knows —— for he sings like a Scritch-Owle, and
95 never touch'd the Lute.

Millisent. You'le see't perform'd?

Warner. Now I think on't, Madam, this will but retard our enterprise.

Millisent. Either let him do't, or see me no more.

100 *Warner.* Well, it shall be done, Madam; but where's your Father? will not he over-hear it?

Millisent. As good hap is, he's below stairs, talking with a Seaman, that has brought him news from the *East-Indies*.

Warner. What concernment can he have there?

105 *Millisent.* He had a Bastard-Son there, whom he lov'd extreamly: but not having any news from him these

_____

72 one] Q2; *omit* Q1

102 *as good hap is*] fortunately.

many years, concluded him dead; this Son he expects
within these three days.

Warner. When did he see him last?

Millisent. Not since he was seven years old.   110

Warner. A sudden thought comes into my head to make
him appear before his time; let my Master pass for him,
and by that means he may come into the House unsuspected by her Father, or his Rival.   [*To* Rose.]

Millisent. According as he performs his Serenade, I'le talk   115
with you—make haste—I must retire a little.

> *Exit* Millisent *from above.*

Rose. I'le instruct him most rarely, he shall never be found
out; but in the mean time, what wilt thou do with a
Serenade?

Warner. Faith, I am a little non-plus'd on the sudden, but   120
a warm consolation from thy lips, *Rose*, would set my
wits a working again.

Rose. Adieu, *Warner.*   *Exit* Rose.

Warner. Inhumane *Rose*, adieu.

Blockhead *Warner*, into what a premunire hast thou   125
brought thy self? this 'tis to be so forward to promise
for another—but to be Godfather to a Fool, to promise
and vow he should do any thing like a Christian——

> *Enter Sir* Martin.

Sir Martin. Why, how now Bully, in a Brown Study? for
my good I warrant it; there's five shillings for thee,   130
what, we must encourage good wits sometimes.

Warner. Hang your white pelf: sure, Sir, by your largess
you mistake me for *Martin Parker*, the Ballad-Maker;
your covetousness has offended my Muse, and quite
dull'd her.   135

Sir Martin. How angry the poor Devil is? in fine thou art
as cholerick as a Cook by a Fire side.

Warner. I am over-heated, like a Gun, with continual
discharging my wit: 'slife, Sir, I have rarifi'd my brains
for you, till they are evaporated; but come, Sir, do   140
something for your self like a man, I have engag'd you
shall give to your Mistress a Serenade in your proper
person: I'le borrow a Lute for you.

---

125 *premunire*] *praemunire*, penalties incurred whereby the offender
loses all his goods. Used here, humorously to indicate the fix that
Warner is in.

132 *white pelf*] silver money.

133 *Martin Parker*] the popular royalist ballad writer. The point here
is that ballad makers sold their works in the streets, a penny each, like
newspapers.

145

Sir Martin. I'le warrant thee, I'le do't man.

Warner. You never learn't, I do not think you know one stop.

Sir Martin. 'Tis no matter for that, Sir, I'le play as fast as I can, and never stop at all.

150

Warner. Go to, you are an invincible Fool I see; get up into your Window, and set two Candles by you, take my Land-lord's Lute in your hand, and fumble on't, and make grimmaces with your mouth, as if you sung; in the mean time, I'le play in the next Room in the dark, and consequently your Mistress, who will come to her Balcone over against you, will think it to be you; and at the end of every Tune, I'le ring the Bell that hangs between your Chamber and mine, that you may know when to have done.

155

Sir Martin. Why, this is fair Play now, to tell a man before-hand what he must do; Gramercy i'faith, Boy, now if I fail thee ———

160

Warner. About your business then, your Mistress and her Maid appear already: I'le give you the sign with the Bell when I am prepar'd, for my Lute is at hand in the Barber's shop.   *Exeunt.*

165

Enter Millisent, Rose, *with a Candle by 'em above.*

Rose. We shall have rare Musick.

Millisent. I wish it prove so; for I suspect the Knight can neither play nor sing.

170

Rose. But if he does, you're bound to pay the Musick, Madam.

Millisent. I'le not believe it, except both my Ears and Eyes are Witnesses.

Rose. But 'tis night, Madam, and you cannot see 'em; yet he may play admirably in the dark.

175

Millisent. Where's my Father?

Rose. You need not fear him, he's still employ'd with that same Sea-man, and I have set Mistress *Christian* to watch their discourse, that betwixt her and me *Warner* may have wherewithal to instruct his Master.

180

Millisent. But yet there's fear my Father will find out the Plot.

Rose. Not in the least, for my old Lady has provided two rare disguises for the Master and the Man.

Millisent. Peace, I hear them beginning to tune the Lute.

154 who] Q2; who who Q1

165 *Barber's shop*] Various stringed instruments were kept in barber shops for the patrons' use while waiting.

Rose. And see, Madam, where your true Knight Sir *Martin*   185
is plac'd yonder like *Apollo*, with his Lute in his hand and
his Rays about his head.

> Sir Martin *appears at the adverse window, a Tune play'd;*
> *when it is done,* Warner *rings, and Sir Martin holds.*

Did he not play most excellently, Madam?
Millisent. He play'd well, and yet methinks he held his
Lute but untowardly.   190
Rose. Dear Madam, peace; now for the Song.

The SONG.

Blind Love to this hour
Had never like me, a slave under his power.
　　Then blest be the Dart
　　That he threw at my heart,
　　　For nothing can prove   195
A joy so great as to be wounded with love.

My Days and my Nights
Are fill'd to the purpose with sorrows and frights;
　　From my heart still I sigh
　　And my Eyes are ne're dry,   200
　　　So that Cupid *be prais'd,*
I am to the top of Love's happiness rais'd.

My Soul's all on fire,
So that I have the pleasure to doat and desire,   205
　　Such a pretty soft pain
　　That it tickles each vein;
　　　'Tis the dream of a smart,
Which makes me breath short when it beats at my heart.

Sometimes in a Pet,   210
When I am despis'd, I my freedom would get;

187.1 *Sir Martin appears*] This scene, which seems crude and hack-
neyed to us after repeated exposure to Rostand's *Cyrano de Bergerac*,
must have been effective on the Restoration stage, as evidenced by the
number of contemporary allusions to it (see Summers, II, 480–81).

187.1 *adverse window*] The proscenium arch, in Restoration theaters,
was pierced by two doors, with windows or rather balconies above
each, facing each other. Presumably Sir Martin was in the balcony
opposite Millisent. (See Richard Southern, *Changeable Scenery*, 1952,
plate 28.)

192–221] The song is spaced out to cover exactly two sides of the
leaf H5. The original H4 has been canceled and a half sheet, H4 and H5,
inserted in Q1 (see the introduction to this play), suggesting that something was at first left out or something was expanded at the last minute.

> But streight a sweet smile
> Does my anger beguile,
> And my heart does recall,
> Then the more I do struggle, the lower I fall.

215

> Heaven does not impart
> Such a grace as to love unto ev'ry one's heart;
> For many may wish
> To be wounded and miss:
> Then blest be love's Fire,
> And more blest her Eyes that first taught me desire.

220

The Song being done, Warner *rings agen; but Sir*
Martin *continues fumbling, and gazing on his Mistress.*

Millisent. A pretty humour'd Song:—but stay, methinks
he plays and sings still, and yet we cannot hear him.—
Play louder, Sir *Martin,* that we may have the fruits on't.

225 *Warner (peeping).* Death! this abominable Fool will spoil
all agen. Dam him, he stands making his Grimaces
yonder, and he looks so earnestly upon his Mistress, that
he hears me not. *Rings agen.*

Millisent. Ah, ah! have I found you out, Sir? now as I live
230 and breathe, this is pleasant, *Rose,*—his man play'd and
sung for him, and he, it seems, did not know when he
should give over. Millisent *and* Rose *laugh.*

Warner. They have found him out, and laugh yonder as
if they would split their sides. Why Master Fool, Oafe,
235 Coxcomb, will you hear none of your names?

Millisent. Sir *Martin,* Sir *Martin,* take your man's counsel,
and keep time with your Musick.

Sir Martin (peeping). Ha! what do you say, Madam? how
does your Ladiship like my Musick?

240 *Millisent.* O most heavenly! just like the Harmony of the
Spheres that is to be admired, and never heard.

Warner. You have ruin'd all by your not leaving off in
time.

Sir Martin. What the Devil would you have a man do
245 when my hand is in! well o' my conscience I think there
is a Fate upon me. *Noise within.*

Millisent. Look, *Rose,* what's the matter.

Rose. 'Tis Sir *John Swallow* pursu'd by the Bailiffs, Madam,
according to our plot; it seems they have dog'd him
250 thus late to his Lodging.

Millisent. That's well! for though I begin not to love this
Fool; yet I am glad I shall be rid on him.

Exeunt Millisent, Rose.

Enter Sir John *pursu'd by three Bailiffs over the Stage.*

Sir Martin. Now I'le redeem all agen, my Mistress shall
see my Valour, I'm resolv'd on't. Villains, Rogues,
Poultroons! what? three upon one? in fine, I'le be with   255
you immediately.   *Exit.*

Warner. Why, Sir, are you stark mad? have you no grain
of sense left? he's gone! now is he as earnest in the
quarrel as Cokes among the Poppits; 'tis to no purpose
whatever I do for him.   *Exit* Warner.   260

Enter Sir John *and Sir* Martin (*having driven away the
Bailiffs*). *Sir* Martin *flourisheth his Sword.*

Sir Martin. Victoria! Victoria! what heart, Sir *John,* you
have received no harm, I hope?

Sir John. Not the least, I thank you Sir for your timely
assistance, which I will requite with any thing but the
resigning of my Mistress.—Dear Sir *Martin,* a good   265
night.

Sir Martin. Pray let me wait upon you in Sir *John.*

Sir John. I can find my way to Mistress *Millisent* without
you, Sir, I thank you.

Sir Martin. But pray, what were you to be arrested for?   270

Sir John. I know no more than you; some little debts,
perhaps, I left unpaid by my negligence: once more
good night, Sir.   *Exit.*

Sir Martin. He's an ungrateful Fellow; and so in fine, I
shall tell him when I see him next———   275

Enter Warner.

Monsieur *Warner,* A propos! I hope you'l applaud me
now, I have defeated the Enemy, and that in sight of
my Mistress; Boy, I have charm'd her, i'faith, with my
Valour.

Warner. I, just as much as you did e'ne now with your   280
Musick; go, you are so beastly a Fool, that a Chiding is
thrown away upon you.

Sir Martin. Fool in your face, Sir; call a man of Honour,
Fool, when I have just atchieved such an Enterprise—
Gad now my blood's up, I am a dangerous person, I can   285
tell you that, *Warner.*

Warner. Poor Animal, I pity thee.

Sir Martin. I grant I am no Musician, but you must allow
me for a Sword-man, I have beat 'em bravely; and in

---

259 *Cokes among the Poppits*] Bartholomew Cokes, the fool, at the
puppet show, an allusion to *Bartholomew Fair,* Act V.

163

290   fine, I am come off unhurt, save only a little scratch
i'th' head.

         Warner. That's impossible, thou hast a Scull so thick, no
Sword can pierce it; but much good may't d'ye, Sir,
with the fruits of your Valour: you rescu'd your Rival

295   when he was to be arrested on purpose to take him off
from your Mistress.

         Sir Martin. Why, this is ever the Fate of ingenious men;
nothing thrives they take in hand.

Enter Rose.

         Rose. Sir *Martin*, you have done your business with my

300   Lady, she'l never look upon you more; she says, she's
so well satisfied of your Wit and Courage, that she will
not put you to any further tryal.

         Sir Martin. *Warner*, is there no hopes, *Warner*?

         Warner. None that I know.

305   *Sir Martin.* Let's have but one civil plot more before we
part.

         Warner. 'Tis to no purpose.

         Rose. Yet if he had some golden Friends that would engage
for him the next time ———

310   *Sir Martin.* Here's a Jacobus and a Carolus will enter into
Bonds for me.

         Rose. I'le take their Royal words for once.

She fetches two disguises.

         Warner. The meaning of this, dear *Rose*?

         Rose. 'Tis in pursuance of thy own invention, *Warner*; a

315   child which thy wit hath begot upon me: but let us
lose no time, Help! Help! dress thy Master, that he may
be *Anthony*, old *Moody*'s Bastard, and thou his man
come from the *East-Indies*.

         Sir Martin. Hey-tarock it—now we shall have *Rose*'s

320   device too, I long to be at it, pray let's hear more on't.

         Rose. Old *Moody* you must know in his younger years,
when he was a *Cambridge*-Scholar, made bold with a
Towns-man's Daughter there, by whom he had a
Bastard whose name was *Anthony*, whom you Sir

325   *Martin*, are to represent.

         Sir Martin. I warrant you, let me alone for *Tony*: but
pray go on, *Rose*.

---

317 man] *omit* Qq,F

297 *ingenious*] possessed of genius.

310 *Jacobus . . . Carolus*] twenty-shilling gold pieces.

319 *Hey-tarock it*] meaning uncertain, possibly a cry of delight: "Hey trump it," our trump card, from the Italian *tarrocare*.
Tarock is an English word for the tarot deck of playing cards.

164

Rose. This Child in his Father's time he durst not own, but
bred him privately in the Isle of *Ely*, till he was seven
years old, and from thence sent him with one *Bonaven-*   330
ture a Merchant for the *East-Indies.*
Warner. But will not this over-burden your memory, Sir?
Sir Martin. There's no answering thee any thing, thou
think'st I am good for nothing.
Rose. Bonaventure dy'd at *Surat* within two years, and this   335
Anthony has liv'd up and down in the *Mogul's* Country
unheard of by his Father till this night, and is expected
within these three days: now if you can pass for him,
you may have admittance into the house, and make an
end of all the business before the other *Anthony* arrives.   340
Warner. But hold, *Rose,* there's one considerable point
omitted; what was his Mother's name?
Rose. That indeed I had forgot; her name was *Dorothy,*
Daughter to one *Draw-water* a Vintner at the *Rose.*
Warner. Come, Sir, are you perfect in your Lesson?   345
Anthony Moody born in *Cambridge,* bred in the Isle of
Ely, sent into the *Mogul's* Country at seven years old
with one *Bonaventure* a Merchant, who dy'd within two
years; your Mother's name *Dorothy Draw-water* the
Vintner's Daughter at the *Rose.*   350
Sir Martin. I have it all *ad unguem*—what, do'st think I'm
a Sot? but stay a little, how have I liv'd all this while
in that same Country?
Warner. What Country?—Pox, he has forgot already.—
Rose. The *Mogul's* Country.   355
Sir Martin, I, I, the *Mogul's* Country! what a Devil, any
man may mistake a little; but now I have it perfect: but
what have I been doing all this while in the *Mogul's*
Country? He's a Heathen Rogue, I am afraid I shall
never hit upon his name.   360
Warner. Why, you have been passing your time there, no
matter how.
Rose. Well, if this passes upon the Old man, I'le bring
your business about agen with my Mistress, never fear
it; stay you here at the door, I'le go tell the Old man of   365
your arrival.
Warner. Well, Sir, now play your part exactly, and I'le
forgive all your former errours.————

349–50 *Dorothy Draw-water . . . Rose*] "Away to Cambridge, it
being foul, rainy weather, and there did take up at the Rose, for the
sake of Mrs. Dorothy Drawwater, the vintner's daughter, which is
mentioned in the play of Sir Martin Marral" (Pepys, *Diary*, October 8,
1667).
351 *ad unguem*] to a hair, perfectly.

370

Sir Martin. Hang 'em, they were only slips of Youth—
how peremptory and domineering this Rogue is! now
he see's I have need of his service: would I were out of
his power agen, I would make him lye at my feet like
any Spaniel.

Enter Moody, *Sir* John, *Lord* [Dartmouth], *Lady* Dupe,
Millisent, Christian, Rose.

375

Moody. Is he here already, say'st thou? which is he?
Rose. That Sun-burn'd Gentleman.
Moody. My dear Boy *Anthony*, do I see thee agen before
I dye? welcome, welcome.
Sir Martin. My dear Father, I know it is you by instinct;
for methinks I am as like you as if I were spit out of

380

your mouth.
Rose. Keep it up I beseech your Lordship.
Aside to the Lord.
Lord Dartmouth. He's wond'rous like indeed.
Lady Dupe. The very image of him.
Moody. Anthony, you must salute all this Company: this is

385

my Lord *Dartmouth*, this my Lady *Dupe*, this her Niece
Mistress *Christian*. *He salutes them.*
Sir Martin. And that's my Sister, methinks I have a good
resemblance of her too: honest Sister, I must need kiss
you Sister.

390

Warner. This fool will discover himself, I foresee it already,
by his carriage to her.
Moody. And now *Anthony*, pray tell's a little of your
Travels.
Sir Martin. Time enough for that, forsooth Father, but I

395

have such a natural affection for my Sister, that methinks
I could live and dye with her: give me thy hand sweet
Sister.
Sir John. She's beholding to you, Sir.
Sir Martin. What if she be Sir, what's that to you Sir?

400

Sir John. I hope, Sir, I have not offended you?
Sir Martin. It may be you have, and it may be you have
not, Sir; you see I have no mind to satisfie you, Sir:
what a Devil! a man cannot talk a little to his own flesh
and blood, but you must be interposing, with a murrain

405

to you.
Moody. Enough of this, good *Anthony*, this Gentleman is
to marry your Sister.

379–80 *spit out of your mouth*] a spitting image.
404 *murrain*] see IV.i.122.

Sir Martin. He marry my Sister! ods foot, Sir, there are
some Bastards, that shall be nameless, that are as well
worthy to marry her, as any man; and have as good   410
blood in their veins.

Sir John. I do not question it in the least, Sir.

Sir Martin. 'Tis not your best course, Sir; you marry my
Sister! what have you seen of the world, Sir? I have
seen your Hurricanoes, and your Calentures, and your   415
Eclipticks, and your Tropick Lines, Sir, an' you go to
that, Sir.

Warner. You must excuse my Master, the Sea's a little
working in his brain, Sir.

Sir Martin. And your *Prester Johns* o'th' *East-Indies*, and   420
your Great Turk of *Rome* and *Persia*.

Moody. Lord, what a thing it is to be Learned, and a
Traveller! Bodikins it makes me weep for joy; but,
Anthony, you must not bear your self too much upon
your Learning, Child.   425

Millisent. Pray Brother be civil to this Gentleman for my
sake.

Sir Martin. For your sake, Sister *Millisent*, much may be
done, and here I kiss your hand on't.

Warner. Yet again stupidity?   430

Millisent. Nay, pray Brother hands off, now you are too
rude.

Sir Martin. Dear Sister, as I am a true *East-India* Gentleman——

Moody. But pray, Son *Anthony*, let us talk of other matters,   435
and tell me truly, had you not quite forgot me? and yet
I made woundy much of you when you were young.

Sir Martin. I remember you as well as if I saw you but
yesterday: A fine grey-headed—grey-bearded old
Gentleman as ever I saw in all my life.   440

Warner (aside). Grey-bearded old Gentleman! when he
was a Scholar at *Cambridge*.

Moody. But do you remember where you were bred up?

Sir Martin. O yes, Sir, most perfectly, in the Isle—stay—
let me see, oh—now I have it—in the Isle of *Silly*.   445

Moody. In the Isle of *Ely*, sure you mean?

Warner. Without doubt he did, Sir, but this damn'd Isle
of *Silly* runs in's head ever since his Sea-Voyage.

Moody. And your Mother's name was—come pray let me
examine you—for that I'm sure you cannot forget.   450

---

415 *Calentures*] fevers suffered by sailors in tropical climates.
437 *woundy*] excessively.
445 *Silly*] The Scilly Islands off the coast of Cornwall, site of many
shipwrecks.

Sir Martin [*aside*]. *Warner*! what was it *Warner*?

Warner. Poor Mistress *Dorothy Draw-water*, if she were now alive, what a joyful day would this be to her?

Moody. Who the Devil bid you speak, Sirrah?

455 *Sir Martin.* Her name, Sir, was Mistress *Dorothy Draw-water*.

Sir John. I'le be hang'd if this be not some Cheat.

Millisent. He makes so many stumbles, he must needs fall at last.

460 *Moody.* But you remember, I hope, where you were born?

Warner. Well, they may talk what they will of *Oxford* for an University, but *Cambridge* for my Money.

Moody. Hold your tongue you scanderbag Rogue you,
465 this is the second time you have been talking when you should not.

Sir Martin. I was born at *Cambridge*, I remember it as perfectly as if it were but yesterday.

Warner. How I sweat for him! he's remembring ever since
470 he was born.

Moody. And who did you go over withall to the *East-Indies*?

Sir Martin [*aside*]. *Warner*!

Warner. 'Twas a happy thing, Sir, you lighted upon so
475 honest a Merchant as Master *Bonaventure*, to take care of him.

Moody. Sawcy Rascal! this is past all sufferance.

Rose. We are undone *Warner*, if this discourse go on any further.

480 *Lord Dartmouth.* Pray, Sir, take pity o'th' poor Gentleman, he has more need of a good Supper, than to be ask'd so many Questions.

Sir John. These are Rogues, Sir, I plainly perceive it; pray let me ask him one question—which way did you come
485 home Sir?

Sir Martin. We came home by Land, Sir.

Warner. That is, from *India* to *Persia*, from *Persia* to *Turkey*, from *Turkey* to *Germany*, from *Germany* to *France*.

490 *Sir John.* And from thence, over the narrow Seas on Horse-back.

Moody. 'Tis so, I discern it now, but some shall smoke for't.
Stay a little *Anthony*, I'le be with you presently.

Exit Moody.

---

492 *smoke*] be beaten, suffer.

Warner (aside). That wicked old man is gone for no good,
   I'm afraid, would I were fairly quit of him.   495
Millisent (aside). Tell me no more of Sir *Martin, Rose*, he
   wants natural sence, to talk after this rate; but for this
   Warner, I am strangely taken with him, how hand-
   somly he brought him off?

   Enter Moody *with two Cudgels.*

Moody. Among half a score tough Cudgels I had in my   500
   Chamber, I have made choice of these two as best able
   to hold out.
Millisent. Alas! poor *Warner* must be beaten now for all
   his wit, would I could bear it for him.
Warner. But to what end is all this preparation, Sir?   505
Moody. In the first place, for your Worship, and in the
   next, for this *East-Indian* Apostle, that will needs be my
   Son *Anthony.*
Warner. Why, d'ye think he is not?
Moody. No, thou wicked Accomplice in his designs, I   510
   know he is not.
Warner. Who, I his Accomplice? I beseech you, Sir, what
   is it to me, if he should prove a Counterfeit; I assure
   you he has cozen'd me in the first place.
Sir John. That's likely, i'faith, cozen his own Servant?   515
Warner. As I hope for mercy, Sir, I am an utter stranger
   to him, he took me up but yesterday, and told me the
   story word for word as he told it you.
Sir Martin. What will become of us two now? I trust to
   the Rogue's wit to bring me off.   520
Moody. If thou wou'dst have me believe thee, take one of
   these two Cudgels, and help me to lay it on soundly.
Warner. With all my heart.
Moody. Out you Cheat, you Hypocrite, you Imposter!
   do you come hither to cozen an honest man?   525
                                             Beats him.
Sir Martin. Hold, hold, Sir.
Warner. Do you come hither with a lye to get a Father,
   Master *Anthony* of *East-India*?   [*Beats him.*]
Sir Martin. Hold you inhumane Butcher.
Warner. I'le teach you to counterfeit again, Sir.   530
Sir Martin. The Rogue will murder me.
         Exit Sir Martin [Warner *beating him out*].
Moody. A fair riddance of 'em both: let's in and laugh at
   'em.
                                             Exeunt.

   Enter again Sir Martin, *and* Warner.

535

Sir Martin. Was there ever such an affront put upon a man, to be beaten by his Servant?

Warner. After my hearty salutations upon your back-side, Sir, may a man have leave to ask you, what news from the *Mogul's* Country?

540

Sir Martin. I wonder where thou hadst the impudence to move such a question to me, knowing how thou hast us'd me.

Warner. Now, Sir, you may see what comes of your indiscretion and stupidity: I always gave you warning of it, but for this time I am content to pass it by without

545

more words, partly, because I have already corrected you, though not so much as you deserve.

Sir Martin. Do'st thou think to carry it off at this rate, after such an injury?

Warner. You may thank your self for't; nay 'twas very

550

well I found out that way, otherwise I had been suspected as your Accomplice.

Sir Martin. But you laid it on with such a vengeance, as if you were beating of a Stock-fish.

Warner. To confess the truth on't, you had anger'd me,

555

and I was willing to evaporate my choler; if you will pass it by, so; I may chance to help you to your Mistress: no more words of this business, I advise you, but go home and grease your back.

Sir Martin. In fine, I must suffer it at his hands; for if my

560

shoulders had not paid for this fault, my purse must have sweat blood for't: the Rogue has got such a hank upon me ———

Enter Rose.

Warner. So, so, here's another of our Vessels come in after the storm that parted us: what comfort, *Rose*, no

565

harbour near?

Rose. My Lady, as you may well imagine, is most extreamly incens'd against Sir *Martin*; but she applauds your ingenuity to the Skies. I'le say no more, but thereby hangs a Tale.

570

Sir Martin. I am considering with my self about a Plot, to bring all about agen.

Rose. Yet again plotting! if you have such a mind to't, I

553 *Stock-fish*] codfish which was cured by beating with cudgels and drying hard in the cold air.
561 *hank*] a restraining hold.

know no way so proper for you as to turn Poet to
Pugenello.

Warner. Hark! is not that Musick in your house?   575
                            Musick plays.

Rose. Yes, Sir *John* has given my Mistress the Fiddles, and
our Old man is as jocund yonder, and does so hug himself to think how he has been reveng'd upon you.

Warner. Why, he does not know 'twas we, I hope?

Rose. 'Tis all one for that.   580

Sir Martin. I have such a Plot; I care not, I will speak an'
I were to be hang'd for't—shall I speak, dear *Warner*?
let me now; it does so wamble within me, just like a
Clyster, i'faith law, and I can keep it no longer for my
heart.   585

Warner, Well, I am indulgent to you; out with it boldly
in the name of Non-sense.

Sir Martin. We two will put on Vizards, and with the
help of my Landlord, who shall be of the party, go a
Mumming there, and by some device of dancing, get   590
my Mistress away unsuspected by 'em all.

Rose. What if this should hit now, when all your projects
have fail'd, *Warner*?

Warner. Would I were hang'd if it be not somewhat
probable: nay, now I consider better on't—exceeding   595
probable, it must take, 'tis not in Nature to be avoided.

Sir Martin. O must it so, Sir! and who may you thank
for't?

Warner. Now am I so mad he should be the Author of this
device. How the Devil, Sir, came you to stumble on't?   600

Sir Martin. Why should not my brains be as fruitful as
yours or any man's?

Warner. This is so good, it shall not be your Plot, Sir,
either disown it, or I will proceed no further.

Sir Martin. I would not lose the credit of my Plot, to gain   605
my Mistress: the Plot's a good one, and I'le justifie it
upon any ground of *England*; an' you will not work
upon't, it shall be done without you.

Rose. I think the Knight has reason.

Warner. Well, I'le order it however to the best advantage: 610
hark you, *Rose.*   *Whispers.*

Sir Martin. If it miscarry by your ordering, take notice
'tis your fault, 'tis well invented I'le take my Oath on't.

574 *Pugenello*] Punchinello, the name of the principal character in a
puppet show of Italian origin, the prototype of Punch. Hence Martin
would write dialogue for puppets.

583 *wamble*] roll about as though in nausea.

584 *Clyster*] a suppository or injection for costiveness.

615

Rose. I must in to 'em, for fear I should be suspected; but I'le acquaint my Lord, my old Lady, and all the rest who ought to know it, with your design.

Warner. We'll be with you in a twinkling: you and I, *Rose*, are to follow our Leaders, and be pair'd to night.—

Rose. To have, and to hold, are dreadful words, *Warner*; but for your sake I'le venture on 'em.

620

Exeunt.

[ACT V. SCENE 2]

Enter Lord [Dartmouth], *Lady* Dupe, *and* Christian.

Lady Dupe. Nay! good my Lord be patient.

Lord Dartmouth. Does he think to give Fiddles and Treatments in a house where he has wrong'd a Lady? I'le never suffer it.

5

Lady Dupe. But upon what ground will you raise your quarrel?

Lord Dartmouth. A very just one, as I am her Kinsman.

Lady Dupe. He does not know yet why he was to be arrested; try that way agen.

10

Lord Dartmouth. I'le hear of nothing but revenge.

Enter Rose.

Rose. Yes, pray hear me one word, my Lord, Sir *Martin* himself has made a Plot.

Christian. That's like to be a good one.

Rose. A Fool's Plot may be as lucky as a Fool's Handsel;

15

'tis a very likely one, and requires nothing for your part, but to get a Parson in the next room, we'll find work for him.

Lady Dupe. That shall be done immediately; *Christian*, make haste, and send for Master *Ball* the Non-con-

20

formist, tell him here are two or three Angels to be earn'd.

Christian. And two or three Possets to be eaten: may I not put in that, Madam?

Lady Dupe. Surely you may.   *Exit* Christian.

2–3 *Fiddles and Treatments*] music and feasting.

7 *her Kinsman*] Since there is not other mention of this, it may be a loose end from an earlier draft.

14 *Handsel*] a gift or a ceremony of inauguration, as the first money taken by a trader in the morning. *The luck of a fool's handsel* is said to be a proverb (Jonson, *Bartholomew Fair*, II.ii.138–39).

22 *Possets*] rich concoctions of curdled milk, spices, and wine eaten on a wedding night or other festive occasions.

Rose. Then for the rest—'tis only this—Oh! they are here!   25
   pray take it in a whisper; my Lady knows of it already.

       Enter Moody, *Sir* John, Millisent.

Millisent. Strike up agen, Fiddle, I'le have a French Dance.
Sir John. Let's have the Brawls.
Moody. No, good Sir *John,* no quarrelling among Friends.
Lady Dupe. Your Company is like to be increas'd, Sir;   30
   some Neighbors that heard your Fiddles are come a
   mumming to you.
Moody. Let 'em come in, and we'l be Jovy; an' I had but
   my Hobby-horse at home ——
Sir John. What, are they Men or Women?   35
Lady Dupe. I believe some Prentices broke loose.
Millisent. Rose! go and fetch me down two Indian-gowns
   and Vizard-masks—you and I will disguise too, and be
   as good a Mummery to them as they to us.
                                  Exit Rose.
Moody. That will be most rare.   40

Enter Sir Martin, Warner, Landlord *disguised like a Tony.*

Moody. O here they come! Gentlemen Maskers you are
   welcome.— (Warner *signs to the musick for a Dance.*)
   He signs for a Dance I believe; you are welcome.
   Master Musick, strike up, I'le make one as old as I am.
Sir John. And I'le not be out.   45
            Dance.
Lord Dartmouth. Gentlemen Maskers, you have had the
   Frolick, the next turn is mine; bring two Flute-glasses
   and some stools, Ho, we'll have the Ladies health.
Sir John. But why stools, my Lord?
Lord Dartmouth. That you shall see: the humour is, that   50
   two men at a time are hoysted up; when they are above,
   they name their Ladies, and the rest of the Company
   dance about them while they drink: this they call the
   Frolick of the Altitudes.
Moody. Some High-lander's invention, I'le warrant it.   55

---

   28 *Brawls*] "a brawle, or daunce, wherein many (men and women)
holding by the hands sometimes in a ring, and otherwhiles at length
move altogether." (Cotgrave's *Dictionary*, 1611, *s.v. bransle*).
   33 *Jovy*] jovial.
   40.1 *Tony*] fool, an antic clown.
   47 *Flute-glasses*] wine glasses, tall and slender, used especially for
sparkling wines.
   48 *stools*] Exactly how these were stacked is not clear, but it was
necessary that the two atop the stools could not come down without
assistance.

Lord Dartmouth. Gentlemen-maskers, you shall begin.
> *They hoyst Sir* Martin *and* Warner.

Sir John. Name the Ladies.

Lord Dartmouth. They point to Mistress *Millisent* and Mistress *Christian,* Allon's, Touche! Touche!
> *While they drink the Company dances and sings: they are*
> *taken down.*

60 *Moody.* A rare toping health this: come Sir *John,* now you and I will be in our altitudes.
> *When they are up, the Company dances about 'em: then*
> *dance off. Tony dances a Jig.*

Sir John. What new device is this tro?

Moody. I know not what to make on't.

Sir John (to Tony). Pray, Master Fool, where's the rest o'
65 your Company? I would fain see 'em again.

Landlord. Come down and tell 'em so, *Cudden.*

Sir John. I'le be hang'd if there be not some plot in't, and this Fool is set here to spin out the time.

Moody. Like enough: undone! undone! my Daughter's
70 gone, let me down, Sirrah.

Landlord. Yes, *Cudden.*

Sir John. My Mistress is gone, let me down first.

Landlord. This is the quickest way, *Cudden.*
> *He offers to pull down the stools.*

Sir John. Hold! Hold! or thou wilt break my neck.

75 *Landlord.* And you will not come down, you may stay there, *Cudden.*   *Exit Landlord dancing.*

Moody. O Scanderbag Villains!

Sir John. Is there no getting down?

Moody. All this was long of you Sir *Jack.*

80 *Sir John.* 'Twas long of your self to invite them hither.

Moody. O you young Coxcombs, to be drawn in thus!

Sir John. You old Sot you, to be caught so sillily!

Moody. Come but an inch nearer, and I'le so claw thee.

Sir John. I hope I shall reach to thee.

85 *Moody.* And 'twere not for thy wooden breast-work there.

Sir John. I hope to push thee down from *Babylon.*

> *Enter Lord* [Dartmouth], *Lady* Dupe, *Sir* Martin,
> Warner, Rose, Millisent *vail'd,* Landlord.

Lord Dartmouth. How, Gentlemen! what, quarrelling among your selves!

---

59 Allon's] A Lou's Q1; A Lon's Q2–5,F
62 *tro*] do you suppose.
66 *Cudden*] a born fool, a feeble-minded person.
79 *long of*] because of.

Moody. Coxnowns! help me down, and let me have fair
    play, he shall never marry my Daughter. 90
Sir Martin (leading Rose). No I'le be sworn that he shall
    not, therefore never repine, Sir, for Marriages you know
    are made in Heaven: in fine, Sir, we are joyn'd together
    in spight of Fortune.
Rose (pulling off her mask). That we are indeed, Sir *Martin*, 95
    and these are Witnesses; therefore in fine never repine,
    Sir, for marriages you know are made in Heaven.
Omnes. Rose!
Warner. What, is *Rose* split in two? sure I ha' got one
    Rose! 100
Millisent. I, the best *Rose* you ever got in all your life.
                                   Pulls off her Mask.
Warner. This amazeth me so much, I know not what to
    say or think.
Moody. My Daughter married to *Warner!*
Sir Martin. Well, I thought it impossible any man in 105
    England should have over-reach'd me: sure *Warner* there
    was some mistake in this: prithee *Billy* let's go to the
    Parson to set all right again, that every man may have
    his own before the matter go too far.
Warner. Well, Sir! for my part I will have nothing 110
    farther to do with these Women, for I find they will
    be too hard for us, but e'ne sit down by the loss, and
    content my self with my hard fortune: But, Madam, do
    you ever think I will forgive you this, to cheat me into
    an Estate of two thousand pounds a year? 115
Sir Martin. And I were as thee, I would not be so serv'd
    Warner!
Millisent. I have serv'd him but right for the cheat he put
    upon me, when he perswaded me you were a Wit—
    now there's a trick for your trick, Sir. 120
Warner. Nay, I confess you have out-witted me.
Sir John. Let me down, and I'le forgive all freely.
                              They let him down.
Moody. What am I kept here for?
Warner. I might in policy keep you there, till your
    Daughter and I had been in private, for a little con- 125
    summation: But for once, Sir, I'le trust your good
    nature.   *Takes him down too.*
Moody. And thou wert a Gentleman it would not grieve
    me!
Millisent. That I was assur'd of before I married him, by 130
    my Lord here.
Lord Dartmouth. I cannot refuse to own him for my Kins-

man, though his Father's sufferings in the late times hath ruin'd his Fortunes.

135 *Moody.* But yet he has been a Serving-man.

Warner. You are mistaken, Sir, I have been a Master, and besides there's an Estate of eight hundred pounds a year, only it is mortgaged for six thousand pounds.

Moody. Well, we'll bring it off, and for my part, I am glad 140 my Daughter has miss'd *in fine*, there.

Sir John. I will not be the only man that must sleep without a Bedfellow to night, if this Lady will once again receive me.

Lady Dupe. She's yours, Sir.

145 *Lord Dartmouth.* And the same Parson, that did the former execution, is still in the next Chamber; what with Cawdels, Wine, and Quidding, which he has taken in abundance, I think he will be able to wheadle two more of you into matrimony.

150 *Millisent.* Poor Sir *Martin* looks melancholly! I am half afraid he is in love.

Warner. Not with the Lady that took him for a wit, I hope.

Rose. At least, Sir *Martin* can do more than you Master 155 *Warner*, for he can make me a Lady, which you cannot my Mistress.

Sir Martin. I have lost nothing but my man, and in fine, I shall get another.

Millisent. You'll do very well, Sir *Martin*, for you'll never 160 be your own man, I assure you.

Warner. For my part I had lov'd you before if I had follow'd my inclination.

Millisent. But now I am afraid you begin of the latest, except your love can grow up like a Mushroom at a 165 night's warning.

Warner. For that matter never trouble your self, I can love as fast as any man, when I am nigh possession; my love falls heavy, and never moves quick till it comes near the Centre; he's an ill Falconer that will unhood before the 170 quarry be in sight.

Love's an high mettal'd Hawk that beats the Air,
But soon grows weary when the Game's not near.

147 *Cawdels*] warm, sweet drinks, made of gruel and wine or ale.

147 *Quidding*] perhaps chewing tobacco, the earliest recorded quotations are from the early eighteenth century. Saintsbury says "stuffing, food."

176

Epilogue

As Country Vicars, when the Sermon's done,
Run hudling to the Benediction;
Well knowing, though the better sort may stay,
The Vulgar Rout will run unblest away:
So we, when once our Play is done, make haste   5
With a short Epilogue to close your taste.
In thus withdrawing we seem mannerly,
But when the Curtain's down we peep, and see
A Jury of the Wits who still stay late,
And in their Club decree the poor Play's fate;   10
Their verdict back is to the Boxes brought,
Thence all the Town pronounces it their thought.
Thus, Gallants, we like *Lilly* can foresee,
But if you ask us what our doom will be,
We by to morrow will our Fortune cast,   15
As he tells all things when the Year is past.

   2 *hudling*] disorderly hurrying.
  13 *Lilly*] William Lilly, an astrologer and almanac maker.

I.i.9 comes.] ~,   36 it?] ~.   41–42 easie: ... her,] ~, ... ~ :
123 Fox's subtlety] Foxes subtlety   169 gaming.] ~,   199 then;
... *Canterbury*,] ~, ... 1;   233 since,] ~ ,   244 Mistress's]
Mistresses   272 So,] ~ ,   291 thank] Thank   298 on't] ont
304 why,] ~ ,   309 Father.] Q1 *cw*; ~ : *text* 309 But] but   321
within.] ~,   330–31 Loggar- / head] Loggar-head
II.i.1 would;] ~,   8 Gold,] ~ ,   29 me.] ~,   65 one?] ~ ,
86 fly.] ~ :
II.ii.2 Chamber.] ~,   6 Lodgings.] ~, 25 him.] ~ ;   43 you—] ~.
72 innocent?] ~.   154 Sir.] ~ ;   352 what,] ~ , 354 as] As
III.i.36 Sir.] ~,   112 What,] ~ ,   129 born,] ~ ,
III.ii.45 happy,—] ~ , ,
III.iii.61 enough; what,] ~, ~ ,   68 Sir!] ~ ?   77 way,] ~ ,
IV.i.8 man,] ~.   39 overgrown] over- / grown   42 time;] ~,
48 Scanderbag-] Scander-bag-   133 imagination).] ~) ,   168
Wind- / mill] Wind-mill   187 insupportable;] ~,   189 Purse-
strings] Purse- / strings   198 What,] ~,   204 pounds!] ~ ,
370 before-hand] before- / hand   371 you; ... one,] ~ , ... ~ ;
386 afterwards;] ~,   532 Pox,] ~ ,   536 what,] ~ ,   552
Servant?] ~.
V.i.55 *Rose*,] ~ ,   154 who] who who   160 before-hand] before- /
hand   276 Mounsieur,] ~ —   318 *East-Indies*] ~ , ~   390
already,] ~ ,   404 interposing,] ~ ,   556 by, so;] ~ , ~,   589
Landlord] Lordland   605 Plot,] ~ ,
V.ii.43 welcome.] ~,   87 what,] ~ ,

Press Variants in Q1
Sheet D (inner forme)
Corrected: DFo[1, 3–4]
Uncorrected: CLUC, DFo[2]

Sig. D1ᵛ
II.ii.115 you make] you I make
131 *Warn. entring.*] *Warn.*
131.1 *omit*] *Enter* Millisent.
138*cw* Our] *Mill.*
Sig. D4
II.ii.300 you] you you
319 Repast?] Repast.
324 Sir.] ~ ;
327 Rogue,] ~ ,

Sheet F (inner forme)
Corrected: CLUC, DFo[2–4]
Uncorrected: DFo[1]

Sig. F1ᵛ
III.iii.71 love] are

An Evening's Love

An Evening's Love, or The Mock Astrologer, acted for the first time June 12, 1668, by the King's Company, at the Bridges Street theater, Drury Lane, received mixed comments, as it has from most critics and editors since that time. Although the world commended it, Pepys and his wife did not, "it being very smutty, and nothing so good as 'The Maiden Queen,' or 'The Indian Emperour.'"[1] "Calling this day at Herringman's [Dryden's publisher] he tells me Dryden do himself call it but a fifth-rate play" (June 22). "Often seen . . . but an ordinary play" (March 8, 1669). John Evelyn thought it "a foolish plot, and very profane, so as it afflicted me to see how the stage was degenerated and poluted by the licentious times."[2] And in his prologue and epilogue Dryden deprecates his work. Nevertheless the play had a considerable number of performances, and it continues to be interesting, if only as a problem.

Although the received text may have had some of the profane and smutty talk expunged, *An Evening's Love* still seems, to N. B. Allen, inferior writing, because "Dryden, tired of dramatic work and disillusioned as to the value of trying to do more than please, gave the public a little of each kind of thing that it had applauded during recent years, not even taking the trouble to combine carefully what he borrowed from his various sources."[3] The scenes involving Wildblood's affair with Jacinta are "largely his own," but they were suggested by Molière's *Le Dépit amoureux* (1656). Dryden added "many passages of excellent raillery," such as II.i.1–204 and the disguises in III.ii.451–700, IV.i.29–170, as well as the foolish conversation between Alonzo and Lopez, III.ii.334–407. The other action, involving Bellamy's duping of Alonzo, Don Melchor's wooing of Theodosia and Amelia, and Don Lopez' interest in Aurelia are heavily indebted to Thomas Corneille's *Le Feint astrologue* (1648) and no doubt Madeleine de Scudéry's *Ibrahim* (1641, English 1652).[4] Dryden invented most of the assembly scene in Act V, although the pretense that the people are ghosts may have been suggested by Philippe Quinault's *L'Amant indiscret*, which he had used for *Sir Martin Mar-All*. Allen thinks that Dryden grew tired

[1] *Diary*, ed. Wheatley, June 19, 20, 1668.
[2] *Diary*, ed. De Beer, June 19, 1668.
[3] *The Sources of Dryden's Comedies*, pp. 169–70, and some additional observations in Allen's "The Sources of Dryden's *The Mock Astrologer*," *PQ*, XXXVI (1957), 453–64.
[4] Both of which are derived from Calderón's *Astrológo Fingido*, which Dryden apparently did not consult.

of Wildblood and Jacinta after Act II, and he put Jacinta through a series of disguises to make up for "the lack of wit by intrigue," and the faults of the whole play lie in the incompatibility of intrigue, borrowed from Corneille, wit combats of Jacinta and Wildblood, and farce of Acts IV and V. For proof that such elements can be successfully combined and are not intrinsically discordant, we need look only at *Twelfth Night* or *As You Like It*. The problem remains, then, how Dryden succeeded or failed to integrate his material and specifically we must question the supposed inconsistency in Wildblood.

The scenes of disguise in Acts III and IV have, it seems to me, a distinct dramatic point that grows out of the first two acts. Wildblood wants to be a rake-hell lover, and during the carnival season, he feels a necessity to be daring and live high, proving that Jacinta means little to him. Yet every woman who attracts him, be she fair or brown or black, turns out to be another manifestation of his mistress. He is, in effect, acting out a sexual fantasy: he enjoys inconstancy but in spite of himself he is constant. Like the speaker in Donne's "The Indifferent," he boasts of catholic taste, but is tied to a woman who is true. The implications, however, go beyond Donne's poem, for Jacinta is too much for Wildblood. Her constancy and vigilance surprise him, and her bewildering range of attributes and talents fulfills, in an unexpected way, the ideal of a libertine's mistresses, qualities he had sought and found in a dozen or a hundred women, but never in one. Consequently, every act of infidelity, seen from her ironic perspective, is an act of unconscious faith, and she loves him all the more. Like Mirabell fascinated with Millamant, Jacinta is obsessed with Wildblood's faults, so she keeps hunting them compulsively; she is indeed, as Beatrix says, a "bleeding gamester who will obstinately pursue a losing hand." Both lovers maintain their brisk talk to the end of Act IV, except for one terrible moment, when Wildblood can think of no more excuses (IV.i.743–53), and Jacinta has him almost to his knees. If he submits, she will not love him, so he brazens it out, with the help of Maskall. The scene then closes with some of their best gay conversation, where they seem to renounce all love for each other, but in fact they cement the bond even firmer. The passage is a model of facetious dialogue.

The real difficulty with Act IV is merely that the other action is not funny, the scenes are uninventive and over-written; neither Bellamy, Melchor, Alonzo, Aurelia, Theo-dosia, nor Lopez show the slightest spark of mind or character. Therefore, the final assembly in Act V, with its romping foolishness, comes as a relief, saving their story from utter tedium. And Dryden outdid himself in this scene; with "too gross artifice," as Alonzo says, he manipulated the entire cast, keeping everyone confined to the garden. The broken key to the garden gate, the absurdity of the conjuration, the attempted escape, the huddled-up marriage agreements, and the easy disposal of Don Melchor must be taken in the spirit of make believe, and they may work on the stage, suitably capped by the song of Jacinta and Wildblood.[5] This song epitomizes their charming selfconsciousness in a parody of a pastoral singing bout; it is a competition between a husband and wife to see who shall dominate, like a Thurber battle of the sexes, in which the opponents throw flowers at each other. The audience, therefore, should receive a final impression of the forced gaiety of *An Evening's Love*, the masking that seems to dominate the action, and the playful carnival atmosphere powerful enough to encompass the intrigue, wit, and high-jinks, such as we find in *Les enfants du paradis*.[6] The connections are weak, but the gusto and degagé air of the whole are powerful.

Although it was entered at Stationers' Hall on November 20, 1668, the play, dedicated to the Duke of Newcastle, was not published until 1671 (Term Catalogue, February 13). The present text is based on the Newberry copy of Q1 (Macd. 75a, W & M 409), which has been compared with the Claremont College and five Texas copies, revealing press correction in four different forms. Dryden does not appear to have been responsible for any new readings in the subsequent reprints: Q2 1671 (Macd. 75b, W & M 410), Q3 1691, and F 1701. Any conscientious printer could have made the few corrections that come in Q2. The supposed edition of 1675 (Macd. 75c, W & M 411) was a reissue of Q2 with a new title page.

[5] The original music of this song does not survive, according to C. L. Day, *The Songs of John Dryden* (1932), but Day reprints the airs for two other songs in the play: "After the pangs of a desperate Lover" and "Calm was the even, and clear was the Skie" set by Alphonso Marsh, from *Choice Songs and Ayres* (1673), pp. 8–9.

[6] One of the play's court performances occurred on February 16, 1685/86, at the end of the carnival celebration at Court (*London Stage*, I.347).

A N
Evening's Love,
OR THE
Mock-Aſtrologer.

Acted at the **THEATER ROYAL,**

BY HIS

MAJESTIES SERVANTS.

WRITTEN BY

ƒOHN DRYDEN,

Servant to His Majeſty.

Mallem Convivis quàm placuiſſe Cocis. Mart.

In the *SAVOY,*

Printed by *T. N.* for *Henry Herringman,* and are to be
ſold at the Anchor in the lower Walk of
the *New Exchange,* 1671.

Preface

I had thought, Reader, in this Preface to have written somewhat concerning the difference betwixt the Playes of our Age,
and those of our Predecessors on the *English* Stage: to have
shewn in what parts of Dramatick Poesie we were excell'd by
Ben. Johnson, I mean, humour, and contrivance of Comedy;
and in what we may justly claim precedence of *Shakespear* and
Fletcher, namely in Heroick Playes: but this design I have
wav'd on second considerations; at least deferr'd it till I publish the *Conquest of Granada*, where the discourse will be
more proper. I had also prepar'd to treat of the improvement
of our Language since *Fletcher's* and *Johnson's* dayes, and consequently of our refining the Courtship, Raillery, and Conversation of Playes: but as I am willing to decline that envy
which I shou'd draw on my self from some old Opiniatre
judges of the Stage; so likewise I am prest in time so much
that I have not leisure, at present, to go thorough with it.
Neither, indeed, do I value a reputation gain'd from Comedy,
so far as to concern my self about it any more than I needs
must in my own defence: for I think it, in it's own nature,
inferiour to all sorts of Dramatick writing. Low Comedy
especially requires, on the Writer's part, much of conversation
with the vulgar: and much of ill nature in the observation of
their follies. But let all men please themselves according to
their several tastes: that which is not pleasant to me may be
to others who judge better: and, to prevent an accusation
from my enemies, I am sometimes ready to imagine that my
disgust of low Comedy proceeds not so much from my judgement as from my temper; which is the reason why I so seldom
write it; and that when I succeed in it, (I mean so far as to
please the Audience) yet I am nothing satisfi'd with what I
have done; but am often vex'd to hear the people laugh, and
clap, as they perpetually do, where I intended 'em no jest;
while they let pass the better things without taking notice of
them. Yet even this confirms me in my opinion of slighting
popular applause, and of contemning that approbation which
those very people give, equally with me, to the Zany of a
Mountebank; or to the appearance of an Antick on the
Theatre, without wit on the Poet's part, or any occasion of
laughter from the Actor, besides the ridiculousness of his habit
and his Grimaces.

14 *Opiniatre*] opinionated.
36–37 *Zany . . . Mountebank*] A mountebank was a quack, often
attended by a clown, called a zany, who helped to attract a crowd for
the mountebank's spiel.
37 *Antick*] clown.

But I have descended before I was aware, from Comedy to Farce; which consists principally of Grimaces. That I admire not any Comedy equally with Tragedy, is, perhaps, from the sullenness of my humor; but that I detest those Farces, which
45 are now the most frequent entertainments of the Stage, I am sure I have reason on my side. Comedy consists, though of low persons, yet of natural actions, and characters; I mean such humours, adventures, and designes, as are to be found and met with in the world. Farce, on the other side, consists
50 of forc'd humours, and unnatural events: Comedy presents us with the imperfections of humane nature. Farce entertains us with what is monstruous and chimerical: the one causes laughter in those who can judge of men and manners, by the lively representation of their folly or corruption; the other
55 produces the same effect in those who can judge of neither, and that only by its extravagances. The first works on the judgment and fancy; the latter on the fancy only: There is more of satisfaction in the former kind of laughter, and in the latter more of scorn. But, how it happens that an impossible
60 adventure should cause our mirth, I cannot so easily imagine. Something there may be in the oddness of it, because on the Stage it is the common effect of things unexpected to surprize us into a delight: and that is to be ascrib'd to the strange appetite, as I may call it, of the fancy; which, like that of a
65 longing Woman, often runs out into the most extravagant desires; and is better satisfi'd sometimes with Loam, or with the Rinds of Trees, than with the wholsome nourishments of life. In short, there is the same difference betwixt Farce and Comedy, as betwixt an Empirique and a true Physitian: both
70 of them may attain their ends; but what the one performs by hazard, the other does by skill. And as the Artist is often unsuccessful, while the Mountebank succeeds; so Farces more commonly take the people than Comedies. For to write unnatural things, is the most probable way of pleasing them,
75 who understand not Nature. And a true Poet often misses of applause, because he cannot debase himself to write so ill as to please his Audience.

After all, it is to be acknowledg'd, that most of those Comedies, which have been lately written, have been ally'd
80 too much to Farce: and this must of necessity fall out till we forbear the translation of *French Plays*: for their Poets wanting judgement to make, or to maintain true characters, strive to cover their defects with ridiculous Figures and Grimaces.

44 *sullenness*] seriousness.
65 *longing Woman*] pregnant woman, from the fanciful cravings said to be characteristic.
69 *Empirique*] quack.

While I say this I accuse my self as well as others: and this
very play would rise up in judgment against me, if I would   85
defend all things I have written to be natural: but I confess
I have given too much to the people in it, and am asham'd for
them as well as for my self, that I have pleas'd them at so
cheap a rate: not that there is any thing here which I would
not defend to an ill-natur'd judge: (for I despise their censures,   90
who I am sure wou'd write worse on the same subject:) but
because I love to deal clearly and plainly, and to speak of my
own faults with more criticism, then I would of another
Poet's. Yet I think it no vanity to say that this Comedy has as
much of entertainment in it as many other which have bin   95
lately written: and, if I find my own errors in it, I am able
at the same time to arraign all my Contemporaries for
greater. As I pretend not that I can write humour, so none of
them can reasonably pretend to have written it as they ought.
Johnson was the only man of all Ages and Nations who has   100
perform'd it well; and that but in three or four of his
Comedies: the rest are but a *Crambe bis cocta*; the same
humours a little vary'd and written worse: neither was it
more allowable in him, than it is in our present Poets, to
represent the follies of particular persons; of which many   105
have accus'd him. *Parcere personis dicere de vitiis* is the rule of
Plays. And *Horace* tells you that the old Comedy amongst
the *Grecians* was silenc'd for the too great liberties of the
Poets.

> ———— *In vitium libertas excidit et vim*   110
> *Dignam lege regi: lex est accepta chorusque*
> *Turpiter obticuit, sublato jure nocendi.*

Of which he gives you the reason in another place: where
having given the precept,

> *Neve immunda crepent, ignominiosáque dicta:*   115

He immediately subjoyns,

> *Offenduntur enim, quibus est equus, et pater, et res.*

But *Ben. Johnson* is to be admir'd for many excellencies;
and can be tax'd with fewer failings than any *English* Poet. I

___

95 it as] Q2; as it Q1

102 *Crambe bis cocta*] cabbage twice baked.

106 *Parcere personis dicere de vitiis*] refrain from speaking of living
persons.

110–12 *In . . . nocendi*] liberty turned to licence, and to an excess
that called for legal restraint. A law was passed, and, the right of libel
gone, the chorus to its shame fell silent (Horace, *Ars Poetica*, 282–84).

115–17 *Neve . . . res*] nor should they give way to foul and scurrilous
expressions, for rank, birth, and fortune are offended by them (Horace,
Ars Poetica, 247–48).

120   know I have been accus'd as an enemy of his writings; but
without any other reason than that I do not admire him
blindly, and without looking into his imperfections. For why
should he only be exempted from those frailties, from which
Homer and *Virgil* are not free? Or why should there be any
125   *ipse dixit* in our Poetry, any more than there is in our Philosophy? I admire and applaud him where I ought: those who
do more do but value themselves in their admiration of him:
and, by telling you they extoll *Ben. Johnson's* way, would
insinuate to you that they can practice it. For my part I declare
130   that I want judgement to imitate him: and shou'd think it a
great impudence in my self to attempt it. To make men appear
pleasantly ridiculous on the Stage was, as I have said, his
talent: and in this he needed not the acumen of wĩt, but that
of judgement. For the characters and representations of folly
135   are only the effects of observation; and observation is an
effect of judgment. Some ingenious men, for whom I have a
particular esteem, have thought I have much injur'd *Ben.
Johnson* when I have not allow'd his wit to be extraordinary:
but they confound the notion of what is witty with what is
140   pleasant. That *Ben. Johnson's* Playes were pleasant he must
want reason who denyes: But that pleasantness was not
properly wit, or the sharpness of conceit; but the natural
imitation of folly: which I confess to be excellent in it's kind,
but not to be of that kind which they pretend. Yet if we will
145   believe *Quintilian* in his Chapter *de Movendo risu*, he gives his
opinion of both in these following words. *Stulta reprehendere
facillimum est; nam per se sunt ridicula: et a derisu non procul
abest risus: sed rem urbanam facit aliqua ex nobis adjectio.*
    And some perhaps wou'd be apt to say of *Johnson* as it was
150   said of *Demosthenes*; *Non displicuisse illi jocos, sed non contigisse.*
I will not deny but that I approve most the mixt way of
Comedy; that which is neither all wit, nor all humour, but
the result of both. Neither so little of humour as *Fletcher*
shews, nor so little of love and wit, as *Johnson*. Neither all
155   cheat, with which the best Playes of the one are fill'd, nor
all adventure, which is the common practice of the other. I
would have the characters well chosen, and kept distant from
interfaring with each other; which is more than *Fletcher* or
Shakespear did: but I would have more of the *Urbana, venusta,*

146–48 *Stulta . . . adjectio*] It is easy to make fun of folly, for folly
is ridiculous in itself; but something of our own makes the joke urbane
(Quintilian, *Institutio Oratoria*, VI.iii.71).

150 *Non . . . contigisse*] not to have disliked jokes, but to have
lacked the power to make them (*Inst.* VI.iii.2).

159–60 *Urbana . . . faceta*] the language of the cities and polite
learning, graceful, salty, and playfully elegant (*Inst.* VI.iii.17–20).

salsa, faceta and the rest which *Quintilian* reckons up as the
ornaments of wit; and these are extremely wanting in *Ben.
Johnson.* As for repartie in particular; as it is the very soul of
conversation, so it is the greatest grace of Comedy, where it
is proper to the Characters: there may be much of acuteness
in a thing well said; but there is more in a quick reply: *sunt,
enim, longè venustiora omnia in respondendo quàm in provocando.*
Of one thing I am sure, that no man ever will decry wit, but
he who despairs of it himself; and who has no other quarrel
to it but that which the Fox had to the Grapes. Yet, as Mr.
Cowley, (who had a greater portion of it than any man I know)
tells us in his Character of Wit, rather than all wit let there
be none; I think there's no folly so great in any Poet of our
Age as the superfluity and wast of wit was in some of our
predecessors: particularly we may say of *Fletcher* and of
Shakespear, what was said of *Ovid, In omni ejus ingenio, facilius
quod rejici, quàm quod adjici potest, invenies.* The contrary of
which was true in *Virgil* and our incomparable *Johnson.*

Some enemies of Repartie have observ'd to us, that there is
a great latitude in their Characters, which are made to speak
it: And that it is easier to write wit than humour; because in
the characters of humour, the Poet is confin'd to make the
person speak what is only proper to it. Whereas all kind of
wit is proper in the Character of a witty person. But, by their
favour, there are as different characters in wit as in folly.
Neither is all kind of wit proper in the mouth of every
ingenious person. A witty Coward and a witty Brave must
speak differently. *Falstaffe* and the *Lyar,* speak not like *Don
John* in the *Chances,* and *Valentine* in *Wit without Money.* And
Johnson's Truwit in the *Silent Woman,* is a Character different
from all of them. Yet it appears that this one Character of
Wit was more difficult to the Author, than all his images of
humour in the Play: For those he could describe and manage
from his observation of men; this he has taken, at least a
part of it, from books: witness the Speeches in the first
Act, translated *verbatim* out of *Ovid de Arte Amandi.* To omit
what afterwards he borrowed from the sixth Satyre of
Juvenal against Women.

However, if I should grant, that there were a greater latitude in Characters of Wit, than in those of Humour; yet that

160

165

170

175

180

185

190

195

194 the Speeches] Q1(c); the long Speeches Q1(u)

165–66 *sunt . . . provocando*] for wit always looks more graceful in
reply than in attack (*Inst.* VI.iii.13).

175–76 *In . . . invenies*] In all his wit you will find it easier to reject
than to add (*Inst.* VI.iii.5).

187 *the Lyar*] Dorante in *The Lyar,* acted in 1661, a translation of
Corneille's *Le Menteur* (Summers).

188 *Chances . . . Money*] two comedies by Fletcher.

200 latitude would be of small advantage to such Poets who have too narrow an imagination to write it. And to entertain an Audience perpetually with Humour, is to carry them from the conversation of Gentlemen, and treat them with the follies and extravagances of *Bedlam*.

205 I find I have launch'd out farther than I intended in the beginning of this Preface. And that in the heat of writing, I have touch'd at something, which I thought to have avoided. 'Tis time now to draw homeward: and to think rather of defending my self, than assaulting others. I have already

210 acknowledg'd that this Play is far from perfect: but I do not think my self oblig'd to discover the imperfections of it to my Adversaries, any more than a guilty person is bound to accuse himself before his Judges. 'Tis charg'd upon me that I make debauch'd persons (such as they say my Astrologer

215 and Gamester are) my Protagonists, or the chief persons of the *Drama*; and that I make them happy in the conclusion of my Play; against the Law of Comedy, which is to reward virtue and punish vice. I answer first, that I know no such law to have been constantly observ'd in Comedy, either by

220 the Ancient or Modern Poets. *Chærea* is made happy in the *Eunuch*, after having deflour'd a Virgin: and *Terence* generally does the same through all his Plays, where you perpetually see, not only debauch'd young men enjoy their Mistresses, but even the Courtezans themselves rewarded and honour'd

225 in the Catastrophe. The same may be observ'd in *Plautus* almost every where. *Ben. Johnson* himself, after whom I may be proud to erre, has given me more than once the example of it. That in the *Alchemist* is notorious, where *Face*, after having contriv'd and carried on the great cozenage of the

230 Play, and continued in it without repentance to the last, is not only forgiven by his Master, but inrich'd by his consent, with the spoiles of those whom he had cheated. And, which is more, his Master himself, a grave man, and a Widower, is introduc'd taking his Man's counsel, debauching the Widow

235 first, in hope to marry her afterward. In the *Silent Woman*, *Dauphine*, (who with the other two Gentlemen, is of the same Character with my *Celadon* in the *Maiden Queen*, and with *Wildblood* in this) professes himself in love with all the Collegiate Ladies: and they likewise are all of the same

240 Character with each other, (excepting only Madam *Otter*, who has something singular:) yet this naughty *Dauphine* is crown'd in the end with the possession of his Uncle's Estate, and with the hopes of enjoying all his Mistresses. And his friend Master *Truwit* (the best Character of a Gentleman which *Ben.*

245 *Johnson* ever made) is not asham'd to pimp for him. As for *Beaumont* and *Fletcher*, I need not alledge examples out of

them; for that were to quote almost all their Comedies. But now it will be objected that I patronize vice by the authority of former Poets, and extenuate my own faults by recrimination. I answer that as I defend my self by their example; so that example I defend by reason, and by the end of all Dramatique Poesie. In the first place therefore give me leave to shew you their mistake who have accus'd me. They have not distinguish'd, as they ought, betwixt the rules of Tragedy and Comedy. In Tragedy, where the Actions and Persons are great, and the crimes horrid, the laws of justice are more strictly to be observ'd: and examples of punishment to be made to deterre mankind from the pursuit of vice. Faults of this kind have been rare amongst the Ancient Poets: for they have punish'd in *Oedipus*, and in his posterity, the sinne which he knew not he had committed. *Medea* is the only example I remember at present, who escapes from punishment after murder. Thus Tragedie fulfils one great part of its institution; which is by example to instruct. But in Comedy it is not so; for the chief end of it is divertisement and delight: and that so much, that it is disputed, I think, by *Heinsius*, before *Horace* his art of Poetry, whether instruction be any part of its employment. At least I am sure it can be but its secondary end: for the business of the Poet is to make you laugh: when he writes humour he makes folly ridiculous; when wit, he moves you, if not always to laughter, yet to a pleasure that is more noble. And if he works a cure on folly, and the small imperfections in mankind, by exposing them to publick view, that cure is not perform'd by an immediate operation. For it works first on the ill nature of the Audience; they are mov'd to laugh by the representation of deformity; and the shame of that laughter, teaches us to amend what is ridiculous in our manners. This being, then, establish'd, that the first end of Comedie is delight, and instruction only the second; it may reasonably be inferr'd that Comedy is not so much oblig'd to the punishment of the faults which it represents, as Tragedy. For the persons in Comedy are of a lower quality, the action is little, and the faults and vices are but the sallies of youth, and the frailties of humane nature, and not premeditated crimes: such to which all men are obnoxious, not such, as are attempted only by few, and those abandonn'd to all sense of vertue: such as move pity and commiseration; not detestation and horror; such in short as may be forgiven, not such as must of necessity be punish'd. But, lest any man should think

250

255

260

265

270

275

280

285

266 *Heinsius*] Daniel Heinsius, in his edition of Horace's *Works*, says no such thing.

290 that I write this to make libertinism amiable; or that I car'd
not to debase the end and institution of Comedy, so I might
thereby maintain my own errors, and those of better Poets; I
must farther declare, both for them and for my self, that we
make not vicious persons happy, but only as heaven makes
295 sinners so: that is by reclaiming them first from vice. For so
'tis to be suppos'd they are, when they resolve to marry; for
then enjoying what they desire in one, they cease to pursue
the love of many. So *Chærea* is made happy by *Terence*, in
marrying her whom he had deflour'd: And so are *Wildblood*
300 and the *Astrologer* in this Play.

    There is another crime with which I am charg'd, at which
I am yet much less concern'd, because it does not relate to my
manners, as the former did, but only to my reputation as a
Poet: A name of which I assure the Reader I am nothing
305 proud; and therefore cannot be very solicitous to defend it.
I am tax'd with stealing all my Playes, and that by some who
should be the last men from whom I would steal any part of
'em. There is one answer which I will not make; but it has
been made for me by him to whose Grace and Patronage I
310 owe all things.

        Et spes et ratio studiorum, in Cæsare *tantum.*

    And without whose command they shou'd no longer be
troubl'd with any thing of mine, that he only desir'd that
they who accus'd me of theft would always steal him Playes
315 like mine. But though I have reason to be proud of this
defence, yet I should wave it, because I have a worse opinion
of my own Comedies than any of my Enemies can have.
'Tis true, that where ever I have lik'd any story in a Romance,
Novel, or forreign Play, I have made no difficulty, nor ever
320 shall, to take the foundation of it, to build it up, and to make
it proper for the *English* Stage. And I will be so vain to say
it has lost nothing in my hands: But it always cost me so
much trouble to heighten it, for our Theatre (which is incom-
parably more curious in all the ornaments of Dramatick
325 Poesie, than the *French* or *Spanish*) that when I had finish'd
my Play, it was like the Hulk of *Sir Francis Drake*, so strangely
alter'd, that there scarce remain'd any Plank of the Timber
which first built it. To witness this I need go no farther than

309 *him*] almost certainly the Duke of Newcastle, to whom this
play is dedicated.
311 *Et . . . tantum*] on Caesar alone all the hopes and prospects of
scholars depend (Juvenal, *Satires*, VII.i).
324 *curious*] careful as to the standard of excellence.
326 *Hulk*] *The Golden Hind*, preserved at the dock at Deptford.

this Play: It was first *Spanish*, and call'd *El Astrologo fingido*; then made *French* by the younger *Corneille*: and is now translated into *English*, and in print, under the name of the *Feign'd Astrologer*. What I have perform'd in this will best appear by comparing it with those: you will see that I have rejected some adventures which I judg'd were not divertising: that I have heightned those which I have chosen, and that I have added others which were neither in the *French* nor *Spanish*. And besides you will easily discover that the Walk of the *Astrologer* is the least considerable in my Play: for the design of it turns more on the parts of *Wildblood* and *Jacinta*, who are the chief persons in it. I have farther to add, that I seldom use the wit and language of any Romance, or Play which I undertake to alter: because my own invention (as bad as it is) can furnish me with nothing so dull as what is there. Those who have call'd *Virgil*, *Terence*, and *Tasso Plagiaries* (though they much injur'd them,) had yet a better colour for their accusation: For *Virgil* has evidently translated *Theocritus*, *Hesiod*, and *Homer*, in many places; besides what he has taken from *Ennius* in his own language. *Terence* was not only known to translate *Menander*, (which he avows also in his Prologues) but was said also to be help'd in those Translations by *Scipio* the *African*, and *Lælius*. And *Tasso*, the most excellent of modern Poets, and whom I reverence next to *Virgil*, has taken both from *Homer* many admirable things which were left untouch'd by *Virgil*, and from *Virgil* himself where *Homer* cou'd not furnish him. Yet the bodies of *Virgil's* and *Tasso's* Poems were their own: and so are all the Ornaments of language and elocution in them. The same (if there were any thing commendable in this Play) I could say for it. But I will come nearer to our own Countrymen. Most of *Shakespear's* Playes, I mean the Stories of them, are to be found in the *Hecatommithi*, or hundred Novels of *Cinthio*. I have, my self, read in his *Italian*, that of *Romeo and Juliet*, the *Moor of Venice*, and many others of them. *Beaumont* and *Fletcher* had most of theirs from *Spanish Novels*: witness the *Chances*, the *Spanish Curate*, *Rule a Wife and have a Wife*, the *Little French Lawyer*, and so many others of them as compose the greatest part of their Volume in folio. *Ben. Johnson*, indeed, has design'd his Plots himself; but no man has borrow'd so much from the Ancients as he has done: And he did well in it, for he has thereby beautifi'd our language.

330

335

340

345

350

355

360

365

370

331–32 *Feign'd Astrologer*] See the introduction to this play for comments on the sources.

337 *Walk*] course of action.

362 *Romeo and Juliet*] Dryden may have seen the tale in Bandello's *Nouvelle*, but not in Cinthio.

But these little Criticks do not well consider what is the work of a Poet, and what the Graces of a Poem. The Story is the least part of either: I mean the foundation of it, before it is modell'd by the art of him who writes it; who formes it
375 with more care, by exposing only the beautiful parts of it to view, than a skilful Lapidary sets a Jewel. On this foundation of the Story the Characters are rais'd: and, since no Story can afford Characters enough for the variety of the *English* Stage, it follows that it is to be alter'd, and inlarg'd, with new
380 persons, accidents, and designes, which wil almost make it new. When this is done, the forming it into Acts, and Scenes, disposing of actions and passions into their proper places, and beautifying both with descriptions, similitudes, and propriety of language, is the principal employment of the Poet; as
385 being the largest field of fancy, which is the principall quality requir'd in him: For so much the word ποιητὴς imployes. Judgement, indeed, is necessary in him; but 'tis fancy that gives the life touches, and the secret graces to it; especially in serious Plays, which depend not much on
390 observation. For to write humour in Comedy (which is the theft of Poets from mankind) little of fancy is requir'd; the Poet observes only what is ridiculous, and pleasant folly, and by judging exactly what is so, he pleases in the representation of it.

395 But in general, the employment of a Poet, is like that of a curious Gunsmith, or Watchmaker: the Iron or Silver is not his own; but they are the least part of that which gives the value: The price lyes wholly in the workmanship. And he who works dully on a Story, without moving laughter in a
400 Comedy, or raising concernments in a serious Play, is no more to be accounted a good Poet, than a Gunsmith of the *Minories* is to be compar'd with the best workman of the Town.

But I have said more of this than I intended; and more, perhaps, than I needed to have done: I shall but laugh at them
405 hereafter, who accuse me with so little reason; and withall contemn their dulness, who, if they could ruine that little reputation I have got, and which I value not, yet would want both wit and learning to establish their own; or to be remem-berd in after ages for any thing, but only that which makes
410 them ridiculous in this.

386 ποιητὴς] poet, maker.
387 *imployes*] i.e., implies.
401 *Gunsmith . . . Minories*] The Minories was a street in the City of London occupied by gunsmiths. Dryden implies inferior workmen came from there.

Persons Represented

MEN

Wildblood,⎫
Bellamy, ⎬ Two young English Gentlemen.
Maskall, Their Servant.
Don Alonzo de Ribera, an old Spanish Gentleman.
Don Lopez de Gamboa, a young Noble Spaniard.
Don Melchor de Guzman, A Gentleman of a great Family; but of a decay'd fortune.

WOMEN

Donna Theodosia,⎫
Donna Jacinta, ⎬ Daughters to *Don Alonzo.*
Donna Aurelia, Their Cousin.
Beatrix, Woman and Confident to the two Sisters.
Camilla, Woman to *Aurelia.*

Servants to *Don Lopez,* and *Don Alonzo.*

The Scene *Madrid,* in the Year 1665.

The Time the last Evening of the Carnival.

The original cast listed in Q1 supplemented by Downes: *Wildblood,* Charles Hart; *Bellamy,* Michael Mohun; *Maskall,* Robert Shatterel; *Alonzo,* William Wintershall; *Lopez,* Nicholas Burt; *Melchor,* Edward Lydall; *Theodosia,* Margaret Hughes, later Elizabeth Boutell; *Jacinta,* Nell Gwyn; *Aurelia,* Anne Marshall Quin, and later, Rebecca Marshall; *Beatrix,* Mrs. Knep; *Camilla,* Betty Slade.

Prologue

When first our Poet set himself to write,
Like a young Bridegroom on his Wedding-night
He layd about him, and did so bestir him,
His Muse could never lye in quiet for him:
But now his Honey-moon is gone and past,
Yet the ungrateful drudgery must last:
And he is bound, as civil Husbands do,
To strain himself, in complaisance to you:
To write in pain, and counterfeit a bliss,
Like the faint smackings of an after kiss.
But you, like Wives ill pleas'd, supply his want;
Each writing Monsieur is a fresh Gallant:
And though, perhaps, 'twas done as well before,
Yet still there's something in a new amour.
Your several Poets work with several tools,
One gets you wits, another gets you fools:
This pleases you with some by-stroke of wit,
This finds some cranny that was never hit.
But should these janty Lovers daily come
To do your work, like your good man at home,
Their fine small-timber'd wits would soon decay;
These are Gallants but for a Holiday.
Others you had who oftner have appear'd,
Whom, for meer impotence you have cashier'd:
Such as at first came on with pomp and glory,
But, overstraining, soon fell flat before yee.
Their useless weight with patience long was born,
But at the last you threw 'em off with scorn.
As for the Poet of this present night,
Though now he claims in you an Husband's right,
He will not hinder you of fresh delight.
He, like a Seaman, seldom will appear;
And means to trouble home but thrice a year:
That only time from your Gallants he'll borrow;
Be kind to day, and Cuckold him to morrow.

5

10

15

20

25

30

35

19 *janty*] genteel.

194

An Evening's Love,
or the
Mock-Astrologer

ACT I. SCENE I

Don Lopez, *and a Servant, walking over the Stage.*
Enter another Servant, and follows him.

Servant. Don *Lopez?*
Lopez. Any new business?
Servant. My Master had forgot this Letter;
    Which he conjures you, as you are his friend,
    To give *Aurelia* from him.   5
Lopez. Tell *Don Melchor* 'tis a hard task which he enjoyns
    me:
    He knows I love her, and much more than he;
    For I love her alone, but he divides
    His passion betwixt two. Did he consider
    How great a pain 'tis to dissemble love,   10
    He would never practise it.
Servant. He knows his fault; but cannot mend it.
Lopez. To make the poor *Aurelia* believe
    He's gone for *Flanders,* whiles he lies conceal'd,
    And every night makes visits to her Cousin.   15
    When will he leave this strange extravagance?
Servant. When he can love one more, or t'other less.
Lopez. Before I lov'd my self, I promis'd him
    To serve him in his love; and I'll perform it,
    How e're repugnant to my own concernments.   20
Servant. You are a noble Cavalier.   *Exit Servant.*

    Enter Bellamy, Wildblood, Maskall.

2nd Servant. Sir, your Guests of the *English* Embassador's
    Retinue.
Lopez. Cavaliers, will you please to command my Coach
    to take the air this Evening?   25
Bellamy. We have not yet resolv'd how to dispose of our
    selves; but however we are highly acknowledging to
    you for your civility.
Lopez. You cannot more oblige me then by laying your
    commands on me.   30

Wildblood. We kiss your hands.   *Exit* Lopez *cum Servo.*

Bellamy. Give the Don his due, he entertain'd us nobly this
Carnival.

Wildblood. Give the Devil the Don for any thing I lik'd in
his Entertainment.

Bellamy. I hope we had variety enough.

Wildblood. I, it look'd like variety, till we came to taste it;
there were twenty several dishes to the eye, but in the
pallat nothing but Spices. I had a mind to eat of a
Pheasant, and as soon as I got it into my mouth, I found
I was chawing a limb of Cinamon; then I went to cut
a piece of Kid, and no sooner it had touch'd my lips,
but it turn'd to red Pepper: at last I began to think my
self another kind of *Midas*, that every thing I touch'd
should be turn'd to Spice.

Bellamy. And for my part, I imagin'd his Catholick
Majesty had invited us to eat his *Indies*. But prethee let's
leave the discourse of it, and contrive together how we
may spend the Evening; for in this hot Country, 'tis as
in the Creation, the Evening and the Morning make the
Day.

Wildblood. I have a little serious business.

Bellamy. Put it off till a fitter season: for the truth is,
business is then only tollerable, when the world and the
flesh have no baits to set before us for the day.

Wildblood. But mine perhaps is publick business.

Bellamy. Why, is any business more publick than drinking
and wenching? Look on those grave plodding fellows,
that pass by us as though they were meditating the
reconquest of *Flanders*: fly 'em to a Mark, and I'll undertake three parts of four are going to their Courtezans.
I tell thee, *Jack*, the whisking of a Silk-Gown, and the
rash of a Tabby-Pettycoat, are as comfortable sounds
to one of these rich Citizens, as the chink of their
Pieces of Eight.

Wildblood. This being granted to be the common design of
humane kind, 'tis more than probable 'tis yours; therefore I'll leave you to the prosecution of it.

Bellamy. Nay, good *Jack*, mine is but a Mistress in Embrio;
the possession of her is at least some ten dayes off, and
till that time, thy company will be pleasant, and may be
profitable to carry on the work. I would use thee like
an under kind of Chymist, to blow the coals; 'twill be

60 *fly . . . Mark*] a hawking expression; let 'em loose to find
their quarry.
63 *rash . . . Pettycoat*] the rustle of a taffeta pettycoat.

time enough for me to be alone when I come to pro-
jection.   75
Wildblood. You must excuse me, *Franck*; I have made an
appointment at the Gameing-house.
Bellamy. What to do there I prethee? To mis-spend that
money which kind fortune intended for a Mistress? or
to learn new Oaths and Curses to carry into *England*?   80
That is not it. —— I heard you were to marry when
you left home: perhaps that may be still running in
your head, and keep you vertuous.
Wildblood. Marriage quoth a! what, dost thou think I have
been bred in the Desarts of *Africk*, or among the Savages   85
of *America*? nay, if I had, I must needs have known
better things than so; the light of Nature would not
have let me gone so far astray.
Bellamy. Well! what think you of the *Prado* this Evening?
Wildblood. Pox upon't, 'tis worse than our contemplative   90
Hide-Park.
Bellamy. O! but we must submit to the Custom of the
Country for courtship: what ever the means are, we
are sure the end is still the same in all places. But who
are these?   95

> *Enter* Don Alonzo de Ribera, *with his two Daughters*
> Theodosia *and* Jacinta, *and* Beatrix *their Woman,*
> *passing by.*

Theodosia. Do you see those strangers, Sister, that eye us
so earnestly?
Jacinta. Yes, and I guess 'em to be feathers of the *English*
Embassador's Train; for I think I saw 'em at the grand
Audience. —— And have the strangest temptation in   100
the world to talk to 'em: A mischief on this modesty.
Beatrix. A mischief of this Father of yours that haunts you
so.
Jacinta. 'Tis very true *Beatrix*; for though I am the younger
Sister, I should have the grace to lay modesty first aside: 105
however, Sister, let us pull up our Vails and give 'em
an Essay of our faces.
> *They pull up their Vails, and pull 'em down agen.*
Wildblood. Ah *Bellamy*! undone, undone! dost thou see
those Beauties?

74–75 *projection*] change. The whole sentence is an analogy with
alchemy. The term *projection* means literally that moment when the
alchemist casts the powder of projection upon a metal to transmute it
into gold.
98 *feathers*] beaus, gallants.

110   *Bellamy.* Prethee *Wildblood* hold thy tongue, and do not
         spoil my contemplation; I am undoing my self as fast
         as e're I can too.
         Wildblood. I must go to 'em.
         Bellamy. Hold Madman; dost thou not see their father?

115   hast thou a mind to have our throats cut?
         Wildblood. By a Hector of fourscore? Hang our throats;
         what, a Lover and cautious?   *Is going towards them.*
         Alonzo. Come away Daughters, we shall be late else.
         Bellamy. Look you, they are on the wing already.

120   *Wildblood.* Prethee, dear *Frank*, let's follow 'em: I long to
         know who they are.
         Maskall. Let me alone, I'll dog 'em for you.
         Bellamy. I am glad on't, for my shooes so pinch me, I can
         scarce go a step farther.

125   *Wildblood.* Cross the way there lives a Shoomaker: away
         quickly, that we may not spoil our man's design.
                            Exeunt Bellamy, Wildblood.
         Alonzo (offers to go off). Now friend! what's your business
         to follow us?
         Maskall. Noble *Don*; 'tis only to recommend my service

130   to you: A certain violent passion I have had for your
         worship since the first moment that I saw you.
         Alonzo. I never saw thee before to my remembrance.
         Maskall. No matter Sir; true love never stands upon
         ceremony.

135   *Alonzo.* Prethee begone my sawcie companion, or I'll clap
         an Alguazile upon thy heels; I tell thee I have no need
         of thy service.
         Maskall. Having no servant of your own, I cannot in good
         manners leave you destitute.

140   *Alonzo.* I'll beat thee if thou follow'st me.
         Maskall. I am your Spaniel Sir, the more you beat me, the
         better I'll wait on you.
         Alonzo. Let me intreat thee to be gone; the boyes will
         hoot at me to see me follow'd thus against my will.

145   *Maskall.* Shall you and I concern our selves for what the
         Boyes do, Sir? Pray do you hear the news at Court?
         Alonzo. Prethee what's the news to thee or me?
         Maskall. Will you be at the next *Juego de cannas*?
         Alonzo. If I think good.

116 *Hector*] bully.
136 *Alguazile*] constable.
148 *Juego de cannas*] *juego de cané*, a gambling game played with
cards. Saintsbury, quoting "The flying skirmish of the darted cane"
(*Conquest of Granada*, Part I, I.i.10), says this refers to javelin play,
but I have been unable to find that meaning for *Juego de cannas*.

Maskall. Pray go on Sir, we can discourse as we walk   150
    together: And whither were you now a going, Sir?
Alonzo. To the Devil I think.
Maskall. O! not this year or two, Sir, by your age.
Jacinta. My Father was never so match'd for talking in all
    his life before; he who loves to hear nothing but him-   155
    self: Prethee, *Beatrix*, stay behind, and see what this
    impudent *Englishman* would have.
Beatrix. Sir! if you'll let my Master go, I'll be his pawn.
Maskall. Well, Sir, I kiss your hand, in hope to wait on
    you another time.   160
Alonzo. Let us mend our pace to get clear of him.
Theodosia. If you do not, he'll be with you agen, like
    Atalanta in the fable, and make you drop another of your
    golden Apples.
                   Exeunt Alonzo, Theodosia, Jacinta.
                   Maskall *whispers* Beatrix *the while.*
Beatrix. How much good language is here thrown away to   165
    make me betray my Ladies?
Maskall. If you will discover nothing of 'em, let me dis-
    course with you a little.
Beatrix. As little as you please.
Maskall. They are rich I suppose.   170
Beatrix. Now you are talking of them agen: but they are
    as rich, as they are fair.
Maskall. Then they have the *Indies*: well, but their Names
    my sweet Mistress.
Beatrix. Sweet Servant their Names are ——   175
Maskall. Their Names are —— out with it boldly ——
Beatrix. A secret not to be disclos'd.
Maskall. A secret say you? Nay, then I conjure you as you
    are a Woman tell it me.
Beatrix. Not a syllable.   180
Maskall. Why then as you are a Waiting-woman: as you
    are the Sieve of all your Ladies Secrets tell it me.
Beatrix. You lose your labour: nothing will strain through
    me.
Maskall. Are you so well stop'd i'th' bottom?   185
Beatrix. It was enjoyn'd me strictly as a Secret.
Maskall. Was it enjoyn'd thee strictly, and can'st thou hold
    it? Nay then thou art invincible: but, by that face, that
    more than ugly face, which I suspect to be under thy
    Vaile, disclose it to me.   190
Beatrix. By that Face of thine, which is a Natural Visor: I
    will not tell thee.

191 *Visor*] mask.

Maskall. By thy ———

Beatrix. No more Swearing I beseech you.

195 *Maskall.* That Woman's worth little that is not worth an Oath: well, get thee gone, now I think on't thou shalt not tell me.

Beatrix. Shall I not? Who shall hinder me? They are *Don Alonzo de Ribera's* Daughters.

200 *Maskall.* Out, out: I'le stop my Eares.

Beatrix. ——— They live hard by, in the *Calle major.*

Maskall. O infernal Tongue ———

Beatrix. And are going to the next Chappel with their Father.

205 *Maskall.* Wilt thou never have done tormenting me? in my Conscience anon thou wilt blab out their Names too.

Beatrix. Their Names are *Theodosia* and *Jacinta.*

Maskall. And where's your great Secret now?

Beatrix. Now I think I am reveng'd on you for running 210 down my poor old Master.

Maskall. Thou art not fully reveng'd till thou hast told me thy own Name too.

Beatrix. 'Tis *Beatrix*, at your service, Sir, pray remember I wait on 'em.

215 *Maskall.* Now I have enough, I must be going.

Beatrix. I perceive you are just like other Men; when you have got your ends you care not how soon you are going. ——— ——— Farewell, ——— you'l be constant to me ———

220 *Maskall.* If thy face, when I see it, do not give me occasion to be otherwise.

Beatrix. You shall take a Sample that you may praise it when you see it next.   *She pulls up her Vail.*

Enter Wildblood *and* Bellamy.

Wildblood. Look, there's your Dog with a Duck in's 225 mouth. ——— Oh she's got loose and div'd again.———
                                                    Exit Beatrix.

Bellamy. Well *Maskall*, What newes of the Ladies of the Lake?

Maskall. I have learn'd enough to embarque you in an Adventure; they are Daughters to one *Don Alonzo de* 230 *Ribera* in the *Calle major*, their Names *Theodosia* and *Jacinta*, and they are going to their Devotions in the next Chappel.

---

201 *Calle major*] Calle Mayor, a street near the center of Madrid, and the resort of gallants.

Wildblood. Away then, let us lose no time, I thank Heaven
I never found my self better enclin'd to Godliness than
at this present. ———   235

Exeunt.

[ACT I.] SCENE 2

A Chappel

Enter Alonzo, Theodosia, Jacinta, Beatrix, *other* Ladies
and Cavaliers *as at their Devotion.*

Alonzo. By that time you have told your Beads I'll be agen
with you.   *Exit.*
Jacinta. Do you think the *English* Men will come after us?
Beatrix. Do you think they can stay from you?
Jacinta. For my part I feel a certain qualm upon my heart,   5
which makes me believe I am breeding Love to one of
'em.
Theodosia. How, Love, *Jacinta*, in so short a time? *Cupid's*
Arrow was well feather'd to reach you so suddenly.
Jacinta. Faith as good at first as at last Sister, 'tis a thing that   10
must be done, and therefore 'tis best dispatching it out
o'th' way.
Theodosia. But you do not mean to tell him so whom you
love?
Jacinta. Why should I keep my self and Servant in pain for   15
that which may be cur'd at a dayes warning?
Beatrix. My Lady tells you true, Madam, long tedious
Courtship may be proper for cold Countries, where
their Frosts are long a thawing; but Heaven be prais'd
we live in a warm Climate.   20
Theodosia. The truth is, in other Countries they have opportunities for Courtship, which we have not; they are not
mew'd up with double Locks and Grated Windows,
but may receive Addresses at their leisure.
Jacinta. But our Love here is like our Grass; if it be not   25
mow'd quickly 'tis burnt up.

Enter Bellamy, Wildblood, Maskall: *they look
about 'em.*

Theodosia. Yonder are your Gallants, send you comfort of
'em: I am for my Devotions.
Jacinta. Now for my heart can I think of no other Prayer,
but only that they may not mistake us. ——— Why   30
Sister, Sister, ——— will you Pray? What injury have

201

I ever done you, that you should Pray in my company?
If your servant *Don Melchor* were here, we should have
you mind Heaven as little as the best on's.

35   *Beatrix.* They are at a loss, Madam, shall I put up my Vail
that they may take aime?

Jacinta. No, let 'em take their Fortune in the dark: we shall
see what Archers these *English* are.

Bellamy. Which are they think'st thou?

40   *Wildblood.* There's no knowing them, they are all Children
of darkness.

Bellamy. I'll besworn they have one sign of Godliness
among 'em, there's no distinction of persons here.

Wildblood. Pox o'this blind-man's-buffe; they may be

45   asham'd to provoke a man thus by their keeping themselves so close.

Bellamy. You are for the youngest you say; 'tis the eldest
has smitten me. And here I fix; if I am right ——— happy
man be his dole.   *By* Theodosia.

50   *Wildblood.* I'll take my fortune here.   *By* Jacinta.
Madam, I hope a stranger may take the libertie without
offence to offer his devotions by you.

Jacinta. That, Sir, would interrupt mine, without being any
advantage to your own.

55   *Wildblood.* My advantage, Madam, is very evident; for the
kind Saint to whom you pray, may by the neighbour-
hood mistake my devotions for yours.

Jacinta. O Sir! our Saints can better distinguish between the
prayers of a Catholick and a Lutheran.

60   *Wildblood.* I beseech you, Madam, trouble not your self
for my Religion; for though I am a Heretick to the men
of your Country, to your Ladies I am a very zealous
Catholick: and for fornication and adulterie, I assure
you I hold with both Churches.

65   *Theodosia (to Bellamy).* Sir, if you will not be more devout,
be at least more civil, you see you are observ'd.

Bellamy. And pray, Madam, what do you think the lookers
on imagine I am imploy'd about?

Theodosia. I will not trouble my self to guess.

70   *Bellamy.* Why, by all circumstances, they must conclude
that I am making love to you: and methinks it were
scarce civil to give the opinion of so much good company the lye.

Theodosia. If this were true, you would have little reason

75   to thank 'em for their Divination.

Bellamy. Meaning I should not be lov'd again.

Theodosia. You have interpreted my riddle, and may take
it for your pains.

Enter Alonzo, (*and goes apart to his devotion.*)

Beatrix. Madam, your Father is return'd.

Bellamy. She has nettled me, would I could be reveng'd on   80
her.

Wildblood. Do you see their Father? let us make as though
we talk'd to one another, that we may not be suspected.

Beatrix. You have lost your *Englishmen*.

Jacinta. No, no, 'tis but design I warrant you: you shall see   85
these Island Cocks wheel about immediately.

Beatrix. Perhaps they thought they were observ'd.

    The English gather up close to them.

Wildblood (*to Bellamy*). Talk not of our Countrie Ladies: I
declare my self for the *Spanish* Beauties.

Bellamy. Prethee tell me what thou canst find to doat on in   90
these *Castilians*.

Wildblood. Their wit and beauty.

Theodosia. Now for our Champion St. *Jago* for *Spain* there.

Bellamy. Faith I can speak no such miracles of either; for
their beautie 'tis much as the *Moores* left it; not altogether   95
so deep a black as the true *Æthiopian*: A kind of beautie
that is too civil to the lookers on to do them any mischief.

Jacinta. This was your frowardness that provok'd him,
Sister.   100

Theodosia. But they shall not carry it off so.

Bellamy. As for their wit, you may judge it by their
breeding, which is commonly in a Nunnerie; where the
want of mankind while they are there, makes them value
the blessing ever after.   105

Theodosia. Prethee dear *Jacinta* tell me, what kind of
creatures were those we saw yesterday at the Audience?
Those I mean that look'd so like *Frenchmen* in their
habits, but only became their Apishness so much worse.

Jacinta. Englishmen I think they call'd 'em.   110

Theodosia. Crie you mercy; they were of your wild *English*
indeed, that is a kind of Northern Beast, that is taught
its feats of activity in *Monsieurland*, and for doing 'em
too lubberly, is laugh'd at all the world over.

Bellamy. Wildblood, I perceive the women understand little   115
of discourse; their Gallants do not use 'em to't: they get
upon their Gennits, and prance before their Ladies
windows; there the Palfray curvets and bounds, and in
short entertains 'em for his Master.

93 *St. Jago*] St. James of Compostella, whose spirit rallied the
Spanish to fight for independence from the Moors.
114 *lubberly*] clumsily.

120   *Wildblood.* And this horse-play they call making love.
     Beatrix. Your Father, Madam ———
     Alonzo. Daughters! what Cavaliers are those which were
     talking by you?
     Jacinta. Englishmen, I believe Sir, at their devotions:
125   Cavalier, would you would try to pray a little better
     then you have railly'd.   *Aside to* Wildblood.
     Wildblood. Hang me if I put all my devotions out of order
     for you: I remember I pray'd but on Tuesday last, and
     my time comes not till Tuesday next.
130   *Maskall.* You had as good pray, Sir; she will not stir till
     you have: Say any thing.
     Wildblood. Fair Lady, though I am not worthy of the least
     of your favours, yet give me the happiness this Evening
     to see you at your father's door, that I may acquaint you
135   with part of my sufferings.   *Aside to* Jacinta.
     Alonzo. Come Daughters, have you done?
     Jacinta. Immediately Sir. ———
     Cavalier, I will not fail to be there at the time appointed,
     if it be but to teach you more wit, henceforward, then
140   to engage your heart so lightly.   *Aside to* Wildblood.
     Wildblood. I have engag'd my heart with so much zeal and
     true devotion to your divine beauty, that ———
     Alonzo. What means this Cavalier?
     Jacinta. Some zealous ejaculation.
145   *Alonzo.* May the Saint hear him.
     Jacinta. I'll answer for her. ———
                           Exeunt Father and Daughters.
     Wildblood. Now *Bellamy*, what success?
     Bellamy. I pray'd to a more Marble Saint than that was in
     the Shrine; but you, it seems, have been successful.
150   *Wildblood.* And so shalt thou; let me alone for both.
     Bellamy. If you'll undertake it, I will make bold to indulge
     my love; and within this two hours be a desperate
     Inamorado. I feel I am coming apace to it.
     Wildblood. Faith I can love at any time with a wish at my
155   rate: I give my heart according to the old law of pawns,
     to be return'd me before sun-set.
     Bellamy. I love only that I may keep my heart warm; for
     a man's a pool if love stir him not; and to bring it to
     that pass, I first resolve whom to love, and presently

155 *law of pawns*] "if thou at all take thy neighbor's raiment
to pledge, thou shalt deliver it unto him by that the sun goeth
down: for that is his covering only, it is his raiment for his skin:
wherein shall he sleep?" (*Exodus* 22: 26–27).
158 *pool*] dormant as a calm pool, used as a synonym for "sleepy
vigour of the soul" in Dryden's "Cymon and Iphigenia," 27–30.

after imagine I am in love; for a strong imagination is 160
requir'd in a Lover as much as in a Witch.
Wildblood. And is this all your Receipt?
Bellamy. These are my principal ingredients; as for Piques,
Jealousies, Duels, Daggers, and Halters, I let 'em alone
to the vulgar. 165
Wildblood. Prethee let's round the street a little; till *Maskall*
watches for their Woman.
Bellamy. That's well thought on: he shall about it imme-
diately.
We will attempt the Mistress by the Maid: 170
Women by women still are best betray'd.

Exeunt.

ACT II. [SCENE 1]

[*Enter*] Wildblood, Bellamy, Maskall.

Wildblood. Did you speak with her Woman?
Maskall. Yes, but she was in hast, and bid me wait her
hereabouts when she return'd.
Bellamy. Then you have discover'd nothing more?
Maskall. Only, in general, that *Donna Theodosia* is engag'd 5
elsewhere; so that all your Courtship will be to no
purpose.
(*To Wildblood*). But for your Mistress, Sir, she is waded
out of her depth in love to you already.
Wildblood. That's very hard, when I am scarce knee-deep 10
with her: 'tis true, I have given her hold of my heart,
but if she take not heed it will slip through her fingers.
Bellamy. You are Prince of the Soil, Sir, and may take your
pleasure when you please; but I am the Eve to your
Holy-day, and must fast for being joyn'd to you. 15
Wildblood. Were I as thou art, I would content my self
with having had one fair flight at her, without wearying
my self on the wing for a retrieve; for when all's done
the Quarry is but woman.
Bellamy. Thank you, Sir, you would fly 'em both your 20
self, and while I turn tail, we should have you come
gingling with your bells in the neck of my Patridge; do
you remember who incourag'd me to love, and promis'd me his assistance?
Wildblood. I, while there was hope *Frank*, while there was 25
hope; but there's no contending with one's destiny.
Bellamy. Nay, it may be I care as little for her as another

13 *Prince of the Soil*] owner of the estate.
22 *Patridge*] i.e., partridge.

205

man; but while she flies before me I must follow: I can leave a woman first with ease, but if she begins to fly before me, I grow opiniatre as the Devil.

Wildblood. What a secret have you found out? Why 'tis the nature of all mankind: we love to get our Mistresses, and purr over 'em, as Cats do over Mice, and then let 'em go a little way; and all the pleasure is, to pat 'em back again: But yours, I take it, *Frank*, is gone too far; prethee how long dost thou intend to love at this rate?

Bellamy. Till the evil constellation be past over me: yet I believe it would hasten my recovery if I knew whom she lov'd.

Maskall. You shall not be long without that satisfaction.

Wildblood. 'St, the door opens; and two women are coming out.

Bellamy. By their stature they should be thy gracious Mistress and *Beatrix*.

Wildblood. Methinks you should know your Q. then and withdraw.

Bellamy. Well, I'll leave you to your fortune; but if you come to close fighting, I shall make bold to run in and part you.

> Bellamy *and* Maskall *withdraw.*

Wildblood. Yonder she comes with full sails i'faith; I'll hail her amain for *England*.

> *Enter* Jacinta *and* Beatrix *at the other end of the Stage.*

Beatrix. You do love him then?

Jacinta. Yes, most vehemently.

Beatrix. But set some bounds to your affection.

Jacinta. None but fools confine their pleasure: what Usurer ever thought his Coffers held too much? No, I'll give my self the swinge, and love without reserve. If I'll keep a passion, I'll never starve it in my service.

Beatrix. But are you sure he will deserve this kindness?

Jacinta. I never trouble my self so long beforehand: Jealousies and disquiets are the dregs of an amour; but I'll leave mine before I have drawn it off so low: when it once grows troubled I'll give vent to a fresh draught.

Beatrix. Yet it is but prudence to try him first; no Pilot ventures on an unknown Coast without sounding.

Jacinta. Well, to satisfie thee I am content; partly too because I find a kind of pleasure in laying baits for him.

30 *opiniatre*] wilfull, obstinate.
41 *'St*] hush, whist.
45 *Q.*] cue.
57 *swinge*] complete freedom of action.

Beatrix. The two great vertues of a Lover are constancy
  and liberality; if he profess those two, you may be
  happy in him.   70
Jacinta. Nay, if he be not Lord and Master of both those
  qualities I disown him. ———— But who goes there?
Beatrix. He, I warrant you, Madam; for his Servant told
  me he was waiting hereabout.
Jacinta. Watch the door, give me notice if any come.   75
Beatrix. I'll secure you, Madam. ————   *Exit* Beatrix.
Jacinta (*to Wildblood*). What, have you laid an ambush for
  me?
Wildblood. Only to make a Reprisal of my heart.
Jacinta. 'Tis so wild, that the Lady who has it in her   80
  keeping, would be glad she were well rid on't: it does
  so flutter about the Cage. 'Tis a meer *Bajazet*; and if it
  be not let out the sooner, will beat out the brains
  against the Grates.
Wildblood. I am afraid the Lady has not fed it, and 'tis   85
  wild for hunger.
Jacinta. Or perhaps it wants company; shall she put
  another to it?
Wildblood. I; but then 'twere best to trust 'em out of the
  Cage together; let 'em hop about at libertie.   90
Jacinta. But if they should lose one another in the wide
  world!
Wildblood. They'll meet at night I warrant 'em.
Jacinta. But is not your heart of the nature of those Birds
  that breed in one Countrie, and goe to winter in   95
  another?
Wildblood. Suppose it does so; yet I take my Mate along
  with me. And now to leave our parables, and speak in
  the language of the vulgar, what think you of a voyage
  to merry *England*?   100
Jacinta. Just as *Æsop's* Frog did, of leaping into a deep Well
  in a drought: if he ventur'd the leap, there might be
  water; but if there were no water, how should he get
  out again?
Wildblood. Faith we live in a good honest Country, where   105
  we are content with our old vices, partly because we
  want wit to invent more new. A Colonie of *Spaniards*,
  or spiritual *Italians* planted among us would make us
  much more racy. 'Tis true, our variety is not much;
  but to speak nobly of our way of living, 'tis like that   110

82 *Bajazet*] Tamburlaine's prisoner who despairingly dashed his
head against the bars of his cage.

of the Sun, which rises, and looks upon the same things
he saw yesterday, and goes to bed again.

Jacinta. But I hear your women live most blessedly; there's
no such thing as jealousie among the Husbands; if any
115   man has horns, he bears 'em as loftily as a Stag, and as
inoffensively.

Wildblood. All this I hope gives you no ill Character of the
Country.

Jacinta. But what need we go into another Climate? as our
120   love was born here; so let it live and die here, and be
honestly buried in its native Country.

Wildblood. Faith agreed with all my heart. For I am none
of those unreasonable lovers, that propose to themselves the loving to eternity; the truth is, a month is
125   commonly my stint; but in that month I love so dread-
fully, that it is after a twelve-month's rate of common
love.

Jacinta. Or would not a fortnight serve our turn? for in
troth a month looks somewhat dismally; 'tis a whole
130   *Ægyptian* year. If a Moon changes in my love I shall
think my *Cupid* grown dull, or fallen into an Apoplexie.

Wildblood. Well, I pray heaven we both get off as clear as
we imagine; for my part I like your humour so damnably well, that I fear I am in for a week longer than I
135   propos'd; I am half afraid your *Spanish* Planet, and my
English one have been acquainted, and have found out
some by-room or other in the twelve houses: I wish
they have been honorable.

Jacinta. The best way for both were to take up in time; yet
140   I am afraid our forces are engag'd so far, that we must
make a battel on't. What think you of disobliging one
another from this day forward; and shewing all our ill
humours at the first; which Lovers use to keep as a
reserve till they are married?

145   *Wildblood.* Or let us encourage one another to a breach by
the dangers of possession: I have a Song to that purpose.

Jacinta. Pray let me hear it: I hope it will go to the tune of
one of our *Passa-calles*.

SONG

You charm'd me not with that fair face
150   *Though it was all divine:*

115 *loftily*] well, proudly.
130 *Ægyptian year*] the full 365-day year.
139 *take up*] make up, arrange our quarrel amicably.
148 *Passa-calles*] literally "walk the streets," a slow dance tune,
played by street musicians.

> To be another's is the Grace,
>   That makes me wish you mine.
> The Gods and Fortune take their part
>   Who like young Monarchs fight;
> And boldly dare invade that heart   155
>   Which is another's right.
> First mad with hope we undertake
>   To pull up every barr;
> But once possess'd, we faintly make
>   A dull defensive warr.   160
> Now every friend is turn'd a foe
>   In hope to get our store:
> And passion makes us Cowards grow,
>   Which made us brave before.

Jacinta. Believe it, Cavalier, you are a dangerous person: 165
do you hold forth your gifts in hopes to make me love
you less?

Wildblood. They would signifie little, if we were once
married: those gayeties are all nipt, and frost-bitten in
the Marriage-bed, i'faith.   170

Jacinta. I am sorry to hear 'tis so cold a place: but 'tis all
one to us who do not mean to trouble it: the truth is,
your humor pleases me exceedingly; how long it will
do so, I know not; but so long as it does, I am resolv'd
to give my self the content of seeing you. For if I should 175
once constrain my self, I might fall in love in good
earnest: but I have stay'd too long with you, and would
be loth to surfeit you at first.

Wildblood. Surfet me, Madam, why you have but Tanta-
liz'd me all this while.   180

Jacinta. What would you have?

Wildblood. A hand, or lip, or any thing that you can spare;
when you have Conjur'd up a Spirit he must have some
employment, or he'll tear you a pieces.

Jacinta. Well, Here's my Picture; to help your contempla-   185
tion in my absence.

Wildblood. You have already the Original of mine: but
some revenge you must allow me: a Locket of Dia-
monds, or some such trifle, the next time I kiss your
hand.   190

Jacinta. Fie, fie; you do not think me mercinary! Yet now
I think on't, I'll put you into our *Spanish* Mode of Love:
our Ladies here use to be the Banquiers of their Servants,
and to have their Gold in keeping.

195   *Wildblood.* This is the least trial you could have made of me:
I have some three hundred Pistols by me; those I'll send
you by my servant.

    Jacinta. Confess freely; you mistrust me: but if you find
the least qualme about your Gold, pray keep it for a
200   Cordial.

    Wildblood. The Cordial must be apply'd to the heart, and
mine's with you Madam. Well; I say no more; but
these are dangerous beginings for holding on: I find my
moneth will have more then one and thirty dayes in't.

Enter Beatrix *running*.

205   *Beatrix.* Madam, your Father calls in hast for you; and is
looking you about the house.

    Jacinta. Adieu Servant, be a good manager of your stock
of Love, that it may hold out your Moneth; I am afraid
you'll wast so much of it before to morrow night, that
210   you'll shine but with a quarter Moon upon me.

    Wildblood. It shall be a Crescent.

Exit Wildblood, Jacinta *severally*,
Beatrix *is going, and* Maskall *runs and stops her*.

    Maskall. Pay your ransome; you are my Prisoner.

    Beatrix. What, do you fight after the *French* Fashion; take
Towns before you declare a Warr?

215   *Maskall.* I should be glad to imitate them so far, to be in
the middle of the Country before you could resist me.

    Beatrix. Well, what composition Monsieur?

    Maskall. Deliver up your Lady's secret; what makes her so
cruel to my Master?

220   *Beatrix.* Which of my Ladies, and which of your Masters?
For I suppose we are Factors for both of them.

    Maskall. Your eldest Lady, *Theodosia*.

    Beatrix. How dare you press your Mistress to an incon-
venience?

225   *Maskall.* My Mistress? I understand not that language; the
fortune of the Valet ever follows that of the Master;
and his is desperate; if his fate were alter'd for the better,
I should not care if I ventur'd upon you for the worse.

    Beatrix. I have told you already *Donna Theodosia* loves
230   another.

    Maskall. Has he no name?

---

196 *Pistols*] quarter doubloons, each worth about $4.00.
200 *Cordial*] a medicine which stimulates the heart.
213 *French Fashion*] possibly a reference to Louis XIV's military
adventures in the Low Countries.
217 *composition*] terms of surrender.

Beatrix. Let it suffice he is born noble, though without a
fortune. His povertie makes him conceal his love from
her Father; but she sees him every night in private: and
to blind the world about a fortnight agoe, he took a   235
solemn leave of her, as if he were going into *Flanders*:
in the mean time he lodges at the house of *Don Lopez
de Gamboa*; and is himself call'd *Don Melchor de Guzman*.

Maskall. Don Melchor de Guzman! O heavens!

Beatrix. What amazes you!   240

Theodosia (within). Why, *Beatrix*, where are you?

Beatrix. You hear I am call'd; Adieu; and be sure you keep
my Counsel.   *Exit* Beatrix.

Maskall. Come, Sir, you see the Coast is clear.

Enter Bellamy.

Bellamy. Clear, dost thou say? no 'tis full of Rocks and   245
Quicksands: yet nothing vexes me so much as that she
is in love with such a poor Rogue.

Maskall. But that he should lodge privately in the same
house with us! 'twas odly contriv'd of fortune.

Bellamy. Hang him Rogue, methinks I see him perching   250
like an Owle by day, and not daring to flutter out till
Moon-light. The Rascal invents love, and brews his
complements all day, and broaches 'em at night; just
as some of our dry wits do their stories before they come
into company. Well, if I could be reveng'd on either   255
of 'em.

Maskall. Here she comes again with *Beatrix*; but good Sir
moderate your passion.

Enter Theodosia *and* Beatrix.

Bellamy. Nay, Madam, you are known; and must not pass
till I have spoke with you.   260
                    Bellamy *lifts up* Theodosia's *Vail.*

Theodosia. This rudeness to a person of my quality may
cost you dear. Pray when did I give you encouragement
for so much familiarity?

Bellamy. When you scorn'd me in the Chappel.

Theodosia. The truth is, I deny'd you as heartily as I could;   265
that I might not be twice troubled with you.

Bellamy. Yet you have not this aversion for all the world:
however I was in hope though the day frown'd, the
night might prove as propitious to me as it is to others.

Theodosia. I have now a quarrell both to the Sun and Moon,   270
because I have seen you by both their lights.

Bellamy. Spare the Moon I beseech you, Madam, she is a
very trusty Planet to you.

Beatrix. O *Maskall* you have ruin'd me.

275 *Maskall.* Dear Sir, hold yet.

Bellamy. Away.

Theodosia. Pray, Sir, expound your meaning; for I confess
I am in the dark.

Bellamy. Methinks you should discover it by Moon-light.

280 Or if you would have me speak clearer to you, give me
leave to wait on you at a midnight assignation; and
that it may not be discover'd, I'll feign a voyage beyond
sea, as if I were gone a Captaining to *Flanders.*

Maskall. A pox on's memory, he has not forgot one

285 syllable.

Theodosia. Ah *Beatrix*, you have betray'd and sold me.

Beatrix. You have betray'd and sold your self, Madam,
by your own rashness to confess it; Heaven know's I
have serv'd you but too faithfully.

290 *Theodosia.* Peace, impudence; and see my face no more.

Maskall. Do you know what work you have made, Sir?

Bellamy. Let her see what she has got by slighting me.

Maskall. You had best let *Beatrix* be turn'd away for me to
keep: if you do, I know whose purse shall pay for't.

295 *Bellamy.* That's a curse I never thought on: cast about
quickly and save all yet. Range, quest, and spring a lie
immediately.

Theodosia (to Beatrix). Never importune me farther; you
shall go; there's no removing me.

300 *Beatrix (going).* Well; this is ever the reward of innocence.

Maskall. Stay, guiltless Virgin, stay; thou shalt not go.

Theodosia. Why, who should hinder it?

Maskall. That will I in the name of truth. (If this hard-
bound lie would but come from me:) Madam, I must

305 tell you it lies in my power to appease this tempest with
one word.

Beatrix. Would it were come once.

Maskall. Nay, Sir, 'tis all one to me, if you turn me away
upon't; I can hold no longer.

310 *Theodosia.* What does the fellow mean?

Maskall. For all your noddings, and your Mathematical
grimaces, in short, Madam, my Master has been conversing with the Planets; and from them has had the
knowledge of your affairs.

315 *Bellamy.* This Rogue amazes me.

Maskall. I care not, Sir, I am for truth; that will shame you
and all your Devils: in short, Madam, this Master of
mine that stands before you, without a word to say for

himself, so like an Oph, as I may say with reverence to
him ——— 320

Bellamy. The Raskal makes me mad.

Maskall. Is the greatest *Astrologer* in Christendome.

Theodosia. Your Master an *Astrologer*?

Maskall. A most profound one.

Bellamy. Why you dog, do you consider what an improb- 325
able lie this is; which you know I can never make good:
disgorge it you Cormorant, or I'll pinch your throat
out. ——— *Takes him by the throat.*

Maskall. 'Tis all in vain, Sir, you are and shall be an
Astrologer what e're I suffer: you know all things, see 330
into all things, foretell all things; and if you pinch more
truth out of me, I will confess you are a Conjurer.

Bellamy. How, sirrah, a Conjurer?

Maskall. I mean, Sir, the Devil is in your fingers: own it
you had best, Sir, and do not provoke me farther; 335
what, did not I see you an hour ago, turning over a
great Folio with strange figures in it, and then muttering
to your self like any Poet, and then naming *Theodosia*,
and then staring up in the skie, and then poring upon
the ground; so that betwixt God and the Devil, Madam, 340
he came to know your love.

While he is speaking, Bellamy *stops his mouth by fits.*

Bellamy. Madam, if ever I knew the least term in Astrologie, I am the arrantest Son of a whore breathing.

Beatrix. O, Sir, for that matter you shall excuse my Lady:
Nay hide your tallents if you can, Sir. 345

Theodosia. The more you pretend ignorance, the more we
are resolv'd to believe you skilfull.

Bellamy. You'll hold your tongue yet.

Maskall. You shall never make me hold my tongue, except
you conjure me to silence: what, did you not call me to 350
look into a Chrystal, and there shew'd me a fair Garden,
and a *Spaniard* stalking in his narrow breeches, and
walking underneath a window; I should know him agen
amongst a thousand.

Beatrix. Don Melchor, in my conscience, Madam. 355

Bellamy. This Rogue will invent more stories of me, than
e're were father'd upon *Lilly*.

Maskall. Will you confess then; do you think I'll stain my
honor to swallow a lie for you?

Bellamy. Well, a pox on you, I am an Astrologer. 360

319 *Oph*] i.e., oaf.
357 *Lilly*] William Lilly (1602–81), astrologer.

213

Beatrix. O, are you so, Sir?

Theodosia. I hope then, learned Sir, as you have been curious in enquiring into my secrets, you will be so much a Cavalier as to conceal 'em.

365 *Bellamy.* You need not doubt me, Madam; I am more in your power than you can be in mine: besides, if I were once known in Town, the next thing, for ought I know, would be to bring me before the fathers of the Inquisition.

370 *Beatrix.* Well, Madam, what do you think of me now; I have betray'd you, I have sold you; how can you ever make me amends for this imputation? I did not think you could have us'd me so. ————

Cries and claps her hands at her.

Theodosia. Nay, prethee *Beatrix* do not crie; I'll leave of
375 my new Gown to morrow, and thou shalt have it.

Beatrix. No, I'll crie eternally; you have taken away my good name from me; and you can never make me recompence ———— except you give me your new Gorget too.

380 *Theodosia.* No more words; thou shalt have it Girle.

Beatrix. O, Madam, your Father has surpriz'd us!

Enter Don Alonzo, *and frowns.*

Bellamy. Then I'll begone to avoid suspicion.

Theodosia. By your favour, Sir, you shall stay a little; the happiness of so rare an acquaintance, ought to be
385 cherish'd on my side by a longer conversation.

Alonzo. Theodosia, what business have you with this Cavalier?

Theodosia. That, Sir, which will make you as ambitious of being known to him as I have been: under the habit of
390 a Gallant he conceals the greatest *Astrologer* this day living.

Alonzo. You amaze me Daughter.

Theodosia. For my own part I have been consulting with him about some particulars of my fortunes past and
395 future; both which he has resolv'd me with that admirable knowledge ————

Bellamy. Yes, faith, Sir, I was foretelling her of a disaster that severely threatn'd her: ———— and (one thing I foresee already by my starrs, that I must bear up boldly,
400 or I am lost.)

379 *Gorget*] an article of feminine dress which covers the throat. Perhaps a wimple.

Maskall (to Bellamy). Never fear him, Sir; he's an ignorant
fellow, and credulous I warrant him.

Alonzo. Daughter be not too confident in your belief;
there's nothing more uncertain than the cold Prophecies
of these *Nostradamusses*; but of what nature was the   405
question which you ask'd him?

Theodosia. What should be my fortune in marriage.

Alonzo. And, pray, what did you answer, Sir?

Bellamy. I answer'd her the truth, that she is in danger of
marrying a Gentleman without a fortune.   410

Theodosia. And this, Sir, has put me into such a fright ——

Alonzo. Never trouble your self about it, Daughter;
follow my advice and I warrant you a rich Husband.

Bellamy. But the starrs say she shall not follow your advice:
if it happens otherwise I'll burn my folio Volumes, and   415
my Manuscripts too, I assure you that, Sir.

Alonzo. Be not too confident, young man; I know somewhat in *Astrologie* my self; for in my younger years I
study'd it; and though I say it, made some small pro-
ficience in it.   420

Bellamy (aside). Marry Heaven forbid. ——

Alonzo. And I could only find it was no way demonstrative, but altogether fallacious.

Maskall. On what a Rock have we split our selves!

Bellamy. Now my ignorance will certainly come out!   425

Beatrix. Sir, remember you are old and crazie, Sir; and if
the Evening Air should take you —— beseech you
Sir retire.

Alonzo. Knowledge is to be prefer'd before health; I must
needs discusse a point with this learned Cavalier, con-   430
cerning a difficult question in that Art, which almost
gravels me.

Maskall. How I sweat for him, *Beatrix*, and my self too,
who have brought him into this *Præmunire*!

Beatrix. You must be impudent; for our old man will stick   435
like a burre to you, now he's in a dispute.

Alonzo. What Judgment may a man reasonably form from
the trine Aspect of the two Infortunes in Angular
houses?

405 *Nostradamusses*] after Michel Notre-Dame (1503–66), the most
famous judicial astrologer in Europe.
426 *crazie*] full of cracks and flaws; apt to break or fall to pieces.
432 *gravels*] confounds, perplexes.
434 *Præmunire*] predicament. See note on *Sir Martin Mar-All*.
438–39 *trine . . . houses*] "The trine aspect is the aspect of two
heavenly bodies which are a third part of the Zodiac, i.e., 120°, distant
from each other. An infortune is an infortunate or malevolent planet.
The two infortunes are Saturn and Mars" (Summers).

440   *Bellamy.* That's a matter of nothing, Sir; I'll turn my man
        loose to you for such a question.

                                            Puts Maskall *forward.*

    Alonzo. Come on, Sir, I am the quærent.

    Maskall. Meaning me, Sir! I vow to God, and your
        Worship knows it, I never made that Science my study
445   in the least, Sir.

    Bellamy. The gleanings of mine are enough for that: why,
        you impudent rogue you, hold forth your gifts, or
        I'll ———— What a devil must I be pester'd with every
        trivial question, when there's not a Master in Town of
450   any Science, but has his Usher for these mean offices?

    Theodosia. Trie him in some deeper question, Sir; you see
        he will not put himself forth for this.

    Alonzo. Then I'll be more abstruse with him: what think
        you, Sir, of the taking *Hyleg*? or of the best way of
455   rectification for a Nativity? have you been conversant
        in the *Centiloquium* of *Trismegistus*: what think you of
        Mars in the tenth when 'tis his own House, or of
        Jupiter configurated with malevolent Planets?

    Bellamy. I thought what your skill was! to answer your
460   question in two words, *Mars* rules over the Martial, and
        Jupiter over the Jovial; and so of the rest, Sir.

    Alonzo. This every School-boy could have told me.

    Bellamy. Why then you must not ask such School-boyes
        questions. (But your Carkase, Sirrah, shall pay for this.)
465   ————   *Aside to* Maskall.

    Alonzo. You seem not to understand the Terms, Sir.

    Bellamy. By your favour, Sir, I know there are five of 'em;
        do not I know your Michaelmas, your Hillary, your
        Easter, your Trinity, and your Long Vacation term,
470   Sir?

    Alonzo. I do not understand a word of this *Jargon.*

    Bellamy. It may be not, Sir; I believe the terms are not the
        same in *Spain* they are in *England.*

    Maskall. Did one ever hear so impudent an ignorance?
475   *Alonzo.* The terms of Art are the same every where.

    Bellamy. Tell me that! you are an old man, and they are
        alter'd since you studied them.

    442 *quærunt*] "that man or woman who propounds anything"
to an astrologer (William Lilly, *Christian Astrology*, VI, 49; cited by
Summers).

    454 *taking Hyleg*] "Hyleg is a nativity; the ruling planet of a
nativity" (Summers).

    455 *rectification*] setting right of the globe for a nativity.

    456 *Centiloquium of Trismegistus*] The Hundred Aphorisms
of Hermes Tristmegistus, presumed to have been written by the
god Thoth, in ancient Egypt.

Alonzo. That may be I must confess; however if you please
to discourse something of the Art to me, you shall
find me an apt Scholar.   480

Enter a Servant *to* Alonzo.

Servant. Sir, ———   *Whispers.*
Alonzo. Sir, I am sorry a business of importance calls me
hence; but I'll wait on you some other time, to discourse more at large of *Astrologie.*
Bellamy. Is your business very pressing?   485
Alonzo. It is, I assure you, Sir.
Bellamy. I am very sorry for I should have instructed you
in such rare secrets; I have no fault, but that I am too
communicative.
Alonzo. I'll dispatch my business, and return immediately; 490
come away Daughter.
               Exeunt Alonzo, Theodosia, Beatrix, *Servus.*
Bellamy. A Devil on's learning; he had brought me to my
last legs; I was fighting as low as ever was Squire
Widdrington.
Maskall. Who would have suspected it from that wicked   495
Elder?
Bellamy. Suspected it? why 'twas palpable from his very
Physnomy; he looks like *Haly*, and the spirit *Fircu* in
the Fortune-book.

Enter Wildblood.

Wildblood. How now *Bellamy*, in wrath? prethee, what's   500
the matter?
Bellamy. The story is too long to tell you; but this Rogue
here has made me pass for an errant Fortune-teller.
Maskall. If I had not, I am sure he must have past for an
errant Mad-man; he had discover'd, in a rage, all that   505
Beatrix had confess'd to me concerning her Mistresse's
love; and I had no other way to bring him off, but to
say he knew it by the Planets.
Wildblood. And art thou such an Oph to be vext at this?
As the adventure may be manag'd it may make the most   510
pleasant one in all the Carnival.

493–94 *Squire Widdrington*] Roger Widdrington, the hero of the old
ballad *Chevy Chase*, who fought on his stumps after his legs were
severed.

498–99 *Haly . . . Fortune-book*] A reference to Hali, the chief astro-
nomer at the court of Abul Abbas Abdallah Mamoun, A.D. 786–835.
Fircu is a name given to a familiar spirit mentioned in old almanacs
(Summers).

Bellamy. Death! I shall have all *Madrid* about me within these two dayes.

Wildblood. Nay, all *Spain*, i'faith, as fast as I can divulge
515   thee: not a Ship shall pass out from any Port, but shall ask thee for a wind; thou shalt have all the trade of *Lapland* within a Month.

Bellamy. And do you think it reasonable for me to stand defendant to all the impertinent questions that the Town
520   can ask me.

Wildblood. Thou shalt do't boy: pox on thee, thou dost not know thine own happiness; thou wilt have the Ladies come to thee; and if thou dost not fit them with fortunes, thou art bewitch'd.

525   *Maskall.* Sir, 'tis the easiest thing in Nature; you need but speak doubtfully, or keep your self in general terms, and for the most part tell good rather than bad fortune.

Wildblood. And if at any time thou ventur'st at particulars, have an evasion ready like *Lilly*; as thus, it will infallibly
530   happen if our sins hinder not. I would undertake with one of his Almanacks to give very good content to all Christendom, and what good luck fell not out in one Kingdom, should in another.

Maskall. The pleasure on't will be to see how all his
535   Customers will contribute to their own deceiving; and verily believe he told them that, which they told him.

Bellamy. Umh! now I begin to taste it; I am like the drunken Tinker in the Play, a great Prince, and never knew it.

540   *Wildblood.* A great Prince, a great Turk; we shall have thee within these two dayes, do grace to the Ladies by throwing out a handkerchief; 'lif, I could feast upon thy fragments.

Bellamy. If the women come you shall be sure to help me
545   to undergo the burden; for though you make me an *Astronomer* I am no *Atlas*, to bear all upon my back. But who are these?

Enter Musicians with disguises; and some in their hands.

Wildblood. You know the men if their Masquing habits were off; they are the Musick of our Embassador's
550   Retinue: my project is to give our Mistresses a Serenade;

516–17 *trade of Lapland*] selling winds, as the witches of Lapland were thought to do.
538 *drunken . . . Prince*] a reference to *The Taming of the Shrew.*
542 *throwing out a handkerchief*] an invitation to a lady to share the king's bed.

218

this being the last Evening of the Carnival; and to prevent discovery here are disguises for us too. ————
Bellamy. 'Tis very well; come *Maskall* help on with 'em,
while they tune their Instruments.
Wildblood. Strike up Gentlemen; we'll entertain 'em with   555
a song *al' Angloise*, pray be ready with your *Chorus*.

SONG

After the pangs of a desperate Lover,
When day and night I have sigh'd all in vain,
Ah what a pleasure it is to discover
In her eyes pity, who causes my pain!   560

2

When with unkindness our love at a stand is,
And both have punish'd our selves with the pain,
Ah what a pleasure the touch of her hand is,
Ah what a pleasure to press it again!

3

When the denyal comes fainter and fainter,   565
And her eyes give what her tongue does deny,
Ah what a trembling I feel when I venture,
Ah what a trembling does usher my joy!

4

When, with a Sigh, she accords me the blessing,
And her eyes twinkle 'twixt pleasure and pain;   570
Ah what a joy 'tis beyond all expressing,
Ah what a joy to hear, shall we again!

[*Enter*] Theodosia *and* Jacinta *above*.
Jacinta *throws down her handkerchief with a Favour ty'd*
                                   to it.
Jacinta. Ill Musicians must be rewarded: there, Cavalier,
'tis to buy your silence.
                            Exeunt women from above.
Wildblood. By this light, which at present is scarce an oath,   575
an handkerchief and a favour.
    Musick and Guittars tuning on the other side of the Stage.
Bellamy. Hark, *Wildblood*, do you hear; there's more
melody; on my life some *Spaniards* have taken up this
Post for the same design.   580
Wildblood. I'll be with their Cats-guts immediately.
Bellamy. Prethee be patient; we shall lose the sport else.

[*Enter*] Don Lopez *and* Don Melchor *disguis'd, with*
            Servants, and Musicians on the other side.

Wildblood. 'Tis some Rival of yours or mine, *Bellamy*: for
he addresses to this window.

Bellamy. Damn him, let's fall on then.

> *The two* Spaniards *and the* English *fight: the* Spaniards *are beaten off the Stage; the Musicians on both sides and Servants fall confusedly one over the other. They all get off, only* Maskall *remains upon the ground.*

585 *Maskall (rising).* So, all's past, and I am safe: a pox on these fighting Masters of mine, to bring me into this danger with their valours and magnanimities. When I go a Serenading again with 'em, I'll give 'em leave to make Fiddle-strings of my small-guts.

> *To him* Don Lopez.

590 *Lopez.* Who goes there?

Maskall. 'Tis *Don Lopez* by his voice.

Lopez. The same; and by yours you should belong to my two English Ghests. Did you hear no tumult hereabouts?

595 *Maskall.* I heard a clashing of swords, and men a fighting.

Lopez. I had my share in't; but how came you here?

Maskall. I came hither by my Master's order to see if you were in any danger.

Lopez. But how could he imagine I was in any?

600 *Maskall.* 'Tis all one for that, Sir, he knew it, by—Heaven, what was I agoing to say, I had like to have discover'd all!

Lopez. I find there is some secret in't; and you dare not trust me.

605 *Maskall.* If you will swear on your honor to be very secret, I will tell you.

Lopez. As I am a Cavalier, and by my Beard, I will.

Maskall. Then, in few words, he knew it by *Astrologie*, or Magick.

610 *Lopez.* You amaze me! Is he conversant in the occult Sciences?

Maskall. Most profoundly.

Lopez. I always thought him an extraordinary person; but I could never imagine his head lay that way.

615 *Maskall.* He shew'd me yesterday in a glass a Ladies Maid at *London*, whom I well knew; and with whom I us'd to converse on a Pallet in a drawing-room, while he was paying his devotions to her Lady in the Bed-chamber.

620 *Lopez.* Lord, what a treasure for a State were here! and how much might we save by this man, in Forreign Intelligence!

Maskall. And just now he shew'd me how you were
    assaulted in the dark by Foreigners.
Lopez. Could you guess what Countrymen?
Maskall. I imagin'd them to be *Italians.*   625
Lopez. Not unlikely; for they play'd most furiously at our
    back-sides.
Maskall. I will return to my Master with the good news of
    your safety; but once again be secret; or disclose it to
    none but friends. ——— So, there's one Woodcock   630
    more in the Springe. ———   *Exit.*
Lopez. Yes, I will be very secret; for I will tell it only to
    one person; but she is a woman. I will to *Aurelia,* and
    acquaint her with the skill of this rare Artist: she is
    curious as all women are; and, 'tis probable, will desire   635
    to look into the Glass to see *Don Melchor,* whom she
    believes absent. So that by this means, without breaking
    my oath to him, he will be discover'd to be in Town.
    Then his intrigue with *Theodosia* will come to light
    too, for which *Aurelia* will, I hope, discard him, and   640
    receive me. I will about it instantly:
        Success, in love, on diligence depends;
        No lazie Lover e're attain'd his ends.
                                Exit.

ACT III. [Scene 1]

Enter Bellamy, Maskall.

Bellamy. Then, they were certainly *Don Lopez* and *Don
    Melchor* with whom we fought!
Maskall. Yes, Sir.
Bellamy. And when you met *Lopez* he swallow'd all you
    told him?   5
Maskall. As greedily, as if it had been a new Saint's miracle.
Bellamy. I see 'twill spread.
Maskall. And the fame of it will be of use to you in your
    next amour: for the women you know run mad after
    Fortune-tellers and Preachers.   10
Bellamy. But for all my bragging this amour is not yet
    worn off. I find constancy, and once a night, come
    naturally upon a man towards thirty: only we set a
    face on't; and call our selves unconstant for our reputa-
    tion.   15
Maskall. But, What say the Starrs, Sir?
Bellamy. They move faster than you imagine; for I have

1–2 *Don Melchor*] Q2; *Don Mel-* / Melchor Q1

20

got me an *Argol*, and an *English-Almanack*; by help of
which in one half-hour I have learnt to Cant with an
indifferent good grace: *Conjunction, Opposition, Trine,
Square* and *Sextile*, are now no longer Bug-bears to me,
I thank my Starrs for't.

Enter Wildblood.

——— Monsieur *Wildblood*, in good time! What, you
have been taking pains too, to divulge my Tallent?

25

Wildblood. So successfully, that shortly there will be no
talk in Town but of you onely: another Miracle or two,
and a sharp Sword, and you stand fair for a New
Prophet.

Bellamy. But where did you begin to blow the Trumpet.

30

Wildblood. In the Gaming-house: where I found most of
the Town-wits; the Prose-wits playing, and the Verse-
wits rooking.

Bellamy. All sorts of Gamesters are so Superstitious, that I
need not doubt of my reception there.

35

Wildblood. From thence I went to the latter end of a
Comedy, and there whisper'd it to the next Man I knew
who had a Woman by him.

Maskall. Nay, then it went like a Train of Powder, if once
they had it by the end.

40

Wildblood. Like a Squib upon a Line, i'faith, it ran through
one row, and came back upon me in the next: at my
going out I met a knot of *Spaniards*, who were formally
listening to one who was relating it: but he told the
Story so ridiculously, with his Marginal Notes upon it,

45

that I was forc'd to contradict him.

Bellamy. 'Twas discreetly done.

Wildblood. I, for you, but not for me: What, says he,
must such Borachio's as you, take upon you to villifie
a Man of Science? I tell you, he's of my intimate

50

Acquaintance, and I have known him long, for a prodigious person. ——— When I saw my *Don* so fierce,
I thought it not wisdom to quarrel for so slight a
matter as your Reputation, and so withdrew.

Bellamy. A pox of your success! Now shall I have my

55

Chamber besieg'd to morrow morning: there will be

18 *Argol*] Andrea Argoli, a celebrated astrologer. Since many
little annual almanacks were published, which extracted from his
work, they were known as "Argols" (Summers).

27 *sharp Sword*] defending your interpretations, as fanatics
fought for their readings of Scripture.

40 *Squib*] a small firecracker.

48 *Borachios*] common fellows, drunkards.

no stiring out for me; but I must be fain to take up their
Questions in a cleft-Cane, or a Begging-box, as they do
Charity in Prisons.

Wildblood. Faith, I cannot help what your Learning has
brought you to: Go in and study; I foresee you will   60
have but few Holy-dayes: in the mean time I'll not
fail to give the World an account of your indowments.
Fare-well: I'll to the Gaming house.   *Exit* Wildblood.

Maskall. O, Sir, here is the rarest adventure, and which is
more, come home to you.   65

Bellamy. What is it?

Maskall. A fair Lady and her Woman, wait in the outer
Room to speak with you.

Bellamy. But how know you she is fair?

Maskall. Her Woman pluck'd up her Vaile when she   70
spake to me; so that having seen her this evening, I know
her Mistress to be *Donna Aurelia*, Cousin to your
Mistress *Theodosia*, and who lodges in the same House
with her: she wants a Starr or two I warrant you.

Bellamy. My whole Constellation is at her service: but   75
what is she for a Woman?

Maskall. Fair enough, as *Beatrix* has told me; but sufficiently impertinent. She is one of those Ladies who make
ten Visits in an afternoon; and entertain her they see,
with speaking ill of the last from whom they parted: 80
in few words, she is one of the greatest Coquette's in
Madrid: and to show she is one, she cannot speak ten
words without some affected phrase that is in fashion.

Bellamy. For my part I can suffer any impertinence from a
woman, provided she be handsome: my business is with   85
her Beauty, not with her Morals: let her Confessor look
to them.

Maskall. I wonder what she has to say to you?

Bellamy. I know not; but I sweat for fear I should be
gravell'd.   90

Maskall. Venture out of your depth, and plunge boldly
Sir; I warrant you will swimm.

Bellamy. Do not leave me I charge you; but when I look
mournfully upon you help me out.

Enter Aurelia *and* Camilla.

Maskall. Here they are already.   95
　　　　　　　Aurelia *plucks up her vail.*
Aurelia. How am I drest to night, *Camilla*? is nothing dis-
order'd in my head?

57–58 *cleft-Cane*] which was thrust through the bars.

Camilla. Not the least hair, Madam.

Aurelia. No? let me see: give me the Counsellor of the
Graces.

Camilla. The Counsellor of the Graces, Madam?

Aurelia. My Glass I mean: what, will you never be so
spiritual as to understand refin'd language?

Camilla. Madam!

Aurelia. Madam me no Madam, but learn to retrench your
words; and say Mam; as yes Mam, and no Mam, as
other Ladies Women do. Madam! 'tis a year in pro-
nouncing.

Camilla. Pardon me Madam.

Aurelia. Yet again ignorance: par-don Madam, fie fie,
what a superfluity is there, and how much sweeter the
Cadence is, parn me Mam! and for your Ladyship,
your Laship. ———— Out upon't, what a furious indi-
gence of Ribands is here upon my head! This dress is
a Libel to my beauty; a meer Lampoon. Would any
one that had the least revenue of common sense have
done this?

Camilla. Mam, the Cavalier approaches your Laship.

Bellamy (to Maskall). Maskall, pump the woman; and see
if you can discover any thing to save my credit.

Aurelia. Out upon it; now I should speak I want assurance.

Bellamy. Madam, I was told you meant to honor me with
your Commands.

Aurelia. I believe, Sir, you wonder at my confidence in this
visit: but I may be excus'd for waving a little modesty
to know the only person of the Age.

Bellamy. I wish my skill were more to serve you, Madam.

Aurelia. Sir, you are an unfit judge of your own merits:
for my own part I confess I have a furious inclination
for the occult Sciences; but at present 'tis my misfortune ———— *Sighs.*

Bellamy. But why that sigh, Madam?

Aurelia. You might spare me the shame of telling you;
since I am sure you can divine my thoughts: I will
therefore tell you nothing.

Bellamy (aside). What the Devil will become of me now!

Aurelia. You may give me an Essay of your Science, by
declaring to me the secret of my thoughts.

Bellamy. If I know your thoughts, Madam, 'tis in vain for
you to disguise them to me: therefore as you tender
your own satisfaction lay them open without bashfulness.

124 *confidence*] presumption.

Aurelia. I beseech you let us pass over that chapter; for I
am shamefac'd to the last point: Since therefore I cannot
put off my modesty, succour it, and tell me what I think.   145
Bellamy. Madam, Madam, that bashfulness must be laid
aside: not but that I know your business perfectly; and
will if you please unfold it to you all, immediately.
Aurelia. Favour me so far, I beseech you, Sir; for I furiously
desire it.   150
Bellamy. But then I must call up before you a most dreadful Spirit, with head upon head, and horns upon horns:
therefore consider how you can endure it.
Aurelia. This is furiously furious; but rather than fail of my
expectances, I'll try my assurance.   155
Bellamy. Well, then, I find you will force me to this un-
lawful, and abominable act of Conjuration: remember
the sin is yours too.
Aurelia. I espouse the crime also.
Bellamy. I see when a woman has a mind to't, she'll never   160
boggle at a sin. Pox on her, what shall I do? ————
Well, I'll tell you your thoughts, Madam; but after
that expect no farther service from me; for 'tis your
confidence must make my Art successful: ———— Well,
you are obstinate, then; I must tell you your thoughts?   165
Aurelia. Hold, hold, Sir, I am content to pass over that
chapter rather than be depriv'd of your assistance.
Bellamy. 'Tis very well; what need these circumstances
between us two? Confess freely, is not love your
business?   170
Aurelia. You have touch'd me to the quick, Sir.
Bellamy. La you there; you see I knew it; nay, I'll tell you
more, 'tis a man you love.
Aurelia. O prodigious Science! I confess I love a man most
furiously, to the last point, Sir.   175
Bellamy. Now proceed Lady, your way is open; I am
resolv'd I'll not tell you a word farther.
Aurelia. Well, then, since I must acquaint you with what
you know much better than my self; I will tell you I
lov'd a Cavalier, who was noble, young, and handsome;   180
this Gentleman is since gone for *Flanders*; now whether
he has preserv'd his passion inviolate or not, is that which
causes my inquietude.
Bellamy. Trouble not your self, Madam; he's as constant as
a Romance Hero's.   185
Aurelia. Sir, your good news has ravish'd me most furiously; but that I may have a confirmation of it, I beg

186 me] S-S; *omit* Qq,F

225

only, that you would lay your commands upon his *Genius*, or *Idea*, to appear to me this night, that I may have my sentence from his mouth. This, Sir, I know is a slight effect of your Science, and yet will infinitely oblige me.

Bellamy (aside). What the Devil does she call a slight effect! Why Lady, do you consider what you say? you desire me to shew you a man whom your self confess to be in *Flanders.*

Aurelia. To view him in a glass is nothing, I would speak with him in person, I mean his *Idea*, Sir.

Bellamy. I but Madam, there is a vast sea betwixt us and *Flanders*; and water is an enemy to Conjuration: A witches horse you know, when he enters into water, returns into a bottle of hay again.

Aurelia. But, Sir, I am not so ill a *Geographer*, or to speak more properly, a *Chorographer*, as not to know there is a passage by land from hence to *Flanders.*

Bellamy. That's true, Madam, but Magick works in a direct line. Why should you think the Devil such an Ass to goe about? 'gad he'll not stir a step out of his road for you or any man.

Aurelia. Yes, for a Lady, Sir; I hope he's a person that wants not that civility for a Lady: especially a spirit that has the honor to belong to you, Sir.

Bellamy. For that matter he's your Servant, Madam; but his education has been in the fire, and he's naturally an enemy to water I assure you.

Aurelia. I beg his pardon for forgetting his Antipathy; but it imports not much, Sir; for I have lately receiv'd a letter from my Servant, that he is yet in *Spain*; and stays for a wind in St. *Sebastian's.*

Bellamy (aside). Now I am lost past all redemption. ——— *Maskall* ——— must you be smickering after Wenches while I am in calamity?

Maskall (aside). It must be he, I'll venture on't. Alas Sir, I was complaining to my self of the condition of poor *Don Melchor*, who you know is windbound at St. *Sebastian's.*

Bellamy. Why you impudent Villain, must you offer to name him publickly, when I have taken so much care to conceal him all this while?

Aurelia. Mitigate your displeasure I beseech you; and without making farther testimony of it, gratifie my expectances.

221 *smickering*] ogling.

Bellamy. Well, Madam, since the Sea hinders not, you shall
   have your desire. Look upon me with a fix'd eye ———
   so ——— or a little more amorously if you please. ———   235
   Good. Now favour me with your hand.

Aurelia. Is it absolutely necessary you should press my hand
   thus?

Bellamy. Furiously necessary, I assure you, Madam; for
   now I take possession of it in the name of the *Idea* of   240
   Don Melchor. Now, Madam, I am farther to desire of
   you, to write a Note to his Genius, wherein you desire
   him to appear, and this, we Men of Art, call a Compact
   with the *Idea's*.

Aurelia. I tremble furiously.   245

Bellamy. Give me your hand, I'll guide it.   *They write.*

Maskall (to Camilla). Now, Lady mine, what think you of
   my Master?

Camilla. I think I would not serve him for the world: nay,
   if he can know our thoughts by looking on us, we   250
   women are hypocrites to little purpose.

Maskall. He can do that and more; for by casting his eyes
   but once upon them, he knows whether they are Maids,
   better than a whole Jury of Midwives.

Camilla. Now Heaven defend me from him.   255

Maskall. He has a certain small Familiar which he carries
   still about him, that never fails to make discovery.

Camilla. See, they have done writing; not a word more,
   for fear he knows my voice.

Bellamy. One thing I had forgot, Madam, you must   260
   subscribe your name to't.

Aurelia. There 'tis; farewell Cavalier, keep your promise,
   for I expect it furiously.

Camilla. If he sees me I am undone.   *Hiding her face.*

Bellamy. Camilla!   265

Camilla (starts and schreeks). Ah he has found me; I am
   ruin'd!

Bellamy. You hide your face in vain; for I see into your heart.

Camilla. Then, sweet Sir, have pity on my frailty; for if
   my Lady has the least inkling of what we did last night,   270
   the poor Coachman will be turn'd away.
                                 Exit after her Lady.

Maskall. Well, Sir, how like you your New Profession?

Bellamy. Would I were well quit on't; I sweat all over.

Maskall. But what faint-hearted Devils yours are that will
   not go by water? Are they all *Lancashire* Devils, of the   275

brood of *Tybert* and *Grimalkin*, that they dare not wet their feet?

Bellamy. Mine are honest land Devils, good plain foot Posts, that beat upon the hoof for me: but to save their labour, here take this, and in some disguise deliver it to *Don Melchor.*

Maskall. I'll serve it upon him within this hour, when he sallyes out to his assignation with *Theodosia*: 'tis but counterfeiting my voice a little; for he cannot know me in the dark. But let me see, what are the words?

Reads.

Don Melchor, *if the Magique of love have any power upon your spirit, I conjure you to appear this night before me: you may guess the greatness of my passion, since it has forc'd me to have recourse to Art: but no shape which resembles you can fright*

Aurelia.

Bellamy. Well, I am glad there's one point gain'd; for by this means he will be hindred to night from entertaining *Theodosia.* —— Pox on him, is he here again?

Enter Don Alonzo.

Alonzo. Cavalier *Ingles* I have been seeking you: I have a Present in my Pocket for you; read it by your Art and take it.

Bellamy. That I could do easily;—but to shew you I am generous, I'll none of your Present; do you think I am mercenary?

Alonzo. I know you will say now 'tis some Astrological question, and so 'tis perhaps.

Bellamy. I, 'tis the Devil of a question without dispute.

Alonzo. No 'tis within dispute: 'tis a certain difficulty in the Art; a Problem which you and I will discuss, with the arguments on both sides.

Bellamy. At this time I am not problematically given; I have a humour of complaisance upon me, and will contradict no man.

Alonzo. We'll but discuss a little.

Bellamy. By your favour I'll not discusse; for I see by the Stars that if I Dispute to day, I am infallibly threatned to be thought ignorant all my life after.

276 *Tybert* ... *Grimalkin*] Tibert is the name of the cat in the apologue of Reynard the Fox ... Grimalkin ... is an old she cat. Cats are proverbially connected with witches, and in the Lancashire of 1612 Elizabeth Sothernes, alias Old Dembdike, confessed ... that she entertained a spirit "called *Tibb*, in the shape of a black cat" (Summers).

Alonzo. Well, then, we'll but cast an eye together, upon
   my eldest Daughter's Nativity.   315
Bellamy. Nativity! ———
Alonzo. I know what you would say now, that there wants
   the Table of Direction for the five Hylegiacalls; the
   Ascendant, *Medium Cœli*, Sun, Moon, and *Sors*: but
   we'll take it as it is.   320
Bellamy. Never tell me that, Sir ———
Alonzo. I know what you would say again, Sir ———
Bellamy (*aside*). 'Tis well you do, for I'll besworn I do
   not. ———
Alonzo. You would say, Sir ———   325
Bellamy. I say, Sir, there is no doing without the Sun and
   Moon, and all that, Sir. And so you may make use of
   your Paper for your occasions. Come to a man of Art
   without the Sun and Moon, and all that, Sir ———
                                     Tears it.
Alonzo. 'Tis no matter; this shall break no squares betwixt   330
   us: *Gathers up the Torne Papers.*
   I know what you would say now, that Men of parts are
   alwayes cholerick; I know it by my self, Sir.
                  He goes to match the Papers.

            Enter Don Lopez.

Lopez. Don Alonzo in my house! This is a most happy
   opportunity to put my other design in execution; for if   335
   I can perswade him to bestow his Daughter on *Don*
   Melchor, I shall serve my Friend, though against his will:
   and, when *Aurelia* sees she cannot be his, perhaps she
   will accept my Love.
Alonzo. I warrant you, Sir, 'tis all piec'd right, both top,   340
   sides and bottom; for, look you, Sir, here was *Alde-*
   boran, and there *Cor Scorpii* ———
Lopez. Don Alonzo, I am happy to see you under my Roof:
   and shall take it ———
Alonzo. I know what you would say, Sir, that though I am   345
   your neighbour, this is the first time I have been here.

---

318 *Table of Direction*] a chart of the heavens with the stars duly
arranged in their places as at the hour of a person's birth.
   318 *Hylegiacals*] the ruling astronomical bodies and configurations
that are significant in casting a nativity. The ascendant is the sign of the
zodiac that is on the horizon. *Medium coeli* is the tenth house (a division
of the heavens). *Sors* is the "fortune" of every place in the heavens.
S-S emended *sors* to *stars*, which is meaningless.
   330 *break no squares*] do no harm, make no difference.
   342 *Cor Scorpii*] Antares.

(*To Bellamy*) But, come, Sir, by *Don Lopez* his permission let us return to our Nativity.

Bellamy (*aside*). Would thou wert there, in thy Mother's
350   Belly again.

Lopez (*to Alonzo*). But *Sennor* ———

Alonzo. It needs not *Sennor*; I'll suppose your Compliment;
you would say that your house and all things in it are at
my service: [*to Bellamy*] but let us proceed without his
355   interruption.

Bellamy. By no means, Sir; this Cavalier is come on purpose to perform the civilities of his house to you.

Alonzo. But, good Sir ———

Bellamy. I know what you would say, Sir.

                          Exeunt Bellamy *and* Maskall.

360   *Lopez*. No matter, let him go, Sir; I have long desir'd this
opportunity to move a Sute to you in the behalf of a
Friend of mine: if you please to allow me the hearing
of it.

Alonzo. With all my heart, Sir.

365   *Lopez*. He is a person of worth and vertue, and is infinitely
ambitious of the honour ———

Alonzo. Of being known to me; I understand you, Sir.

Lopez. If you will please to favour me with your patience,
which I beg of you a second time ———

370   *Alonzo*. I am dumb, Sir.

Lopez. This Cavalier of whom I was speaking, is in Love—

Alonzo. Satisfie your self, Sir, I'll not interrupt you.

Lopez. Sir, I am satisfied of your promise.

Alonzo. If I speak one Syllable more the Devil take me:
375   speak when you please.

Lopez. I am going, Sir ———

Alonzo. You need not speak twice to me to be silent:
though I take it somewhat ill of you to be tutor'd ———

Lopez (*aside*). This eternal old Man will make me mad.

380   *Alonzo*. Why, when do you begin, Sir? How long must
a man wait for you? pray make an end of what you
have to say quickly, that I may speak in my turn too.

Lopez. This Cavalier is in Love ———

Alonzo. You told me that before, Sir; Do you speak
385   Oracles that you require this strict attention? either let
me share the talk with you or I am gone.

Lopez. Why, Sir, I am almost mad to tell you, and you will
not suffer me.

Alonzo. Will you never have done, Sir; I must tell you,
390   Sir, you have tatled long enough; and 'tis now good
Manners to hear me speak. Here's a Torrent of words

indeed; a very *impetus dicendi*. Will you never have done?

Lopez. I will be heard in spight of you.

> *This next Speech of* Lopez, *and the next of* Alonzo's, *with both their Replies, are to be spoken at one time; both raising their voices by little and little, till they baul, and come up close to shoulder one another.*

Lopez. There's one *Don Melchor de Guzman*, a Friend and 395
Acquaintance of mine, that is desperately in Love with your eldest Daughter *Donna Theodosia*.

Alonzo (at the same time). 'Tis the sentence of a Philosopher, *Loquere ut te videam*; Speak that I may know thee; now if you take away the power of speaking from me —— 400
> *Both pause a little; then speak together again.*

Lopez. I'll try the Language of the Law; sure the Devil cannot out-talke that Gibberish. —— For this *Don Melchor* of *Madrid* aforesaid, as premised, I request, move, and supplicate, that you would give, bestow, Marry, and give in Mariage, this your Daughter afore- 405
said, to the Cavalier aforesaid. —— Not yet? thou Devil of a Man thou shalt be silent. ——
> *Exit* Lopez *running.*

Alonzo (at the same time with Lopez his last speech, and after Lopez is run out). Oh, how I hate, abominate, detest and abhor, these perpetual Talkers, Disputants, Contro- 410
verters, and Duellers of the Tongue! But, on the other side, if it be not permitted to prudent men to speak their minds, appositely, and to the purpose and in few words —— If, I say, the prudent must be Tongue-ty'd; then let Great Nature be destroy'd; let the order of all things 415
be turn'd topsy-turvy; let the Goose devour the Fox; let the Infants preach to their Great-Grandsires; let the tender Lamb pursue the Woolfe, and the Sick prescribe to the Physician. Let Fishes live upon dry-land, and the Beasts of the Earth inhabit in the Water. —— Let the 420
fearful Hare ——

> *Enter* Lopez *with a Bell, and rings it in his ears.*

Alonzo. Help, help, murder, murder, murder.
> *Exit* Alonzo *running.*

Lopez. There was no way but this to be rid of him.

> *Enter a Servant.*

392 *impetus dicendi*] violence of language.

425

Servant. Sir, there are some Women without in Masquerade; and, I believe, persons of Quality, who are come to Play here.

Lopez. Bring 'em in with all respect.

Enter again the Servant, after him, Jacinta, Beatrix, and other Ladies and Gentlemen; all Masqued.

Lopez. Cavaliers, and Ladies, you are welcome: I wish I had more company to entertain you: ——— Oh, here comes one sooner then I expected.

430

Enter Wildblood *and* Maskall.

Wildblood. I have swept your Gaming-house, i'faith, *Ecce signum.*   *Shows Gold.*

Lopez. Well, here's more to be had of these Ladies, if it be your fortune.

435

Wildblood. The first Stakes I would play for, should be their Vailes, and Visor Masques.

Jacinta (to Beatrix). Do you think he will not know us?

Beatrix. If you keep your Design of passing for an *African.*

Jacinta. Well, now I shall make an absolute trial of him; for, being thus incognita, I shall discover if he make Love to any of you. As for the Gallantry of his Serenade, we will not be indebted to him, for we will make him another with our Guittars.

440

Beatrix. I'll whisper your intention to the Servant, who shall deliver it to *Don Lopez.*

445

        Beatrix *whispers to the Servant.*

Servant (to Lopez). Sir, the Ladies have commanded me to tell you, that they are willing, before they Play, to present you with a Dance; and to give you an Essay of their Guittars.

450

Lopez. They much honor me.

A DANCE

After the Dance the Cavaliers take the Ladies and Court them. Wildblood *takes* Jacinta.

Wildblood. While you have been Singing, Lady, I have been Praying: I mean, that your Face and Wit may not prove equal to your Dancing; for, if they be, there's a heart gone astray to my knowledge.

455

Jacinta. If you pray against me before you have seen me, you'll curse me when you have look'd on me.

Wildblood. I believe I shall have cause to do so, if your Beauty be as killing as I imagine it.

Jacinta. 'Tis true, I have been flatter'd in my own Country,

with an opinion of a little handsomness; but, how it will   460
pass in *Spain* is a question.

Wildblood. Why Madam, Are you not of *Spain*?

Jacinta. No, Sir, of *Marocco*: I onely came hither to see some
of my Relations who are setled here, and turn'd *Chris-*
tians, since the expulsion of my Countrymen the *Moors*.   465

Wildblood. Are you then a *Mahometan*?

Jacinta. A *Musullman* at your service.

Wildblood. A *Musullwoman* say you? I protest by your voice
I should have taken you for a *Christian* Lady of my
acquaintance.   470

Jacinta. It seems you are in love then: if so, I have done
with you. I dare not invade the Dominions of another
Lady; especially in a Country where my Ancestors have
been so unfortunate.

Wildblood. Some little liking I might have, but that was   475
onely a morning-dew, 'tis drawn up by the Sun-shine
of your Beauty: I find your *African-Cupid* is a much
surer Archer then ours of *Europe*. Yet would I could see
you; one look would secure your victory.

Jacinta. I'll reserve my Face to gratifie your imagination   480
with it, make what head you please, and set it on my
Shoulders.

Wildblood. Well, Madam, an eye, a nose, or a lip shall
break no squares: the Face is but a span's breadth of
beauty; and where there is so much besides, I'll never   485
stand with you for that.

Jacinta. But, in earnest, Do you love me?

Wildblood. I, by *Alha* do I, most extreamly: you have Wit
in abundance, you Dance to a Miracle, you Sing like
an Angel, and I believe you look like a Cherubim.   490

Jacinta. And can you be constant to me?

Wildblood. By *Mahomet*, can I.

Jacinta. You Swear like a *Turk*, Sir; but, take heed: for our
Prophet is a severe punisher of Promise-breakers.

Wildblood. Your Prophet's a Cavalier; I honour your   495
Prophet and his Law, for providing so well for us
Lovers in the other World, Black Eyes, and Fresh-
Maidenheads every day; go thy way little *Mahomet*,
i'faith thou shalt have my good word. But, by his
favour Lady, give me leave to tell you, that we of the   500
Uncircumcised, in a civil way, as Lovers, have some-
what the advantage of your *Musullman*.

Jacinta. The Company are rejoyn'd, and set to play; we
must go to 'em: Adieu, and when you have a thought
to throw away, bestow it on your Servant *Fatyma*.   505

                    She goes to the Company.

Wildblood. This Lady *Fatyma* pleases me most infinitely: now am I got among the *Hamets*, the *Zegrys*, and the *Bencerrages.* Hey, What work will the *Wildbloods* make among the *Cids* and the *Bens* of the *Arabians*!

510 *Beatrix (to Jacinta).* False, or true, Madam?

Jacinta. False as Hell; but by Heaven I'll fit him for't: Have you the high-running Dice about you?

Beatrix. I got them on purpose, Madam.

Jacinta. You shall see me win all their Mony; and when I
515 have done, I'll return in my own person, and ask him for the money which he promis'd me.

Beatrix. 'Twill put him upon a streight to be so surpriz'd: but, let us to the Table; the Company stayes for us.

The Company sit.

Wildblood. What is the Ladies Game, Sir?

520 *Lopez.* Most commonly they use Raffle. That is, to throw with three Dice, till Duplets and a chance be thrown; and the highest Duplets wins except you throw *In* and *In*, which is call'd Raffle; and that wins all.

Wildblood. I understand it: Come, Lady, 'tis no matter
525 what I lose; the greatest stake, my heart, is gone already.

To Jacinta.

They play: and the rest by couples.

Wildblood. So, I have a good chance, two quaters and a sice.

Jacinta. Two sixes and a trey wins it.   *Sweeps the money.*

Wildblood. No matter; I'll try my fortune once again:
530 what have I here, two sixes and a quater? ——— an hundred Pistols on that throw.

Jacinta. I take you, Sir. ——— [*Aside*] *Beatrix* the high running Dice.—

Beatrix. Here Madam. ———

535 *Jacinta.* Three fives: I have won you Sir.

Wildblood. I, the pox take me for't, you have won me: it would never have vex'd me to have lost my money to a Christian; but to a Pagan, an Infidel ———

Maskall. Pray, Sir, leave off while you have some money.

540 *Wildblood.* Pox of this Lady *Fatyma*! Raffle thrice together, I am out of patience.

Maskall (to him). Sir, I beseech you if you will lose, to lose *en Cavalier.*

Wildblood. Tol de ra, tol de ra—pox and curse—tol de ra,

---

512 *high-running*] loaded.
522–23 *In and In*] all three dice are the same number.
526–27 *two . . . sice*] *quatre et sice*, two fours and a six.

&c. What the Devil did I mean to play with this Brunet 545
of *Afrique*?   *The Ladies rise.*
Wildblood. Will you be gone already, Ladies?
Lopez. You have won our money; but however we are
acknowledging to you for the honor of your company.
                Jacinta makes a sign of farewel to Wildblood.
Wildblood. Farewell Lady *Fatyma.* 550
                Exeunt all but Wildblood *and* Maskall.
Maskall. All the company took notice of your concernment.
Wildblood. 'Tis no matter; I do not love to fret inwardly,
as your silent losers do, and in the mean time be ready
to choak for want of vent. 555
Maskall. Pray consider your condition a little; a younger
Brother in a foreign Country, living at a high rate,
your money lost, and without hope of a supply. Now
curse if you think good.
Wildblood. No, now I will laugh at my self most unmerci- 560
fully: for my condition is so ridiculous that 'tis past
cursing. The pleasantest part of the adventure is, that I
have promis'd three hundred pistols to *Jacinta*: but
there is no remedy, they are now fair *Fatyma's.*
Maskall. Fatyma! 565
Wildblood. I, I, a certain *African* Lady of my acquaintance
whom you know not.
Maskall. But who is here, Sir!

Enter Jacinta *and* Beatrix *in their own shapes.*

Wildblood. Madam, what happy star has conducted you
hither to night! (*Aside*) A thousand Devils of this fortune! 570
Jacinta. I was told you had Ladies here and fiddles; so I
came partly for the divertisement, and partly out of
jealousie.
Wildblood. Jealousie! why sure you do not think me a
Pagan, an Infidel? But the company's broke up you see. 575
Am I to wait upon you home, or will you be so kind
to take a hard lodging with me to night?
Jacinta. You shall have the honor to lead me to my Father's.
Wildblood. No more words then, let's away to prevent
discovery. 580
Beatrix. For my part I think he has a mind to be rid of you.
Wildblood. No: but if your Lady should want sleep,
'twould spoil the lustre of her eyes to morrow. There
were a Conquest lost.
Jacinta. I am a peaceable Princess, and content with my 585
own; I mean your heart, and purse; for the truth is, I

235

have lost my money to night in *Masquerade*, and am
come to claim your promise of supplying me.

Wildblood. You make me happy by commanding me: to
morrow morning my servant shall wait upon you with
three hundred pistols.

Jacinta. But I left my company with promise to return to
play.

Wildblood. Play on tick, and lose the *Indies*, I'll discharge
it all to morrow.

Jacinta. To night, if you'll oblige me.

Wildblood. Maskall, go and bring me three hundred pistols
immediately.

Maskall. Are you mad Sir?

Wildblood. Do you expostulate you rascall! how he stares;
I'll be hang'd if he have not lost my gold at play: if you
have, confess you had best, and perhaps I'll pardon you;
but if you do not confess I'll have no mercy: did you
lose it?

Maskall. Sir, 'tis not for me to dispute with you.

Wildblood. Why then let me tell you, you did lose it.

Jacinta. I, as sure as e're he had it I dare swear for him: but
commend to you for a kind Master, that can let your
Servant play off three hundred pistols, without the least
sign of anger to him.

Beatrix. 'Tis a sign he has a greater banck in store to comfort him.

Wildblood. Well, Madam, I must confess I have more then
I will speak of at this time; but till you have given me
satisfaction ———

Jacinta. Satisfaction; why, are you offended, Sir?

Wildblood. Heaven! that you should not perceive it in me:
I tell you I am mortally offended with you.

Jacinta. Sure 'tis impossible.

Wildblood. You have done nothing I warrant to make a
man jealous: going out a gaming in *Masquerade*, at unseasonable hours, and losing your money, at play; that
loss above all provokes me.

Beatrix (*aside*). I believe you; because she comes to you for
more.

Jacinta. Is this the quarrel? I'll clear it immediately.

Wildblood. 'Tis impossible you should clear it; I'll stop my
ears if you but offer it. There's no satisfaction in the
point.

Jacinta. You'll hear me? ———

Wildblood. To do this in the beginning of an amour, and

to a jealous servant as I am; had I all the wealth of *Peru*,
I would not let go one Maravedis to you.

Jacinta. To this I answer ———

Wildblood. Answer nothing, for it will but inflame the
quarrel betwixt us: I must come to my self by little and
little; and when I am ready for satisfaction I will take it:
but at present it is not for my honor to be friends.

Beatrix. Pray let us neighbour Princes interpose a little.

Wildblood. When I have conquer'd, you may interpose;
but at the present the mediation of all Christendome
would be fruitless.

Jacinta. Though Christendome can do nothing with you,
yet I hope an *African* may prevail. Let me beg you for
the sake of the Lady *Fatyma*.

Wildblood. I begin to suspect that Lady *Fatyma* is no better
than she should be. If she be turn'd Christian again I am
undone.

Jacinta. By *Alha* I am afraid on't too: By *Mahomet* I am.

Wildblood. Well, well, Madam, any man may be overtaken with an oath; but I never meant to perform it with
her: you know no oathes are to be kept with Infidels.
But ———

Jacinta. No, the love you made was certainly a design of
charitie you had to reconcile the two Religions. There's
scarce such another man in *Europe* to be sent Apostle to
convert the *Moor* Ladies.

Wildblood. Faith I would rather widen their breaches then
make 'em up.

Jacinta. I see there's no hope of a reconcilement with you;
and therefore I give it o're as desperate.

Wildblood. You have gain'd your point, you have my
money; and I was only angry because I did not know
'twas you who had it.

Jacinta. This will not serve your turn, Sir; what I have got
I have conquer'd from you.

Wildblood. Indeed you use me like one that's conquer'd;
for you have plunder'd me of all I had.

Jacinta. I only disarm'd you for fear you should rebell
again; for if you had the sinews of warr I am sure you
would be flying out.

Wildblood. Dare but to stay without a new Servant till I am
flush again, and I will love you, and treat you, and
present you at that unreasonable rate; that I will make
you an example to all unbelieving Mistresses.

635

640

645

650

655

660

665

670

675

633 *Maravedis*] an old Spanish copper coin, about one-sixth of a
penny.

Jacinta. Well, I will trie you once more; but you must make
  haste then, that we may be within our time; methinks
  our love is drawn out so subtle already, that 'tis near
  breaking.

680   *Wildblood.* I will have more care of it on my part, than the
  kindred of an old Pope have to preserve him.

Jacinta. Adieu; for this time I wipe off your score.
  Till you're caught tripping in some new amour.

Exeunt Women.

Maskall. You have us'd me very kindly, Sir, I thank you.

685   *Wildblood.* You deserv'd it for not having a lye ready for
  my occasions. A good Servant should be no more without it, than a Souldier without his armes. But prethee
  advise me what's to be done to get *Jacinta.*

Maskall. You have lost her, or will lose her by your sub-

690   mitting: if we men could but learn to value our selves,
  we should soon take down our Mistresses from all their
  Altitudes, and make 'em dance after our Pipes, longer
  perhaps than we had a mind to't. ——— But I must
  make haste, or I shall lose *Don Melchor.* ———

695   *Wildblood.* Call *Bellamy*, we'll both be present at thy enterprise: then I'll once more to the Gaming-house with my
  small stock, for my last refuge: if I win, I have wherewithall to mollifie *Jacinta.*

  If I throw out I'll bear it off with huffing;

700   And snatch the money like a Bulli-Ruffin.

Exeunt.

ACT IV. [Scene 1]

[*Enter*] Bellamy, Wildblood: Maskall *in a visor.*

Bellamy. Here comes one, and in all probability it must be
  Don Melchor going to *Theodosia.*

Maskall. Stand close, and you shall see me serve the Writ
  upon him.

Enter Don Melchor.

5   *Wildblood.* Now, *Maskall.*

Maskall. I stay'd here, Sir, by express order from the Lady
  Aurelia, to deliver you this Note; and to desire you from
  her to meet her immediately in the Garden.

Melchor. Do you hear friend!

699 *throw out*] make a losing throw in dice play.
699 *huffing*] bluster, arrogance.
700 *Bulli-Ruffin*] a footpad or highwayman, who, to the injury
of robbery, added the insult of coarse invective (Farmer).

Maskall. Not a syllable more, Sir, I have perform'd my   10
  orders.   *Maskall retires to his Masters.*

Melchor. He's gone; and 'tis in vain for me to look after
  him. What envious Devil has discover'd to *Aurelia* that
  I am in Town? it must be *Don Lopez*, who to advance
  his own pretensions to her, has endeavour'd to ruine   15
  mine.

Wildblood. It works rarely.

Melchor. But I am resolv'd to see *Aurelia*; if it be but to
  defeat him.   *Exit* Melchor.

Wildblood. Let's make haste after him; I long to see the   20
  end of this adventure.

Maskall. Sir, I think I see some women coming yonder.

Bellamy. Well; I'll leave you to your adventures; while I
  prosecute my own.

Wildblood. I warrant you have made an assignation to   25
  instruct some Lady in the Mathematicks.

Bellamy. I'll not tell you my design; because if it does not
  succeed you shall not laugh at me.   *Exit* Bellamy.

    Enter Beatrix; *and* Jacinta *in the habit of a Mulatta.*

Wildblood. Let us withdraw a little, and see if they will come
  this way.   30

Beatrix. We are right, Madam, 'tis certainly your *Englishman*, and his Servant with him. But why this second
  triall, when you engag'd to break with him, if he fail'd
  in the first?

Jacinta. 'Tis true, he has been a little inconstant; cholerick,   35
  or so.

Beatrix. And it seems you are not contented with those
  vices; but are searching him for more. This is the folly
  of a bleeding Gamester, who will obstinately pursue a
  losing hand.   40

Jacinta. On t'other side you would have me throw up my
  Cards before the game be lost: let me make this one
  more triall, when he has money whether he will give it
  me, and then if he fails ———

Beatrix. You'l forgive him agen.   45

Jacinta. He's already in Purgatory; but the next offence
  shall put him in the pit past all redemption; prethee
  sing to draw him nearer: Sure he cannot know me in
  this disguise.

Beatrix. Make haste then; for I have more Irons in the fire: 50
  when I have done with you I have another assignation
  of my Lady *Theodosia's* to *Don Melchor.*

    26 *Mathematicks*] astrology.

SONG

Calm was the Even, and cleer was the Skie,
And the new budding flowers did spring,
55 *When all alone went* Amyntas *and I*
To hear the sweet Nightingale sing;
I sate, and he laid him down by me;
But scarcely his breath he could draw;
For when with a fear he began to draw near,
60 *He was dash'd with A ha ha ha ha!*

2

He blush'd to himself, and lay still for a while,
And his modesty curb'd his desire;
But streight I convinc'd all his fear with a smile,
Which added new flames to his fire.
65 *O* Sylvia, *said he, you are cruel,*
To keep your poor Lover in awe;
Then once more he prest with his hand to my brest,
But was dash'd with A ha ha ha ha.

3

I knew 'twas his passion that caus'd all his fear;
70 *And therefore I pity'd his case:*
I whisper'd him softly there's no body near,
And layd my cheek close to his face:
But as he grew bolder and bolder,
A Shepherd came by us and saw;
75 *And just as our bliss we began with a kiss,*
He laughed out with A ha ha ha ha.

Wildblood. If you dare be the *Sylvia*, Lady, I have brought
you a more confident *Amyntas*, than that bashful Gentleman in your Song. ——— *Goes to lay hold of her.*
80 *Jacinta.* Hold, hold; Sir, I am only an Ambassadress sent
you from a Lady, I hope you will not violate the Laws
of Nations.
Wildblood. I was only searching for your Letters of Cre-
dence: but methinks with that beauty you look more like
85 a Herauld that comes to denounce war to all mankind. ———
Jacinta. One of the Ladies in the Masque to night has taken
a liking to you; and sent you by me this purse of gold,
in recompence of that she saw you lose.
90 *Wildblood.* And she expects in return of it, that I should
wait on her; I'll do't. Where lives she? I am desperately
in love with her.
Jacinta. Why, Can you love her unknown?

63 *convinc'd*] conquered.

Wildblood. I have a Banque of Love, to supply every one's
occasions; some for her, some for another, and some for   95
you; charge what you will upon me, I pay all at sight,
and without questioning who brought the Bill.

Jacinta. Heyday, You dispatch your Mistresses as fast, as if
you meant to o're-run all Woman-kind: sure you aime
at the Universal-Monarchy.   100

Wildblood. Now I think on't, I have a foolish fancy to
send thy Lady a taste of my love by thee.

Jacinta. 'Tis impossible your love should be so humble, to
descend to a *Mulatta.*

Wildblood. One would think so, but I cannot help it. Gad,   105
I think the reason is because there's something more of
sin in thy colour then in ours. I know not what's the
matter, but a *Turky-Cock* is not more provok'd at red,
then I bristle at the sight of black. Come, be kinder to
me. Young, and slip an opportunity? 'Tis an Evening   110
lost out of your life.

Jacinta. These fine things you have said over a thousand
times; your cold Compliment's the cold Pye of love
which you serve up to every new guest whom you
invite.   115

Wildblood. Come; because thou art very moving, here's
part of the Gold, which thou brought'st to corrupt me
for thy Lady: truth is, I had promis'd a summ to a
Spanish Lady ——— but thy eyes have allur'd it from
me.   120

Jacinta. You'll repent to morrow.

Wildblood. Let to morrow starve: or provide for himself,
as to night has done: to morrow is a cheat in love, and
I will not trust it.

Jacinta. I, but Heaven that sees all things ———   125

Wildblood. Heaven that sees all things will say nothing:
that is, all eyes and no tongue; *Et la lune et les estoiles,*
——— you know the Song.

Jacinta. A poor slave as I am ———

Wildblood. It has been alwayes my humour to love down-   130
ward. I love to stoop to my prey, and to have it in my
power to Sowse at whom I please. When a man comes
to a great Lady, he is fain to approach her with fear and
reverence; methinks there's something of Godliness in't.

Jacinta. Yet I cannot believe, but the meanness of my habit   135
must needs scandalize you.

---

132 whom] when Qq,F

127 *Et . . . estoiles*] an unidentified song.
132 *Sowse*] to swoop down on a prey. Said of a hawk.

Wildblood. I'll tell thee my friend and so forth, that I exceedingly honour course Linnen; 'tis as proper sometimes in an under Garment, as a course Towel is to rub
140   and scrub me.

Jacinta. Now I am altogether of the other side, I can love no where but above me: methinks the ratling of a Coach and six, sounds more eloquently, then the best Harrangue a Wit could make me.

145 *Wildblood.* Do you make no more esteem of a Wit then?

Jacinta. His commendations serve onely to make others have a mind to me; He does but say Grace to me like a *Chaplain*; and like him is the last that shall fall on. He ought to get no more by it, then a poor Silk-weaver
150   does by the Ribband which he workes, to make a Gallant fine.

Wildblood. Then what is a Gentleman to hope from you?

Jacinta. To be admitted to pass my time with, while a better comes: to be the lowest step in my Stair-case, for
155   a Knight to mount upon him, and a Lord upon him, and a Marquess upon him, and a Duke upon him, till I get as high as I can climb.

Wildblood. For ought I see, the Great Ladies have the Appetites which you Slaves should have; and you Slaves the
160   Pride which ought to be in Ladies. For, I observe, that all women of your condition are like the women of the Play-house, still Piquing at each other, who shall go the best Drest, and in the Richest Habits: till you work up one another by your high flying, as the *Heron* and
165   *Jerfalcon* do. If you cannot outshine your fellow with one Lover, you fetch her up with another: and in short, all you get by it is onely to put Finery out of countenance; and to make the Ladies of Quality go plain, because they will avoid the Scandal of your bravery.

170 *Beatrix* (*running in*). Madam, come away; I hear company in the Garden.   [*Aside.*]

Wildblood. You are not going?

Jacinta. Yes, to cry out a Rape if you follow me.

Wildblood. However, I am glad you have left your treasure
175   behind you: farewel Fairie.

Jacinta. Farewel Changeling.—[*Aside*] Come *Beatrix*.
                                Exeunt Women.

Maskall. Do you know how you came by this money, Sir? you think, I warrant, that it came by fortune.

Wildblood. No, Sirrah, I know it came by my own industry.
180   Did not I come out diligently to meet this gold, in the

154 *my Stair-case*] alluding to Nell Gwyn's ambitions.
165 *Jerfalcon*] gyrfalcon.

very way it was to come? what could Fate do less for me? they are such thoughtless, and undesigning rogues as you, that make a drudge of poor providence, and set it a shifting for you. Give me a brave fellow like my self; that if you throw him down into the world, lights every where upon his legs, and helps himself without being beholding to Fate, that is the Hospital of fools.

Maskall. But after all your jollitie, what think you if it was *Jacinta* that gave it you in this disguise? I am sure I heard her call *Beatrix* as she went away.

Wildblood. Umh! thou awaken'st a most villainous apprehension in me! methought indeed I knew the voice; but the face was such an evidence against it! if it were so she is lost for ever.

Maskall. And so is *Beatrix*!

Wildblood. Now could I cut my throat for madness.

Maskall. Now could I break my neck for despair; if I could find a precipice absolutely to my liking.

Wildblood. 'Tis in vain to consider on't. There's but one way; go you *Maskall*, and find her out, and invent some excuse for me, and be sure to beg leave I may come and wait upon her with the gold before she sleeps.

Maskall. In the mean time you'l be thinking at your lodging.

Wildblood. But make haste then to relieve me; for I think over all my thoughts in half an hour.   *Exit* Maskall.

Wildblood (solus). Hang't, now I think on't, I shall be but melancholique at my Lodging, I'll go pass my hour at the Gaming-house, and make use of this money while I have tools, to win more to it. Stay, let me see, I have the box and throw. My *Don* he sets me ten pistols; I nick him: ten more, I sweep them too. Now in all reason he is nettled, and sets me twenty: I win them too. Now he kindles, and butters me with forty. They are all my own: in fine, he is vehement, and bleeds on to fourscore or an hundred; and I not willing to tempt fortune, come away a moderate winner of two hundred pistols.

The Scene opens and discovers Aurelia *and* Camilla: *behind them a Table and lights set on it. The Scene is a Garden with an Arbour in it.*

The Garden dore opens! How now, *Aurelia* and *Camilla* in expectation of *Don Melchor* at the Garden door; I'll away lest I prevent the designe, and within this half

185

190

195

200

205

210

215

220

214 *butters*] increases the bet by doubling or tripling it.

hour come sailing back with full pockets, as wantonly
as a laden Galleon from the *Indies*. *Exit.*

225 *Aurelia.* But dost thou think the *Englishman* can keep his
promise? for I confess I furiously desire to see the *Idea*
of *Don Melchor.*

Camilla. But, Madam, if you should see him, it will not
be he, but the Devil in his likeness; and then why should
you desire it?

230 *Aurelia.* In effect 'tis a very dark *Enigma*; and one must be
very spiritual to understand it. But be what it will,
bodie or fantome, I am resolv'd to meet it.

Camilla. Can you do it without fear?

Aurelia. No; I must avow it, I am furiously fearful; but yet
235 I am resolv'd to sacrifice all things to my love. Therefore
let us pass over that chapter. Don Melchor *without.*

Camilla. Do you hear, Madam, there's one treading
already; how if it be he?

Aurelia. If it be he; that is to say his Specter, that is to say
240 his Fantome, that is to say his *Idea*, that is to say, He
and not he.

Camilla (crying out). Ah, Madam, 'tis he himself; but he's
as big again as he us'd to be, with eyes like sawcers.
—— I'll save my self. *Runs under the table.*

Enter Don Melchor: *they both shreek.*

245 *Aurelia.* Oh heaven! humanitie is not able to support it.
Running.

Melchor. Dear *Aurelia,* what mean you?

Aurelia. The Tempter has imitated his voice too; avoid,
avoid Specter.

Camilla. If he should find me under the table now!

250 *Melchor.* Is it thus my Dear that you treat your Servant?

Aurelia. I am not thy Dear; I renounce thee, spirit of
darkness.

Melchor. This Spirit of darkness is come to see an Angel of
light by her command; and to assure her of his con-
255 stancy, that he will be hers eternally.

Aurelia. Away Infernal, 'tis not thee, 'tis the true *Don
Melchor* that I would see.

Melchor. Hell and Furies.

Aurelia. Heaven and Angels! Ah ——
Runs out shreeking.

260 *Melchor.* This is a riddle past my finding out, to send for
me, and then to shun me, but here's one shall resolve it
for me: *Camilla,* what dost thou there?

Camilla. Help, help, I shall be carried away, bodily.

She rises up, overthrows the Table and lights, and runs out.
The Scene Shuts.

Melchor (alone). Why *Aurelia*, *Camilla*! they are both run
out of hearing! This amazes me; what can the meaning   265
of it be? Sure she has heard of my unfaithfulness, and
was resolv'd to punish me by this contrivance! to put
an affront upon me by this abrupt departure, as I did
on her by my seeming absence.

Enter Theodosia *and* Beatrix.

Theodosia. Don *Melchor*! is it you my Love that have   270
frighted *Aurelia* so terribly?
Melchor. Alas, Madam, I know not; but coming hither by
your appointment, and thinking my self secure in the
night without disguise, perhaps it might work upon her
fancie, because she thought me absent.   275
Theodosia. Since 'tis so unluckily fallen out that she knows
you are at *Madrid*, it can no longer be kept a secret; therefore you must now pretend openly to me, and run the
risque of a denial from my Father.
Melchor. O, Madam, there's no question but he'll refuse   280
me: for alas, what is it he can see in me worthy of that
honor? or if he should be so partial to me, as some in
the world are, to think me valiant, learned, and not
altogether a fool, yet my want of fortune would weigh
down all.   285
Theodosia. When he has refus'd you his consent, I may with
Justice dispose of my self; and that, while you are
constant, shall never be to any but your self: in witness
of which, accept this Diamond as a Pledge of my heart's
firmness to you.   290
Beatrix. Madam, Your Father is coming this way.
Theodosia. 'Tis no matter; do not stir; since he must know
you are return'd, let him now see you.

Enter Don Alonzo.

Alonzo. Daughter, What make you here at this unseason-
able hour?   295
Theodosia. Sir, ———
Alonzo. I know what you would say, That you heard a
noise, and ran hither to see what it might be. ———
Bless us! Who is this with you?
Melchor. 'Tis your servant *Don Melchor*; just return'd from 300
St. Sebastian's.
Alonzo. But, Sir, I thought you had been upon the Sea for
Flanders.

Melchor. I had so design'd it.

305   *Alonzo.* But, Why came you back from *St. Sebastian's*?

Melchor. As for that, Sir, 'tis not material ———

Theodosia. An unexpected Law Sute has call'd him back from *St. Sebastian's*.

Alonzo. And, How fares my Son-in-Law that lives there?

310   *Melchor.* In Catholique health, Sir.

Alonzo. Have you brought no Letters from him?

Melchor. I had, Sir, but I was set on by the way, by Pickerons: and, in spight of my resistance, rob'd, and my Portmantue taken from me.

315   *Theodosia.* And this was that which he was now desiring me to excuse to you.

Alonzo. If my Credit, Friends, or Counsel can do you any service in your Sute, I hope you will command them freely.

320   *Melchor.* When I have dispatch'd some private business I shall not fail to trouble you; till then, humbly kisses your hands, the most oblig'd of your servants. ———

                                 Exit Melchor.

Alonzo. Daughter, now this Cavalier is gone, What occasion brought you out so late? I know what you would say, That it is Melancholy; a Tincture of the

325   Hypocondriaque you mean: but, What cause have you for this Melancholy? give me your hand, and answer me without Ambages or Ambiguities.

Theodosia. He will find out I given away my Ring

330   ——— I must prevent him. ——— Sir, I am asham'd to confess it to you; but, in hope of your indulgence, I have lost the Table Diamond you gave me.

Alonzo. You would say, The fear of my displeasure has caus'd this perturbation in you; well, do not disquiet

335   your self too much, you say 'tis gone; I say so too. 'Tis stollen; and that by some Thief I take it: but, I will go and consult the *Astrologer* immediately.   *He is going.*

Theodosia (aside). What have I done? to avoid one inconvenience, I have run into another: this Devil of an

340   *Astrologer* will discover that *Don Melchor* has it.

Alonzo. When did you lose this Diamond? The minute and second I should know; but the hour will serve for the Degree ascending.

Theodosia. Sir, the precise time I know not; but, it was

345   betwixt six and seven this evening, as near as I can guess.

312–13 *Pickerons*] highwaymen.
328 *Ambages*] equivocation, circumlocution.
332 *Table Diamond*] a diamond with a large *table* or upper flat facet.

Alonzo. 'Tis enough; by all the Stars I'll have it for you: Therefore go in, and suppose it on your finger.

Beatrix (aside). I'll watch you at a distance, Sir, that my *Englishman* may have wherewithall to answer you.

Exit Theodosia, Beatrix.

Alonzo. This melancholy wherewith my Daughter   350 laboureth, is ——— a ——— I know what I would say, is a certain species of the Hysterical Diseases; or a certain motion, caused by a certain appetite, which at a certain time heaveth in her, like a certain motion of an Earthquake. ———   355

Enter Bellamy.

Bellamy. This is the place, and very near the time that *Theodosia* appoints her meeting with *Don Melchor*. He is this night otherwise dispos'd of with *Aurelia*: 'Tis but trying my fortune to tell her of his Infidelity, and my love. If she yields she makes me happy; if not, I shall be   360 sure *Don Melchor* has not planted the Armes of *Spain* in the Fort before me. However, I'll push my Fortune as sure as I am an *Englishman*.

Alonzo. Sennor *Ingles*, I know your voice, though I cannot perfectly discern you.   365

Bellamy. How the Devil come he to cross me?

Alonzo. I was just coming to have ask'd another Favour of you.

Bellamy. Without Ceremony command me, Sir.

Alonzo. My Daughter *Theodosia* has lost a fair Diamond   370 from her finger, the time betwixt six and seven this evening; now I desire you, Sir, to erect a Scheme for it, and if it be lost, or stollen, to restore it to me. ——— This is all, Sir.

Bellamy (aside). There is no end of this old Fellow; thus will   375 he baite me from day to day, till my ignorance be found out.———

Alonzo (aside). Now is he casting a Figure by the Art of Memory, and making a Judgment of it to himself. This *Astrology* is a very mysterious speculation. ———   380

Bellamy (aside). 'Tis a madness for me to hope I can deceive him longer. Since then he must know I am no Astrologer, I'll discover it my self to him, and blush once for all.

Alonzo. Well, Sir, and what do the Stars hold forth? What   385 sayes nimble Master *Mercury* to the matter?

Bellamy. Sir, not to keep you longer in ignorance, I must

---

372 *erect a Scheme*] draw up a diagram of the heavens.

ingeniously declare to you that I am not the man for whom you take me. Some smattering in *Astrology* I have; which my Friends, by their indiscretion, have blown abroad, beyond my intentions. But, you are not a person to be impos'd on like the vulgar: therefore, to satisfie you in one word, my skill goes not farr enough to give you knowledge of what you desire from me.

Alonzo. You have said enough, Sir, to perswade me of your Science; if Fame had not publish'd it, yet this very humility of yours were enough to confirm me in the beliefe of it.

Bellamy. Death, you make me mad, Sir: Will you have me Swear? As I am a Gentleman, a man of the Town, one who wears good Cloathes, Eates, Drinks, and Wenches abundantly; I am a damn'd ignorant, and senceless Fellow.

Enter Beatrix.

Alonzo. How now Gentlewoman. ⸺⸺ What, Are you going to reliefe by Moonshine?

Beatrix. I was going on a very charitable Office, to help a Friend that was gravell'd in a very doubtful business.

Bellamy. Some good newes, Fortune, I beseech thee.

Beatrix. But now I have found this learned Gentleman, I shall make bold to propound a Question to him from a Lady.

Alonzo. I will have my own Question first resolv'd.

Bellamy. O, Sir, 'tis from a Lady ⸺⸺

Beatrix. If you please, Sir, I'll tell it in your eare. ⸺⸺ (*In whisper*) My Lady has given *Don Melchor* the Ring; in whose company her Father found her but just now at the Garden door.

Bellamy (*aloud*). Come to me to morrow, and you shall receive an answer. ⸺⸺

Beatrix. Your Servant, Sir. ⸺⸺   *Exit* Beatrix.

Alonzo. Sir, I shall take it very unkindly if you satisfie any other, and leave me in this perplexity.

Bellamy. Sir, if my knowledge were according ⸺⸺

Alonzo. No more of that, Sir, I beseech you.

Bellamy. Perhaps I may know something by my Art concerning it; but, for your quiet, I wish you would not press me.

Alonzo. Do you think I am not Master of my Passions?

Bellamy. Since you will needs know what I would willingly

405 *reliefe*] give aid.

have conceal'd, the person who has your Diamond, is he   430
whom you saw last in your Daughter's company.
Alonzo. You would say 'tis *Don Melchor de Guzman*. Who
the Devil would have suspected him of such an action?
But he is of a decay'd Family, and poverty it seems has
inforc'd him to it: now I think on't better he has e'en   435
stoln it for a fee to bribe his Lawyer; to requite a lye
with a theft. I'll seek him out, and tell him part of my
mind before I sleep.   *Exit* Alonzo.
Bellamy. So, once more I am at liberty: but this *Astrologie*
is so troublesome a Science —— would I were well   440
rid on't.

        Enter Don Lopez *and a* Servant.

Lopez. Astrologie does he say? O Cavalier is it you; not
finding you at home I came on purpose to seek you out:
I have a small request to the Stars by your mediation.
Bellamy. Sir, for pity let 'em shine in quiet a little; for what   445
for Ladies and their Servants, and younger Brothers,
they scarce get a Holy-day in a twelvemoneth.
Lopez. Pray pardon me, if I am a little curious of my
destiny, since all my happiness depends on your answer.
Bellamy. Well, Sir, what is it you expect?   450
Lopez. To know whether my love to a Lady will be
succesful.
Bellamy (aside). 'Tis *Aurelia* he means. —— Sir, in one
word I answer you, that your Mistress loves another:
one who is your friend: but comfort your self; the   455
Dragon's tail is between him and home, he never shall
enjoy her.
Lopez. But what hope for me?
Bellamy. The Stars have partly assur'd me you shall be
happy, if you acquaint her with your passion, and with   460
the double dealing of your friend, who is false to her.
Lopez. You speak like an Oracle. But I have engag'd my
promise to that friend to serve him in his passion to my
Mistress.
Bellamy. We *English* seldom make such scruples; Women   465
are not compris'd in our Laws of friendship: they are
feræ naturæ; our common game, like Hare and Patridge:
every man has equal right to them, as he has to the Sun
and Elements.
Lopez. Must I then betray my friend?   470
Bellamy. In that case my friend is a Turk to me, if he will
be so barbarous as to retain two women to his private

467 *feræ-naturæ*] wild creatures.

use; I will be factious for all distressed Damsels; who
would much rather have their cause try'd by a full Jury,
475   then a single Judge.

Lopez. Well, Sir, I will take your counsel; and if I erre, the
fault be on love and you. ———   *Exit* Lopez.

Bellamy. Were it not for love I would run out of the Town,
that's the short on't; for I have engag'd my self in so
480   many promises for the Sun and Moon, and those little
minc'd-meats of 'em, that I must hide before my day of
payment comes. In the mean time I forget *Theodosia*;
but now I defie the Devil to hinder me.

As he is going out he meets Aurelia, *and almost justles
her down. With her* Camilla *enters.*

Aurelia. What rudeness is this?
485   *Bellamy.* Madam *Aurelia*, is it you?

Aurelia. Monsieur *Bellamy*!

Bellamy. The same, Madam.

Aurelia. My Unkle told me he left you here: and indeed I
came hither to complain of you: for you have treated
490   me so inhumanely that I have some reason to resent it.

Bellamy. What occasion can I have given you for a complaint?

Aurelia. Don Melchor, as I am inform'd by my Uncle, is
effectively at *Madrid*: so that it was not his *Idea*, but
495   himself in person whom I saw: and since you knew
this, why did you conceal it from me?

Bellamy. When I spoke with you I knew it not: but I discover'd it in the erecting of my figure. Yet if instead of
his *Idea* I constrain'd himself to come, in spight of his
500   resolution to remain conceal'd, I think I have shown a
greater effect of my art then what I promis'd.

Aurelia. I render my self to so convincing an argument:
but by over-hearing a discourse just now betwixt my
Cousin *Theodosia* and her Maid, I find that he has con-
505   ceal'd himself upon her account, which has given me
jealousie to the last point; for to avow an incontestable
truth, my Cousin is furiously handsome.

Bellamy. Madam, Madam, trust not your ears too far; she
talk'd on purpose that you might hear her: but I assure
510   you the true cause of *Don Melchor's* concealment, was
not love of her, but jealousie of you: he staid in private
to observe your actions: build upon't Madam, he is
inviolably yours.

Aurelia. Then will he sacrifice my Cousin to me?
515   *Bellamy.* 'Tis furiously true Madam.

Aurelia. O most agreeable assurance!

Camilla. Albricias Madam, for my good news; *Don Melchor* is coming this way; I know him by his voice; but he is in company with another person.

Aurelia. It will not be convenient to give him any umbrage   520
by seeing me with another person; therefore I will go before; do you stay here and conduct him to my Appartment. Good-night Sir.   *Exit.*

Bellamy. I have promis'd *Don Lopez* he shall possess her; and I have promis'd her she shall possess *Don Melchor*:   525
'tis a little difficult I confess, as to the Matrimonial part of it: but if *Don Melchor* will be civil to her, and she be civil to *Don Lopez*, my credit is safe without the benefit of my Clergie. But all this is nothing to *Theodosia*.
                                        Exit Bellamy.
            Enter Don Alonzo *and* Don Melchor.

Camilla. Don Melchor, a word in private.   530

Melchor. Your pleasure, Lady; Sir, I will wait on you immediately.

Camilla. I am sent to you from a fair Lady, who bears you no ill will. You may guess whom I mean.

Melchor. Not by my own merits, but by knowing whom   535
you serve: but I confess I wonder at her late strange usage when she fled from me.

Camilla. That was only a mistake; but I have now, by her command, been in a thousand places in quest of you.

Melchor. You overjoy me.   540

Camilla. And where amongst the rest do you think I have been looking you?

Melchor. Pray refresh my memory.

Camilla. In that same street, by that same shop; you know where by a good token.

Melchor. By what token?   545

Camilla. Just by that shop where, out of your nobleness, you promis'd me a new Silk Gown.

Melchor. O, now I understand you.

Camilla. Not that I press you to a performance ———

Melchor. Take this, and please your self in the choice of   550
it. ———   *Gives her money.*

Camilla. Nay, dear Sir, now you make me blush; in faith I—am asham'd—I swear 'tis only because I would keep something for your sake.—But my Lady expects you immedeiately in her Appartment.   555

Melchor. I'll wait on her if I can possibly. ———
                                        Exit Camilla.

529 is] Q2; *omit* Q1

517 *Albricias*] largesse, a reward to the bearer of good news.

(*Aside*) But if I can prevail with *Don Alonzo* for his
Daughter, then will I again consider, which of the
Ladies best deserves me. ———

560 (*To Alonzo*) Sir, I beg your pardon for this rudeness in
leaving you.

Alonzo (*aside*). I cannot possibly resolve with my self to
tell him openly he is a thief; but I'll guild the pill for him
to swallow.

565 *Melchor* [*aside*]. I believe he has discover'd our amour: how
he surveys me for a Son in law!

Alonzo. Sir, I am sorry for your sake, that true nobility is
not always accompanied with riches to support it in
it's lustre.

570 *Melchor*. You have a just exception against the Capri-
chiousness of destiny; yet if I were owner of any noble
qualities, (which I am not) I should not much esteem
the goods of fortune.

Alonzo. But pray conceive me, Sir, your father did not
575 leave you flourishing in wealth.

Melchor. Only a very fair Seat in *Andalusia*, with all the
pleasures imaginable about it: that alone, were my poor
deserts according, which I confess they are not, were
enough to make a woman happy in it.

580 *Alonzo*. But give me leave to come to the point I beseech
you, Sir. I have lost a Jewel which I value infinitely, and
I hear it is in your possession: but I accuse your wants,
not you, for it.

Melchor. Your Daughter is indeed a Jewel, but she were not
585 lost, were she in possession of a man of parts.

Alonzo. A precious Diamond Sir. ———

Melchor. But a man of honor, Sir.

Alonzo. I know what you would say, Sir, that a man of
honor is not capable of an unworthy action; but there-
590 fore I do not accuse you of the theft, I suppose the
Jewel was only put into your hands.

Melchor. By honorable wayes I assure you Sir.

Alonzo. Sir, Sir, will you restore my Jewel?

Melchor. Will you please, Sir, to give me leave to be the
595 unworthy possessor of her? I know how to use her with
that respect ———

Alonzo. I know what you would say, Sir, but if it belongs
to our Family; otherwise I assure you it were at your
service.

600 *Melchor*. As it belongs to your Family I covet it; not that
I plead my own deserts, Sir.

Alonzo. Sir, I know your deserts; but, I protest I cannot

part with it: for, I must tell you, this Diamond Ring
was originally my Great Grandfather's.

Melchor. A Diamond Ring, Sir, do you mean? ———   605

Alonzo. By your patience, Sir, when I have done you may
speak your pleasure. I onely lent it to my Daughter;
but, how she lost it, and how it came upon your Finger,
I am yet *in tenebris.*

Melchor. Sir ———   610

Alonzo. I know it, Sir; but spare your self the trouble, I'll
speak for you; you would say you had it from some
other hand; I believe it, Sir.

Melchor. But, Sir ———

Alonzo. I warrant you, Sir, Ile bring you off without your   615
speaking; from another hand you had it; and now Sir,
as you say, Sir, and as I am saying for you, Sir, you are
loath to part with it.

Melchor. Good Sir, ——— let me ———

Alonzo. I understand you already, Sir, that you have taken   620
a fancy to it, and would buy it; but, to that I answer as
I did before, that it is Relique of my family: now, Sir,
if you can urge ought farther, you have liberty to speak
without interruption.

Melchor. This Diamond you speak on I confess ———   625

Alonzo. But, What need you confess, Sir, before you are
accus'd?

Melchor. You promis'd you would hear me in my turn,
Sir, but ———

Alonzo. But, as you were saying, it is needless, because I   630
have already spoken for you.

Melchor. The truth is, Sir, I was too presumptuous to take
this Pledge from *Theodosia* without your knowledge;
but, you will pardon the invincible necessity, when I
tell you ———   635

Alonzo. You need not tell me, I know your necessity was
the reason of it, and that place and opportunity have
caus'd your error.

Melchor. This is the goodest old man I ever knew; he prevents me in my motion for his Daughter. Since, Sir,   640
you know the cause of my errors, and are pleas'd to lay
part of the blame upon Youth and Opportunity; I
beseech you favour me so far, to accept me as fair
Theodosia already has ———

Alonzo. I conceive you, Sir, that I would accept of your   645
excuse: why, restore the Diamond and 'tis done.

Melchor. More joyfully then I receiv'd it: and with it I

609 *in tenebris*] in the dark.

beg the honour to be receiv'd by you as your Son in Law.

650   *Alonzo.* My Son in Law! this is the most pleasant Proposition I ever heard.

Melchor. I am proud you think it so; but, I protest I think not I deserve this honor.

Alonzo. Nor I, I assure you, Sir; marry my daughter ———

655   ha, ha, ha.

Melchor. But, Sir ———

Alonzo. I know what you would say, Sir, that there is too much hazard in the Profession of a Thief, and therefore you would Marry my Daughter to become rich, with-

660   out venturing your Neck for't. I beseech you, Sir, steal on, be apprehended, and if you please, be hang'd, it shall make no breach betwixt us. For my part, I'll keep your Counsel, and so good night, Sir.   *Exit* Alonzo.

Melchor. Is the Devil in this old man, first to give me

665   occasion to confess my Love, and, when he knew it, to promise he would keep my Counsel? But, Who are these? I'll not be seen; but to my old appointment with *Theodosia*, and desire her to unriddle it. ———

                                    Exit Melchor.

Enter Maskall, Jacinta, Beatrix.

Maskall. But, Madam, Do you take me for a man of

670   Honour?

Jacinta. No.

Maskall. Why there's it; if you had, I would have sworn that my Master has neither done nor intended you any injury; I suppose you'll grant he knew you in your dis-

675   guise?

Beatrix. Nay, to know her, and use her so, is an aggravation of his Crime.

Maskall. Unconscionable *Beatrix*! Would you two have all the Carnival to your selves? He knew you, Madam, and

680   was resolv'd to countermine you in all your Plots. But, when he saw you so much piqued, he was too good natur'd to let you sleep in wrath, and sent me to you to disabuse you: for, if the business had gone on till to morrow, when *Lent* begins, you would have grown

685   so peevish (as all good Catholicks are with fasting) that the quarrel would never have been ended.

Jacinta. Well; this mollifies a little: I am content he shall see me.

Maskall. But, that you may be sure he knew you, he will

690   bring the Certificate of the Purse along with him.

Jacinta. I shall be glad to find him innocent.

Enter Wildblood *at the other end of the Stage.*

Wildblood. No mortal man ever threw out so often. It could not be me, it must be the Devil that did it: he took all the Chances, and chang'd 'em after I had thrown 'em: but, I'le be even with him; for, I'll never throw one of 695 his Dice more.

Maskall. Madam, 'tis certainly my Master; and he is so zealous to make his peace, that he could not stay till I call'd him to you. —— Sir ——

Wildblood. Sirrah, I'll teach you more manners then to 700 leave me another time: you Rogue, you have lost me two hundred Pistolls, you and the Devil your accomplice; you, by leaving me to my self, and he by tempting me to Play it off.

Maskall. Is the wind in that door? here's like to be fine 705 doings.

Wildblood (aside). Oh mischiefe! am I fallen into her ambush? I must face it out with another quarrel. ——

Jacinta. Your man has been treating your Accommodation; 'tis half made already. 710

Wildblood. I, On your part it may be.

Jacinta. He sayes you knew me.

Wildblood. Yes; I do know you so well, that my poor heart akes for't: I was going to bed without telling you my mind; but, upon consideration I am come. 715

Jacinta. To bring the Money with you.

Wildblood. To declare my grievances, which are great, and many.

Maskall. Well, for impudence, let thee alone.

Wildblood. As in the first place —— 720

Jacinta. I'll hear no Grievances; Where's the Money?

Beatrix. I; keep to that, Madam.

Wildblood. Do you think me a person to be so us'd?

Jacinta. We will not quarrel; Where's the Money?

Wildblood. By your favour we will quarrel. 725

Beatrix. Money, Money ——

Wildblood. I am angry, and can hear nothing.

Beatrix. Money, Money, Money, Money.

Wildblood. Do you think it a reasonable thing to put on two disguises in a Night, to tempt a man? (Help me, 730 *Maskall*, for I want Arguments abominably.) I thank Heaven I was never so barbarously us'd in all my life.

Jacinta. He begins to anger me in good earnest.

Maskall. A thing so much against the Rules of Modesty: so undecent a thing. 735

Wildblood. I, so undecent a thing: nay, now I do not

255

wonder at my self for being angry. And then to wonder
I should love her in those disguises? to quarrel at the
natural desires of humane kind, assaulted by powerful
740   temptations; I am inrag'd at that. ———

Jacinta. Heyday! you had best quarrel too for my bringing
you the Money!

Wildblood. I have a grudging to you for't: (*Maskall,* the
Money, *Maskall;* now help or we are gone.)

745   *Maskall.* Would she offer to bring Money to you? first to
affront your poverty ———

Wildblood. I; to affront my poverty. But, that's no great
matter; and then—

Maskall. And then, to bring you Money (I stick fast, Sir.)

750   *Wildblood.* (Forward, you Dog, and invent, or I'll cut your
throat;) and then as I was saying, to bring me Money

———

Maskall Which is the greatest and most sweet of all
temptations; and to think you could resist it: being also
755   aggravated by her handsomeness who brought it.

Wildblood. Resist it? no; I would she would understand it,
I know better what belongs to flesh and blood then so.

Beatrix (to Jacinta). This is plain confederacie; I smoak it;
he came on purpose to quarrel with you; break first with
760   him and prevent it.

Jacinta [*to Beatrix*]. If it be come to that once, the Devill
take the hindmost; I'll not be last in love; for that will be
a dishonour to my Sex.

Wildblood. And then ———

765   *Jacinta.* Hold Sir; there needs no more: you shall fall out;
and I'll gratifie you with a new occasion: I only try'd
you in hope you would be false; and rather than fail of
my design, brought gold to bribe you to't.

Beatrix. As people when they have an ill bargain, are con-
770   tent to lose by't, that they may get it off their hands.

Maskall. *Beatrix,* while our principals are engag'd, I hold it
not for our honor to stand idle.

Beatrix. With all my heart: please you let us draw off to
some other ground.

775   *Maskall.* I dare meet you on any Spot, but one.

Wildblood. I think we shall do well to put it to an issue;
this is the last time you shall ever be troubled with my
addresses.

Jacinta. The favour had been greater to have spar'd this too.

780   *Maskall.* *Beatrix,* let us dispatch; or they'll break off before
us.

758 *smoak*] understand.

Beatrix. Break as fast as thou wilt, I am as brittle as thou
art for thy heart.

Wildblood. Because I will absolutely break off with you, I
will keep nothing that belongs to you: therefore take   785
back your Picture, and your Handkerchief.

Jacinta. I have nothing of yours to keep; therefore take back
your liberal promises. Take 'em in imagination.

Wildblood. Not to be behind hand with you in your
frumps, I give you back your Purse of Gold: take you   790
that ——— in imagination.

Jacinta. To conclude with you, take back your oathes and
protestations; they are never the worse for the wearing
I assure you: therefore take 'em, spick and span new, for
the use of your next Mistress.   795

Maskall. *Beatrix,* follow your leader; here's the sixpenny
whittle you gave me, with the Mutton haft: I can spare
it, for knives are of little use in *Spain.*

Beatrix. There's your Cizars with the stinking brass chain
to 'em: 'tis well there was no love betwixt us; for they   800
had been too dull to cut it.

Maskall. There's the dandriffe Comb you lent me.

Beatrix. There's your ferret Ribbaning for garters.

Maskall. I would never have come so near as to have taken
'em from you.   805

Beatrix. For your Letter I have it not about me; but upon
reputation I'll burn it.

Maskall. And for yours, I have already put it to a fitting
imployment. ——— Courage, Sir; how goes the battel
on your wing?   810

Wildblood. Just drawing off on both sides. Adieu *Spain.*

Jacinta. Farewel old *England.*

Beatrix. Come away in Triumph; the day's your own
Madam.

Maskall. I'll bear you off upon my shoulders, Sir; we have   815
broke their hearts.

Wildblood. Let her go first then; I'll stay, and keep the
honor of the Field.

Jacinta. I'll not retreat, if you stay till midnight.

Wildblood. Are you sure then we have done loving?   820

Jacinta. Yes, very sure; I think so.

Wildblood. 'Tis well you are so; for otherwise I feel my
stomack a little maukish. I should have doubted another
fit of love were coming up.

---

798 *knives*] for meat was scarce and heavily taxed (Summers).
799 *stinking*] disgusting, contemptible.
803 *ferret Ribbaning*] strong silk or cotton ribbon.

825   *Jacinta.* No, no; your inconstancy secures you enough for
       that.

       Wildblood. That's it which makes me fear my own return-
       ing: nothing vexes me, but that you should part with
       me so slightly, as though I were not worth your keep-
830   ing; well, 'tis a sign you never lov'd me.

       Jacinta. 'Tis the least of your care whether I did or did not:
       it may be it had been more for the quiet of my self, if
       I ——— but 'tis no matter, I'll not give you that satis-
       faction.

835   *Wildblood.* But what's the reason you will not give it me?
       Jacinta. For the reason that we are quite broke off.
       Wildblood. Why, are we quite broke off?
       Jacinta. Why, are we not?
       Wildblood. Well, since 'tis past, 'tis past; but a pox of all
840   foolish quarrelling for my part.

       Jacinta. And a mischief of all foolish disguisements for my
       part.

       Wildblood. But if it were to do again with another Mistress,
       I would e'en plainly confess I had lost my money.

845   *Jacinta.* And if I had to deal with another Servant, I would
       learn more wit then to tempt him in disguises: for that's
       to throw a Venice-glass to the ground, to try if it would
       not break.

       Wildblood. If it were not to please you, I see no necessity of
850   our parting.

       Jacinta. I protest I do it only out of complaisance to you.
       Wildblood. But if I should play the fool and ask you pardon,
       you would refuse it.

       Jacinta. No, never submit, for I should spoil you again with
855   pardoning you.

       Maskall. Do you hear this, *Beatrix*? they are just upon the
       point of accommodation; we must make haste or they'll
       make a peace by themselves; and exclude us from the
       Treaty.

860   *Beatrix.* Declare your self the Aggressor then; and I'll take
       you into mercy.

       Wildblood. The worst that you can say of me is that I have
       lov'd you thrice over.

       Jacinta. The prime Articles between *Spain* and *England* are
865   seal'd; for the rest concerning a more strict alliance, if
       you please we'll dispute them in the Garden.

       Wildblood. But in the first place let us agree on the Article
       of Navigation I beseech you.

       Beatrix. These Leagues offensive and defensive will be too
870   strict for us, *Maskall*: a Treaty of commerce will serve
       our turn.

Maskall. With all my heart; and when our loves are veering,
We'll make no words, but fall to privateering.
Exeunt, the men leading the women.

ACT V. [SCENE 1]

[*Enter*] Lopez, Aurelia, *and* Camilla.

Lopez. 'Tis true, if he had continu'd constant to you, I
should have thought my self oblig'd in honor to be his
friend; but I could no longer suffer him to abuse a person
of your worth and beauty with a feign'd affection.

Aurelia. But is it possible *Don Melchor* should be false to 5
love? I'll be sworn I did not imagine such a treacherie
could have been in nature; especially to a Lady who had
so oblig'd him.

Lopez. 'Twas this, Madam, which gave me the confidence
to wait upon you at an hour which would be otherwise 10
unseasonable.

Aurelia. You are the most obliging person in the world.

Lopez. But to clear it to you that he is false; he is at this
very minute at an assignation with your Cousin in the
Garden; I am sure he was endeavouring it not an hour 15
ago.

Aurelia. I swear this Evening's Air begins to incommode
me extremely with a cold; but yet in hope of detecting
this perjur'd man I am content to stay abroad.

Lopez. But withall you must permit me tell you, Madam, 20
that it is but just I should have some share in a heart
which I endeavour to redeem: in the Law of Arms you
know that they who pay the ransome have right to
dispose of the prisoner.

Aurelia. The prize is so very inconsiderable that 'tis not 25
worth the claiming.

Lopez. If I thought the boon were small, I would not
importune my Princess with the asking it: but since my
life depends upon the grant ———

Camilla. Mam, I must needs tell your Laship that *Don Lopez* 30
has deserv'd you: for he has acted all along like a
Cavalier; and more for your interest than his own;
besides Mam *Don Melchor* is as poor as he is false: for my
part I shall ne're endure to call him Master.

Aurelia. Don Lopez go along with me, I can promise 35
nothing, but I swear I will do my best to disingage my
heart from this furious tender which I have for him.

---

10 you] Q2; *omit* Q1
37 *tender*] a tender feeling.

259

Camilla. If I had been a man I could never have forsaken
you: Ah those languishing casts, Mam; and that pouting
40   lip of your Laship, like a Cherry-bough weigh'd down
with the weight of fruit.
Aurelia. And that sigh too I think is not altogether disagreeable: but something *charmante* and *mignonne*.
Camilla. Well, *Don Lopez*, you'l be but too happy.
45   *Lopez.* If I were once possessor ———

Enter Bellamy *and* Theodosia.

Theodosia. O we are surpriz'd.
Bellamy. Fear nothing, Madam, I think I know 'em: *Don
Lopez?*
Lopez. Our famous *Astrologer*, how come you here!
50   *Bellamy.* I am infinitely happy to have met you with *Donna
Aurelia*, that you may do me the favour to satisfie this
Lady of a truth which I can scarce perswade her to
believe.
Lopez. I am glad our concernments are so equal: for I have
55   the like Favour to ask from *Donna Theodosia.*
Theodosia. *Don Lopez* is too noble to be refus'd any thing
within my power; and I am ready to do him any service
after I have ask'd my Cousin if ever *Don Melchor* pretended to her?
60   *Aurelia.* 'Tis the very question which I was furiously
resolv'd to have ask'd of you.
Theodosia. I must confess he has made some professions to
me: and withall I will acknowledge my own weakness
so far as to tell you I have given way he should often
65   visit me when the world believ'd him absent.
Aurelia. O Cavalier *Astrologer*; how have you betrayd me!
did you not assure me that *Don Melchor's* tender and
inclination was for me only?
Bellamy. I had it from his Star, Madam, I do assure you,
70   and if that twinkled false, I cannot help it. The truth is
there's no trusting the Planet of an inconstant man: his
was moving to you when I look'd on't, and if since it
has chang'd the course, I am not to be blam'd for't.
Lopez. Now, Madam, the truth is evident. And for this
75   Cavalier he might easily be deceiv'd in *Melchor*, for I
dare affirm it to you both, he never knew to which of
you he was most inclin'd: for he visited one, and writ
letters to the other.
Bellamy (to Theodosia). Then Madam I must claim your
80   promise: (since I have discover'd to you that *Don*

39 *casts*] glances.

Melchor is unworthy of your favours) that you would make me happy, who amongst my many imperfections can never be guilty of such a falsehood.

Theodosia. If I have been deceiv'd in *Melchor* whom I have known so long, you cannot reasonably expect I should trust you at a dayes acquaintance.   85

Bellamy. For that, Madam, you may know as much of me in a day as you can in all your life: all my humours circulate like my blood, at farthest within twenty-four hours. I am plain and true like all my Countrymen; you   90 see to the bottom of me as easily as you do to the gravel of a clear stream in Autumn.

Lopez. You plead so well, Sir, that I desire you would speak for me too: my cause is the same with yours, only it has not so good an Advocate.   95

Aurelia. Since I cannot make my self happy, I will have the glory to felicitate another: and therefore I declare I will reward the fidelity of *Don Lopez*.

Theodosia. All that I can say at present is, that I will never be *Don Melchor's*: the rest, time and your service must   100 make out.

Bellamy. I have all I can expect, to be admitted as eldest Servant; as preferment falls I hope you will remember my seniority.

Camilla. Mam, *Don Melchor*.   105

Aurelia. Cavaliers retire a little; we shall see to which of us he will make his Court. ——— *The men withdraw.*

Enter Don Melchor.

Don Melchor, I thought you had been a bed before this time.

Melchor. Fair *Aurelia*, this is a blessing beyond expectation   110 to see you agen so soon.

Aurelia. What important business brought you hither?

Melchor. Onely to make my peace with you before I slept. You know you are the Saint to whom I pay my devotions.   115

Aurelia. And yet it was beyond your expectances to meet me? This is furiously incongruous.

Theodosia (advancing). Don *Melchor*, whither were you bound so late?

Melchor (aside). What shall I say? I am so confounded that   120 I know not to which of them I should excuse my self.

Theodosia. Pray answer me truly to one question: did you never make any addresses to my Cousin?

125   *Melchor.* Fie, fie, Madam, there's a question indeed.
         Aurelia. How, Monster of ingratitude, can you deny the
            Declaration of your passion to me?
         Melchor. I say nothing Madam.
         Theodosia. Which of us is it for whom you are concern'd?
130   *Melchor.* For that Madam, you must excuse me; I have
            more discretion then to boast a Ladies favour.
         Aurelia. Did you counterfeit an address to me?
         Melchor. Still I say nothing, Madam; but I will satisfie
            either of you in private; for these matters are too tender
135   for publick discourse. ———

       Enter Lopez *and* Bellamy *hastily with their swords drawn.*

       Bellamy *and* Lopez! This is strange!
       Lopez. Ladies, we would not have disturb'd you, but as
            we were walking to the Garden-door, it open'd suddenly
            against us, and we confusedly saw by Moon-light, some
140   persons entring, but who they were we know not.
       Bellamy. You had best retire into the Garden-house, and
            leave us to take our fortunes, without prejudice to your
            reputations.

         Enter Wildblood, Maskall, Jacinta, Beatrix.

       Wildblood (*to Jacinta entring*). Do not fear, Madam, I think I
145   heard my friend's voice.
       Bellamy. Marry hang you, is it you that have given us this
            hot alarme.
       Wildblood. There's more in't than you imagine, the whole
            house is up: for seeing you two, and not knowing you
150   after I had entred the Garden-door, I made too much
            haste to get out again, and have left the key broken in
            it. With the noise one of the Servants came running in,
            whom I forc'd back; and doubtless he is gone for com-
            pany, for you may see lights running through every
155   Chamber.
       Theodosia. } What will become of us?
       Jacinta.   }
       Bellamy. We must have recourse to our former resolution.
            Let the Ladies retire into the Garden-house. And now
            I think on't you Gentlemen shall go in with 'em, and
160   leave me and *Maskall* to bear the brunt on't.
       Maskall. Me, Sir? I beseech you let me go in with the
            Ladies too; dear *Beatrix* speak a good word for me, I
            protest 'tis more out of love to thy company than for
            any fear I have.
165   *Bellamy* (*to Maskall*). You Dog I have need of your wit and

counsel. We have no time to deliberate. Will you stay, Sir?

Maskall. No Sir, 'tis not for my safety.

Bellamy (to Melchor). Will you in Sir?

Melchor. No Sir, 'tis not for my honor, to be assisting to   170
you: I'll to *Don Alonzo*, and help to revenge the injury
you are doing him.

Bellamy. Then we are lost, I can do nothing.

Wildblood. Nay, and you talk of honor, by your leave Sir.
I hate your *Spanish* honor ever since it spoyl'd our   175
English Playes, with faces about and t'other side.
                   Falls upon him and throws him down.

Melchor. What do you mean, you will not murder me?
Must valour be oppress'd by multitudes?

Wildblood. Come yarely my mates, every man to his share
of the burthen. Come yarly hay.   180
   The four men take him each by a limb, and carry him out,
                                he crying murder.

Theodosia. If this *Englishman* save us now I shall admire his
wit.

Beatrix. Good wits never think themselves admir'd till they
are well rewarded: you must pay him in *specie*, Madam,
give him love for his wit.   185

                  Enter the Men again.

Bellamy. Ladies fear nothing, but enter into the Garden-
house with these Cavaliers. ———

Maskall. Oh that I were a Cavalier too!
                        Is going with them.

Bellamy. Come you back Sirrah. ———   *Stops him.*
Think your selves as safe as in a Sanctuary, only keep   190
quiet what ever happens.

Jacinta. Come away then, they are upon us.
                Exeunt all but Bellamy *and* Maskall.

Maskall. Hark, I hear the foe coming: methinks they
threaten too, Sir; pray let me go in for a Guard to the
Ladies and poor *Beatrix.* I can fight much better when   195
there is a wall betwixt me and danger.

Bellamy. Peace, I have occasion for your wit to help me lie.

Maskall. Sir, upon the faith of a sinner you have had my
last lye already; I have not one more to do me credit
as I hope to be sav'd, Sir.   200

Bellamy. Victore, victore; knock under you rogue, and confess me Conquerour, and you shall see I'll bring all off.

---

179 *yarely*] briskly, nimbly.
201 *knock under*] yield, as defeated in a drinking bout.

Enter Don Alonzo *and six Servants; with lights
and swords drawn.*

Alonzo. Search about there.

Bellamy. Fear nothing, do but vouch what I shall say.

205 *Maskall.* For a passive lye I can yet do something.

Alonzo. Stand: who goes there?

Bellamy. Friends.

Alonzo. Friends? who are you?

Bellamy. Noble *Don Alonzo*, such as are watching for your
210 good.

Alonzo. Is it you, Sennor *Ingles*? why all this noise and
tumult? where are my Daughters and my Neece? But
in the first place, though last nam'd, how came you
hither, Sir.

215 *Bellamy.* I came hither ———— by Astrologie, Sir.

Maskall. My Master's in, heavens send him good shipping
with his lye, and all kind Devils stand his friends.

Alonzo. How, by Astrologie, Sir? meaning you came
hither by Art Magick?

220 *Bellamy.* I say by pure Astrologie Sir, I foresaw by my Art
a little after I had left you that your Neece and Daughters
would this night run a risque of being carried away from
this very Garden.

Alonzo. O the wonders of this speculation!

225 *Bellamy.* Thereupon I call'd immediately for my sword and
came in all haste to advertise you; but I see there's no
resisting Destiny, for just as I was entring the Garden-
door I met the Women with their Gallants all under sail
and outward bound.

230 *Maskall.* Thereupon what does me he but draws by my
advice ————

Bellamy. How now Master Raskall? are you itching to be
in?

Maskall. Pray, Sir, let me go snip with you in this lye, and
235 be not too covetous of honor? you know I never stood
with you; now my courage is come to me I cannot
resist the temptation.

Bellamy. Content; tell on.

Maskall. So in short Sir we drew, first I, and then my
240 Master; but, being overpower'd, they have escap'd us,
so that I think you may go to bed and trouble your self
no further, for gone they are.

Bellamy. You tell a lye! you have curtail'd my invention:
you are not fit to invent a lye for a Bawd when she
245 would whedle a young Squire.

234 *go snip*] go shares.

Alonzo. Call up the Officers of Justice, I'll have the Town search'd immediately.

Bellamy. 'Tis in vain, Sir; I know by my Art you'll never recover 'em: besides, 'tis an affront to my friends the Stars, who have otherwise dispos'd of 'em.   250

Enter a Servant.

Servant. Sir, the key is broken in the Garden-door, and the door lock'd, so that of necessitie they must be in the Garden yet.

Alonzo. Disperse your selves, some into the Wilderness, some into the Allyes, and some into the Parterre: you   255
Diego, go trie to get out the key, and run to the Corigi-dore for his assistance: in the mean time I'll search the Garden-house my self.

Exeunt all the Servants but one.

Maskall (to Bellamy aside). I'll be unbetted again if you please Sir, and leave you all the honor of it.   260

Alonzo. Come Cavalier, let us in together.

Bellamy (holding him). Hold Sir for the love of heaven, you are not mad.

Alonzo. We must leave no place unsearch'd. A light there.

Bellamy. Hold I say, do you know what you are under-   265
taking? and have you arm'd your self with resolution for such an adventure?

Alonzo. What adventure?

Bellamy. A word in private. ———— The place you would go into is full of enchantments; there are at this time,   270
for ought I know, a Legion of spirits in it.

Alonzo. You confound me with wonder, Sir!

Bellamy. I have been making there my Magical operations, to know the event of your Daughter's flight: and, to perform it rightly, have been forc'd to call up Spirits of   275
several Orders: and there they are humming like a swarm of Bees, some stalking about upon the ground, some flying, and some sticking upon the walls like Rear-mice.

Maskall. The Devil's in him, he's got off again.   280

Alonzo. Now Sir I shall trie the truth of your friendship to

---

254 *Wilderness*] a part of a large garden, planted with trees, and laid out in the form of a maze or labyrinth.

255 *Allyes*] walks generally bordered by trees or bushes.

255 *Parterre*] a level space occupied by ornamental flower beds.

256–57 *Corigidore*] a Spanish magistrate, chief justice or governor of a town.

259 *unbetted*] freed from a bet (this passage the only example in *OED*).

279 *Rear-mice*] bats.

me. To confess the secret of my soul to you, I have all
my life been curious to see a Devil: And to that purpose
have con'd *Agrippa* through and through, and made
285   experiment of all his rules, *Pari die et incremento Lunæ*,
and yet could never compass the sight of one of these
Dæmoniums: if you will ever oblige me let it be on this
occasion.

Maskall. There's another storm arising.

290   *Bellamy.* You shall pardon me, Sir, I'll not expose you to
that perril for the world without due preparations of
ceremony.

Alonzo. For that, Sir, I alwayes carry a Talisman about me;
that will secure me: and therefore I will venture in a
295   God's name, and defie 'em all at once.   *Going in.*

Maskall. How the pox will he get off from this?

Bellamy. Well, Sir, since you are so resolv'd, send off your
Servant that there may be no noise made on't, and we'll
take our venture.

300   *Alonzo.* *Pedro*, leave your light, and help the fellows
search the Garden.   *Exit Servant.*

Maskall. What does my incomprehensible Master mean?

Bellamy. Now I must tell you Sir, you will see that which
will very much astonish you if my Art fail me not.
     Goes to the door.

305   You Spirits and Intelligences that are within there, stand
close, and silent, at your perril, and fear nothing, but
appear in your own shapes, boldly.—*Maskall* open the
door.

> Maskall *goes to one side of the Scene, which draws,*
> *and discovers* Theodosia, Jacinta, Aurelia, Bea-
> trix, Camilla, Lopez, Wildblood *standing all*
> *without motion in a rank.*

Now Sir what think you?

310   *Alonzo.* They are here, they are here: we need search no
farther. Ah you ungratious baggages!
     Going toward them.

Bellamy. Stay, or you'll be torn in pieces: these are the
very shapes I Conjur'd up, and truly represent to you in
what company your Niece and Daughters are, this very
315   moment.

307–8 *Maskall* open the door.] Q3; Q1–2,F *print as stage-direction*

284 *Agrippa*] scientist and humanist Henry Cornelius Agrippa
(1486–1535). His *De occulta philosophia* (1533, English translation,
1651) gave him a reputation as a magician.

285 *Pari . . . Lunæ*] choose the day and the proper phase of the
moon: apparently these are instructions for conjuring.

Alonzo. Why, are they not they? I durst have sworn that
some of 'em had been my own flesh and blood. ———
Look; one of them is just like that rogue your Camrade.
   Wildblood *shakes his head and frowns at him.*
Bellamy. Do you see how you have provok'd that *English*
 Devil: take heed of him; if he gets you once into his   320
 clutches: ———   Wildblood *embracing* Jacinta.
Alonzo. He seems to have got possession of the Spirit of
 my *Jacinta* by his hugging her.
Bellamy. Nay, I imagin'd as much: do but look upon his
 physiognomy, you have read *Baptista Porta*: has he not   325
 the leer of a very lewd debauch'd Spirit?
Alonzo. He has indeed: Then there's my Neece *Aurelia*,
 with the Spirit of *Don Lopez*; but that's well enough;
 and my Daughter *Theodosia* all alone: pray how comes
 that about?   330
Bellamy. She's provided for with a Familiar too: one that
 is in this very room with you, and by your Elbow; but
 I'll shew you him some other time.
Alonzo. And that Baggage *Beatrix*, how I would swinge
 her if I had her here; I lay my life she was in the Plot   335
 for the flight of her Mistresses.
     Beatrix *claps her hands at him.*
Bellamy. Sir you do ill to provoke her: for being the Spirit
 of a Woman, she is naturally mischievous: you see she
 can scarce hold her hands from you already.
Maskall. Let me alone to revenge your quarrel upon   340
 Beatrix: if e're she come to light I'll take a course with
 her I warrant you Sir.
Bellamy. Now come away Sir, you have seen enough: the
 Spirits are in pain whilst we are here: we keep 'em too
 long condens'd in bodies: if we were gone they would   345
 rarifie into air immediately. *Maskall* shut the door.
   Maskall *goes to the Scene and it closes.*
Alonzo. Monstrum hominis! O prodigie of Science!

  Enter two Servants with Don Melchor.

Bellamy. Now help me with a lye *Maskall*, or we are lost.
Maskall. Sir, I could never lie with man or woman in a
 fright.   350
Servant. Sir, we found this Gentleman bound and gagg'd,
 and he desir'd us to bring him to you with all haste
 imaginable.

 325 *Baptista Porta*] Giovanni Battista della Porta (*ca.* 1538–1615), the
most influential leader of the science of physiognomy, author of *De
humana physiognomonia* (1591).
 334 *swinge*] beat.

355

Melchor. O Sir, Sir, your two Daughters and your Niece ——

Bellamy. They are gone, he knows it: but are you mad Sir to set this pernicious wretch at libertie?

Melchor. I endeavour'd all that I was able ——

Maskall. Now Sir I have it for you. ——

Aside to his Master.

360   He was endeavouring indeed to have got away with 'em: for your Daughter *Theodosia* was his prize: but we prevented him, and left him in the condition in which you see him.

Alonzo. I thought somewhat was the matter that *Theodosia*

365   had not a Spirit by her, as her Sister had.

Bellamy. This was he I meant to shew you.

Melchor. Do you believe him Sir?

Bellamy. No, no, believe *him*, Sir: you know his truth ever since he stole your Daughter's Diamond.

370   *Melchor.* I swear to you by my honor.

Alonzo. Nay, a thief I knew him, and yet after that, he had the impudence to ask me for my Daughter.

Bellamy. Was he so impudent? The case is plain Sir, put him quickly into custody.

375   *Melchor.* Hear me but one word Sir, and I'll discover all to you.

Bellamy. Hear him not Sir: for my Art assures me if he speaks one syllable more, he will cause great mischief.

Alonzo. Will he so? I'll stop my ears, away with him.

380   *Melchor.* Your Daughters are yet in the Garden, hidden by this fellow and his accomplices.

Alonzo (*at the same time drowning him*). I'll stop my ears, I'll stop my ears.

Bellamy [*and*] *Maskall* (*at the same time also*). A thief, a thief,

385   away with him.   *Servants carry* Melchor *off struggling.*

Alonzo. He thought to have born us down with his confidence.

Enter another Servant.

Servant. Sir, with much ado we have got out the key and open'd the door.

390   *Alonzo.* Then, as I told you, run quickly to the Corigidor, and desire him to come hither in person to examine a malefactor.   Wildblood *sneezes within.*

Alonzo. Hark, what noise is that within? I think one sneezes.

395   *Bellamy.* One of the Devils I warrant you has got a cold with being so long out of the fire.

Alonzo. Bless his Devilship as I may say.

Wildblood sneezes again.

Servant (*to Don Alonzo*). This is a man's voice, do not suffer your self to be deceiv'd so grosly, Sir.

Maskall. A man's voice, that's a good one indeed! that you   400
should live to these years and yet be so silly as not to
know a man from a Devil.

Alonzo. There's more in't than I imagin'd: hold up your
Torch and go in first, *Pedro*, and I'll follow you.

Maskall. No, let me have the honor to be your Usher.   405

Takes the Torch and goes in.

Maskall (*within*). Help, help, help.

Alonzo. What's the matter?

Bellamy. Stir not upon your life Sir.

Enter Maskall *again without the Torch.*

Maskall. I was no sooner entred, but a huge Giant seiz'd
my Torch, and fell'd me along, with the very whiffe of   410
his breath as he past by me.

Alonzo. Bless us!

Bellamy (*at the door, to them within*). Pass out now while you
have time in the dark: the Officers of Justice will be here
immediately, the Garden-door is open for you.   415

Alonzo. What are you muttering there Sir?

Bellamy. Only dismissing these Spirits of darkness, that
they may trouble you no further: go out I say.

They all come out upon the Stage, groaping their way.

Wildblood falls into Alonzo's *hands.*

Alonzo. I have caught some body; are these your Spirits?
Another light quickly, *Pedro*.   420

Maskall (*slipping between Alonzo and Wildblood*). 'Tis *Maskall* you have caught, Sir; do you mean to strangle me
that you press me so hard between your Arms?

Alonzo (*letting Wildblood go*). Is it thee *Maskall*? I durst
have sworn it had been another.   425

Bellamy. Make haste now before the Candle comes.

Aurelia *falls into* Alonzo's *armes.*

Alonzo. Now I have another.

Aurelia. 'Tis *Maskall* you have caught Sir.

Alonzo. No I thank you Niece, this artifice is too gross! I
know your voice a little better. What ho, bring lights   430
there.

Bellamy. Her impertinence has ruin'd all.

Enter Servants with lights and swords drawn.

410 *along*] flat. The reading of Q2 *all along* is not a necessary correction, for *along* was frequently used alone in this sense.

Servant. Sir, the Corigidor is coming according to your desire: in the mean time we have secur'd the Garden doors.

435

Alonzo. I am glad on't: I'll make some of 'em severe examples.

Wildblood. Nay then as we have liv'd merrily, so let us die together: but we'll shew the *Don* some sport first.

440

Theodosia. What will become of us!

Jacinta. We'll die for company: nothing vexes me but that I am not a man to have one thrust at that malicious old father of mine before I go.

Lopez. Let us break our way through the Corigidor's band.

445

Jacinta. A match i'faith: we'll venture our bodies with you: you shall put the baggage in the middle.

Wildblood. He that pierces thee, I say no more, but I shall be somewhat angry with him: (*to Alonzo*) in the mean time I arrest you Sir, in the behalf of this good company. As the Corigidor uses us, so we'll use you.

450

Alonzo. You do not mean to murder me!

Bellamy. You murder your self if you force us to it.

Wildblood. Give me a Razor there, that I may scrape his weeson, that the bristles may not hinder me when I come to cut it.

455

Bellamy. What need you bring matters to that extremity? you have your ransome in your hand: here are three men, and there are three women; you understand me.

Jacinta. If not, here's a sword and there's a throat: you understand me.

460

Alonzo. This is very hard!

Theodosia. The propositions are good, and marriage is as honorable as it us'd to be.

Beatrix. You had best let your Daughers live branded with the name of Strumpets: for what ever befalls the men, that will be sure to be their share.

465

Alonzo. I can put them into a Nunnery.

All the Women. A Nunnery!

Jacinta. I would have thee to know, thou graceless old man, that I defie a Nunnery: name a Nunnery once more, and I disown thee for my Father.

470

Lopez. You know the Custome of the Country, in this case Sir: 'tis either death or marriage: the business will certainly be publick; and if they die they have sworn you shall bear 'em company.

475

Alonzo. Since it must be so, run *Pedro* and stop the Corigi-

454 *weeson*] throat, weasand.

dor: tell him it was only a Carnival merriment, which I
mistook for a Rape and Robbery.

Jacinta. Why now you are a dutiful Father again, and I
receive you into grace.   480

Bellamy. Among the rest of your mistakes, Sir, I must
desire you to let my *Astrologie* pass for one: my Mathematicks, and Art Magick were only a Carnival device;
and now that's ending, I have more mind to deal with
the flesh than with the devil.   485

Alonzo. No Astrologer! 'tis impossible!

Maskall. I have known him, Sir, this seven years, and dare
take my oath he has been always an utter stranger to
the Stars: and indeed to any thing that belongs to
heaven.   490

Lopez. Then I have been cozen'd among the rest.

Theodosia. And I; but I forgive him.

Beatrix. I hope you will forgive me, Madam; who have
been the cause on't; but what he wants in Astrologie he
shall make up to you some other way, I'll pass my word   495
for him.

Alonzo. I hope you are both Gentlemen?

Bellamy. As good as the Cid himself, Sir.

Alonzo. And for your Religion, right Romanes ———

Wildblood. As ever was *Marc Anthony.*   500

Alonzo. For your fortunes and courages ———

Maskall. They are both desperate, Sir; especially their
fortunes.

Theodosia (to Bellamy). You should not have had my consent so soon, but only to revenge my self upon the   505
falseness of *Don Melchor.*

Aurelia. I must avow that gratitude for *Don Lopez* is as
prevalent with me as revenge against *Don Melchor.*

Alonzo. Lent you know begins to morrow; when that's
over marriage will be proper.   510

Jacinta. If I stay till after Lent, I shall be to marry when I
have no love left: I'll not bate you an Ace of to night,
Father: I mean to bury this man e're Lent be done, and
get me another before Easter.

Alonzo. Well, make a night on't then.   515

> *Giving his Daughters.*

Wildblood. Jacinta Wildblood, welcome to me: since our
Starres have doom'd it so we cannot help it: but 'twas
a meer trick of Fate to catch us thus at unawares: to
draw us in with a what do you lack as we pass'd by:

---

519 *what ... lack*] the cry of peddlars and shopkeepers.

271

520   had we once separated to night, we should have had
more wit than ever to have met again to morrow.

Jacinta. 'Tis true we shot each other flying: we were both
upon wing I find; and had we pass'd this Critical
525   minute, I should have gone for the *Indies*, and you for
Greenland e're we had met in a bed upon consideration.

Maskall. You have quarrell'd twice to night without
bloodshed, 'ware the third time.

Jacinta. A propos! I have been retrieving an old Song of a
Lover that was ever quarrelling with his Mistress: I
530   think it will fit our amour so well, that if you please I'll
give it you for an Epithalamium: and you shall sing it.
Gives him a Paper.

Wildblood. I never sung in all my life; nor ever durst trie
when I was alone, for fear of braying.

Jacinta. Just me, up and down; but for a frolick let's sing
535   together: for I am sure if we cannot sing now, we shall
never have cause when we are married.

Wildblood. Begin then; give me my Key, and I'll set my
voice to't.

Jacinta. Fa la, fa la, fa la.
540   *Wildblood.* Fala, fala, fala. Is this your best upon the faith
of a Virgin?

Jacinta. I by the Muses, I am at my pitch.

Wildblood. Then do your worst: and let the company be
judge who sings worst.
545   *Jacinta.* Upon condition the best singer shall wear the
breeches: prepare to strip Sir; I shall put you into your
drawers presently.

Wildblood. I shall be reveng'd with putting you into your
smock anon; St. *George* for me.
550   *Jacinta.* St. *James* for me: come start Sir.

SONG

Damon.   Celimena, *of my heart,*
None shall e're bereave you:
If, with your good leave, I may
Quarrel with you once a day,
555   *I will never leave you.*

2

Celimena. *Passion's but an empty name*
Where respect is wanting:
Damon *you mistake your ayme;*
Hang your heart, and burn your flame,
560   *If you must be ranting.*

3

Damon.	*Love as dull and muddy is,*
	As decaying liquor:
	Anger sets it on the lees,
	And refines it by degrees,
	Till it workes it quicker. 565

4

Celimena.	*Love by quarrels to beget*
	Wisely you endeavour;
	With a grave Physician's wit
	Who to cure an Ague fit
	Put me in a Feavor. 570

5

Damon.	*Anger rouzes love to fight,*
	And his only bayt is,
	'Tis the spurre to dull delight,
	And is but an eager bite,
	When desire at height is. 575

6

Celimena.	*If such drops of heat can fall*
	In our wooing weather;
	If such drops of heat can fall,
	We shall have the Devil and all
	When we come together. 580

Wildblood. Your judgement Gentlemen: a Man or a Maid?

Bellamy. And you make no better harmony after you are married then you have before, you are the miserablest couple in Christendome.

Wildblood. 'Tis no great matter; if I had had a good voice   585
she would have spoil'd it before to morrow.

Bellamy. When *Maskall* has married *Beatrix*, you may learn of her.

Maskall. You shall put her life into a Lease then.

Wildblood. Upon condition that when I drop into your   590
house from hunting, I may set my slippers at your door, as a *Turk* does at a *Jew's*, that you may not enter.

Beatrix. And while you refresh your self within, he shall wind the horn without.

Maskall. I'll throw up my Lease first.   595

Bellamy. Why, thou would'st not be so impudent, to marry *Beatrix* for thy self only?

Beatrix. For all his ranting and tearing now, I'll pass my word he shall degenerate into as tame and peaceable a Husband as a civil Woman would wish to have.   600

---

589 *put . . . Lease*] be granted possession of her.

Enter Don Melchor *with a Servant.*

Melchor. Sir ——

Alonzo. I know what you would say, but your discoverie
    comes too late now.

Melchor. Why, the Ladies are found.

605   Aurelia. But their inclinations are lost I can assure you.

Jacinta. Look you Sir, there goes the game: your Plate-fleet
    is divided; half for *Spain*, and half for *England*.

Theodosia. You are justly punish'd for loving two.

Melchor. Yet I have the comfort of a cast Lover: I will think

610   well of my self; and despise my Mistresses.   *Exit.*

DANCE

Bellamy. Enough, enough; let's end the Carnival abed.

Wildblood. And for these Gentlemen, when e're they try,
    May they all speed as soon, and well as I.

                         Exeunt Omnes.

606 *Plate-fleet*] returning with the annual yield of the silver mines in
America.

Epilogue

My part being small, I have had time to day,
To mark your various censures of our Play:
First, looking for a Judgement or a Wit,
Like *Jews* I saw 'em scatter'd through the Pit:
And where a knot of Smilers lent an eare   5
To one that talk'd, I knew the foe was there.
The Club of jests went round; he who had none
Borrow'd o'th' next, and told it for his own:
Among the rest they kept a fearfull stir,
In whisp'ring that he stole th'Astrologer;   10
And said, betwixt a *French* and *English* Plot
He eas'd his half-tir'd Muse, on pace and trot.
Up starts a Monsieur new come o're; and warm
In the *French* stoop; and the pull-back o'th' arm;
Morbleu dit il, and cocks, I am a rogue   15
But he has quite spoil'd the *feint Astrologue.*
Pox, sayes another; here's so great a stir
With a son of a whore Farce that's regular,
A rule where nothing must decorum shock!
Dam' me 'ts as dull as dining by the clock.   20
An Evening! why the devil should we be vext
Whether he gets the Wench this night or next?
When I heard this, I to the Poet went,   ⎫
Told him the house was full of discontent,   ⎬
And ask'd him what excuse he could invent.   ⎭ 25
He neither swore nor storm'd as Poets do,
But, most unlike an Author, vow'd 'twas true.
Yet said, he us'd the *French* like Enemies,
And did not steal their Plots, but made 'em prize.
But should he all the pains and charges count   30
Of taking 'em, the bill so high wou'd mount,
That, like Prize-goods, which through the Office come,
He could have had 'em much more cheap at home.
He still must write; and Banquier-like, each day
Accept new Bills, and he must break, or pay.   35
When through his hands such sums must yearly run,
You cannot think the Stock is all his own.
His haste his other errors might excuse;
But there's no mercy for a guilty Muse:
For like a Mistress, she must stand or fall,   40
And please you to a height, or not at all.

7 *Club of jests*] jests shared jointly and retold as if one's own.
14 *French stoop*] bow.

CHANGES IN ACCIDENTALS

Preface 9 *Conquest of*] Conquest of 10 improvement] improvemeni
19 nature] noture 53 manners,] ~ ; 114 precept,] ~. 150 *conigisse.*]
~, 186 witty Brave] wity Brave 221 *Eunuch*] Eunuch 240 (except-
ing] ˆ~ 350 help'd] help' 361 *Hecatommithi*] *Hecatommuthi*
I.i.3 Letter;] ~. 9 twó.] ~ : 78 To] to 81 That] that 84
what,] ~ˆ 116 throats;] ~, 117 what,] ~ ;
I.ii.22–23 not; . . . Windows,] ~, . . . ~ ; 48 fix;] ~, 121 Father,]
~ˆ
II.i.31 Why] why 77 What,] ~ˆ 130 year. If] year, if 191 Yet]
yet 202 Madame.] ~ : 213 What,] ~ˆ 255 company. Well]
company: well 336 what,] ~ˆ 398 her:—] ~ :ˆ 500 wrath?]
~, 596 here?] ~ : 601 discover'd] disover'd
III.i.12 night,] ~ˆ 48 Borachio's] Boracho's 54 Now] now 102
what,] ~ˆ 118 Mam,] ~ˆ 134 since] sioce 185 Hero's] Heros
299 your] yonr 319 *Sors*] Sors 334 This] this 369 time—] ~.
376 Sir—] ~ ; 392 *dicendi.*] ~, 406 aforesaid.— Not yet?]
~ˆ — not yet, 510 true,] ~ˆ 530 here,] ~ˆ
IV.i.91 do't.] ~, 242 himself] nimself 396 Science;] ~, 437
theft.] ~ ; 646 why,] ~ˆ 699 you.— Sir,] ~ˆ — ~. 837,
838 Why,] ~ˆ 865 alliance,] ~ ;
V.i.70 it.] ~ : 100 rest,] ~ˆ 107 Court.—] ~.ˆ 108 *Melchor,*]
~ˆ 124 cousin?] ~. 126 How,] ~ˆ 135 discourse.—] ~.ˆ
138 Garden-door] ~ˆ~ 152 running] runing 189 Sirrah.—]
~.ˆ 219 Magick?] ~. 227 Garden-door] ~ˆ~ 336.1 claps]
Claps 356 gone,] ~ˆ 405 No,] ~ˆ 430 ho,] ~ˆ 495 way,]
~ˆ 507 gratitude,] ~, 596 Why,] ~ˆ 597 *Beatrix,*] ~ :
604 Why,] ~ˆ
Epilogue 8, 14 o'th'] oth' 16 *feint Astrologue*] feint Astrologue 22
Whether] Whither

Press Variants in Q1
Sheet a (inner forme)
Corrected: CCC, TxU[1,4,5]
Uncorrected: ICN, TxU[2,3]

Sig. a2
Preface 194 the Speeches] the long Speeches

Sheet b (outer forme)
Corrected: CCC, TxU[5]
Uncorrected: ICN, TxU[1–4]

Sig. b2[v]
catchword Persons] *Peersons*

Sheet F (inner forme)
Corrected: CCC, CSmH, TxU[1–5]
Uncorrected: ICN

Sig. F1[v]
III.i.443 Guit- / tars] Gui- / tars
449 Guittars] Guittarrs
Sig. F3[v]
III.i.597 *Maskall,*] *Maskall*
Sig. F4
III.i.617 Heaven!] Heaven,
632 *Peru,*] *Perue*

Sheet K (outer forme)
Corrected: CCC, ICN, TxU[1–3,5]
Uncorrected: CSmH, TxU[4]

Sig. K3
V.i.178 Must] *Meleh.* Must

Marriage a-la-Mode

The design of *Marriage a-la-Mode* is subject to the same aesthetic principles as an elegant geometric garden: symmetry, balance, contrast, clarity, and above all, style—the maximum amount of artifice that can be attained with material drawn from nature. The romantic and antiromantic actions explicitly set each other off in alternating scenes, showing the varieties of love in contrasting circumstances: in public life, where political interests impinge upon an idealized passion, and in private life, where wit and passion try to preserve the excitement of a courtship under the official sanction of marriage. Leonidas and Palmyra, "two miricles, of different sexes but of equal form," are prevented from achieving their fondest purpose and fulfilling their love in marriage, because political power first encircles one and then the other, creating an unequal match. If Leonidas falls heir to the throne, his father would force him to marry Almathea; if Palmyra is the princess, she must marry Argelon; both matches are for reasons of state. Consequently, only armed rebellion can set things straight, by overthrowing the usurping tyrant. Similarly, in the other action, two love triangles involving four people illustrate the contradictions between love and marriage. The battle of the sexes has been continuous during four acts, and only an elaborate truce between factions can make peace. The domestic civil war is settled after each has consented to the other's provisos; then Rhodophil and Palamede prove they are men by drawing their swords and fighting for the rightful faction in the great rebellion. The whole play suggests that a limited number of possible situations may be invented, and Dryden gives the impression that their potential variations have all been worked out to the fullest.

He skillfully sets forth complementary episodes with their exquisitely defined tones, a balance of whimsy and seriousness, of self-mockery and sentimentalism, of tough reasonableness and slight lyrical grace. Nowhere do they blend, except in the insinuations of the dialogue, as mentioned in the general introduction.[1] Evidence of Dryden's use of sources helps us to see his manipulation of tone, because almost every important departure from source heightens the analogy between the two plots and increases the audience's awareness of the subtext. The story of Sesostris and Timareta in Madeleine de Scudéry's *Artamène, ou le Grand Cyrus*[2] sug-

---

[1] For another view of the "hidden metaphor" in the play, see Bruce King's "Dryden's *Marriage a la Mode*," *Drama Survey*, IV (1965), 28–37.
[2] Published 1648–53, in English 1653–54, VI, 2.

gested the romantic action, but Dryden cut the tale severely and made two major inventions, according to N. B. Allen (pp. 100–106). Rather than allow the king to have a gradual change of heart, as in the source, Leonidas seizes the kingdom by force. The other significant change is the action of III.i, where Polydamas has decided to cast Palmyra adrift in a boat, to die for the love of Leonidas; all the grand posturing by Leonidas and Palmyra are thus Dryden's addition, and all the elaborate comments on dying first, dying later, and dying together are his. Allen thinks that this scene "shows how badly he could 'improve' on his sources" (p. 265), but it is a striking instance of a thematic echo of the other action.

No significant literary parallels, outside of Dryden's previous comedies, have been found for the antiromantic action, except for the character of Melantha. Dryden changed Mascarille of Molière's *Les Précieuses ridicules* from one who affected the jargon of *préciosité* into a more lighthearted and self-aware female fop. She is no mere fool, and although she is frivolous, she does not deceive herself when she is slighted by the court. Her favorite phrase, "Let me die," varies the usual expression, "Let me perish," and has no counterpart in Molière.

The notorious song (IV.ii) comes from a French madrigal, found in *Recueil de quelques pieces nouvelles et galantes, tant en prose qu'en vers* (1664, cited by Allen, p. 115–16), the last seven lines of which read:

> Meurs, mon Tirsis; car je me meurs aussi.
> Soudain ce Berger tout en flâme,
> Luy réspond, come toy je me meurs, je me pâme.
> Ainsi dans les ravissemens
> Moururent ces heureux Amans;
> Mais d'une mort si douce & si digne d'envie,
> Que pour mourir encour ils reprirent la vie.

Dryden's final couplet, his invention, adds the ironic twist, implying the eventual superiority of the woman.

> Then often they di'd; but the more they did so,
> The Nymph di'd more quick, and the Shepherd more slow.

This presents an appropriate analogy with the love game; although the men seem to be the aggressors and great braggarts about their sexual prowess, the women conquer with love and marriage. And in the romantic action, Leonidas wins a crown, only to restrain his power. He will not execute the father of his mistress, and his last speech emphasizes his subordinate position in love:

Beyond my Crown, I have one joy in store;
To give that Crown to her whom I adore.

The dedication to the Earl of Rochester, not reprinted in
the present edition because of its slight literary interest, says
that the play "receiv'd amendment" from the earl, who furthermore "commended it to the view" of the king. Charles'
"approbation of it in Writing, made way for its kind reception on the *Theatre*." Dryden goes on to say that the play's
good qualities are the result of his being admitted to Rochester's conversation, and that the best comic writers of the age
acknowledge "that they have copy'd the Gallantries of Courts,
the Delicacy of Expression, and the Decencies of Behaviour"
from Rochester, "with more success, then if they had taken
their Models from the Court of *France*" (1673 edition, sig.
B2ᵛ). The play was, Dryden thought, perhaps "the best of my
Comedies" (sig. B4). At any rate, it was finished presumably
by the summer of 1671,[3] acted by the King's Company probably about April, 1672.[4] The recorded performances, includ-
ing revivals in April, 1674; July, 1675; and June, 1697, mean
that the play was at least moderately successful. And contemporary allusions suggest some notoriety, as the remark of a
"Country Gentleman" in 1674, that Dryden has celebrated
love and marriage and he does not endeavor to prove that
love and lust are the same passion.

> What is either wicked or silly in modish colours he has so
> well painted, as would divert any person that is owner
> of the least enginuity, from both: more particularly this
> of shunning Marriage, and being entred perfidiously to
> break a vow so easy to be kept, in his Play of *Marriage
> a-la-Mode*: a more gentile Satyre against this sort of folly,
> no Pen can write, where he brings the very assignations
> that are commonly used about Town upon the stage: and
> to see both Boxes and Pitt so damnably crouded, in order
> to see themselves abused, and yet neither to be angry nor
> ashamed, argues such excess of stupidity, that this great
> Pen it self . . . would be put to a nonplus to express it.[5]

The song "Whil'st Alexas lay" was quickly printed in *Covent
Garden Drollery* (1672), *New Court Songs and Poems* (1672), and

---

[3] C. E. Ward, *The Life of John Dryden* (1961), p. 85.
[4] Ward thinks it was acted first in late 1671 (p. 83).
[5] *Marriage Asserted: In Answer to a Book Entitled Conjugium Conjurgium
written by a "Country Gentleman"* (1674); cited by Harold Brooks,
"Some Notes on Dryden, Cowley and Shadwell," N & Q, CLXVIII
(1935), 94.

Westminster Drollery (1672), and both songs, with musical settings, in *Choice Songs and Ayres* (1673).[6]

Entered under the title "Amorous adventures, or marriage á lá mode" in the Stationers' Register, March 18, 1673, and in the Term Catalogue, June 16, 1673, the first quarto was printed in that spring. The University of Chicago Library copy of Q1 (Macd. 77a, W & M 432), the basis of this edition, has been compared with the Newberry, Huntington, Texas, Claremont College, British Museum[1] (1174.e.15), and British Museum[2] (1174.g.10) copies, but few press variants were found. Collation of subsequent editions of Q2 1684, Q3 1691, Q4 1698, and F 1701 revealed no new authority for the text. Melantha's French has been allowed to stand as it was printed in Q1, except that acute accents have been supplied, because they influence the pronunciation.

[6] Reprinted by Cyrus L. Day, *The Songs of John Dryden* (1932), pp. 41–43.

MARRIAGE
A-la-Mode.

A
COMEDY.

As it is Acted at the

THEATRE-ROYAL.

Written by *JOHN DRYDEN*, Servant
to His Majesty.

———————— *Quicquid ſum ego, quamvis
Infra Lucilli cenſum ingeniumque, tamen me
Cum magnis vixiſſe, invita fatebitur uſque
Invidia, & fragili quærens illidere dentem
Offendet ſolido.*

Horat. Serm.

LONDON,

Printed by *T. N.* for *Henry Herringman*, and are to be
ſold at the *Anchor* in the Lower Walk of
the *New Exchange.* 1673.

Persons Represented

MEN

Polydamas, Usurper of *Sicily*.
Leonidas, the Rightful Prince, unknown.
Argaleon, Favourite to *Polydamas*.
Hermogenes, Foster-father to *Leonidas*.
Eubulus, his Friend and Companion.
Rhodophil, Captain of the Guards.
Palamede, a Courtier.
[*Straton*, Servant to *Palamede*.]

WOMEN

Palmyra, Daughter to the Usurper.
Amalthea, Sister to *Argaleon*.
Doralice, Wife to *Rhodophil*.
Melantha, an Affected Lady.
Philotis, Woman to *Melantha*.
Beliza, Woman to *Doralice*.
Artemis, a Court-Lady.

Scene, *Sicilie*.

The original cast as listed in Q1: *Polydamus*, William Wintershall;
Leonidas, Edward Kynaston; *Argaleon*, Edward Lydall; *Hermogenes*,
William Cartwright; *Eubulus*, Marmaduke Watson; *Rhodophil*,
Michael Mohun; *Palamede*, Charles Hart; *Palmyra*, Elizabeth Cox;
Almathea, Elizabeth James; *Doralice*, Rebecca Marshall; *Melantha*,
Elizabeth Boutell; *Philotis*, Anne Reeves (rumored to be Dryden's
mistress); *Beliza*, Elizabeth Slade; *Artemis*, Susanna Uphill.

Prologue

Lord, how reform'd and quiet we are grown,
Since all our Braves and all our Wits are gone:
Fop-corner now is free from Civil War:
White-Wig and Vizard make no longer jar.
France, and the Fleet, have swept the Town so clear,   5
That we can Act in peace, and you can hear.
'Twas a sad sight, before they march'd from home, ⎫
To see our Warriours, in Red Wastecoats, come,   ⎬
With hair tuck'd up, into our Tireing-room.   ⎭
But 'twas more sad to hear their last Adieu,   10
The Women sob'd, and swore they would be true;
And so they were, as long as e're they cou'd: ⎫
But powerful *Guinnee* cannot be withstood,   ⎬
And they were made of Play-house flesh and bloud. ⎭
Fate did their Friends for double use ordain,   ⎫   15
In Wars abroad, they grinning Honour gain,   ⎬
And Mistresses, for all that stay, maintain.   ⎭
Now they are gone, 'tis dead Vacation here,
For neither Friends nor Enemies appear.
Poor pensive Punk now peeps ere Plays begin,   20
Sees the bare Bench, and dares not venture in:
But manages her last Half-crown with care,
And trudges to the *Mall*, on foot, for Air.
Our City Friends so far will hardly come,

1–37] There are many insignificant variants in the first printing of the prologue in *Covent Garden Drollery* 1672 (Wing STC C 6624A). If the additional couplet following l. 6, "Those that durst fight are gone to get renown, / And those that durst not, blush to stand in Town," is by Dryden, I am inclined to think it was deleted as unsuitable to the trend of the argument. L. 7 refers to only those who "went from home," not those who stayed behind. Except for *Masks* (for *make*) in l. 4, the other variants in *CGD* are obvious errors. In *CGD* the prologue is said to be spoken "*by Mr.* Heart," who played Palamede.

3 *Fop-corner*] a corner in the pit where fops resorted.

5 *France, and the Fleet*] an allusion to the equipment of the fleet in preparation for the third Dutch War. The first engagement was on March 13, 1672. A major battle took place May 28.

16 *grinning Honour*] grinning corpses, see Falstaff's remark about Sir Walter Blunt, *1 Henry IV*, V.iii.62, "I like not such grinning honour."

22 *her last Half-crown*] the price of admission to the pit. Since there are no young sparks present, as in normal times, a prostitute will not waste her money.

24 *so far*] The Theatre Royal in Drury Lane had burned in the beginning of 1672, causing the players to perform in the old theater in Lincoln's Inn Fields, a longer journey from the city.

25 They can take up with Pleasures nearer home;
And see gay Shows; and gawdy Scenes elsewhere:
For we presume they seldom come to hear.
But they have now ta'n up a glorious Trade,
And cutting *Moorcraft*, struts in Masquerade.
30 There's all our hope, for we shall show to day,
A Masquing Ball, to recommend our Play:
Nay, to endear 'em more, and let 'em see,
We scorn to come behind in Courtesie,
We'll follow the new Mode which they begin,
35 And treat 'em with a Room, and Couch within:
For that's one way, how e're the Play fall short,
T'oblige the Town, the City, and the Court.

26 *elsewhere*] an allusion to the Dorset Garden Theatre, which opened November 9, 1671, with Dryden's *Sir Martin Mar-all*. This playhouse of the Duke's Company was more elaborately equipped for spectacle than any other in London.

29 *Moorcraft*] a usurer turned gallant in Beaumont and Fletcher's *The Scornful Lady. Cutting* means swaggering.

35 *a Room, and Couch within*] It is not clear which scene of this play requires the couch within, but it would be suitable for V.i.233–34.

Marriage
A-la-Mode

ACT I. Scene 1

Walks near the Court.

Enter Doralice *and* Beliza.

Doralice. Beliza, bring the Lute into this Arbor, the Walks
are empty: I would try the Song the Princess *Amalthea*
bad me learn.

They go in, and sing.

1.

Why should a foolish Marriage Vow
  Which long ago was made,
Oblige us to each other now   5
  When Passion is decay'd?
We lov'd, and we lov'd, as long as we cou'd,
  Till our love was lov'd out in us both:
But our Marriage is dead, when the Pleasure is fled: 10
  'Twas Pleasure first made it an Oath.

2.

If I have Pleasures for a Friend,
  And farther love in store,
What wrong has he whose joys did end,
  And who cou'd give no more?   15
'Tis a madness that he should be jealous of me,
  Or that I shou'd bar him of another:
For all we can gain, is to give our selves pain,
  When neither can hinder the other.

Enter Palamede, *in Riding Habit, and hears the Song.*

Re-enter Doralice *and* Beliza.

Beliza. Madam, a Stranger.   20
Doralice. I did not think to have had witnesses of my bad
  singing.
Palamede. If I have err'd, Madam, I hope you'l pardon the
  curiosity of a Stranger; for I may well call my self so,
  after five years absence from the Court: But you have   25
  freed me from one error.
Doralice. What's that, I beseech you?
Palamede. I thought good voices, and ill faces, had been

inseparable; and that to be fair and sing well, had been
30   onely the priviledge of Angels.

Doralice. And how many more of these fine things can you
say to me?

Palamede. Very few, Madam, for if I should continue to
see you some hours longer: You look so killingly, that
35   I should be mute with wonder.

Doralice. This will not give you the reputation of a Wit
with me: you travelling Monsieurs live upon the stock
you have got abroad, for the first day or two: to repeat
with a good memory, and apply with a good grace, is
40   all your wit. And, commonly, your Gullets are sew'd
up, like Cormorants: When you have regorg'd what
you have taken in, you are the leanest things in Nature.

Palamede. Then, Madam, I think you had best make that
use of me; let me wait on you for two or three days
45   together, and you shall hear all I have learnt of extraordinary, in other Countreys: And one thing which I
never saw till I came home, that is, a Lady of a better
voice, better face, and better wit, than any I have seen
abroad. And, after this, if I should not declare my self
50   most passionately in love with you, I should have less
wit than yet you think I have.

Doralice. A very plain, and pithy Declaration. I see, Sir,
you have been travelling in *Spain* or *Italy*, or some of
the hot Countreys, where men come to the point
55   immediately. But are you sure these are not words of
course? For I would not give my poor heart an occasion
of complaint against me, that I engag'd it too rashly,
and then could not bring it off.

Palamede. Your heart may trust it self with me safely; I
60   shall use it very civilly while it stays, and never turn it
away, without fair warning to provide for it self.

Doralice. First, then, I do receive your passion with as little
consideration, on my part, as ever you gave it me, on
yours. And now see what a miserable wretch you have
65   made your self.

Palamede. Who, I miserable? Thank you for that. Give me
love enough, and life enough, and I defie *Fortune*.

    40–41 *sew'd up, like Cormorants*] referring to the practice of
using cormorants to catch fish. "For this purpose a leather thong
was tied round the lower part of their necks, that they might not
swallow the fish. When cormorants had caught several fish, their
keepers called them back—'and, one after another [they] vomit up
all their fish, a little bruised with the first nip, given in catch-
ing them.'" (Goldsmith's *History of Animated Nature* (1832), vol. III,
Book vii, chap. iv. Cited by Sutherland.)

Doralice. Know then, thou man of vain imagination, know, to thy utter confusion, that I am vertuous.

Palamede. Such another word, and I give up the ghost.   70

Doralice. Then, to strike you quite dead, know, that I am marry'd too.

Palamede. Art thou marry'd; O thou damnable vertuous Woman?

Doralice. Yes, marry'd to a Gentleman; young, handsome,   75
rich, valiant, and with all the good qualities that will make you despair, and hang your self.

Palamede. Well, in spight of all that, I'll love you: *Fortune* has cut us out for one another; for I am to be marry'd within these three days. Marry'd past redemption, to a   80
young, fair, rich, and vertuous Lady: And, it shall go hard, but I will love my Wife as little, as I perceive you do your Husband.

Doralice. Remember I invade no propriety: My servant you are onely till you are marry'd.   85

Palamede. In the mean time, you are to forget you have a Husband.

Doralice. And you, that you are to have a Wife.

Beliza (aside to her Lady). O Madam, my Lord's just at the end of the Walks; and, if you make not haste, will dis-   90
cover you.

Doralice. Some other time, new Servant, we'll talk further of the premisses; in the mean while, break not my first commandment, that is, not to follow me.

Palamede. But where, then, shall I find you again?   95

Doralice. At Court. Yours for two days, Sir.

Palamede. And nights, I beseech you, Madam.
                              Exit Doralice *and* Beliza.

Palamede. Well, I'll say that for thee, thou art a very dextrous Executioner; thou hast done my business at one stroke: Yet I must marry another ——— and yet   100
I must love this; and if it lead me into some little inconveniencies, as jealousies, and duels, and death, and so forth; yet while sweet love is in the case, *Fortune* do thy worst, and avant Mortality.

Enter Rodophil, *who seems speaking to one within.*

Rhodophil. Leave 'em with my Lieutenant, while I fetch   105
new Orders from the King. How? *Palamede*!
                              Sees Palamede.

Palamede. Rhodophil!

84 *propriety*] property.
93 *premisses*] the aforementioned.

Rhodophil. Who thought to have seen you in *Sicily*?

Palamede. Who thought to have found the Court so far
110   from *Syracuse*?

Rhodophil. The King best knows the reason of the progress.
But answer me, I beseech you, what brought you home
from travel?

Palamede. The commands of an old rich Father.

115 *Rhodophil.* And the hopes of burying him?

Palamede. Both together, as you see, have prevail'd on my
good nature. In few words, My old man has already
marry'd me; for he has agreed with another old man,
as rich and as covetous as himself; the Articles are drawn,
120   and I have given my consent, for fear of being dis-
inherited; and yet know not what kind of woman I am
to marry.

Rhodophil. Sure your Father intends you some very ugly
wife; and has a mind to keep you in ignorance, till you
125   have shot the gulf.

Palamede. I know not that; but obey I will, and must.

Rhodophil. Then, I cannot chuse but grieve for all the
good Girls and Curtizans of *France* and *Italy*: They have
lost the most kind-hearted, doting, prodigal, humble
130   servant, in *Europe*.

Palamede. All I could do in these three years, I stay'd
behind you, was to comfort the poor Creatures, for the
loss of you. But what's the reason that in all this time,
a friend could never hear from you?

135 *Rhodophil.* Alass, dear *Palamede*, I have had no joy to write,
nor indeed to do any thing in the World to please me:
The greatest misfortune imaginable is faln upon me.

Palamede. Prithee, what's the matter?

Rhodophil. In one word, I am marry'd; wretchedly
140   marry'd; and have been above these two years. Yes,
faith, the Devil has had power over me, in spight of my
Vows and Resolutions to the contrary.

Palamede. I find you have sold your self for filthy lucre;
she's old, or ill-condition'd.

145 *Rhodophil.* No, none of these: I'm sure she's young; and,
for her humor, she laughs, sings, and dances eternally;
and, which is more, we never quarrel about it, for I do
the same.

Palamede. You're very unfortunate indeed: Then the case
150   is plain, she is not handsome.

Rhodophil. A great Beauty too, as people say.

125 *shot the gulf*] succeeded in bringing off this dangerous enterprise

Palamede. As people say? Why, you should know that
  best your self.
Rhodophil. Ask those, who have smelt to a strong perfume
  two years together, what's the scent.   155
Palamede. But here are good qualities enough for one
  woman.
Rhodophil. Ay, too many, *Palamede*, if I could put 'em into
  three or four women, I should be content.
Palamede. O, now I have found it, you dislike her for no   160
  other reason, but because she's your wife.
Rhodophil. And is not that enough? All that I know of
  her perfections now, is only by memory; I remember,
  indeed, that about two years ago I lov'd her passionately;
  but those golden days are gone, *Palamede*: Yet I lov'd her   165
  a whole half year, double the natural term of any
  Mistress, and think in my conscience I could have held
  out another quarter; but then the World began to laugh
  at me, and a certain shame of being out of fashion,
  seiz'd me: At last, we arriv'd at that point, that there   170
  was nothing left in us to make us new to one another:
  yet still I set a good face upon the matter, and am
  infinite fond of her before company; but, when we are
  alone, we walk like Lions in a room, she one way, and I
  another: and we lie with our backs to each other so   175
  far distant, as if the fashion of great Beds was onely
  invented to keep Husband and Wife sufficiently asunder.
Palamede. The truth is, your disease is very desperate; but,
  though you cannot be cur'd, you may be patch'd up a
  little; you must get you a Mistress, *Rhodophil*: that,   180
  indeed, is living upon Cordials; but, as fast as one fails,
  you must supply it with another. You're like a Gamester,
  who has lost his estate; yet, in doing that, you have
  learn'd the advantages of Play, and can arrive to live
  upon't.   185
Rhodophil. Truth is, I have been thinking on't, and have
  just resolv'd to take your counsel; and, faith, considering the damn'd disadvantages of a marry'd man, I
  have provided well enough, for a poor humble sinner,
  that is not ambitious of great matters.   190
Palamede. What is she, for a Woman?
Rhodophil. One of the Stars of *Syracuse*, I assure you:

176 *great Beds*] oversized beds, such as the great bed of Ware, had
been notorious for orgies in the earlier part of the century, but Rhodophil seems to refer to double beds that were appearing in roomier
Restoration houses.
  181 *Cordials*] comforting, exhilarating drinks, which stimulated the
heart.

Young enough, fair enough, and, but, for one quality, just such a woman as I would wish.

195 *Palamede.* O Friend, this is not an age to be critical in Beauty: when we had good store of handsome women, and but few Chapmen, you might have been more curious in your choice; but now the price is enhanc'd upon us, and all Mankind set up for Mistresses, so that 200 poor little creatures, without beauty, birth, or breeding, but onely impudence, go off at unreasonable rates: and a man, in these hard times, snaps at 'em, as he does at Broad-gold, never examines the weight, but takes light, or heavy, as he can get it.

205 *Rhodophil.* But my Mistris has one fault that's almost unpardonable; for, being a Town-Lady, without any relation to the Court, yet she thinks her self undone, if she be not seen there three or four times a day, with the Princess *Amalthea.* And for the King, she haunts, and 210 watches him so narrowly in a morning, that she prevents even the Chymists who beset his Chamber, to turn their Mercury into his Gold.

Palamede. Yet, hitherto, me-thinks, you are no very unhappy man.

215 *Rhodophil.* With all this, she's the greatest Gossip in Nature; for, besides the Court, she's the most eternal Visiter of the Town: and yet manages her time so well, that she seems ubiquitary. For my part, I can compare her to nothing but the Sun; for, like him, she takes no rest, 220 nor ever sets in one place, but to rise in another.

Palamede. I confess she had need be handsome with these qualities.

Rhodophil. No Lady can be so curious of a new Fashion, as she is of a new French-word; she's the very Mint of the 225 Nation; and as fast as any Bullion comes out of *France*, coins it immediately into our Language.

Palamede. And her name is ———

Rhodophil. No naming; that's not like a Cavalier: Find her, if you can, by my description; and I am not 230 so ill a painter, that I need write the name beneath the Picture.

197 *Chapmen*] customers.
203 *Broad-gold*] A twenty-shilling piece of James' and Charles' time which was thinner and broader than the newer coinage. The broad pieces were much subject to clipping (Noyes).
211 *Chymists*] alchemists. Charles II was especially interested in curious chemical experiments, but the insinuation here is that the king was being treated for venereal disease with mercury and paying for it with his gold (Sutherland).
213 *hitherto*] thus far.

Palamede. Well, then, how far have you proceeded in your
love?

Rhodophil. 'Tis yet in the bud, and what fruit it may bear
I cannot tell; for this insufferable humour, of haunting   235
the Court, is so predominant, that she has hitherto
broken all her assignations with me, for fear of missing
her visits there.

Palamede. That's the hardest part of your adventure: but,
for ought I see, Fortune has us'd us both alike; I have a   240
strange kind of Mistris too in Court, besides her I am to
marry.

Rhodophil. You have made haste to be in love then; for, if
I am not mistaken, you are but this day arriv'd.

Palamede. That's all one, I have seen the Lady already, who   245
has charm'd me, seen her in these Walks, courted her,
and receiv'd, for the first time, an answer that does not
put me into despair.

      To them, Argaleon, Amalthea, Artemis.

I'll tell you at more leisure my adventures. The Walks
fill apace, I see. Stay, is not that the young Lord *Argaleon,*   250
the King's Favourite?

Rhodophil. Yes, and as proud as ever, as ambitious, and as
revengeful.

Palamede. How keeps he the King's favour with these
qualities?   255

Rhodophil. Argaleon's father help'd him to the Crown:
besides, he gilds over all his vices to the King, and,
standing in the dark to him, sees all his inclinations,
interests and humours, which he so times and sooths,
that, in effect, he reigns.   260

Palamede. His sister *Amalthea,* who, I ghess, stands by him,
seems not to be of his temper.

Rhodophil. O, she's all goodness and generosity.

Argaleon. Rhodophil, the King expects you earnestly.

Rhodophil. 'Tis done, my Lord, what he commanded: I   265
onely waited his return from Hunting. Shall I attend
your Lordship to him?

Argaleon. No; I go first another way.   *Exit hastily.*

Palamede. He seems in haste, and discompos'd.

Amalthea (to Rhodophil after a short whisper). Your friend?
then he must needs be of much merit.   270

Rhodophil. When he has kis'd the King's hand, I know he'll
beg the honour to kiss yours. Come, *Palamede.*
     Exeunt Rhodophil *and* Palamede *bowing to* Amalthea.

259 *times*] marks the rhythm or measure of.

        Artemis. Madam, you tell me most surprising news.

275   *Amalthea.* The fear of it, you see,
         Has discompos'd my brother; but to me
         All that can bring my Country good, is welcome.
        Artemis. It seems incredible, that this old King,
         Whom all the world thought childless,

280   Should come to search the farthest parts of *Sicily*,
         In hope to find an Heir.
        Amalthea. To lessen your astonishment, I will
         Unfold some private passages of State,
         Of which you yet are ignorant: Know, first,

285   That this *Polydamas*, who Reigns, unjustly
         Gain'd the Crown.
        Artemis. Somewhat of this I have confus'dly heard.
        Amalthea. I'll tell you all in brief: *Theagenes*,
         Our last great King,

290   Had, by his Queen, one onely Son, an Infant
         Of three years old, call'd, after him, *Theagenes*:
         The General, this *Polydamas*, then marri'd;
         The publick Feasts for which were scarcely past,
         When a Rebellion in the heart of *Sicily*

295   Call'd out the King to Arms.
        Artemis.   *Polydamas*
         Had then a just excuse to stay behind.
        Amalthea. His temper was too warlike to accept it:
         He left his Bride, and the new joys of marriage,
         And follow'd to the Feild. In short, they fought,

300   The Rebels were o'rcome; but in the Fight
         The too bold King receiv'd a mortal wound.
         When he perceiv'd his end approaching near,
         He call'd the General, to whose care he left
         His Widow Queen, and Orphan Son; then dy'd.

305   *Artemis.* Then false *Polydamas* betray'd his trust?
        Amalthea. He did; and with my father's help, for which
         Heav'n pardon him, so gain'd the Soldiers hearts,
         That in few days he was saluted King:
         And when his crimes had impudence enough

310   To bear the eye of day,
         He march'd his Army back to *Syracuse*.
         But see how heav'n can punish wicked men
         In granting their desires: the news was brought him
         That day he was to enter it, that *Eubulus*,

315   Whom his dead Master had left Governour,
         Was fled, and with him bore away the Queen,
         And Royal Orphan; but, what more amaz'd him,
         His wife, now big with child, and much detesting

Her husband's practises, had willingly
Accompani'd their flight. 320
Artemis. How I admire her vertue!
Amalthea.   What became
Of her, and them, since that, was never known;
Onely, some few days since, a famous Robber
Was taken with some Jewels of vast price,
Which, when they were delivered to the King, 325
He knew had been his Wife's; with these, a Letter,
Much torn, and sulli'd, but which yet he knew
To be her writing.
Artemis.   Sure from hence he learn'd
He had a Son.
Amalthea.   It was not left so plain:
The Paper onely said, she dy'd in childbed: 330
But when it should have mention'd Son, or Daughter,
Just there it was torn off.
Artemis.   Madam, the King.

To them, Polydamas, Argaleon, *Guard, and Attendants.*

Argaleon. The Robber, though thrice Rack'd, confess'd no
     more,
But that he took those Jewels near this place.
Polydamas. But yet the circumstances strongly argue, 335
That those, for whom I search, are not far off.
Argaleon. I cannot easily believe it.
Artemis (aside).   No,
You would not have it so.
Polydamas. Those I employ'd, have, in the neighbouring
     Hamlet,
Amongst the Fishers Cabins, made discovery 340
Of some young persons, whose uncommon beauty,
And graceful carriage, make it seem suspicious
They are not what they seem: I therefore sent
The Captain of my Guards, this morning early,
With orders to secure and bring 'em to me. 345

Enter Rhodophil *and* Palamede.

O here he is. Have you perform'd my will?
Rhodophil. Sir, those whom you commanded me to bring,
Are waiting in the Walks.
Polydamas.   Conduct 'em hither.
Rhodophil. First, give me leave
To beg your notice of this Gentleman. 350
Polydamas. He seems to merit it. His name and quality?
Rhodophil. Palamede, son to Lord *Cleodemus* of *Palermo*,
And new return'd from travel.

Palamede *approaches, and kneels to kiss the King's hand.*
Polydamas. You're welcome.
I knew your father well, he was both brave
355 And honest; we two once were fellow-soldiers
In the last Civil Wars.
Palamede. I bring the same unquestion'd honesty
And zeal to serve your Majesty; the courage
You were pleased to praise in him,
360 Your Royal prudence, and your People's love,
Will never give me leave to try like him
In Civil Wars, I hope it may in Foreign.
Polydamas. Attend the Court, and it shall be my care
To find out some employment, worthy you.
365 Go, *Rhodophil*, and bring in those without.
Exeunt Rhodophil *and* Palamede.

Rhodophil *returns again immediately, and with him*
Enter Hermogenes, Leonidas, *and* Palmyra.

Behold two miracles!
Looking earnestly on Leonidas *and* Palmyra.
Of different sexes, but of equal form:
So matchless both, that my divided soul
Can scarcely ask the Gods a Son, or Daughter,
370 For fear of losing one. If from your hands,
You Powers, I shall this day receive a Daughter,
Argaleon, she is yours; but, if a Son,
Then *Amalthea's* love shall make him happy.
Argaleon. Grant, heav'n, this admirable Nymph may prove
375 That issue which he seeks.
Amalthea. Venus Urania, if thou art a Goddess,
Grant that sweet Youth may prove the Prince of *Sicily*.
Polydamas (to Hermogenes). Tell me, old man, and tell me
true, from whence
Had you that Youth and Maid?
Hermogenes. From whence you had
380 Your Scepter, Sir: I had 'em from the Gods.
Polydamas. The Gods then have not such another gift.
Say who their Parents were.
Hermogenes. My Wife, and I.
Argaleon. It is not likely, a Virgin of so excellent a beauty
Should come from such a Stock.
385 *Amalthea.* Much less, that such a Youth, so sweet, so
graceful,
Should be produc'd from Peasants.

376 *Venus Urania*] daughter of Uranus, presiding over beauty
and generation.

Hermogenes. Why, Nature is the same in Villages,
    And much more fit to form a noble issue
    Where it is least corrupted.
Polydamas. He talks, too like a man that knew the world   390
    To have been long a Peasant. But the Rack
    Will teach him other language. Hence with him.
      As the Guard are carrying him away, his Perruke falls off.
    Sure I have seen that face before. *Hermogenes*!
    'Tis he, 'tis he who fled away with *Eubulus*,
    And with my dear *Eudoxia*.   395
Hermogenes. Yes, Sir, I am *Hermogenes*.
    And if to have been loyal be a crime,
    I stand prepar'd to suffer.
Polydamas. If thou would'st live, speak quickly,
    What is become of my *Eudoxia*?   400
    Where is the Queen and young *Theagenes*?
    Where *Eubulus*? and which of these is mine?
                Pointing to Leonidas *and* Palmyra.
Hermogenes. Eudoxia is dead, so is the Queen,
    The infant King her son, and *Eubulus*.
Polydamas. Traitor, 'tis false: produce 'em, or ———
Hermogenes.   Once more   405
    I tell you, they are dead; but leave to threaten,
    For you shall know no further.
Polydamas. Then prove indulgent to my hopes, and be
    My friend for ever. Tell me, good *Hermogenes*,
    Whose Son is that brave Youth?
Hermogenes.   Sir, he is yours.   410
Polydamas. Fool that I am, thou see'st that so I wish it,
    And so thou flatter'st me.
Hermogenes.   By all that's holy.
Polydamas. Again. Thou canst not swear too deeply.
    Yet hold, I will beleive thee: ——— yet I doubt.
Hermogenes. You need not, Sir.   415
Argaleon. Beleive him not; he sees you credulous,
    And would impose his own base issue on you,
    And fix it to your Crown.
Amalthea. Behold his goodly shape and feature, Sir,
    Methinks he much resembles you.   420
Argaleon. I say, if you have any issue here,
    It must be that fair creature;
    By all my hopes I think so.
Amalthea [*aside*]. Yes, Brother, I believe you by your hopes,
    For they are all for her.
Polydamas.   Call the Youth nearer.   425
Hermogenes. Leonidas, the King would speak with you.

Polydamas. Come near, and be not dazled with the splendor,
And greatness of a Court.
Leonidas. I need not this incouragement.

430   I can fear nothing but the Gods.
And for this glory, after I have seen
The Canopy of State spread wide above
In the Abyss of Heaven, the Court of Stars,
The blushing Morning, and the rising Sun,

435   What greater can I see?
Polydamas. This speaks thee born a Prince, thou art thy
self   *Embracing him.*
That rising Sun, and shalt not see on earth,
A brighter then thy self. ——— All of you witness,
That for my son I here receive this Youth,

440   This brave, this ——— but I must not praise him
further,
Because he now is mine.
Leonidas (kneeling)   I wonnot, Sir,
Believe that I am made your sport;
For I find nothing in my self, but what
Is much above a scorn; I dare give credit

445   To whatsoe'r a King, like you, can tell me.
Either I am, or will deserve to be your Son.
Argaleon. I yet maintain it is impossible
This young man should be yours; for, if he were,
Why should *Hermogenes* so long conceal him

450   When he might gain so much by his discovery?
Hermogenes (to the King). I stay'd a while to make him
worthy, Sir, of you.
But in that time I found
Somewhat within him, which so mov'd my love,
I never could resolve to part with him.

455   *Leonidas (to Argaleon).* You ask too many questions, and are
Too sawcy for a subject.
Argaleon. You rather over-act your part, and are
Too soon a Prince.
Leonidas.   Too soon you'l find me one.
Polydamas. Enough, *Argaleon*;

460   I have declar'd him mine: and you, *Leonidas*,
Live well with him I love.
Argaleon. Sir, if he be your Son, I may have leave
To think your Queen had Twins; look on this Virgin;
Hermogenes would enviously deprive you
Of half your treasure.

465   *Hermogenes.*   Sir, she is my daughter.
I could, perhaps, thus aided by this Lord,

Prefer her to be yours; but truth forbid
I should procure her greatness by a Lie.
Polydamas. Come hither, beauteous Maid: are you not sorry
  Your father will not let you pass for mine?   470
Palmyra. I am content to be what heav'n has made me.
Polydamas. Could you not wish your self a Princess then?
Palmyra. Not to be Sister to *Leonidas.*
Polydamas. Why, my sweet Maid?
Palmyra.   Indeed I cannot tell;
  But I could be content to be his Handmaid.   475
Argaleon (aside). I wish I had not seen her.
Palmyra (to Leonidas). I must weep for your good fortune;
  Pray pardon me, indeed I cannot help it.
  Leonidas, (alas, I had forgot,
  Now I must call you Prince) but must I leave you?   480
Leonidas (aside). I dare not speak to her; for if I should,
  I must weep too.
Polydamas. No, you shall live at Court, sweet Innocence,
  And see him there. *Hermogenes,*
  Though you intended not to make me happy,   485
  Yet you shall be rewarded for th'event.
  Come, my *Leonidas,* let's thank the Gods;
  Thou for a Father, I for such a Son.
               Exeunt all but Leonidas *and* Palmyra.
Leonidas. My dear *Palmyra,* many eyes observe me,
  And I have thoughts so tender, that I cannot   490
  In publick speak 'em to you: some hours hence
  I shall shake off these crowds of fawning Courtiers,
  And then ——————   *Exit* Leonidas.
Palmyra. Fly swift, you hours, you measure time for me in
    vain,
  Till you bring back *Leonidas* again.   495
  Be shorter now; and to redeem that wrong,
  When he and I are met, be twice as long.
                       Exit.

ACT II. Scene 1

[*Enter*] Melantha *and* Philotis.

Philotis. Count *Rhodophil's* a fine Gentleman indeed,
  Madam; and I think deserves your affection.
Melantha. Let me die but he's a fine man; he sings, and
  dances *en Francois,* and writes the *Billets doux* to a
  miracle.   5
Philotis. And those are no small tallents, to a Lady that
  understands, and values the *French* ayr, as your Ladiship
  does.

10

Melantha. How charming is the *French* ayr! and what an *étourdy bete* is one of our untravel'd Islanders! when he would make his Court to me, let me die, but he is just *Æsop's* Ass, that would imitate the courtly *French* in his addresses; but, in stead of those, comes pawing upon me, and doing all things so *mal a droitly*.

15

Philotis. 'Tis great pity *Rhodophil's* a married man, that you may not have an honourable Intrigue with him.

Melantha. Intrigue, *Philotis*! that's an old phrase; I have laid that word by: *Amour* sounds better. But thou art heir to all my cast words, as thou art to my old Ward-

20

robe. Oh Count *Rhodophil*! Ah *mon cher*! I could live and die with him.

Enter Palamede *and a Servant.*

Servant. Sir, this is my Lady.

Palamede. Then this is she that is to be Divine, and Nymph, and Goddess, and with whom I am to be desperately in

25

love.   *Bows to her, delivering a Letter.*
This Letter, Madam, which I present you from your father, has given me both the happy opportunity, and the boldness, to kiss the fairest hands in *Sicily*.

Melantha. Came you lately from *Palermo*, Sir?

30

Palamede. But yesterday, Madam.

Melantha (Reading the Letter). *Daughter, receive the bearer of this Letter, as a Gentleman whom I have chosen to make you happy;* (O *Venus*, a new Servant sent me! and let me die but he has the ayre of a gallant *homme*) *his father is*

35

the rich Lord Cleodemus, *our neighbour: I suppose you'l find nothing disagreeable in his person or his converse; both which he has improv'd by travel. The Treaty is already concluded, and I shall be in Town within these three days; so that you have nothing to do, but to obey your careful*

40

Father.
(*To Palamede*) Sir, my Father, for whom I have a blind obedience, has commanded me to receive your passion-ate addresses; but you must also give me leave to avow, that I cannot merit 'em, from so accomplish'd a Cavalier.

45

Palamede. I want many things, Madam, to render me accomplish'd; and the first and greatest of 'em, is your favour.

Melantha. Let me die, *Philotis*, but this is extremely *French*;

10 *étourdy bete*] foolish creature.

12 *Æsop's Ass*] the ass who tried to imitate the farmer's lap dog, frisking about and climbing onto the farmer. The moral: Clumsy jesting is no joke.

but yet Count *Rhodophil* ———. A Gentleman, Sir, that
understands the *Grand mond* so well, who has hanted the   50
best conversations, and who (in short) has voyag'd, may
pretend to the good graces of any Lady.

Palamede (aside). Hay day! *Grand mond! conversation!*
voyag'd! and *good graces!* I find my Mistris is one of those
that run mad in new *French* words.   55

Melantha. I suppose, Sir, you have made the *Tour* of
France; and having seen all that's fine there, will make a
considerable reformation in the rudeness of our Court:
for, let me die, but an unfashion'd, untravel'd, meer
Sicilian, is a *Bete*; and has nothing in the world of an   60
honete homme.

Palamede. I must confess, Madam, that ———

Melantha. And what new *Minouets* have you brought over
with you! their *Minouets* are to a miracle! and our
Sicilian Jigs are so dull and sad to 'em!   65

Palamede. For *Minouets*, Madam ———

Melantha. And what new Plays are there in vogue? and
who danc'd best in the last Grand Ballet? Come, sweet
Servant, you shall tell me all.

Palamede (aside). Tell her all? why, she asks all, and will   70
hear nothing. ——— To answer in order, Madam, to
your demands ———

Melantha. I am thinking what a happy couple we shall be!
for you shall keep up your correspondence abroad, and
every thing that's new writ, in *France*, and fine, I mean   75
all that's delicate, and *bien tourné*, we will have first.

Palamede. But, Madam, our fortune ———

Melantha. I understand you, Sir; you'l leave that to me:
for the *ménnage* of a family, I know it better then any
Lady in *Sicily*.   80

Palamede. Alas, Madam, we ———

Melantha. Then, we will never make visits together, nor
see a Play, but always apart; you shall be every day at
the King's *Levé*, and I at the Queen's; and we will never
meet, but in the Drawing-room.   85

Philotis. Madam, the new Prince is just pass'd by the end
of the Walk.

Melantha. The new Prince, say'st thou? Adieu, dear

---

50 *hanted*] frequented.

52 *good graces*] "From the fact that Palamede proceeds to repeat
those words along with the French phrases of Melantha's it may perhaps be presumed that she gives 'graces' an un-English pronunciation"
(Sutherland).

84 *Queen's*] Dryden has forgotten that the king is a widower
(Summers).

90

Servant; I have not made my court to him these two long hours. O, 'tis the sweetest Prince! so *obligeant*, *charmant, ravissant*, that—Well, I'll make haste to kiss his hands; and then make half a score visits more, and be with you again in a twinkling.

Exit, running with Philotis.

95

Palamede (solus). Now heaven, of thy mercy, bless me from this tongue; it may keep the field against a whole Army of Lawyers, and that in their own language, *French Gibberish.* 'Tis true, in the day-time, 'tis tolerable, when a man has field-room to run from it; but, to be shut up in a bed with her, like two Cocks in a pit;

100

humanity cannot support it: I must kiss all night, in my own defence, and hold her down, like a Boy at cuffs, nay, and give her the rising blow every time she begins to speak.

Enter Rhodophil.

But here comes *Rhodophil.* 'Tis pretty odd that my

105

Mistris should so much resemble his: the same News-monger, the same passionate lover of a Court, the same —— But *Basta*, since I must marry her, I'll say nothing, because he shall not laugh at my misfortune.

Rhodophil. Well, *Palamede*, how go the affairs of love?

110

You've seen your Mistris?

Palamede. I have so.

Rhodophil. And how, and how? has the old *Cupid*, your Father, chosen well for you? is he a good Woodman?

Palamede. She's much handsomer then I could have

115

imagin'd: In short, I love her, and will marry her.

Rhodophil. Then you are quite off from your other Mistris?

Palamede. You are mistaken, I intend to love 'em both, as a reasonable man ought to do. For, since all women

120

have their faults, and imperfections, 'tis fit that one of 'em should help out t'other.

Rhodophil. This were a blessed Doctrine, indeed, if our Wives would hear it; but, they're their own enemies: if they would suffer us but now and then to make excur-

97 *French Gibberish*] i.e., legal French. Until the beginning of the eighteenth century, law reports were written in a curious language compounded of English, Latin, and Norman French (Saintsbury).

101 *at cuffs*] fighting.

102 *rising blow*] presumably an uppercut, but with sexual significance as well.

107 *Basta*] enough!

113 *Woodman*] huntsman, wencher, muttonmonger (Farmer).

sions, the benefit of our variety would be theirs; instead 125
of one continu'd, lazy, tyr'd love, they would, in their
turns, have twenty vigorous, fresh, and active loves.

Palamede. And I would ask any of 'em, whether a poor
narrow Brook, half dry the best part of the year, and
running ever one way, be to be compar'd to a lusty 130
Stream, that has Ebbs and Flows?

Rhodophil. Ay; or is half so profitable for Navigation?

Enter Doralice, *walking by, and reading.*

Palamede. Ods my life, *Rhodophil*, will you keep my
counsel?

Rhodophil. Yes: where's the secret? 135

Palamede. There 'tis.   *Showing* Doralice.
I may tell you, as my friend, *sub sigillo*, &c. this is that
very numerical Lady, with whom I am in love.

Rhodophil (*aside*). By all that's vertuous, my Wife!

Palamede. You look strangely: how do you like her? is she 140
not very handsome?

Rhodophil (*aside*). Sure he abuses me.
(*To him*) Why the devil do you ask my judgment?

Palamede. You are so dogged now, you think no man's
Mistris handsome, but your own. Come, you shall hear 145
her talk too; she has wit, I assure you.

Rhodophil. This is too much, *Palamede*.   *Going back,*

Palamede. Prethee do not hang back so: of an old try'd
Lover, thou art the most bashful fellow!
                                        Pulling him forward.

Doralice. Were you so near, and would not speak, dear 150
Husband?   *Looking up.*

Palamede (*aside*). Husband, quoth a! I have cut out a fine
piece of work for myself.

Rhodophil. Pray, Spouse, how long have you been
acquainted with this Gentleman? 155

Doralice. Who, I acquainted with this Stranger?
To my best knowledge, I never saw him before.

Enter Melantha, *at the other end.*

Palamede (*aside*). Thanks, *Fortune*, thou hast help'd me.

Rhodophil. *Palamede*, this must not pass so: I must know
your Mistris a little better. 160

137 *sub sigillo, &c.*] i.e., I swear or sign under a seal, in confidence.
138 *numerical*] particular, the very same.
144 *dogged*] perverse.

Palamede. It shall be your own fault else. Come, I'll introduce you.

Rhodophil. Introduce me! where?

Palamede. There. To my Mistris.

    Pointing to Melantha, *who swiftly passes over the
Stage.*

165   *Rhodophil.* Who? *Melantha!*

O heavens, I did not see her.

Palamede. But I did: I am an Eagle where I love;
I have seen her this half hour.

Doralice (aside). I find he has wit, he has got off so readily;
170   but it would anger me, if he should love *Melantha.*

Rhodophil (aside). Now I could e'en wish it were my Wife
he lov'd: I find he's to be marri'd to my Mistris.

Palamede. Shall I run after, and fetch her back again, to
present you to her?

175   *Rhodophil.* No, you need not; I have the honour to have
some small acquaintance with her.

Palamede (aside). O *Jupiter!* what a blockhead was I not to
find it out! My Wife that must be, is his Mistris. I did
a little suspect it before; well, I must marry her, because
180   she's handsome, and because I hate to be dis-inherited
for a younger Brother, which I am sure I shall be if I
disobey; and yet I must keep in with *Rhodophil*, because
I love his Wife.

    (*To Rhodophil*) I must desire you to make my excuse to
185   your Lady, if I have been so unfortunate to cause any
mistake; and, withall, to beg the honour of being
known to her.

Rhodophil. O, that's but reason. Hark you, Spouse, pray
look upon this Gentleman as my friend; whom, to my
190   knowledge, you have never seen before this hour.

Doralice. I'm so obedient a Wife, Sir, that my Husband's
commands shall ever be a Law to me.

Enter Melantha *again, hastily, and runs to embrace* Doralice.

Melantha. O, my dear, I was just going to pay my devoirs
to you; I had not time this morning, for making my
195   Court to the King, and our new Prince. Well, never
Nation was so happy, and all that, in a young Prince;
and he's the kindest person in the World to me, let me
die, if he is not.

Doralice. He has been bred up far from Court, and there-
200   fore ———

Melantha. That imports not: Though he has not seen the

Grand mond, and all that, let me die but he has the air
of the Court, most absolutely.

Palamede. But yet, Madam, he ———

Melantha. O, Servant, you can testifie that I am in his good   205
Graces. Well, I cannot stay long with you, because I
have promis'd him this Afternoon to ——— But hark
you, my dear, I'll tell you a Secret.

Whispers to Doralice.

Rhodophil (aside). The Devil's in me, that I must love this
Woman.   210

Palamede (aside). The Devil's in me, that I must marry this
Woman.

Melantha (raising her voice). So the Prince and I ——— But
you must make a Secret of this, my dear, for I would
not for the World your Husband should hear it, or my   215
Tyrant, there, that must be.

Palamede (aside). Well, fair impertinent, your whisper is
not lost, we hear you.

Doralice. I understand then, that ———

Melantha. I'll tell you, my dear, the Prince took me by the   220
hand, and press'd it *al a dérobbée*, because the King was
near, made the *doux yeux* to me, and, *in suitte*, said a
thousand Gallanteries, or let me die, my dear.

Doralice. Then I am sure you ———

Melantha. You are mistaken, my dear.   225

Doralice. What, before I speak?

Melantha. But I know your meaning; you think, my dear,
that I assum'd something of *fierté* into my Countenance,
to *rebute* him; but, quite contrary, I regarded him, I
know not how to express it in our dull *Sicilian* Lan-   230
guage, *d'un ayr enjouué*; and said nothing but *a d'autre*,
a d'autre, and that it was all *grimace*, and would not pass
upon me.

Enter Artemis: Melantha *sees her, and runs away from*
Doralice.

231–32 *a d'autre, a d'autre*] S-S; *ad autre, ad autre* Qq,F

---

202 *and all that*] a phrase used frequently by Mr. Bayes in *The
Rehearsal* (December, 1671), suggesting that Buckingham saw the
script of *Marriage a-la-Mode* before its first performance, or else this was
a favorite of Dryden himself. The Prince Prettyman episode in *The
Rehearsal* may ridicule the serious plot of this play.

221 *al a dérobbée*] secretly; *al a: à la.*

222 *doux yeux*] loving glance.

222 *in suitte*] afterward.

228 *fierté*] hautiness.

231 *d'un ayr enjouué*] playfully.

231–2 *a d'autre, a d'autre*] tell it to someone else, to the marines.

232 *grimace*] humbug, affectation.

235   (*To Artemis*) My dear, I must beg your pardon, I was
just making a loose from *Doralice*, to pay my respects to
you: Let me die, if I ever pass time so agreeably as in
your company, and if I would leave it for any Lady's in
Sicily.

Artemis. The Princess *Amalthea* is coming this way.

Enter Amalthea: Melantha *runs to her.*

240   *Melantha.* O dear Madam! I have been at your Lodgings,
in my new *Galeche*, so often, to tell you of a new
Amour, betwixt two persons whom you would little
suspect for it; that, let me die, if one of my Coach-
horses be not dead, and another quite tyr'd, and sunk
245   under the *fatigue.*

Amalthea. O, *Melantha*, I can tell you news, the Prince is
coming this way.

Melantha. The Prince, O sweet Prince! He and I are to
———— and I forgot it. ———— Your pardon, sweet
250   Madam, for my abruptness. Adieu, my dears. Servant,
Rodophil; Servant, Servant, Servant All.   *Exit running.*

Amalthea. *Rodophil*, a word with you.   *Whispers.*

Doralice (*to Palamede*). Why do you not follow your
Mistress, Sir?

255   *Palamede.* Follow her? Why, at this rate she'll be at the
Indies within this half hour.

Doralice. However, if you can't follow her all day, you'll
meet her at night, I hope?

Palamede. But can you, in charity, suffer me to be so
260   mortify'd, without affording me some relief? If it be
but to punish that sign of a Husband there; that lazy
matrimony, that dull insipid taste, who leaves such
delicious fare at home, to dine abroad, on worse meat,
and to pay dear for't into the bargain.

265   *Doralice.* All this is in vain: Assure your self, I will never
admit of any visit from you in private.

Palamede. That is to tell me, in other words, my condition
is desperate.

Doralice. I think you in so ill a condition, that I am resolved
270   to pray for you, this very evening, in the close Walk,
behind the Terras; for that's a private place, and there
I am sure no body will disturb my devotions. And so,
good-night, Sir.   *Exit.*

Palamede. This is the newest way of making an appoint-
275   ment, I ever heard of: let women alone to contrive the

235 *making a loose*] getting away.
241 *Galeche*] caleche, an open carriage.

means; I find we are but dunces to 'em. Well, I will not
be so prophane a wretch as to interrupt her devotions;
but to make 'em more effectual, I'll down upon my
knees, and endeavour to joyn my own with 'em.

Exit.

Amalthea (to Rhodophil). I know already they do not love   280
each other; and that my Brother acts but a forc'd
obedience to the King's commands; so that, if a quarrel
should arise betwixt the Prince and him, I were most
miserable on both sides.

Rhodophil. There shall be nothing wanting in me, Madam,   285
to prevent so sad a consequence.

Enter the King, Leonidas; *the King whispers* Amalthea.

(*To himself*) I begin to hate this *Palamede*, because he is to
marry my Mistris: yet break with him I dare not, for
fear of being quite excluded from her company. 'Tis a
hard case when a man must go by his Rival to his   290
Mistris: but 'tis at worst but using him like a pair of
heavy Boots in a dirty journey; after I have foul'd him
all day, I'll throw him off at night.   *Exit.*

Amalthea (to the King). This honour is too great for me to
hope.

Polydamas. You shall this hour have the assurance of it.   295
    Leonidas, come hither; you have heard,
    I doubt not, that the Father of this Princess
    Was my most faithful friend, while I was yet
    A private man; and when I did assume
    This Crown, he serv'd me in that high attempt.   300
    You see, then, to what gratitude obliges me;
    Make your addresses to her.

Leonidas. Sir, I am yet too young to be a Courtier;
    I should too much betray my ignorance,
    And want of breeding, to so fair a Lady.   305

Amalthea. Your language speaks you not bred up in
    Desarts,
    But in the softness of some *Asian* Court,
    Where luxury and ease invent kind words, .
    To cozen tender Virgins of their hearts.

Polydamas. You need not doubt   310
    But in what words soe're a Prince can offer
    His Crown and Person, they will be receiv'd.
    You know my pleasure, and you know your duty.

Leonidas. Yes, Sir, I shall obey, in what I can.

Polydamas. In what you can, *Leonidas*? Consider,   315
    He's both your King, and Father, who commands you.
    Besides, what is there hard in my injunction?

Leonidas. 'Tis hard to have my inclination forc'd.
   I would not marry, Sir; and, when I do,
320   I hope you'll give me freedom in my choice.
Polydamas. View well this Lady,
   Whose mind as much transcends her beauteous face,
   As that excels all others.
Amalthea. My beauty, as it ne'r could merit love,
325   So neither can it beg: and, Sir, you may
   Beleive that, what the King has offer'd you,
   I should refuse, did I not value more
   Your person then your Crown.
Leonidas.   Think it not pride,
   Or my new fortunes swell me to contemn you;
330   Think less, that I want eyes to see your beauty;
   And least of all think duty wanting in me
   T'obey a father's will: but ———
Polydamas.   But what, *Leonidas*?
   For I must know your reason; and be sure
   It be convincing too.
Leonidas.   Sir, ask the Stars,
335   Which have impos'd love on us, like a fate,
   Why minds are bent to one, and fly another?
   Ask why all Beauties cannot move all hearts?
   For though there may
   Be made a rule for colour, or for feature;
340   There can be none for liking.
Polydamas. *Leonidas*, you owe me more
   Then to oppose your liking to my pleasure.
Leonidas. I owe you all things, Sir; but something too
   I owe my self.
345 *Polydamas.* You shall dispute no more; I am a King,
   And I will be obey'd.
Leonidas. You are a King, Sir; but you are no God;
   Or if you were, you could not force my will.
Polydamas (*aside*). But you are just, you Gods; O you are
   just,
350   In punishing the crimes of my rebellion
   With a rebellious Son!
   Yet I can punish him, as you do me.
   [*To him*] *Leonidas*, there is no jesting with
   My will: I ne'r had done so much to gain
355   A Crown, but to be absolute in all things.
Amalthea. O, Sir, be not so much a King, as to
   Forget you are a Father: Soft indulgence
   Becomes that name. Though Nature gives you pow'r,
   To bind his duty, 'tis with silken Bonds:
360   Command him, then, as you command your self:

He is as much a part of you, as are
  Your Appetite, and Will, and those you force not,
  But gently bend, and make 'em pliant to your Reason.
Polydamas. It may be I have us'd too rough a way:
  Forgive me, my *Leonidas*; I know   365
  I lie as open to the gusts of passion,
  As the bare Shore to every beating Surge:
  I will not force thee, now; but I intreat thee,
  Absolve a Father's vow, to this fair Virgin:
  A vow, which hopes of having such a Son   370
  First caus'd.
Leonidas. Show not my disobedience by your pray'rs,
  For I must still deny you, though I now
  Appear more guilty to my self, than you:
  I have some reasons, which I cannot utter,   375
  That force my disobedience; yet I mourn
  To death, that the first thing you e'r injoyn'd me,
  Should be that onely one command in Nature
  Which I could not obey.
Polydamas. I did descend too much below my self   380
  When I intreated him. Hence, to thy Desart,
  Thou'rt not my son, or art not fit to be.
Amalthea (kneeling). Great Sir, I humbly beg you, make not
    me
  The cause of your displeasure. I absolve
  Your vow: far, far from me, be such designs;   385
  So wretched a desire of being great,
  By making him unhappy. You may see
  Something so noble in the Prince his nature,
  As grieves him more not to obey, then you
  That you are not obey'd.
Polydamas.   Then, for your sake,   390
  I'll give him one day longer, to consider,
  Not to deny; for my resolves are firm
  As Fate, that cannot change.
                        Exeunt King and Amalthea.
Leonidas.   And so are mine.
  This beauteous Princess, charming as she is,
  Could never make me happy: I must first   395
  Be false to my *Palmyra*, and then wretched.
  But, then, a Father's anger!
  Suppose he should recede from his own vow,
  He never would permit me to keep mine.

  Enter Palmyra; Argaleon *following her, a little after.*

  See, she appears!   400

307

I'll think no more of any thing, but her.
Yet I have one hour good ere I am wretched.
But, Oh! *Argaleon* follows her! so night
Treads on the foot-steps of a Winter's Sun,
And stalks all black behind him.

405 *Palmyra.*   O *Leonidas*,
(For I must call you still by that dear name)
Free me from this bad man.

Leonidas. I hope he dares not be injurious to you.

Argaleon. I rather was injurious to my self,
410   Then her.

Leonidas. That must be judg'd when I hear what you said.

Argaleon. I think you need not give your self that trouble:
It concern'd us alone.

Leonidas. You answer sawcily, and indirectly:
415   What interest can you pretend in her?

Argaleon. It may be, Sir, I made her some expressions
Which I would not repeat, because they were
Below my rank, to one of hers.

Leonidas. What did he say, *Palmyra*?

420 *Palmyra.* I'll tell you all: First, he began to look,
And then he sigh'd, and then he look'd again;
At last, he said my eyes wounded his heart:
And, after that, he talk'd of flames, and fires;
And such strange words, that I believ'd he conjur'd.

425 *Leonidas.* O my heart! Leave me, *Argaleon.*

Argaleon. Come, sweet *Palmyra*,
I will instruct you better in my meaning:
You see he would be private.

Leonidas.   Go your self,
And leave her here.

Argaleon.   Alas, she's ignorant,
430   And is not fit to entertain a Prince.

Leonidas. First learn what's fit for you; that's to obey.

Argaleon. I know my duty is to wait on you.
A great King's Son, like you, ought to forget
Such mean converse.

Leonidas.   What? a disputing Subject?
435   Hence; or my sword shall do me justice, on thee.

Argaleon. Yet I may find a time ———   *Going.*

Leonidas.   What's that you mutter,
               Going after him.
To find a time?

Argaleon.   To wait on you again. ———

402 *one hour good*] one hour at least.

(*Softly*) In the mean while I'll watch you.

Exit, and watches during the Scene.

Leonidas. How precious are the hours of Love in Courts!
In Cottages, where Love has all the day,   440
Full, and at ease, he throws it half away.
Time gives himself, and is not valu'd, there;
But sells, at mighty rates, each minute, here.
There, he is lazy, unemploy'd, and slow;
Here, he's more swift; and yet has more to do. 445
So many of his hours in publick move,
That few are left for privacy, and Love.
Palmyra. The Sun, methinks, shines faint and dimly, here;
Light is not half so long, nor half so clear.
But, Oh! when every day was yours and mine, 450
How early up! what haste he made to shine!
Leonidas. Such golden days no Prince must hope to see;
Whose ev'ry Subject is more bless'd then he.
Palmyra. Do you remember, when their tasks were done,
How all the Youth did to our Cottage run?   455
While winter-winds were whistling loud without,
Our chearful hearth was circled round about:
With strokes in ashes Maids their Lovers drew;
And still you fell to me, and I to you.
Leonidas. When Love did of my heart possession take, 460
I was so young, my soul was scarce awake:
I cannot tell when first I thought you fair;
But suck'd in Love, insensibly as Ayre.
Palmyra. I know too well when first my love began,
When, at our Wake, you for the Chaplet ran: 465
Then I was made the Lady of the May,
And, with the Garland, at the Goal did stay:
Still, as you ran, I kept you full in view;
I hop'd, and wish'd, and ran, methought, for you.
As you came near, I hastily did rise,   470
And stretch'd my arm out-right, that held the prize.
The custom was to kiss whom I should crown:
You kneel'd; and, in my lap, your head laid down.
I blush'd, and blush'd, and did the kiss delay:
At last, my Subjects forc'd me to obey;   475
But, when I gave the Crown, and then the kiss,
I scarce had breath to say, Take that ——— and this.
Leonidas. I felt, the while, a pleasing kind of smart;
The kiss went, tingling, to my very heart.

458 *strokes in ashes*] Maidens made random marks or strokes in the
ashes of a hearth, from which they deciphered the initials of their lovers.
465 *Wake . . . Chaplet*] at a rural festival he ran a race for a garland.

480   When it was gone, the sense of it did stay;
        The sweetness cling'd upon my lips all day,
        Like drops of Honey, loath to fall away.
    Palmyra. Life, like a prodigal, gave all his store
        To my first youth, and now can give no more.
485   You are a Prince; and, in that high degree,
        No longer must converse with humble me.
    Leonidas. 'Twas to my loss the Gods that title gave;
        A Tyrant's Son is doubly born a Slave:
        He gives a Crown; but, to prevent my life
490   From being happy, loads it with a Wife.
    Palmyra. Speak quickly; what have you resolv'd to do?
    Leonidas. To keep my faith inviolate to you.
        He threatens me with exile, and with shame,
        To lose my birth-right, and a Prince his name;
495   But there's a blessing which he did not mean,
        To send me back to Love and You again.
    Palmyra. Why was not I a Princess for your sake?
        But Heav'en no more such miracles can make:
        And, since That cannot, This must never be;
500   You shall not lose a Crown for love of me.
        Live happy, and a nobler choice pursue;
        I shall complain of Fate; but not of you.
    Leonidas. Can you so easily without me live?
        Or could you take the counsel which you give?
505   Were you a Princess would you not be true?
    Palmyra. I would; but cannot merit it from you.
    Leonidas. Did you not merit, as you do, my heart;
        Love gives esteem; and then it gives desert.
        But if I basely could forget my vow,
510   Poor helpless Innocence, what would you do?
    Palmyra. In Woods, and Plains, where first my love began,
        There would I live, retir'd from faithless man:
        I'd sit all day within some lonely shade,
        Or that close Arbour which your hands have made:
515   I'd search the Groves, and ev'ry Tree, to find
        Where you had carv'd our names upon the rind:
        Your Hook, your Scrip, all that was yours, I'd keep,
        And lay 'em by me when I went to sleep.
        Thus would I live: and Maidens, when I die,
520   Upon my Hearse white True-love-knots should tie:
        And thus my Tomb should be inscrib'd above,
        Here the forsaken Virgin rests from love.

517 *Hook . . . Scrip*] a shepherd's crook and bag.
520 *Upon my Hearse*] cf. Aspasia's lament in Beaumont and
Fletcher's *The Maid's Tragedy*, II.i.

Leonidas. Think not that time or fate shall e'r divide
    Those hearts, which Love and mutual Vows have ty'd:
    But we must part; farewell, my Love
Palmyra.   Till when?   525
Leonidas. Till the next age of hours we meet agen.
    Mean time ———— we may
    When near each other we in publick stand,
    Contrive to catch a look, or steal a hand:
    Fancy will every touch, and glance improve;   530
    And draw the most spirituous parts of Love.
    Our souls sit close, and silently within;
    And their own Web from their own Intrals spin.
    And when eyes meet far off, our sense is such,
    That, Spider-like, we feel the tender'st touch.   535

                                  Exeunt.

ACT III. Scene 1

    Enter Rhodophil, *meeting* Doralice *and* Artemis.
      Rhodophil *and* Doralice *embrace.*

Rhodophil. My own dear heart!
Doralice. My own true love!   *She starts back.*
    I had forgot my self to be so kind; indeed I am very
    angry with you, dear; you are come home an hour after
    you appointed: If you had staid a minute longer, I was   5
    just considering, whether I should stab, hang, or drown
    my self.   *Embracing him.*
Rhodophil. Nothing but the King's business could have
    hinder'd me; and I was so vext, that I was just laying
    down my Commission, rather then have fail'd my Dear.   10
                           Kissing her hand.
Artemis. Why, this is love as it should be, betwixt Man
    and Wife: such another Couple would bring Marriage
    into fashion again. But is it always thus betwixt you?
Rhodophil. Always thus! this is nothing. I tell you there is
    not such a pair of Turtles in all *Sicily*; there is such an   15
    eternal Cooing and kissing betwixt us, that indeed it is
    scandalous before civil company.
Doralice. Well, if I had imagin'd, I should have been this
    fond fool, I would never have marri'd the man I lov'd:
    I marri'd to be happy; and have made my self miserable,   20
    by over-loving. Nay, and now, my case is desperate;
    for I have been marry'd above these two years, and find
    my self every day worse and worse in love: nothing but
    madness can be the end on't.
Artemis. Doat on, to the extremity, and you are happy.   25

Doralice. He deserves so infinitely much, that, the truth is, there can be no doating in the matter; but to love well, I confess, is a work that pays it self: 'tis telling gold, and after taking it for one's pains.

30 *Rhodophil.* By that I should be a very covetous person; for I am ever pulling out my money, and putting it into my pocket again.

Doralice. O dear *Rhodophil!*

Rhodophil. O sweet *Doralice!*   *Embracing each other.*

35 *Artemis* (*aside*). Nay, I am resolv'd, I'll never interrupt Lovers: I'll leave 'em as happy as I found 'em.

                                                                            Steals away.

Rhodophil. What, is she gone?   *Looking up.*

Doralice. Yes; and without taking leave.

Rhodophil. Then there's enough for this time.

                                                                        Parting from her.

40 *Doralice.* Yes sure, the Scene's done, I take it.

They walk contrary ways on the Stage; he, with his hands in his pocket, whistling: she, singing a dull melancholly Tune.

Rhodophil. Pox o' your dull tune, a man can't think for you.

Doralice. Pox o' your damn'd whistling; you can neither be company to me your self, nor leave me to the freedom of my own fancy.

45 *Rhodophil.* Well, thou art the most provoking Wife!

Doralice. Well, thou art the dullest Husband, thou art never to be provok'd.

Rhodophil. I was never thought dull, till I marry'd thee; and now thou hast made an old knife of me, thou hast

50 whetted me so long, till I have no edge left.

Doralice. I see you are in the Husbands fashion; you reserve all your good humours for your Mistresses, and keep your ill for your wives.

Rhodophil. Prethee leave me to my own cogitations; I am

55 thinking over all my sins, to find for which of them it was I marry'd thee.

Doralice. Whatever your sin was, mine's the punishment.

Rhodophil. My comfort is, thou art not immortal; and when that blessed, that divine day comes, of thy depar-

60 ture, I'm resolv'd I'll make one Holy-day more in the Almanack, for thy sake.

Doralice. Ay, you had need make a Holy-day for me, for I am sure you have made me a Martyr.

Rhodophil. Then, setting my victorious foot upon thy head,

65 in the first hour of thy silence, (that is, the first hour thou art dead, for I despair of it before) I will swear by thy Ghost, an oath as terrible to me, as *Styx* is to the

Gods, never more to be in danger of the Banes of
Matrimony.

Doralice. And I am resolv'd to marry the very same day   70
thou dy'st, if it be but to show how little I'm concern'd
for thee.

Rhodophil. Prethee, *Doralice*, why do we quarrel thus
a-days? ha? this is but a kind of Heathenish life, and
does not answer the ends of marriage. If I have err'd,   75
propound what reasonable atonement may be made,
before we sleep, and I shall not be refractory: but
withall consider, I have been marry'd these three years,
and be not too tyrannical.

Doralice. What should you talk of a peace abed, when you   80
can give no security for performance of Articles?

Rhodophil. Then, since we must live together, and both of
us stand upon our terms, as to matter of dying first,
let us make our selves as merry as we can with our
misfortunes.   85
Why there's the devil on't! if thou couldst make my
enjoying thee but a little less easie, or a little more un-
lawful, thou shouldst see, what a Termagant Lover I
would prove. I have taken such pains to enjoy thee,
Doralice, that I have fanci'd thee all the fine women in   90
the Town, to help me out. But now there's none left
for me to think on, my imagination is quite jaded.
Thou art a Wife, and thou wilt be a Wife, and I can
make thee another no longer.   *Exit* Rhodophil.

Doralice. Well, since thou art a Husband, and wilt be a   95
Husband, I'll try if I can find out another! 'Tis a pretty
time we Women have on't, to be made Widows, while
we are marry'd. Our Husbands think it reasonable to
complain, that we are the same, and the same to them,
when we have more reason to complain, that they are   100
not the same to us. Because they cannot feed on one
dish, therefore we must be starv'd. 'Tis enough that
they have a sufficient Ordinary provided, and a Table
ready spread for 'em: if they cannot fall too and eat
heartily, the fault is theirs; and 'tis pity, me-thinks, that   105
the good creature should be lost, when many a poor
sinner would be glad on't.

Enter Melantha, *and* Artemis *to her.*

Melantha. Dear, my dear, pity me; I am so *chagrin* to day,

68 *Banes*] marriage banns, with a pun on *bane.*
81 *Articles*] the formal agreement.
88 *Termagant*] tyrant.
103 *Ordinary*] regular, daily meal.

and have had the most signal affront at Court! I went
this afternoon to do my devoir to Princess *Amalthea*,
found her, convers'd with her, and help'd to make her
court some half an hour; after which, she went to take
the ayr, chose out two Ladies to go with her, that came
in after me, and left me most barbarously behind her.

Artemis. You are the less to be piti'd, *Melantha*, because you
subject your self to these affronts, by coming perpetually
to Court, where you have no business nor employment.

Melantha. I declare, I had rather of the two, be *railly'd*, nay,
mal traittée at Court, then be Deifi'd in the Town: for,
assuredly, nothing can be so *ridicule*, as a meer Town-
Lady.

Doralice. Especially at Court. How I have seen 'em crowd
and sweat in the Drawing-room, on a Holiday-night!
for that's their time to swarm, and invade the Presence.
O, how they catch at a bow, or any little salute from a
Courtier, to make show of their acquaintance! and
rather then be thought to be quite unknown, they
court'sie to one another; but they take true pains to
come near the Circle, and press and peep upon the
Princess, to write Letters into the Countrey how she
was dress'd, while the Ladies that stand about make their
court to her with abusing them.

Artemis. These are sad truths, *Melantha*; and therefore I
would e'en advise you to quit the Court, and live either
wholly in the Town; or, if you like not that, in the
Countrey.

Doralice. In the Countrey! nay, that's to fall beneath the
Town; for they live there upon our offals here: their
entertainment of wit, is onely the remembrance of what
they had when they were last in Town; they live this
year upon the last year's knowledge, as their Cattel do
all night, by chewing the Cud of what they eat in the
afternoon.

Melantha. And they tell, for news, such unlikely stories; a
letter from one of us is such a present to 'em, that the
poor souls wait for the Carrier's-day with such devotion,
that they cannot sleep the night before.

Artemis. No more then I can, the night before I am to go
a journey.

Doralice. Or I, before I am to try on a new Gown.

Melantha. A Song that's stale here, will be new there a

---

129 *Circle*] surrounding courtiers and ladies in waiting.
146 *Carrier's-day*] when the private, common carrier delivered
the mail from the city.

twelvemoneth hence; and if a man of the Town by
chance come amongst 'em, he's reverenced for teaching
'em the Tune.

Doralice. A friend of mine, who makes Songs sometimes,   155
came lately out of the West, and vow'd he was so put
out of count'nance with a Song of his; for at the first
Countrey-Gentleman's he visited, he saw three Tailors
cross-leg'd upon the Table in the Hall, who were tearing
out as loud as ever they could sing,   160

———— *After the pangs of a desperate Lover, &c.*

and all that day he heard nothing else, but the Daughters
of the house and the Maids, humming it over in every
corner, and the Father whistling it.

Artemis. Indeed I have observ'd of my self, that when I am   165
out of Town but a fortnight, I am so humble, that I
would receive a Letter from my Tailor or Mercer for a
favour.

Melantha. When I have been at grass in the Summer, and
am new come up again, methinks I'm to be turn'd into   170
ridicule by all that see me; but when I have been once or
twice at Court, I begin to value my self again, and to
despise my Countrey-acquaintance.

Artemis. There are places where all people may be ador'd,
and we ought to know our selves so well as to chuse   175
'em.

Doralice. That's very true; your little Courtier's wife, who
speaks to the King but once a moneth, need but go to
a Town-Lady; and there she may vapour, and cry, *The
King and I*, at every word. Your Town-Lady, who is   180
laugh'd at in the Circle, takes her Coach into the City,
and there she's call'd your Honour, and has a Banquet
from the Merchant's Wife, whom she laughs at for
her kindness. And, as for my finical Cit, she removes
but to her Countrey-house, and there insults over the   185
Countrey Gentlewoman that never comes up; who
treats her with Frumity and Custard, and opens her dear
bottle of *Mirabilis* beside, for a Jill-glass of it at parting.

Artemis. At last, I see, we shall leave *Melantha* where we
found her; for, by your description of the Town and   190
Countrey, they are become more dreadful to her, then

160.1 *After . . . Lover &c.*] from Act II of *Evening's Love*, produced
four years before.

187 *Frumity*] a kind of gruel made of hulled wheat boiled in milk,
seasoned with cinnamon and sugar.

188 *Jill-glass*] a half pint, a gill.

188 *Mirabilis*] an invigorating cordial made of wines and spices.

the Court, where she was affronted. But you forget we
are to wait on the Princess *Amalthea*. Come, *Doralice*.

Doralice. Farewell, *Melantha.*

195 *Melantha.* Adieu, my dear.

Artemis. You are out of charity with her, and therefore I
shall not give your service.

Melantha. Do not omit it, I beseech you; for I have such a
tender for the Court, that I love it ev'n from the

200 Drawing-room to the Lobby, and can never be *rebutée*
by any usage. But, hark you, my Dears, one thing I had
forgot of great concernment.

Doralice. Quickly then, we are in haste.

Melantha. Do not call it my service, that's too vulgar; but

205 do my *baise mains* to the Princess *Amalthea*; that is
Spirituelle!

Doralice. To do you service then, we will *prendre* the
Carrosse to Court, and do your *Baise mains* to the
Princess *Amalthea*, in your phrase *Spirituelle*.

> *Exeunt* Artemis *and* Doralice.

Enter Philotis, *with a Paper in her hand.*

210 *Melantha.* O, are you there, Minion? And, well, are not
you a most precious damsel, to retard all my visits for
want of language, when you know you are paid so
well for furnishing me with new words for my daily
conversation? Let me die, if I have not run the risque

215 already, to speak like one of the vulgar; and if I have
one phrase left in all my store that is not thrid-bare *et
usé*, and fit for nothing but to be thrown to Peasants.

Philotis. Indeed, Madam, I have been very diligent in my
vocation; but you have so drain'd all the *French* Plays

220 and Romances, that they are not able to supply you
with words for your daily expences.

Melantha. Drain'd? what a word's there!
Epuisée, you sot you. Come, produce your morning's
work.

225 *Philotis.* 'Tis here, Madam. *Shows the Paper.*

Melantha. O, my *Venus*! fourteen or fifteen words to serve
me a whole day! Let me die, at this rate I cannot last
till night. Come, read your works: twenty to one half
of 'em will not pass muster neither.

---

200 *rebutée*] rebuffed.
205 *baise mains*] compliments.
206–7 *prendre the Carrosse*] take the carriage.
223 *Epuissée*] exhausted.
228 *works*] labors.

Philotis. Sottises.   *Reads.*

Melantha. Sottises: *bon.* That's an excellent word to begin
   withall: as for example; He, or she said a thousand
   Sottises to me. Proceed.

Philotis. Figure: as what a figure of a man is there!
   Naive, and *Naiveté.*   235

Melantha. Naive! as how?

Philotis. Speaking of a thing that was naturally said; It was
   so *naive*: or such an innocent piece of simplicity; 'twas
   such a *naiveté.*

Melantha. Truce with your interpretations: make haste.   240

*Philotis. Foible, Chagrin, Grimace, Embarrassé, Double
   entendre, Equivoque, Esclaircissement, Suitté, Béveue,
   Facòn, Panchant, Coup d'étourdy,* and *Ridicule.*

Melantha. Hold, hold; how did they begin?

Philotis. They began at *Sottises,* and ended *en Ridicule.*   245

Melantha. Now give me your Paper in my hand, and hold
   you my Glass, while I practise my postures for the day.
                                      Melantha *laughs in the Glass.*
   How does that laugh become my face?

Philotis. Sovereignly well, Madam.

Melantha. Sovereignly! Let me die, that's not amiss. That   250
   word shall not be yours; I'll invent it, and bring it up
   my self: my new *Point Gorget* shall be yours upon't:
   not a word of the word, I charge you.

Philotis. I am dumb, Madam.

Melantha. That glance, how sutes it with my face?   255
                                      Looking in the Glass again.

Philotis. 'Tis so *languissant.*

Melantha. Languissant! that word shall be mine too, and
   my last *Indian-Gown* thine for't.
   That sigh?   *Looks again.*

Philotis. 'Twill make many a man sigh, Madam. 'Tis a   260
   meer *Incendiary.*

Melantha. Take my *Guimp* Petticoat for that truth. If thou

---

   230 *Sottises*] the singular form means folly or nonsense, the plural,
insults or abusive language.
   240 *Truce with*] enough of.
   241–43 *Foible . . . Ridicule*] feeble, peevishness, a face or pose,
embarrassed, double meaning, enlightenment, ambiguous, a following,
a blunder, fashion or affectation, a leaning or bent, a silly act: all
reflect upon Melantha's character and interests.
   252 *Point Gorget*] needlework collar or handkerchief covering the
neck or breast.
   256 *languissant*] languishing, dull.
   258 *Indian-Gown*] a dress of Indian pattern usually gaudy, dishabille.
   262 *Guimp*] trimmed with gimp, twisted silk or cotton lacework.

hast more of these phrases, let me die but I could give
away all my Wardrobe, and go naked for 'em.

265 *Philotis.* Go naked? then you would be a *Venus*, Madam.
O *Jupiter*! what had I forgot? this Paper was given me
by *Rhodophil's* Page.

Melantha (reading the Letter). —— Beg the favour from
you. —— Gratifie my passion —— so far ——

270 assignation —— in the Grotto —— behind the
Terras —— clock this evening. —— Well, for the
Billets doux there's no man in *Sicily* must dispute with
Rhodophil; they are so *French*, so *gallant*, and so *tendre*,
that I cannot resist the temptation of the assignation.

275 Now go you away, *Philotis*; it imports me to practise
what I shall say to my Servant when I meet him.

Exit Philotis.

Rhodophil, you'll wonder at my assurance to meet you
here; let me die, I am so out of breath with coming,
that I can render you no reason of it. Then he will make

280 this *repartee*; Madam, I have no reason to accuse you for
that which is so great a favour to me. Then I reply,
But why have you drawn me to this solitary place? let
me die but I am apprehensive of some violence from
you. Then, says he; Solitude, Madam, is most fit for

285 Lovers; but by this fair hand ——. Nay, now I vow
you're rude, Sir. O fie, fie, fie; I hope you'l be honourable? —— You'd laugh at me if I should, Madam.
—— What do you mean to throw me down thus?
Ah me! ah, ah, ah.

Enter Polydamas, Leonidas, *and Guards.*

290 O *Venus*! the King and Court. Let me die but I fear
they have found my *foible*, and will turn me into
ridicule. *Exit running.*

Leonidas. Sir, I beseech you.

Polydamas. Do not urge my patience.

Leonidas. I'll not deny

295 But what your Spies inform'd you of, is true:
I love the fair *Palmyra*; but I lov'd her
Before I knew your title to my bloud.

Enter Palmyra, *guarded.*

See, here she comes; and looks, amid'st her Guards,

---

288 *What do you mean*] Modern editors who put a comma
after *What* alter the meaning. Melantha visualizes the "throwing
down" as an accomplished fact, but with the comma the event is
still incomplete (Sutherland).

Like a weak Dove under the Falcon's gripe.
O heav'n, I cannot bear it.
Polydamas.   Maid, come hither.   300
  Have you presum'd so far, as to receive
  My Son's affection?
Palmyra. Alas, what shall I answer? to confess it
  Will raise a blush upon a Virgin's face;
  Yet I was ever taught 'twas base to lie.   305
Polydamas. You've been too bold, and you must love no
    more.
Palmyra. Indeed I must; I cannot help my love;
  I was so tender when I took the bent,
  That now I grow that way.
Polydamas. He is a Prince; and you are meanly born.   310
Leonidas. Love either finds equality, or makes it:
  Like death, he knows no difference in degrees,
  But plains, and levels all.
Palmyra. Alas, I had not render'd up my heart,
  Had he not lov'd me first; but he prefer'd me   315
  Above the Maidens of my age and rank;
  Still shun'd their company, and still sought mine;
  I was not won by gifts, yet still he gave;
  And all his gifts, though small, yet spoke his love.
  He pick'd the earliest Strawberries in Woods,   320
  The cluster'd Filberds, and the purple Grapes:
  He taught a prating Stare to speak my name;
  And when he found a Nest of Nightingales,
  Or callow Linnets, he would show 'em me,
  And let me take 'em out.   325
Polydamas. This is a little Mistris, meanly born,
  Fit onely for a Prince his vacant hours,
  And then, to laugh at her simplicity,
  Not fix a passion there. Now hear my sentence.
Leonidas. Remember, ere you give it, 'tis pronounc'd   330
  Against us both.
Polydamas.   First, in her hand
  There shall be plac'd a Player's painted Sceptre,
  And, on her head, a gilded Pageant Crown;
  Thus shall she go,   335
  With all the Boys attending on her Triumph:
  That done, be put alone into a Boat,
  With bread and water onely for three days,
  So on the Sea she shall be set adrift,
  And who relieves her, dies.   340
Palmyra. I onely beg that you would execute

322 *Stare*] starling.

319

The last part first: let me be put to Sea;
The bread and water, for my three days life,
I give you back, I would not live so long;
345   But let me scape the shame.
Leonidas.   Look to me, Piety;
And you, O Gods, look to my piety:
Keep me from saying that which misbecomes a son;
But let me die before I see this done.
Polydamas. If you for ever will abjure her sight,
350   I can be yet a father; she shall live.
Leonidas. Hear, O you Pow'rs, is this to be a father?
I see 'tis all my happiness and quiet
You aim at, Sir; and take 'em:
I will not save ev'n my *Palmyra's* life
355   At that ignoble price; but I'll die with her.
Palmyra. So had I done by you,
Had Fate made me a Princess: Death, methinks,
Is not a terrour now;
He is not fierce, or grim, but fawns, and sooths me,
360   And slides along, like *Cleopatra's* Aspick,
Off'ring his service to my troubled breast.
Leonidas. Begin what you have purpos'd when you please,
Lead her to scorn, your triumph shall be doubled.
As holy Priests
365   In pity go with dying malefactours,
So will I share her shame.
Polydamas. You shall not have your will so much; first part 'em,
Then execute your office.
Leonidas.   No; I'll die
In her defence.   *Draws his sword.*
Palmyra.   Ah, hold, and pull not on
370   A curse, to make me worthy of my death:
Do not by lawless force oppose your Father,
Whom you have too much disobey'd for me.
Leonidas. Here, take it, Sir, and with it, pierce my heart:

    Presenting his sword to his father upon his knees.

You have done more, in taking my *Palmyra*.
375   You are my Father, therefore I submit.
Polydamas. Keep him from any thing he may design
Against his life, whil'st the first fury lasts;
And now perform what I commanded you.
Leonidas. In vain; if sword and poison be deni'd me,
380   I'll hold my breath and die.

346 *piety*] filial duty.

Palmyra. Farewell, my last, *Leonidas*; yet live,
  I charge you live, till you believe me dead.
  I cannot die in peace, if you die first.
  If life's a blessing, you shall have it last.
Polydamas. Go on with her, and lead him after me.   385

    Enter Argaleon *hastily, with* Hermogenes.

Argaleon. I bring you, Sir, such news as must amaze you,
  And such as will prevent you from an action
  Which would have rendred all your life unhappy.
Polydamas. Hermogenes, you bend your knees in vain,
                        Hermogenes *kneels.*
  My doom's already past.   390
Hermogenes. I kneel not for *Palmyra*, for I know
  She will not need my pray'rs; but for my self:
  With a feign'd tale I have abus'd your ears,
  And therefore merit death; but since, unforc'd,
  I first accuse my self, I hope your mercy.   395
Polydamas. Haste to explain your meaning.
Hermogenes. Then, in few words, *Palmyra* is your daughter.
Polydamas. How can I give belief to this Impostor?
  He who has once abus'd me, often may.
  I'll hear no more.
Argaleon.   For your own sake, you must.   400
Hermogenes. A parent's love (for I confess my crime)
  Mov'd me to say, *Leonidas* was yours;
  But when I heard *Palmyra* was to die,
  The fear of guiltless bloud so stung my conscience,
  That I resolv'd, ev'n with my shame, to save   405
  Your daughter's life.
Polydamas. But how can I be certain, but that interest,
  Which mov'd you first to say your son was mine,
  Does not now move you too, to save your daughter?
Hermogenes. You had but then my word; I bring you now   410
  Authentick testimonies. Sir, in short,
        Delivers on his knees a Jewel, and a Letter.
  If this will not convince you, let me suffer.
Polydamas. I know this Jewel well; 'twas once my mother's,
              Looking first on the Jewel.
  Which, marrying, I presented to my wife.
  And this, O this, is my *Eudoxia's* hand.   415
  This was the pledge of love given to Eudoxia,   Reads.
  Who, dying, to her young Palmyra *leaves it:*
  And this when you, my dearest Lord, receive,

---

381 last,] ~ ∧ Qq,F

---

381 *my last,*] the last thing she can do, as "This is Timon's last"
(*Timon of Athens*, III.vi.100). S–S emended to *my lost.*

321

      Own her, and think on me, dying Eudoxia.
420   (*To Argaleon*) Take it; 'tis well there is no more to read,
      My eyes grow full, and swim in their own light.
               He embraces Palmyra.
    Palmyra. I fear, Sir, this is your intended Pageant.
      You sport your self at poor *Palmyra's* cost;
      But if you think to make me proud,
425   Indeed I cannot be so: I was born
      With humble thoughts, and lowly, like my birth.
      A real fortune could not make me haughty,
      Much less a feign'd.
    Polydamas.   This was her mother's temper.
      I have too much deserv'd thou shouldst suspect
430   That I am not thy father; but my love
      Shall henceforth show I am. Behold my eyes,
      And see a father there begin to flow:
      This is not feign'd, *Palmyra.*
    Palmyra. I doubt no longer, Sir; you are a King,
435   And cannot lie: falshood's a vice too base
      To find a room in any Royal breast;
      I know, in spight of my unworthiness,
      I am your child; for when you would have kill'd me,
      Methought I lov'd you then.
440   *Argaleon.* Sir, we forget the Prince *Leonidas,*
      His greatness should not stand neglected thus.
    Polydamas. Guards, you may now retire: Give him his
      sword,
      And leave him free.
    Leonidas. Then the first use I make of liberty
445   Shall be, with your permission, mighty Sir,
      To pay that reverence to which Nature binds me.
             Kneels to Hermogenes.
    Argaleon. Sure you forget your birth, thus to misplace
      This act of your obedience; you should kneel
      To nothing but to Heav'n, and to a King.
450   *Leonidas.* I never shall forget what Nature owes,
      Nor be asham'd to pay it; though my father
      Be not a King, I know him brave and honest,
      And well deserving of a worthier son.
    Polydamas. He bears it gallantly.
    Leonidas (*to Hermogenes*). Why would you not instruct me,
455   Sir, before
      Where I should place my duty?
      From which, if ignorance have made me swerve,
      I beg your pardon for an erring son.
    Palmyra. I almost grieve I am a Princess, since
460   It makes him lose a Crown.

Leonidas. And next, to you, my King, thus low I kneel,
   T'implore your mercy; if in that small time
   I had the honour to be thought your son,
   I pay'd not strict obedience to your will:
   I thought, indeed, I should not be compell'd,   465
   But thought it as your son; so what I took
   In duty from you, I restor'd in courage;
   Because your son should not be forc'd.
Polydamas. You have my pardon for it.
Leonidas. To you, fair Princess, I congratulate   470
   Your birth; of which I ever thought you worthy:
   And give me leave to add, that I am proud
   The Gods have pick'd me out to be the man
   By whose dejected fate yours is to rise;
   Because no man could more desire your fortune,   475
   Or franklier part with his to make you great.
Palmyra. I know the King, though you are not his son,
   Will still regard you as my Foster-brother,
   And so conduct you downward from a Throne,
   By slow degrees, so unperceiv'd and soft,   480
   That it may seem no fall: or, if it be,
   May Fortune lay a bed of down beneath you.
Polydamas. He shall be rank'd with my Nobility,
   And kept from scorn by a large pension giv'n him.
Leonidas (*bowing*). You are all great and Royal in your
     gifts;   485
   But at the Donor's feet I lay 'em down:
   Should I take riches from you, it would seem
   As I did want a soul to bear that poverty
   To which the Gods design'd my humble birth:
   And should I take your Honours without merit,   490
   It would appear, I wanted manly courage
   To hope 'em, in your service, from my sword.
Polydamas. Still brave, and like your self.
   The Court shall shine this night in its full splendor,
   And celebrate this new discovery.   495
   Argaleon, lead my daughter: as we go
   I shall have time to give her my commands,
   In which you are concern'd.
                 Exeunt all but Leonidas.
Leonidas. Methinks I do not want
   That huge long train of fawning followers,   500
   That swept a furlong after me.
   'Tis true, I am alone;
   So was the Godhead ere he made the world,

474 *dejected*] humbled.

And better serv'd Himself, then serv'd by Nature.
505 And yet I have a Soul
Above this humble fate. I could command,
Love to do good; give largely to true merit;
All that a King should do: But though these are not
My Province, I have Scene enough within
510 To exercise my vertue.
All that a heart, so fix'd as mine, can move,
Is, that my niggard fortune starves my love.

Exit.

[ACT III.] SCENE 2

Palamede *and* Doralice *meet: she with a Book in her hand,
seems to start at sight of him.*

Doralice. 'Tis a strange thing that no warning will serve
your turn; and that no retirement will secure me from
your impertinent addresses! Did not I tell you, that I
was to be private here at my devotions?
5 *Palamede.* Yes; and you see I have observ'd my Cue
exactly: I am come to releive you from them. Come,
shut up, shut up your Book; the man's come who is
to supply all your necessities.
Doralice. Then, it seems, you are so impudent to think it
10 was an assignation? this, I warrant, was your lewd
interpretation of my innocent meaning.
Palamede. Venus forbid that I should harbour so unreasonable a thought of a fair young Lady, that you should
lead me hither into temptation. I confess I might think
15 indeed it was a kind of honourable challenge, to meet
privately without Seconds, and decide the difference
betwixt the two Sexes; but heaven forgive me if I
thought amiss.
Doralice. You thought too, I'll lay my life on't, that you
20 might as well make love to me, as my Husband does to
your Mistris.
Palamede. I was so unreasonable to think so too.
Doralice. And then you wickedly inferr'd, that there was
some justice in the revenge of it: or at least but little
25 injury; for a man to endeavour to enjoy that, which he
accounts a blessing, and which is not valu'd as it ought
by the dull possessour. Confess your wickedness, did
you not think so?
Palamede. I confess I was thinking so, as fast as I could;

509 *Scene*] theater of action.

324

but you think so much before me, that you will let me   30
     think nothing.

Doralice. 'Tis the very thing that I design'd: I have fore-
     stall'd all your arguments, and left you without a word
     more, to plead for mercy. If you have any thing farther
     to offer, ere Sentence pass ——— Poor Animal, I   35
     brought you hither onely for my diversion.

Palamede. That you may have, if you'll make use of me the
     right way; but I tell thee, woman, I am now past
     talking.

Doralice. But it may be, I came hither to hear what fine   40
     things you could say for your self.

Palamede. You would be very angry, to my knowledge,
     if I should lose so much time to say many of 'em.———
     By this hand you would. ———

Doralice. Fie, *Palamede*, I am a woman of honour.   45

Palamede. I see you are; you have kept touch with your
     assignation: and before we part, you shall find that I am
     a man of honour: ——— yet I have one scruple of
     conscience ———

Doralice. I warrant you will not want some naughty argu-   50
     ment or other to satisfie your self. ——— I hope you are
     afraid of betraying your friend?

Palamede. Of betraying my friend! I am more afraid of
     being betray'd by you to my friend. You women now
     are got into the way of telling first your selves: a man   55
     who has any care of his reputation will be loath to trust
     it with you.

Doralice. O you charge your faults upon our Sex: you men
     are like Cocks, you never make love, but you clap your
     wings, and crow when you have done.   60

Palamede. Nay, rather you women are like Hens; you
     never lay, but you cackle an hour after, to discover your
     Nest. ——— But I'll venture it for once.

Doralice. To convince you that you are in the wrong, I'll
     retire into the dark Grotto, to my devotion, and make   65
     so little noise, that it shall be impossible for you to find
     me.

Palamede. But if I find you ———

Doralice. Ay, if you find me ——— But I'll put you to
     search in more corners then you imagine.   70
                     She runs in, and he after her.

         Enter Rhodophil *and* Melantha.

Melantha. Let me die, but this solitude, and that Grotto are
     scandalous; I'll go no further; besides, you have a sweet
     Lady of your own.

Rhodophil. But a sweet Mistris, now and then, makes my
75   sweet Lady so much more sweet.

Melantha. I hope you will not force me?

Rhodophil. But I will, if you desire it.

Palamede (within). Where the devil are you, Madam?
S'death, I begin to be weary of this hide and seek: if
80   you stay a little longer, till the fit's over, I'll hide in my
turn, and put you to the finding me.

                  He enters, and sees Rhodophil *and* Melantha.

How! *Rhodophil* and my Mistris!

Melantha. My servant to apprehend me! this is *Surprenant
au dernier.*

85   *Rhodophil.* I must on; there's nothing but impudence can
help me out.

Palamede. *Rhodophil,* How came you hither in so good
company?

Rhodophil. As you see, *Palamede*; an effect of pure friend-
90   ship; I was not able to live without you.

Palamede. But what makes my Mistris with you?

Rhodophil. Why, I heard you were here alone, and could
not in civility but bring her to you.

Melantha. You'll pardon the effects of a passion which I
95   may now avow for you, if it transported me beyond the
rules of *bien séance.*

Palamede. But who told you I was here? they that told
you that, may tell you more, for ought I know.

Rhodophil. O, for that matter, we had intelligence.

100 *Palamede.* But let me tell you, we came hither so very
privately, that you could not trace us.

Rhodophil. Us? what us? you are alone.

Palamede. Us! the devil's in me for mistaking: me, I meant.
Or us; that is, you are me, or I you, as we are friends:
105 that's us.

Doralice (within). Palamede, Palamede.

Rhodophil. I should know that voice? who's within there,
that calls you?

Palamede. Faith I can't imagine; I believe the place is
110 haunted.

Doralice (within). Palamede, Palamede, All-cocks hidden.

Palamede. Lord, lord, what shall I do? Well, dear friend,
to let you see I scorn to be jealous, and that I dare trust

83–84 *Surprenant au dernier*] extremely surprising.

96 *bien séance*] decorum.

111 *All-cocks hidden*] possibly a cry in a children's game, as in
hide-and-go-seek (see V.i.339); Sutherland thinks it may refer
to the practice of covering up the cocks just before releasing them
for a fight. At any rate Doralice is telling Palamede that she is ready.

my Mistris with you, take her back, for I would not
willingly have her frighted, and I am resolv'd to see   115
who's there; I'll not be danted with a Bug-bear, that's
certain: prethee dispute it not, it shall be so; nay, do
not put me to swear, but go quickly: there's an effect of
pure friendship for you now.

Enter Doralice, *and looks amaz'd, seeing them.*

Rhodophil. Doralice! I am thunder-struck to see you here.   120
Palamede. So am I! quite thunder-struck. Was it you that
call'd me within? (I must be impudent.)
Rhodophil. How came you hither, Spouse?
Palamede. Ay, how came you hither? And, which is more,
how could you be here without my knowledge?   125
Doralice (*to her husband*). O, Gentleman, have I caught you
i'faith! have I broke forth in ambush upon you! I
thought my suspicions would prove true.
Rhodophil. Suspicions! this is very fine, Spouse!
Prethee what suspicions?   130
Doralice. O, you feign ignorance: why, of you and
Melantha; here have I staid these two hours, waiting
with all the rage of a passionate, loving wife, but
infinitely jealous, to take you two in the manner; for
hither I was certain you would come.   135
Rhodophil. But you are mistaken, Spouse, in the occasion;
for we came hither on purpose to find *Palamede*, on
intelligence he was gone before.
Palamede. I'll be hang'd then if the same party who gave
you intelligence, I was here, did not tell your wife you   140
would come hither: now I smell the malice on't on both
sides.
Doralice. Was it so, think you? nay, then, I'll confess my
part of the malice too. As soon as ever I spi'd my
husband and *Melantha* come together, I had a strange   145
temptation to make him jealous in revenge; and that
made me call *Palamede*, *Palamede*, as though there had
been an Intrigue between us.
Melantha. Nay, I avow, there was an apparence of an
Intrigue between us too.   150
Palamede. To see how things will come about!
Rhodophil. And was it onely thus, my dear *Doralice*?
                                                    Embraces.
Doralice. And did I wrong none, *Rhodophil*, with a false
suspicion?   *Embracing him.*
Palamede (*aside*). Now am I confident we had all four the   155
same design: 'tis a pretty odd kind of game this, where

327

each of us plays for double stakes: this is just thrust and
parry with the same motion; I am to get his Wife, and
yet to guard my own Mistris. But I am vilely suspitious,
160   that, while I conquer in the Right Wing, I shall be
routed in the Left: for both our women will certainly
betray their party, because they are each of them for
gaining of two, as well as we; and I much fear,
    If their necessities and ours were known,
165   They have more need of two, then we of one.
                          Exeunt, embracing one another.

ACT IV. Scene 1

Enter Leonidas, *musing,* Amalthea *following him.*
Amalthea. Yonder he is, and I must speak, or die;
    And yet 'tis death to speak; yet he must know
    I have a passion for him, and may know it
    With a less blush; because to offer it
5   To his low fortunes, shows I lov'd before,
    His person, not his greatness.
Leonidas. First scorn'd, and now commanded from the
    Court!
    The King is good; but he is wrought to this
    By proud *Argaleon's* malice.
10   What more disgrace can Love and Fortune joyn
    T'inflict upon one man? I cannot now
    Behold my dear *Palmyra*: she, perhaps, too
    Is grown asham'd of a mean ill-plac'd love.
Amalthea (aside). Assist me, *Venus,* for I tremble when
15   I am to speak, but I must force my self.
    (*To him*) Sir, I would crave but one short minute with
    you,
    And some few words.
Leonidas (aside).   The proud *Argaleon's* sister!
Amalthea (aside). Alas, it will not out; shame stops my
    mouth.
    [*To him*] Pardon my errour, Sir, I was mistaken,
20   And took you for another.
Leonidas (aside). In spight of all his guards, I'll see *Palmyra*;
    Though meanly born, I have a Kingly Soul yet.
Amalthea (aside). I stand upon a precipice, where fain
    I would retire, but Love still thrusts me on:
25   Now I grow bolder, and will speak to him.
    (*To him*) Sir, 'tis indeed to you that I would speak,
    And if ——

Leonidas.   O, you are sent to scorn my fortunes;
  Your Sex and Beauty are your priviledge;
  But should your Brother ———
Amalthea. Now he looks angry, and I dare not speak.   30
  I had some business with you, Sir,
  But 'tis not worth your knowledge.
Leonidas. Then 'twill be charity to let me mourn
  My griefs alone, for I am much disorder'd.
Amalthea. 'Twill be more charity to mourn 'em with you: 35
  Heav'n knows I pity you.
Leonidas.   Your pity, Madam,
  Is generous, but 'tis unavailable.
Amalthea. You know not till 'tis tri'd.
  Your sorrows are no secret; you have lost
  A Crown, and Mistris.
Leonidas.   Are not these enough?   40
  Hang two such weights on any other soul,
  And see if it can bear 'em.
Amalthea. More; you are banish'd, by my Brother's means,
  And ne'r must hope again to see your Princess;
  Except as Pris'ners view fair Walks and Streets,   45
  And careless Passengers going by their grates,
  To make 'em feel the want of liberty.
  But, worse then all,
  The King this morning has injoyn'd his Daughter
  T'accept my Brother's love.
Leonidas.   Is this your pity?   50
  You aggravate my griefs, and print 'em deeper
  In new and heavier stamps.
Amalthea. 'Tis as Physicians show the desperate ill
  T'indear their Art, by mittigating pains
  They cannot wholly cure: when you despair   55
  Of all you wish, some part of it, because
  Unhop'd for, may be grateful; and some other ———
Leonidas. What other?
Amalthea. Some other may ———
  (*Aside*) My shame again has seiz'd me, and I can go   60
  No farther. ———
Leonidas. These often failing sighs, and interruptions,
  Make me imagine you have grief like mine:
  Have you ne'r lov'd?
Amalthea.   I? never (*aside*) 'tis in vain;
  I must despair in silence.   65

---

  62 failing ‿] F; ~, Q1–2; failings ‿ Q3–4

  37 *unavailable*] of no avail.
  46 *Passengers*] passersby, travelers.
  46 *grates*] prison bars.

Leonidas. You come as I suspected then, to mock,
    At least observe my griefs: take it not ill
    That I must leave you.   *Is going.*
Amalthea. You must not go with these unjust opinions.
70   Command my life, and fortunes; you are wise,
    Think, and think well what I can do to serve you.
Leonidas. I have but one thing in my thoughts and wishes:
    If by your means I can obtain the sight
    Of my ador'd *Palmyra*; or, what's harder,
75   One minute's time, to tell her, I die hers.
                         She starts back.
    I see I am not to expect it from you;
    Nor could, indeed, with reason.
Amalthea. Name any other thing: is *Amalthea*
    So despicable, she can serve your wishes
    In this alone?
80 *Leonidas.*   If I should ask of heav'n,
    I have no other suit.
Amalthea. To show you, then, I can deny you nothing,
    Though 'tis more hard to me then any other,
    Yet I will do't for you.
Leonidas. Name quickly, name the means, speak my good
85   Angel.
Amalthea. Be not so much o'rjoy'd; for, if you are,
    I'll rather dye then do't. This night the Court
    Will be in *Masquerade*;
    You shall attend on me; in that disguise
90   You may both see and speak to her, if you
    Dare venture it.
Leonidas.   Yes, were a God her Guardian,
    And bore in each hand thunder, I would venture.
Amalthea. Farewell then; two hours hence I will expect
    you:
    My heart's so full, that I can stay no longer.   *Exit.*
95 *Leonidas.* Already it grows dusky; I'll prepare
    With haste for my disguise. But who are these?

         Enter Hermogenes *and* Eubulus.

Hermogenes. 'Tis he; we need not fear to speak to him.
Eubulus. Leonidas.
Leonidas.   Sure I have known that voice.
Hermogenes. You have some reason, Sir; 'tis *Eubulus,*
100   Who bred you with the Princess; and, departing,
    Bequeath'd you to my care.
Leonidas. My Foster-Father! let my knees express
    My joys for your return!   *Kneeling.*

Eubulus. Rise, Sir, you must not kneel.
Leonidas.   E'r since you left me,
  I have been wandring in a maze of fate,   105
  Led by false fires of a fantastick glory,
  And the vain lustre of imagin'd Crowns,
  But, ah! why would you leave me? or how could you
  Absent your self so long?
Eubulus. I'll give you a most just account of both: 110
  And something more I have to tell you, which
  I know must cause your wonder; but this place,
  Though almost hid in darkness, is not safe.
  Already I discern some coming towards us
                                    Torches appear.
  With lights, who may discover me. *Hermogenes*,   115
  Your lodgings are hard by, and much more private.
Hermogenes. There you may freely speak.
Leonidas.   Let us make haste;
  For some affairs, and of no small importance,
  Call me another way.
                                    Exeunt.

Enter Palamede *and* Rhodophil, *with Vizor Masques in
    their hands, and Torches before 'em.*

Palamede. We shall have noble sport to night, *Rhodophil*;   120
  this Masquerading is a most glorious invention.
Rhodophil. I believe it was invented first by some jealous
  Lover, to discover the haunts of his Jilting Mistris; or,
  perhaps, by some distressed servant, to gain an opportunity with a jealous man's wife.   125
Palamede. No, it must be the invention of a woman, it has
  so much of subtilty and love in it.
Rhodophil. I am sure 'tis extremely pleasant; for to go unknown, is the next degree to going invisible.
Palamede. What with our antique habits, and feign'd voices,   130
  do you know me? and I know you? methinks we move
  and talk just like so many over-grown Puppets.
Rhodophil. Masquerade is onely Vizor-masque improv'd, a
  heightning of the same fashion.
Palamede. No; Masquerade is Vizor-masque in debauch;   135
  and I like it the better for't: for, with a Vizor-masque,
  we fool our selves into courtship, for the sake of an eye
  that glanc'd; or a hand that stole it self out of the glove
  sometimes, to give us a sample of the skin: but in

131 you? methinks] S-S (~, —~); ~? Methinks Qq; ~;
Methinks F

133 *Vizor-masque*] a face mask.

140   Masquerade there is nothing to be known, she's all
         Terra incognita, and the bold discoverer leaps ashoar, and
         takes his lot among the wild *Indians* and *Salvages*, with-
         out the vile consideration of safety to his person, or of
         beauty, or wholesomeness in his Mistris.

                           Enter Beliza.

145   *Rhodophil. Beliza*, what make you here?
         Beliza. Sir, my Lady sent me after you, to let you know,
               she finds her self a little indispos'd, so that she cannot be
               at Court, but is retir'd to rest, in her own appartment,
               where she shall want the happiness of your dear em-
150   braces to night.
         Rhodophil. A very fine phrase, *Beliza*, to let me know my
               wife desires to lie alone.
         Palamede. I doubt, *Rhodophil*, you take the pains sometimes
               to instruct your wife's Woman in these elegancies.
155   *Rhodophil*. Tell my dear Lady, that since I must be so un-
               happy as not to wait on her to night, I will lament
               bitterly for her absence. 'Tis true, I shall be at Court,
               but I will take no divertisement there; and when I
               return to my solitary bed, if I am so forgetful of my
160   passion as to sleep, I will dream of her; and betwixt
               sleep and waking, put out my foot towards her side,
               for mid-night consolation; and not finding her, I will
               sigh, and imagine my self a most desolate widower.
         Beliza. I shall do your commands, Sir.   *Exit*.
165   *Rhodophil* (*aside*). She's sick as aptly for my purpose, as if
               she had contriv'd it so: well, if ever woman was a help-
               meet for man, my Spouse is so; for within this hour I
               receiv'd a Note from *Melantha*, that she would meet me
               this evening in Masquerade in Boy's habit, to rejoyce
170   with me before she entred into fetters; for I find she
               loves me better then *Palamede*, onely because he's to be
               her husband. There's something of antipathy in the
               word Marriage to the nature of love; marriage is the
               meer Ladle of affection, that cools it when 'tis never so
175   fiercely boiling over.
         Palamede. Dear *Rhodophil*, I must needs beg your pardon;
               there is an occasion fall'n out which I had forgot: I
               cannot be at Court to night.
         Rhodophil. Dear *Palamede*, I am sorry we shall not have one

         _____

         145 *what make you here*] what are you doing here.
         149 *want*] be without.
         153 *I doubt*] I fear.

course together at the herd; but I find your Game lies 180
single: good fortune to you with your Mistris.   *Exit.*
Palamede. He has wish'd me good fortune with his Wife:
there's no sin in this then, there's fair leave given. Well,
I must go visit the sick; I cannot resist the temptations
of my charity. O what a difference will she find betwixt 185
a dull resty Husband, and a quick vigorous Lover! he
sets out like a Carrier's Horse, plodding on, because he
knows he must, with the Bells of Matrimony chiming
so melancholly about his neck, in pain till he's at his
journey's end, and dispairing to get thither, he is fain 190
to fortifie imagination with the thoughts of another
woman: I take heat after heat, like a well-breath'd
Courser, and ——— But hark, what noise is that?
swords!   *Clashing of Swords within.*
Nay, then have with you.   *Exit* Palamede. 195

Re-enter Palamede, *with* Rhodophil: *and* Doralice *in man's
habit.*

Rhodophil. Friend, your relief was very timely, otherwise
I had been oppress'd.
Palamede. What was the quarrel?
Rhodophil. What I did, was in rescue of this Youth.
Palamede. What cause could he give 'em? 200
Doralice. The cause was nothing but onely the common
cause of fighting in Masquerades: they were drunk, and
I was sober.
Rhodophil. Have they not hurt you?
Doralice. No; but I am exceeding ill, with the fright on't. 205
Palamede. Let's lead him to some place where he may
refresh himself.
Rhodophil. Do you conduct him then.
Palamede (*aside*). How cross this happens to my design of
going to *Doralice*! for I am confident she was sick on 210
purpose that I should visit her. Hark you, *Rhodophil*,
could not you take care of the stripling? I am partly
engag'd to night.
Rhodophil. You know I have business: but come, Youth, if
it must be so. 215
Doralice (*to Rhodophil*). No, good Sir, do not give your self
that trouble; I shall be safer, and better pleas'd with your
friend here.

180 *course . . . herd*] an analogy to hunting, coursing game, probably
deer, with hounds.
186 *resty*] lazy or dronish.

Rhodophil. Farewell then; once more I wish you a good
220   adventure.

Palamede. Damn this kindness! now must I be troubled
with this young Rogue, and miss my opportunity with
Doralice.

          Exit Rhodophil *alone,* Palamede *with* Doralice.

[ACT IV.] SCENE 2

Enter Polydamas.

Polydamas. *Argaleon* counsel'd well to banish him,
    He has, I know not what,
    Of greatness in his looks, and of high fate,
    That almost awes me; but I fear my Daughter,
5   Who hourly moves me for him, and I mark'd
    She sigh'd when I but nam'd *Argaleon* to her.
    But see, the Maskers: hence my cares, this night,
    At least take truce, and find me on my pillow.

Enter the Princess in Masquerade, with Ladies: at the other end,
Argaleon *and Gentlemen in Masquerade: then* Leonidas
leading Amalthea. *The King sits. A Dance. After the Dance,*

Amalthea (to Leonidas). That's the Princess;
10   I saw the habit ere she put it on.
Leonidas. I know her by a thousand other signs,
    She cannot hide so much Divinity.
    Disguis'd, and silent, yet some graceful motion
    Breaks from her, and shines round her like a Glory.
                Goes to Palmyra.
15   *Amalthea.* Thus she reveals her self, and knows it not:
    Like Love's Dark-lantern I direct his steps,
    And yet he sees not that which gives him light.
Palmyra (to Leonidas). I know you; but, alas, *Leonidas,*
    Why should you tempt this danger on your self?
20   *Leonidas.* Madam, you know me not, if you believe
    I would not hazard greater for your sake:
    But you, I fear, are chang'd.
Palmyra. No, I am still the same;
    But there are many things became *Palmyra*
    Which ill become the Princess.
25   *Leonidas.*   I ask nothing
    Which Honour will not give you leave to grant:
    One hour's short audience, at my father's house,
    You cannot sure refuse me.
Palmyra. Perhaps I should, did I consult strict vertue;

But something must be given to Love and you.   30
When would you I should come?
Leonidas. This evening, with the speediest opportunity.
I have a secret to discover to you,
Which will surprise, and please you.
Palmyra.   'Tis enough.
Go now; for we may be observ'd and known.   35
I trust your honour; give me not occasion
To blame my self, or you.
Leonidas. You never shall repent your good opinion.
                              Kisses her hand, and Exit.
Argaleon. I cannot be deceiv'd; that is the Princess:
One of her Maids betray'd the habit to me;   40
But who was he with whom she held discourse?
'Tis one she favours, for he kiss'd her hand.
Our shapes are like, our habits near the same:
She may mistake, and speak to me for him.
I am resolv'd, I'll satisfie my doubts,   45
Though to be more tormented.   *Exit.*

SONG.

1.

Whil'st Alexis *lay prest*
In her Arms he lov'd best,
With his hands round her neck,
And his head on her breast,
He found the fierce pleasure too hasty to stay,   50
And his soul in the tempest just flying away.

2.

When Cœlia *saw this,*
With a sigh, and a kiss,
She cry'd, Oh my dear, I am robb'd of my bliss;   55
'Tis unkind to your Love, and unfaithfully done,
To leave me behind you, and die all alone.

3.

The Youth, though in haste,
And breathing his last,
In pity dy'd slowly, while she dy'd more fast;   60
Till at length she cry'd, Now, my dear, now let us go,
Now die, my Alexis, *and I will die too.*

45 *resolved,*] Modern editors punctuate: "I am resolved; I'll
satisfy"; whereas the plainer sense is that Argelon is resolved to satisfy
his doubts, and the comma (Q1) or no punctuation (Sutherland) is
clearer.

4.

Thus intranc'd they did lie,
Till Alexis did try
65   *To recover new breath, that again he might die:*
    Then often they di'd; but the more they did so,
    The Nymph di'd more quick, and the Shepherd more slow.

Another Dance. After it, Argaleon *re-enters, and stands*
by the Princess.

Palmyra (*to Argaleon*). Leonidas, what means this quick
    return?
Argaleon [*aside*]. O heav'n! 'tis what I fear'd.
70 Palmyra. Is ought of moment happen'd since you went?
Argaleon. No, Madam, but I understood not fully
    Your last commands.
Palmyra.   And yet you answer'd to 'em.
    Retire; you are too indiscreet a Lover:
    I'll meet you where I promis'd.   *Exit.*
75 Argaleon. O my curst fortune! what have I discover'd?
    But I will be reveng'd.   *Whispers to the King.*
Polydamas. But are you certain you are not deceiv'd?
Argaleon. Upon my life.
Polydamas.   Her honour is concern'd.
    Somewhat I'll do; but I am yet distracted,
80   And know not where to fix. I wish'd a child,
    And Heav'n, in anger, granted my request.
    So blind we are, our wishes are so vain,
    That what we most desire, proves most our pain.
                    Exeunt omnes.

[ACT IV.] SCENE 3

An Eating-house. Bottles of Wine on the Table. Palamede;
and Doralice *in Man's habit.*

Doralice (*aside*). Now cannot I find in my heart to discover
    my self, though I long he should know me.
Palamede. I tell thee, Boy, now I have seen thee safe, I must
    be gone: I have no leisure to throw away on thy raw
5   conversation: I am a person that understand better
    things, I.
Doralice. Were I a woman, Oh how you'd admire me!
    cry up every word I said, and scrue your face into a
    submissive smile; as I have seen a dull Gallant act Wit,

65 *die*] See the general introduction and the introduction to
this play for comment on the song.

and counterfeit pleasantness, when he whispers to a great 10
Person in a Play-house; smile, and look briskly, when
the other answers, as if something of extraordinary had
past betwixt 'em, when, heaven knows, there was
nothing else but, What a clock does your Lordship
think it is? and my Lord's *repertee* is, 'Tis almost Park- 15
time: or, at most, Shall we out of the Pit, and go behind
the Scenes for an Act or two? And yet such fine things
as these, would be wit in a Mistris's mouth.

Palamede. Ay, Boy; there's Dame Nature in the case: he
who cannot find wit in a Mistris, deserves to find 20
nothing else, Boy. But these are riddles to thee, child,
and I have not leisure to instruct thee; I have affairs to
dispatch, great affairs; I am a man of business.

Doralice. Come, you shall not go: you have no affairs but
what you may dispatch here, to my knowledge. 25

Palamede. I find now, thou art a Boy of more understanding
then I thought thee; a very lewd wicked Boy: o' my
conscience thou wouldst debauch me, and hast some evil
designs upon my person.

Doralice. You are mistaken, Sir; I would onely have you 30
show me a more lawful reason why you would leave
me, then I can why you should not, and I'll not stay
you; for I am not so young, but I understand the
necessities of flesh and bloud, and the pressing occasions
of mankind, as well as you. 35

Palamede. A very forward and understanding Boy! Thou
art in great danger of a Page's wit, to be brisk at fourteen,
and dull at twenty. But I'll give thee no further account;
I must, and will go.

Doralice. My life on't, your Mistris is not at home. 40

Palamede. This Imp will make me very angry.
I tell thee, young Sir, she is at home; and at home for
me; and, which is more, she is abed for me, and sick for
me.

Doralice. For you onely? 45

Palamede. Ay, for me onely.

Doralice. But how do you know she's sick abed?

Palamede. She sent her Husband word so.

Doralice. And are you such a novice in Love, to believe a
Wife's message to her Husband? 50

Palamede. Why, what the devil should be her meaning
else?

Doralice. It may be, to go in Masquerade as well as you;

15–16 *Parktime*] time for riding in the park.

55 to observe your haunts, and keep you company without
your knowledge.

Palamede. Nay, I'll trust her for that: she loves me too
well, to disguise her self from me.

Doralice. If I were she, I would disguise on purpose to try
your wit; and come to my servant like a Riddle, Read
60 me, and take me.

Palamede. I could know her in any shape: my good
Genius would prompt me to find out a handsome
woman: there's something in her, that would attract me
to her without my knowledge.

65 *Doralice.* Then you make a Load-stone of your Mistris?

Palamede. Yes, and I carry Steel about me, which has been
so often touch'd, that it never fails to point to the North
Pole.

Doralice. Yet still my mind gives me, that you have met
70 her disguis'd to night, and have not known her.

Palamede. This is the most pragmatical conceited little
fellow, he will needs understand my business better
then my self. I tell thee, once more, thou dost not know
my Mistris.

75 *Doralice.* And I tell you, once more, that I know her better
then you do.

Palamede. The Boy's resolv'd to have the last word.
I find I must go without reply.   *Exit.*

Doralice. Ah mischief, I have lost him with my fooling.
80 Palamede, Palamede.

> *He returns. She plucks off her Perruke, and puts it on*
> *again when he knows her.*

Palamede. O Heavens! is it you, Madam?

Doralice. Now, where was your good Genius, that would
prompt you to find me out?

Palamede. Why, you see I was not deceiv'd; you, your self,
85 were my good Genius.

Doralice. But where was the Steel, that knew the Load-
stone? ha?

Palamede. The truth is, Madam, the Steel has lost its
vertue; and therefore, if you please, we'll new touch it.

> *Enter Rhodophil; and Melantha in Boy's habit. Rhodophil*
> *sees Palamede kissing Doralice's hand.*

90 *Rhodophil. Palamede* again! am I fall'n into your quarters?
What? ingaging with a Boy? is all honourable?

59–60 *Read me, and take me*] probably a formula from printed
riddles, with a pun on "Ride me, and take me."

Palamede. O, very honourable on my side. I was just
    chastising this young Villain; he was running away,
    without paying his share of the reckoning.
Rhodophil. Then I find I was deceiv'd in him.   95
Palamede. Yes, you are deceiv'd in him: 'tis the archest
    rogue, if you did but know him.
Melantha. Good *Rhodophil*, let us get off *al-a dérobbée*, for
    fear I should be discover'd.
Rhodophil. There's no retiring now; I warrant you for   100
    discovery: now have I the oddest thought, to entertain
    you before your Servant's face, and he never the wiser;
    'twill be the prettiest jugling trick to cheat him when he
    looks upon us.
Melantha. This is the strangest *caprice* in you.   105
Palamede (to Doralice). This *Rhodophil*'s the unluckiest
    fellow to me! this is now the second time he has bar'd
    the Dice when we were just ready to have nick'd him;
    but if ever I get the Box again ———
Doralice. Do you think he will not know me?   110
    Am I like my self?
Palamede. No more then a Picture in the Hangings.
Doralice. Nay, then he can never discover me, now the
    wrong side of the Arras is turn'd towards him.
Palamede. At least, 'twill be some pleasure to me, to enjoy   115
    what freedom I can while he looks on; I will storm the
    Out-works of Matrimony even before his face.
Rhodophil. What Wine have you there, *Palamede*?
Palamede. Old *Chios*, or the rogue's damn'd that drew it.
Rhodophil. Come, to the most constant of Mistresses, that   120
    I believe is yours, *Palamede*.
Doralice. Pray spare your Seconds; for my part I am but a
    weak Brother.
Palamede. Now, to the truest of Turtles; that is your Wife,
    Rhodophil, that lies sick at home in the bed of honour.   125
Rhodophil. Now let's have one common health, and so
    have done.
Doralice. Then, for once, I'll begin it. Here's to him that
    has the fairest Lady of *Sicily* in Masquerade to night.

---

   98 *al-a dérobbée*] secretly.
  100 *I warrant you*] I guarantee we will not be discovered.
  107–8 *bar'd the Dice*] declared the throw void.
  108 *nick'd*] To nick means to make a winning cast, at hazard.
  109 *Box*] Dice were shaken in a box.
  112 *Hangings*] tapestries embroidered on one side, arras.
  119 *Chios*] the wine of the isle of Chios.
  122 *Seconds*] followups, seconding the toast.
  123 *weak Brother*] one of the more timerous members of the party.

130   *Palamede.* This is such an obliging health, I'll kiss thee, dear
        Rogue for thy invention.   *Kisses her.*
        Rhodophil. He who has this Lady, is a happy man, without
        dispute. —— (*aside*) I'm most concern'd in this, I am
        sure.

135   *Palamede.* Was it not well found out, *Rhodophil?*
        Melantha. Ay, this was *bien trouvée* indeed.
        Doralice (to Melantha). I suppose I shall do you a kindness to
        enquire if you have not been in *France*, Sir?
        Melantha. To do you service, Sir.

140   *Doralice.* O, Monsieur, *votre valet bien humble.*
                                    Saluting her.
        Melantha. *Votre esclave, Monsieur, de tout Mon Cœur.*
                                Returning the salute.
        Doralice. I suppose, sweet Sir, you are the hope and joy of
        some thriving Citizen, who has pinch'd himself at
        home, to breed you abroad, where you have learnt your

145   Exercises, as it appears most aukwardly, and are returned
        with the addition of a new-lac'd bosom and a Clap, to
        your good old father, who looks at you with his mouth,
        while you spout *French* with your *Mon Monsieur.*
        Palamede. Let me kiss thee again for that, dear Rogue.

150   *Melantha.* And you, I imagine, are my young Master,
        whom your Mother durst not trust upon salt water,
        but left you to be your own Tutour at fourteen, to be
        very brisk and *entreprenant*, to endeavour to be debauch'd
        ere you have learnt the knack on't, to value your self

155   upon a Clap before you can get it, and to make it the
        height of your ambition to get a Player for your
        Mistris.
        Rhodophil (embracing Melantha). O dear young Bully, thou
        hast tickled him with a *repertee* i'faith.

160   *Melantha.* You are one of those that applaud our Countrey
        Plays, where drums, and trumpets, and bloud, and
        wounds, are wit.
        Rhodophil. Again, my Boy? let me kiss thee most abun-
        dantly.

165   *Doralice.* You are an admirer of the dull *French* Poetry,

---

140 *votre*] S-S; *vot* Qq,F   148 *Mon*] Q4; *Man* Q1–3

146 *Clap*] gonorrhea.

147 *mouth*] uncertain meaning, possibly "with a full mouth,
loudly, railing furiously." Summers and Sutherland think it
means "gapes, stares open-mouthed."

148 *Mon Monsieur*] *Man Monsieur* (Q1–3) could refer to "your
French serving man," but *Mon Monsieur* (Q4) seems more likely to
be what Dryden wrote. Q4's emendation, at any rate, is superior
sense, that a gallant should impudently address his father this way.

which is so thin, that it is the very Leaf-gold of Wit, the
very Wafers and whip'd Cream of sense, for which a
man opens his mouth and gapes, to swallow nothing:
and to be an admirer of such profound dulness, one
must be endow'd with a great perfection of impudence   170
and ignorance.

Palamede. Let me embrace thee most vehemently.

Melantha. I'll sacrifice my life for *French* Poetry.

Advancing.

Doralice. I'll die upon the spot for our Countrey Wit.

Rhodophil (to Melantha). Hold, hold, young *Mars*: Pala-   175
mede, draw back your *Hero*.

Palamede. 'Tis time; I shall be drawn in for a Second else
at the wrong weapon.

Melantha. O that I were a man for thy sake!

Doralice. You'll be a man as soon as I shall.   180

Enter a Messenger to Rhodophil.

Messenger. Sir, the King has instant business with you.
I saw the Guard drawn up by your Lieutenant
Before the Palace-gate, ready to march.

Rhodophil. 'Tis somewhat sodain; say that I am coming.

Exit Messenger.

Now, *Palamede*, what think you of this sport?   185
This is some suddain tumult: will you along?

Palamede. Yes, yes, I will go; but the devil take me if ever
I was less in humour. Why, the pox, could they not
have staid their tumult till to morrow? then I had done
my business, and been ready for 'em. Truth is, I had a   190
little transitory crime to have committed first; and I am
the worst man in the world at repenting, till a sin be
throughly done: but what shall we do with the two
Boys?

Rhodophil. Let them take a lodging in the house till the   195
business be over.

Doralice. What, lie with a Boy? for my part, I own it, I
cannot endure to lie with a Boy.

Palamede. The more's my sorrow, I cannot accommodate
you with a better bed-fellow.   200

Melantha. Let me die, if I enter into a pair of sheets with
him that hates the *French*.

Doralice. Pish, take no care for us, but leave us in the
streets; I warrant you, as late as it is, I'll find my lodging
as well as any drunken Bully of 'em all.   205

Rhodophil (aside). I'll fight in meer revenge, and wreak my
passion
On all that spoil this hopeful assignation.

Palamede. I'm sure we fight in a good quarrel:
    Rogues may pretend Religion, and the Laws;
210   But a kind Mistris is the *Good old Cause.*

                          Exeunt.

[ACT IV.] Scene 4

Enter Palmyra, Eubulus, Hermogenes.

Palmyra. You tell me wonders; that *Leonidas*
    Is Prince *Theagenes*, the late King's Son.
Eubulus. It seem'd as strange to him, as now to you,
    Before I had convinc'd him; But, besides
5   His great resemblance to the King his Father,
    The Queen his Mother lives, secur'd by me
    In a Religious House; to whom each year
    I brought the news of his increasing virtues.
    My last long absence from you both, was caus'd
10   By wounds which, in my journey, I receiv'd,
    When set upon by thieves; I lost those Jewels
    And Letters, which your dying Mother left.
Hermogenes. The same he means, which, since, brought to
    the King,
    Made him first know he had a Child alive:
15   'Twas then my care of Prince *Leonidas*
    Caus'd me to say he was th'Usurper's Son;
    Till, after forc'd by your apparent danger,
    I made the true discovery of your birth,
    And once more hid my Prince's.

             Enter Leonidas.

20 *Leonidas. Hermogenes,* and *Eubulus,* retire;
    Those of our party, whom I left without,
    Expect your aid and counsel.   *Exeunt ambo.*
Palmyra. I should, *Leonidas*, congratulate
    This happy change of your exalted fate;
25   But, as my joy, so you my wonder move;
    Your looks have more of Business, then of Love:
    And your last words some great design did show.
Leonidas. I frame not any to be hid from you.
    You, in my love, all my designs may see;
30   But what have love and you design'd for me?
    Fortune, once more, has set the ballance right:
    First, equall'd us, in lowness; then, in height.
    Both of us have so long, like Gamesters, thrown,

210 *Good old Cause*] the popular satirical name for the rebelling Puritan party in the Civil War, the roundheads.

Till Fate comes round, and gives to each his own.
As Fate is equal, so may Love appear: 35
Tell me, at least, what I must hope, or fear.
Palmyra. After so many proofs, how can you call
My love in doubt? Fear nothing; and hope, all.
Think what a Prince, with honour, may receive,
Or I may give, without a Parent's leave. 40
Leonidas. You give, and then restrain the grace you show;
As ostentatious Priests, when Souls they wooe,
Promise their Heav'n to all, but grant to few.
But do for me, what I have dar'd for you:
I did no argument from duty bring: 45
Duty's a Name; and Love's a Real thing.
Palmyra. Man's love may, like wild torrents, over-flow;
Woman's as deep, but in its banks must go.
My love is mine; and that I can impart;
But cannot give my person, with my heart. 50
Leonidas. Your love is then no gift:
For when the person it does not convey,
'Tis to give Gold, and not to give the Key.
Palmyra. Then ask my Father.
Leonidas.   He detains my Throne:
Who holds back mine, will hardly give his own. 55
Palmyra. What then remains?
Leonidas.   That I must have recourse
To Arms; and take my Love and Crown, by force.
Hermogenes is forming the design;
And with him, all the brave and loyal joyn.
Palmyra. And is it thus you court *Palmyra's* bed? 60
Can she the murd'rer of her Parent wed?
Desist from force: so much you well may give
To Love, and Me, to let my Father live.
Leonidas. Each act of mine my love to you has shown;
But you, who tax my want of it, have none. 65
You bid me part with you, and let him live;
But they should nothing ask, who nothing give.
Palmyra. I give what vertue and what duty can,
In vowing ne'r to wed another man.
Leonidas. You will be forc'd to be *Argaleon's* wife. 70
Palmyra. I'll keep my promise, though I lose my life.
Leonidas. Then you lose Love, for which we both contend;
For Life is but the means, but Love's the end.
Palmyra. Our Souls shall love hereafter.
Leonidas.   I much fear, ⎫
That Soul which could deny the Body here, ⎬ 75
To taste of love, would be a niggard there. ⎭
Palmyra. Then 'tis past hope: our cruel fate, I see,

Will make a sad divorce 'twixt you and me.
For, if you force employ, by Heav'n I swear,
And all bless'd Beings, ———

80   *Leonidas.*   Your rash Oath forbear.
Palmyra. I never ———
Leonidas.   Hold once more. But, yet, as he
Who scapes a dang'rous leap, looks back to see;
So I desire, now I am past my fear,
To know what was that Oath you meant to swear.

85   *Palmyra.* I meant that if you hazarded your life,
Or sought my Father's, ne'r to be your Wife.
Leonidas. See now, *Palmyra*, how unkind you prove!
Could you, with so much ease, forswear my love?
Palmyra. You force me with your ruinous design.

90   *Leonidas.* Your Father's life is more your care, then Mine.
Palmyra. You wrong me: 'tis not; though it ought to be;
You are my Care, heav'n knows, as well as he.
Leonidas. If now the execution I delay.
My Honour, and my Subjects, I betray.

95   All is prepar'd for the just enterprize;
And the whole City will to morrow rise.
The Leaders of the party are within,
And *Eubulus* has sworn that he will bring,
To head their Arms, the person of their King.

100   *Palmyra.* In telling this, you make me guilty too;
I therefore must discover what I know:
What Honour bids you do, Nature bids me prevent;
But kill me first, and then pursue your black intent.
Leonidas. Palmyra, no; you shall not need to die;

105   Yet I'll not trust so strict a piety.
Within there.

Enter Eubulus.

Eubulus, a Guard prepare;
Here, I commit this pris'ner to your care.
                    Kisses Palmyra's *hand; then gives it to* Eubulus.
Palmyra. Leonidas, I never thought these bands
Could e'r be giv'n me by a Lover's hands.
Leonidas (kneeling). Palmyra, thus your Judge himself

110   arraigns;
He who impos'd these bonds, still wears your chains:
When you to Love or Duty false must be,   ⎫
Or to your Father guilty, or to me,   ⎬
These chains, alone, remain to set you free.   ⎭
                              Noise of swords clashing.

115   *Polydamas (within).* Secure these, first; then search the inner
      room.

344

Leonidas. From whence do these tumultuous clamours
    come?

        Enter Hermogenes, *hastily.*

Hermogenes. We are betray'd; and there remains alone
    This comfort, that your person is not known.

   Enter the King, Argaleon, Rhodophil, Palamede, *Guards;*
        some like Citizens as prisoners.

Polydamas. What mean this midnight-consultations here,
    Where I, like an unsummon'd guest, appear?   120
Leonidas. Sir ———
Argaleon.   There needs no excuse; 'tis understood;
    You were all watching, for your Prince's good.
Polydamas. My reverend City-friends, you are well met!
    On what great work were your grave wisdoms set?
    Which of my actions were you scanning here?   125
    What *French* invasion have you found to fear?
Leonidas. They are my friends; and come, Sir, with intent
    To take their leaves before my banishment.
Polydamas. Your exile, in both sexes, friends can find:
    I see the Ladies, like the men, are kind.   130
                Seeing Palmyra.
Palmyra (kneeling). Alas, I came but ———
Polydamas.   Adde not to your crime
    A lie: I'll hear you speak some other time.
    How? *Eubulus!* nor time, nor thy disguise,
    Can keep thee, undiscover'd, from my eyes.
    A Guard there; seize 'em all.   135
Rhodophil. Yield, Sir; what use of valour can be shown?
Palamede. One, and unarm'd, against a multitude!
Leonidas. O for a sword!
    He reaches at one of the Guard's Halberds, and is seiz'd
                 behind.
        I w'not lose my breath
    In fruitless pray'rs; but beg a speedy death.
Palmyra. O spare *Leonidas,* and punish me.   140
Polydamas. Mean Girl, thou want'st an Advocate for thee.
    Now the mysterious knot will be unty'd;
    Whether the young King lives, or where he dy'd:
    To morrow's dawn shall the dark riddle clear;
    Crown all my joys; and dissipate my fear.   145
                Exeunt omnes.

---

  138 *Leonidas.* O for] F; O for Qq
   126 *French invasion*] Londoners, often at odds with Charles II, suspected that the king was selling out their liberty to the French (Noyes).

ACT V. SCENE 1

[Enter] Palamede, Straton. Palamede *with a Letter*
in his hand.

Palamede. This evening, say'st thou? will they both be
here?

Straton. Yes, Sir; both my old Master, and your Mistris's
Father: the old Gentlemen ride hard this journey; they
say, it shall be the last time they will see the Town; and
both of 'em are so pleas'd with this marriage, which they
have concluded for you, that I am afraid they will live
some years longer to trouble you, with the joy of it.

Palamede. But this is such an unreasonable thing, to impose
upon me to be marri'd to morrow; 'tis hurrying a man
to execution, without giving him time to say his
pray'rs.

Straton. Yet, if I might advise you, Sir, you should not
delay it: for your younger Brother comes up with 'em,
and is got already into their favours. He has gain'd much
upon my old Master, by finding fault with Inn-keepers
Bills, and by starving us, and our Horses, to show his
frugality; and he is very well with your Mistris's
Father, by giving him Receipts for the Splene, Gout,
and Scurvy, and other infirmities of old age.

Palamede. I'll rout him, and his Countrey education: Pox
on him, I remember him before I travell'd, he had
nothing in him but meer Jocky; us'd to talk loud, and
make matches, and was all for the crack of the field:
sense and wit were as much banish'd from his discourse,
as they are when the Court goes out of Town to a
Horse-race. Go now and provide your Master's Lodgings.

Straton. I go, Sir.   *Exit.*

Palamede. It vexes me to the heart, to leave all my designs
with *Doralice* unfinish'd; to have flown her so often to
a mark, and still to be bob'd at retrieve: if I had but once
enjoy'd her, though I could not have satisfi'd my

23 *Jocky*] a lad.
24 *matches*] contests with his own horses or dogs against those
of other country sportsmen (Sutherland), bets.
24 *crack of the field*] the favorite.
32 *mark*] the quarry, as in falconry, when a hawk has "put
in" a covy of partridges, he takes a stand, marking the spot
where they disappeared.
32 *bob'd*] cheated, made a fool of, at the second discovery of
a flight of birds.

stomach, with the feast, at least I should have relish'd
my mouth a little; but now ——— 35

Enter Philotis.

Philotis. Oh, Sir, you are happily met; I was coming to
find you.

Palamede. From your Lady, I hope.

Philotis. Partly from her; but more especially from my
self: she has just now receiv'd a Letter from her Father, 40
with an absolute command to dispose her self to marry
you to morrow.

Palamede. And she takes it to the death?

Philotis. Quite contrary: the Letter could never have come
in a more lucky minute; for it found her in an ill 45
humour with a Rival of yours, that shall be nameless,
about the pronunciation of a *French* word.

Palamede. Count *Rhodophil*; never disguise it, I know the
Amour: but I hope you took the occasion to strike in for
me? 50

Philotis. It was my good fortune to do you some small
service in it; for your sake I discommended him all
over: cloaths, person, humour, behaviour, every thing;
and to sum up all, told her, It was impossible to find a
marri'd man that was otherwise; for they were all so 55
mortifi'd at home with their wives ill humours, that
they could never recover themselves to be company
abroad.

Palamede. Most divinely urg'd!

Philotis. Then I took occasion to commend your good 60
qualities: as, the sweetness of your humour, the comeli-
ness of your person, your good Meene, your valour;
but, above all, your liberality.

Palamede. I vow to Gad I had like to have forgot that good
quality in my self, if thou had'st not remember'd me 65
on't: here are five Pieces for thee.

Philotis. Lord, you have the softest hand, Sir! it would do
a woman good to touch it: Count *Rhodophil's* is not half
so soft; for I remember I felt it once, when he gave me
ten Pieces for my New-year's gift. 70

Palamede. O, I understand you, Madam; you shall find my
hand as soft again as Count *Rhodophil's*: there are twenty
Pieces for you. The former was but a Retaining Fee;
now I hope you'l plead for me.

Philotis. Your own merits speak enough. Be sure onely to 75
ply her with *French* words, and I'll warrant you'll do
your business. Here are a list of her phrases for this day:
use 'em to her upon all occasions, and foil her at her own

347

weapon; for she's like one of the old *Amazons*, she'l
80 never marry, except it be the man who has first conquer'd her.

Palamede. I'll be sure to follow your advice: but you'll
forget to further my design.

Philotis. What, do you think I'll be ungrateful? ———
85 ——— But, however, if you distrust my memory, put
some token on my finger to remember it by: that
Diamond there would do admirably.

Palamede. There 'tis; and I ask your pardon heartily for
calling your memory into question: I assure you I'll
90 trust it another time, without putting you to the trouble
of another token.

Enter Palmyra *and* Artemis.

Artemis. Madam, this way the prisoners are to pass;
Here you may see *Leonidas.*

Palmyra. Then here I'll stay, and follow him to death.

Enter Melantha *hastily.*

95 *Melantha.* O, here's her Highness!
Now is my time to introduce my self, and to make my
court to her, in my new *French* phrases. Stay, let me
read my catalogue—*suitte, figure, chagrin, naiveté,* and
let me die for the Parenthesis of all.
100 *Palamede (aside).* Do, persecute her; and I'll persecute thee
as fast in thy own dialect.

Melantha. Madam, the Princess! let me die, but this is a
most horrid spectacle, to see a person who makes so
grand a figure in the Court, without the *Suitte* of a
105 Princess, and entertaining your *Chagrin* all alone;
(*Naiveté* should have been there, but the disobedient
word would not come in.)

Palmyra. What is she, *Artemis*?

Artemis. An impertinent Lady, Madam; very ambitious of
110 being known to your Highness.

Palamede (to Melantha). Let me die, Madam, if I have not
waited you here these two long hours, without so much
as the *Suitte* of a single Servant to attend me; entertaining my self with my own *Chagrin,* till I had the
115 honour to see your Ladiship, who are a person that
makes so considerable a figure in the Court.

Melantha. Truce with your *douceurs,* good servant; you see
I am addressing to the Princess; pray do not *embarrass*
me ——— *embarrass* me! what a delicious *French* word
120 do you make me lose upon you too!
(*To the Princess*) Your Highness, Madam, will please to

pardon the *Beveue* which I made, in not sooner finding
you out to be a Princess: but let me die if this *Eclair-
cissement* which is made this day of your quality, does
not ravish me; and give me leave to tell you ———   125
Palamede. But first give me leave to tell you, Madam, that
I have so great a tender for your person, and such a
panchant to do you service, that ———
Melantha. What, must I still be troubled with your
Sottises? (There's another word lost, that I meant for the   130
Princess, with a mischief to you.) But your Highness,
Madam ———
Palamede. But your Ladiship, Madam ———

    Enter Leonidas *guarded, and led over the Stage.*

Melantha. Out upon him, how he looks, Madam! now he's
found no Prince, he is the strangest figure of a man;   135
how could I make that *Coup d'étourdy* to think him one?
Palamede. Away, impertinent. ——— My dear *Leonidas*!
Leonidas. My dear *Palmyra*!
Palmyra.   Death shall never part us;
  My Destiny is yours.   *He is led off; she follows.*
Melantha. Impertinent! Oh I am the most unfortunate   140
person this day breathing: that the Princess should thus
rompre en visiere, without occasion. Let me die but I'll
follow her to death, till I make my peace.
Palamede (holding her). And let me die, but I'll follow you
to the Infernals till you pity me.   145
Melantha (turning towards him angrily). Ay, 'tis long of you
that this *Malheur* is fall'n upon me; your impertinence
has put me out of the good graces of the Princess, and
all that, which has ruin'd me and all that, and therefore
let me die but I'll be reveng'd, and all that.   150
Palamede. Façon, façon, you must and shall love me, and
all that; for my old man is coming up, and all that; and
I am *désespéré au dernier*, and will not be disinherited, and
all that.
Melantha. How durst you interrupt me so *mal a propos*,   155
when you knew I was addressing to the Princess?
Palamede. But why would you address your self so much *a
contretemps* then?
Melantha. Ah *mal peste*!
Palamede. Ah *l'enragée*!   160

142 *rompre en visiere*] take offence.
151 *façon, façon*] nonsense, fashionable twaddle.
153 *désespéré au dernier*] extremely desperate.
157–58 *a contretemps*] at the wrong time.

  Philotis. Radoucissez vous, de grace, Madame; vous étes bien
  en colere pour peu de chose. Vous n'entendez pas la raillerie
  gallante.
  Melantha. Ad'autres, ad'autres: he mocks himself of me, he
165 abuses me: ah me unfortunate!   *Cries.*
  Philotis. You mistake him, Madam, he does but accom-
  modate his phrase to your refin'd language. *Ah, qu'il est un*
  Cavalier accomply! (*to him*) pursue your point, Sir ——
  Palamede. Ah qu'il fait beau dans ces boccages; *Singing.*
170 *Ah que le ciel donne un beau jour!*
  There I was with you, with a *minouet.*
  Melantha. Let me die now, but this singing is fine, and
  extremely *French* in him: *Laughs.*
  But then, that he should use my own words, as it were
175 in contempt of me, I cannot bear it.   *Crying.*
  Palamede. Ces beaux séjours, ces doux ramages ——
               Singing.
  Melantha. Ces beaux Séjours, ces doux ramages,
           Singing after him.
  Ces beaux sejours, nous invitent a l'amour!
  Let me die but he sings *en Cavalier*, and so humours the
180 Cadence.   *Laughing.*
  Palamede. Voy, ma Clymene, voy soubs ce chesne,
           Singing again.
  S'entrebaiser ces oiseaux amoreux!
  Let me die now, but that was fine. Ah, now, for three
  or four brisk *Frenchmen*, to be put into Masquing habits,
185 and to sing it on a Theatre, how witty it would be!
  and then to dance helter skelter to a *Chanson a boire:*
  toute la terre, toute la terre est a moy! what's matter though
  it were made, and sung, two or three years ago in

161–63 *Radoucissez . . . gallante*] Calm yourself, for mercy's sake, Madame; you are angry for nothing. You don't know how to take a pretty joke.

164 *he mocks himself of me*] "Melantha here carries her affectation to the point of giving her plain English words a French idiom" (Sutherland).

169–70 *Ah . . . jour*] "Ah, the weather is fine in the woods; Ah it is a fine day in the open air." This and the following verses are from the songs of many nations, at the end of Molière's *Le Bourgeois Gentilhomme* (1670).

176 *Ces . . . ramages*] "This is a good place, the sweet songs of the birds tempt us toward love."

179 *en Cavalier*] in the gallant fashion.

181–82 *Voy . . . amoreux*] "See, my Climène, See, under the oak, The love birds kiss one another." *Voy* reads *Vois* in the French text.

186–87 *Chanson . . . moy*] a drinking song: all the world, all the world is mine (unidentified).

Cabarets, how it would attract the admiration, especially
    of every one that's an *éveillé*!   190
Melantha. Well; I begin to have a tender for you; but yet,
    upon condition, that——when we are marri'd, you——
              Palamede *sings, while she speaks.*
Philotis. You must drown her voice: if she makes her
    French conditions, you are a slave for ever.
Melantha. First, will you engage ——— that ———   195
Palamede. Fa, la, la, la, &c.   *Louder.*
Melantha. Will you hear the conditions?
Palamede. No; I will hear no conditions! I am resolv'd to
    win you *en Francais*: to be very aiery, with abundance
    of noise, and no sense: Fa, la, la, la, &c.   200
Melantha. Hold, hold: I am vanquish'd with your *gayeté
    d'esprit.* I am yours, and will be yours, *sans nulle réserve,
    ny condition*: and let me die, if I do not think my self
    the happiest Nymph in *Sicily.* ——— My dear *French*
    Dear, stay but a *minuite*, till I *raccommode* my self with   205
    the Princess; and then I am yours, *jusq'a la mort.
    Allons donc* ———
               Exeunt Melantha, Philotis.
Palamede (*solus, fanning himself with his hat*). I never thought
    before that wooing was so laborious an exercise; if she
    were worth a million, I have deserv'd her; and now,   210
    me-thinks too, with taking all this pains for her, I begin
    to like her. 'Tis so; I have known many, who never
    car'd for Hare nor Partridge, but those they caught
    themselves would eat heartily: the pains, and the story
    a man tells of the taking of 'em, makes the meat go down   215
    more pleasantly. Besides, last night I had a sweet dream
    of her, and, Gad, she I have once dream'd of, I am stark
    mad till I enjoy her, let her be never so ugly.

Enter Doralice.

Doralice. Who's that you are so mad to enjoy, *Palamede*?
Palamede. You may easily imagine that, sweet *Doralice.*   220
Doralice. More easily then you think I can: I met just now
    with a certain man, who came to you with Letters,
    from a certain old Gentleman, yclipped your father;
    whereby I am given to understand, that to morrow you
    are to take an Oath in the Church to be grave hence-   225
    forward, to go ill-dress'd and slovenly, to get heirs for

190 *éveillé*] sprightly fellow, a gallant.
191 *a tender*] tender feelings.
205 *minuite*] This error for *minute* may suggest Melantha's imperfect
command of French.

your estate, and to dandle 'em for your diversion; and, in short, that Love and Courtship are to be no more.

Palamede. Now have I so much shame to be thus appre-
230   hended in the manner, that I can neither speak nor look upon you; I have abundance of grace in me, that I find: But if you have any spark of true friendship in you, retire a little with me to the next room, that has a couch or bed in't, and bestow your charity upon a poor dying
235   man: a little comfort from a Mistris, before a man is going to give himself in Marriage, is as good as a lusty dose of Strong-water to a dying Malefactour; it takes away the sense of hell, and hanging from him.

Doralice. No, good *Palamede*, I must not be so injurious to
240   your Bride: 'tis ill drawing from the Bank to day, when all your ready money is payable to morrow.

Palamede. A Wife is onely to have the ripe fruit, that falls of it self; but a wise man will always preserve a shaking for a Mistris.

245   *Doralice.* But a Wife for the first quarter is a Mistris.

Palamede. But when the second comes.

Doralice. When it does come, you are so given to variety, that you would make a Wife of me in another quarter.

Palamede. No, never, except I were married to you:
250   marri'd people can never oblige one another; for all they do is duty, and consequently there can be no thanks: but love is more frank and generous then he is honest; he's a liberal giver, but a cursed pay-master.

Doralice. I declare I will have no Gallant; but, if I would,
255   he should never be a marri'd man; a marri'd man is but a Mistris's half-servant, as a Clergy-man is but the King's half-subject: for a man to come to me that smells o'th' Wife! 's life, I wou'd as soon wear her old Gown after her, as her Husband.

260   *Palamede.* Yet 'tis a kind of fashion to wear a Princess cast shoes, you see the Countrey Ladies buy 'em to be fine in them.

Doralice. Yes, a Princess shoes may be worn after her, because they keep their fashion, by being so very little
265   us'd; but generally a marri'd man is the creature of the world the most out of fashion; his behaviour is dumpish, his discourse his wife and family, his habit so much neglected, it looks as if that were marri'd too; his Hat is marri'd, his Perruke is marri'd, his Breeches are

---

237 *Strong-water*] spirits, such as were offered criminals as they were carted to the gallows.

marri'd, and if we could look within his Breeches, we   270
should find him marri'd there too.

Palamede. Am I then to be discarded for ever? pray do but
mark how terrible that word sounds; For ever! it has a
very damn'd sound, *Doralice.*

Doralice. Ay, for ever! it sounds as hellishly to me, as it   275
can do to you, but there's no help for't.

Palamede. Yet if we had but once enjoy'd one another; but
then once onely, is worse then not at all: it leaves a man
with such a lingring after it.

Doralice. For ought I know 'tis better that we have not;   280
we might upon trial have lik'd each other less, as many
a man and woman, that have lov'd as desperately as we,
and yet when they came to possession, have sigh'd, and
cri'd to themselves, Is this all?

Palamede. That is onely, if the Servant were not found a   285
man of this world; but if, upon trial, we had not lik'd
each other, we had certainly left loving; and faith, that's
the greater happiness of the two.

Doralice. 'Tis better as 'tis; we have drawn off already as
much of our Love as would run clear; after possessing,   290
the rest is but jealousies, and disquiets, and quarrelling,
and piecing.

Palamede. Nay, after one great quarrel, there's never any
sound piecing; the love is apt to break in the same place
again.   295

Doralice. I declare I would never renew a love; that's like
him who trims an old Coach for ten years together, he
might buy a new one better cheap.

Palamede. Well, Madam, I am convinc'd, that 'tis best for
us not to have enjoy'd; but Gad, the strongest reason is,   300
because I cann't help it.

Doralice. The onely way to keep us new to one another, is
never to enjoy, as they keep grapes by hanging 'em upon
a line, they must touch nothing if you would preserve
'em fresh.   305

Palamede. But then they wither, and grow dry in the very
keeping; however I shall have a warmth for you, and
an eagerness, every time I see you; and if I chance to
out-live *Melantha* ———

Doralice. And if I chance to out-live *Rhodophil* ———   310

Palamede. Well, I'll cherish my body as much as I can upon
that hope. 'Tis true, I would not directly murder the
wife of my bosome; but to kill her civilly, by the way
of kindness, I'll put as fair as another man: I'll begin to

292 *piecing*] making-up.

353

315   morrow night, and be very wrathful with her, that's
                     resolv'd on.

            Doralice. Well, *Palamede,* here's my hand, I'll venture to
                     be your second Wife, for all your threatnings.

            Palamede. In the mean time I'll watch you hourly, as I
320   would the ripeness of a Melon, and I hope you'll give
                     me leave now and then to look on you, and to see if you
                     are not ready to be cut yet.

            Doralice. No, no, that must not be, *Palamede,* for fear the
                     Gardener should come and catch you taking up the
325   glass.

                       Enter Rhodophil.

           Rhodophil (aside). Billing so sweetly! now I am confirm'd
                     in my suspicions; I must put an end to this, ere it go
                     further.

                  (To Doralice) Cry you mercy, Spouse; I fear I have in-
330   terrupted your recreations.

           Doralice. What recreations?

          Rhodophil. Nay, no excuses, good Spouse; I saw fair hand
                     convey'd to lip, and prest, as though you had been
                     squeezing soft wax together for an Indenture. *Palamede,*
335   you and I must clear this reckoning; why would you
                     have seduc'd my wife?

           Palamede. Why would you have debauch'd my Mistris?

          Rhodophil. What do you think of that civil couple, that
                     play'd at a Game call'd, *Hide and Seek,* last evening, in
340   the Grotto?

          Palamede. What do you think of that innocent pair, who
                     made it their pretence to seek for others, but came,
                     indeed, to hide themselves there?

          Rhodophil. All things consider'd, I begin vehemently to
345   suspect, that the young Gentleman I found in your
                     company last night, was a certain youth of my acquaint-
                     ance.

          Palamede. And I have an odd imagination, that you could
                     never have suspected my small Gallant, if your little
350   villanous *Frenchman* had not been a false Brother.

          Rhodophil. Farther Arguments are needless; Draw off; I
                     shall speak to you now by the way of *Bilbo.*
                         Claps his hand to his sword.

---

320 *Melon*] pumpkin.
325 *glass*] glass placed over young plants for their protection.
334 *Indenture*] impression, with a play on sealing an agreement.
352 *Bilbo*] a common fighter's term for a sword.

Palamede. And I shall answer you by the way of Danger-
field.   *Claps his hand on his.*

Doralice. Hold, hold; are not you two a couple of mad   355
fighting fools, to cut one another's throats for nothing?

Palamede. How for nothing? he courts the woman I must
marry.

Rhodophil. And he courts you whom I have marri'd.

Doralice. But you can neither of you be jealous of what   360
you love not.

Rhodophil. Faith I am jealous, and that makes me partly
suspect that I love you better then I thought.

Doralice. Pish! a meer jealousie of honour.

Rhodophil. Gad I am afraid there's something else in't; for   365
Palamede has wit, and if he loves you, there's something
more in ye then I have found: some rich Mine, for ought
I know, that I have not yet discover'd.

Palamede. 'S life, what's this? here's an argument for me to
love *Melantha*; for he has lov'd her, and he has wit too,   370
and, for ought I know, there may be a Mine: but, if
there be, I am resolv'd I'll dig for't.

Doralice (to Rhodophil). Then I have found my account in
raising your jealousie: O! 'tis the most delicate sharp
sawce to a cloy'd stomach; it will give you a new edge,   375
Rhodophil.

Rhodophil. And a new point too, *Doralice*, if I could be
sure thou art honest.

Doralice. If you are wise, believe me for your own sake:
Love and Religion have but one thing to trust to; that's   380
a good sound faith. Consider, if I have play'd false, you
can never find it out by any experiment you can make
upon me.

Rhodophil. No? Why, suppose I had a delicate screw'd
Gun, if I left her clean, and found her foul, I should   385
discover, to my cost, she had been shot in.

Doralice. But if you left her clean, and found her onely
rusty, you would discover, to your shame, she was onely
so for want of shooting.

Palamede. Rhodophil, you know me too well, to imagine I   390
speak for fear; and therefore in consideration of our
past friendship, I will tell you, and bind it by all things
holy, that *Doralice* is innocent.

Rhodophil. Friend, I will believe you, and vow the same

353–54 *Dangerfield*] the conventional name for a bully and braggart.
371 *Mine*] a land mine, a countermine, in the military sense.
384 *screw'd*] having a screwed or helically grooved bore.

395   for your *Melantha*; but the devil on't is, how we shall
    keep 'em so.
    Palamede. What dost think of a blessed community
    betwixt us four, for the solace of the women, and relief
    of the men? Methinks it would be a pleasant kind of
400   life: Wife and Husband for the standing Dish, and
    Mistris and Gallant for the Desert.
    Rhodophil. But suppose the Wife and the Mistris should
    both long for the standing Dish, how should they be
    satisfi'd together?
405   *Palamede.* In such a case they must draw lots: and yet that
    would not do neither; for they would both be wishing
    for the longest cut!
    Rhodophil. Then I think, *Palamede*, we had as good make a
    firm League, not to invade each other's propriety.
410   *Palamede.* Content, say I. From henceforth let all acts of
    hostility cease betwixt us; and that in the usual form of
    Treaties, as well by Sea as by Land, and in all Fresh
    waters.
    Doralice. I will adde but one *Proviso*, That who ever breaks
415   the League, either by war abroad, or by neglect at home,
    both the Women shall revenge themselves, by the help
    of the other party.
    Rhodophil. That's but reasonable. Come away, *Doralice*; I
    have a great temptation to be sealing Articles in private.
420   *Palamede.* Hast thou so?   *Claps him on the shoulder.*
    Fall on, *Machduff*,
    And curst be he that first cries, Hold, enough.

    Enter Polydamas, Palmyra, Artemis, Argaleon: *after them,*
    Eubulus, *and* Hermogenes, *guarded.*

    Palmyra. Sir, on my knees I beg you.
    Polydamas. Away, I'll hear no more.
    Palmyra. For my dead Mother's sake; you say you lov'd
425   her,
    And tell me I resemble her.
    Thus she had begg'd.
    Polydamas.   And thus had I deny'd her.
    Palmyra. You must be merciful.
    Argaleon.   You must be constant.
    Polydamas. Go, bear 'em to the torture; you have boasted
430   You have a King to head you: I would know
    To whom I must resign.

---

407 cut] F; out Qq

421–22 *Fall . . . enough*] a curious misquotation of *Macbeth*, V.viii.
33–34, not so rendered in Restoration printed versions of *Macbeth*.

Eubulus.   This is our recompence
  For serving thy dead Queen.
Hermogenes.   And education
  Of thy daughter.
Argaleon. You are too modest, in not naming all
  His obligations to you: why did you   435
  Omit his Son, the Prince *Leonidas*?
Polydamas. That Imposture
  I had forgot; their tortures shall be doubled.
Hermogenes. You please me, I shall die the sooner.
Eubulus. No; could I live an age, and still be rack'd,   440
  I still would keep the secret.   *As they are going off,*

                Enter Leonidas, *guarded.*

Leonidas. Oh whither do you hurry innocence!
  If you have any justice, spare their lives;
  Or if I cannot make you just, at least
  I'll teach you to more purpose to be cruel.   445
Palmyra. Alas, what does he seek!
Leonidas. Make me the object of your hate and vengeance!
  Are these decrepid bodies worn to ruine,
  Just ready, of themselves, to fall asunder,
  And to let drop the soul,   450
  Are these fit subjects for a Rack, and Tortures?
  Where would you fasten any hold upon 'em?
  Place pains on me; united fix 'em here;
  I have both youth, and strength, and soul to bear 'em:
  And if they merit death, then I much more;   455
  Since 'tis for me they suffer.
Hermogenes.   Heav'n forbid
  We should redeem our pains, or worthless lives,
  By our exposing yours.
Eubulus. Away with us: Farewell, Sir.
  I onely suffer in my fears for you.   460
Argaleon (aside). So much concern'd for him?
  Then my suspicion's true.   *Whispers the King.*
Palmyra. Hear yet my last request, for poor *Leonidas*;
  Or take my life with his.
Argaleon (to the King). Rest satisfi'd; *Leonidas* is he.   465
Polydamas. I am amaz'd: what must be done?
Argaleon. Command his execution instantly;
  Give him not leisure to discover it;
  He may corrupt the Soldiers.
Polydamas. Hence with that Traitour; bear him to his
    death: 470
  Haste there, and see my will perform'd.

Leonidas. Nay, then I'll die like him the Gods have made
    me.
    Hold, Gentlemen; I am ———
                                Argaleon stops his mouth.
Argaleon. Thou art a Traitor; 'tis not fit to hear thee.
475   *Leonidas.* I say I am the ———   *Getting loose a little.*
    Argaleon. So; gag him, and lead him off.
                                 Again stopping his mouth.
      Leonidas, Hermogenes, Eubulus, *led off.* Polydamas
                          and Argaleon *follow.*
Palmyra. Duty and Love, by turns possess my soul,
    And struggle for a fatal victory:
    I will discover he's the King; Ah, no:
480   That will perhaps save him;
    But then I am guilty of a father's ruine.
    What shall I do, or not do? either way
    I must destroy a Parent, or a Lover.
    Break heart; for that's the least of ills to me,
    And Death the onely cure.   *Swoons.*
485   *Artemis.* Help, help the Princess.
    Rhodophil.   Bear her gently hence,
    Where she may have more succour.
                She is born off, Artemis *follows her.*
                Shouts within, and clashing of swords.
    Palamede.   What noise is that?

               Enter Amalthea, *running.*

Amalthea. Oh, Gentlemen, if you have loyalty,
    Or courage, show it now: *Leonidas*
490   Broke on the sudden from his Guards, and snatching
    A sword from one, his back against the Scaffold,
    Bravely defends himself; and owns aloud
    He is our long lost King; found for this moment,
    But, if your valours help not, lost for ever.
495   Two of his Guards, mov'd by the sense of virtue,
    Are turn'd for him, and there they stand at Bay
    Against an host of foes.
    Rhodophil.   Madam, no more;
    We lose time: my command, or my example,
    May move the Soldiers to the better cause.
500   (*To Palamede*) You'll second me?
    Palamede. Or die with you: no Subject e'r can meet
    A nobler fate, then at his Sovereign's feet.
                                  Exeunt.
         Clashing of swords within, and shouts.

Enter Leonidas, Rhodophil, Palamede, Eubulus,
   Hermogenes, *and their party, victorious,*
    Polydamas *and* Argaleon, *disarm'd.*

Leonidas. That I survive the dangers of this day,
  Next to the Gods, brave friends, be yours the honour.
  And let Heav'n witness for me, that my joy   505
  Is not more great for this my right restor'd,
  Than 'tis, that I have power to recompence
  Your Loyalty and Valour. Let mean Princes
  Of abject souls, fear to reward great actions;
  I mean to show, that whatsoe'r subjects,   510
  Like you, dare merit, a King, like me, dares give.———
Rhodophil. You make us blush, we have deserv'd so little.
Palamede. And yet instruct us how to merit more.
Leonidas. And as I would be just in my rewards,
  So should I in my punishments; these two,   515
  This the Usurper of my Crown, the other
  Of my *Palmyra's* love, deserve that death
  Which both design'd for me.
Polydamas.   And we expect it.
Argaleon. I have too long been happy to live wretched.
Polydamas. And I too long have govern'd, to desire   520
  A life without an Empire.
Leonidas. You are *Palmyra's* father; and as such,
  Though not a King, shall have obedience paid
  From him who is one. Father, in that name,
  All injuries forgot, and duty own'd.   *Embraces him.*   525
Polydamas. O, had I known you could have been this King,
  Thus God-like, great and good, I should have wish'd
  T'have been dethron'd before. 'Tis now I live,
  And more then Reign; now all my joys flow pure,
  Unmix'd with cares, and undisturb'd by conscience.   530

     Enter Palmyra, Amalthea, Artemis, Doralice,
       and Melantha.

Leonidas. See, my *Palmyra* comes! the frighted bloud
  Scarce yet recall'd to her pale cheeks,
  Like the first streaks of light broke loose from darkness,
  And dawning into blushes. ——— (*to Polydamas*) Sir,
    you said,
  Your joys were full; Oh, would you make mine so!   535
  I am but half-restor'd without this blessing.

---

525 *injuries*] Possibly this should mean "all injury's forgot" (Sutherland).

Polydamas. The Gods, and my *Palmyra*, make you happy,
As you make me.   *Gives her hand to* Leonidas.
Palmyra.   Now all my prayers are heard:
I may be dutiful, and yet may love.
540   Virtue, and patience, have at length unravell'd
The knots which Fortune ty'd.
Melantha. Let me die, but I'll congratulate his Majesty:
how admirably well his Royalty becomes him!
Becomes! that is *luy sied*, but our damn'd Language
545   expresses nothing.
Palamede. How? does it become him already? 'twas but
just now you said, he was such a figure of a man.
Melantha. True, my dear, when he was a private man he
was a figure; but since he is a King, methinks he has
550   assum'd another figure: he looks so grand, and so
August.   *Going to the King.*
Palamede. Stay, stay; I'll present you when it is more convenient. I find I must get her a place at Court; and when
she is once there, she can be no longer ridiculous; for
555   she is young enough, and pretty enough, and fool
enough, and *French* enough, to bring up a fashion there
to be affected.
Leonidas (to Rhodophil). Did she then lead you to this brave
attempt?
(To Amalthea) To you, fair *Amalthea*, what I am,
560   And what all these, from me, we joyntly owe:
First, therefore, to your great desert, we give
Your Brother's life; but keep him under guard,
Till our new power be setled. What more grace
He may receive, shall from his future carriage
565   Be given, as he deserves.
Argaleon. I neither now desire, nor will deserve it;
My loss is such as cannot be repair'd,
And to the wretched, life can be no mercy.
Leonidas. Then be a prisoner always: thy ill fate,
570   And pride will have it so: but since, in this, I cannot,
Instruct me, generous *Amalthea*, how
A King may serve you.
Amalthea.   I have all I hope,
And all I now must wish; I see you happy.
Those hours I have to live, which Heav'n in pity
575   Will make but few, I vow to spend with Vestals:
The greatest part, in pray'rs for you; the rest
In mourning my unworthiness.
Press me not farther to explain my self;

'Twill not become me, and may cause you trouble.
Leonidas (*aside*). Too well I understand her secret grief,   580
    But dare not seem to know it. ——— (*to Palmyra*) Come,
      my fairest,
    Beyond my Crown, I have one joy in store;
    To give that Crown to her whom I adore.

                            Exeunt omnes.

579 you] your Qq,F

Epilogue

[*Spoken by* Rhodophil.]

Thus have my Spouse and I inform'd the Nation,
And led you all the way to Reformation.
Not with dull Morals, gravely writ, like those,
Which men of easie Phlegme, with care compose.
5   Your Poet's of stiff words, and limber sense,
Born on the confines of indifference.
But by examples drawn, I dare to say,
From most of you, who hear, and see the Play.
There are more *Rhodophils* in this Theatre,
10   More *Palamedes*, and some few Wives, I fear.
But yet too far our Poet would not run,
Though 'twas well offer'd, there was nothing done.
He would not quite the Women's frailty bare,
But stript 'em to the waste, and left 'em there.
15   And the men's faults are less severely shown,
For he considers that himself is one.
Some stabbing Wits, to bloudy Satyr bent,
Would treat both Sexes with less complement:
Would lay the Scene at home, of Husbands tell,
20   For Wenches, taking up their Wives i'th' Mell,
And a brisk bout which each of them did want,
Made by mistake of Mistris and Gallant.
Our modest Authour, thought it was enough
To cut you off a Sample of the stuff:
25   He spar'd my shame, which you, I'm sure, would not,
For you were all for driving on the Plot:
You sigh'd when I came in to break the sport,
And set your teeth when each design fell short.
To Wives, and Servants all good wishes lend,
30   But the poor Cuckold seldom finds a friend.
Since therefore Court and Town will take no pity,
I humbly cast my self upon the City.

---

13 Women's frailty] Woman's frailty Qq,F; Women faulty CGD

0.1 *Rhodophil*] according to *Covent Garden Drollery* (1672) "Mr. Moon" i.e., Michael Mohun, who played Rhodophil.

20 *Mell*] Pall Mall.

Persons Beliza] *Belisa*
Prologue 29 *Moorcraft*] Moorcraft
I.i.16 Q *lines:* . . . *he* / *Should* . . . *me,*   18 Q *lines:* . . . *gain* / *Is* . . .
pain,   120 dis- / inherited] dis-inherited   151 Beauty] beauty
194 just] Just   291 *Theagenes:*] ∼ ;   292 marri'd;] ∼ :   403
Queen,] ∼ .   441–42 Q *lines:* Sir, believe / That
II.i.10 *étourdy*] *etourdy*   79 *ménnage*] *mennage*   98 field- room]
field- / room   105 News- / monger] News-monger   158 *Fortune*]
Fortune   221 *dérobbée*] *derobbée*   243 Coach- / horses] Coach-
horses   337 Beauties] beauties   391 consider,] ∼ ˄
III.i.209 *Spirituelle*] *Spirituellé*   217 *usé*] *use*   241 *Embarrassé*] *Em-
barrasse* 242 *Béveue*] *Beveue* 243 *d'étourdy*] *d'etourdy* 286 rude,] ∼ .
345–46 one line in Q   415 *Eudoxia's*] *Eudocia's*   416, 419 *Eudoxia*]
Eudocia
III.ii.48 honour:] ∼ ˄   96 *séance*] *seance*
IV.i.90–91 Q *lines:* . . . her, / If you . . . it.   102 Foster-Father] ∼ , ∼
166 help- / meet] help-meet   192 I˄] ∼ ,
IV.iii.15 Park- / time] Park- / time   98 *dérobbée*] *derobbée*   141
esclave] *esclaue*
V.i.40 Father] Fathet   98, 106 *naiveté*] *naivete*   99 *let me die*] let me
die   103 Madam,] ∼ ˄   136 *d'étourdi*] *d'etourdi*   153 *désespéré*]
desesperé   160 *l'enragée*] *l'enrage*   171 *minouet*] *minouét*   176, 177
séjours] *sejours*   190 *éveillé*] *eveille*   199 *Francais*] *Francois*
202 *réserve*] *reserve*   354 Danger- / field] Danger-field   407
cut!] ∼ ?   426–27 Q *lines:* And . . . she / Had begg'd.   461–62
Q *lines:* my / Suspicion's   486–87 Q *lines:* Bear . . . may / Have
493 King; . . . moment,]∼, . . . ∼ ;   510–11 Q *lines* show, /
That . . . subjects, / Like . . .   542–43 Q *lines:* Let . . . his / Majesty
. . . Royalty / Becomes . . .

Press Variants in Q1
Sheet F (inner forme)
Corrected: TxU
Uncorrected: CCC, ICU

Sig. F2
III.i.202 concernment] concerment

Sheet K (inner forme)
Corrected: BM², ICU, TxU
Uncorrected: BM¹, CCC

Sig. K1ᵛ
IV.iv.79 *last line unindented*] *last line indented*
Sig. K2
IV.iv.82 a dang'rous] a da dang'rous

Bibliography

ALLEN, NED BLISS. "The Sources of Dryden's *The Mock Astrologer*," *Philological Quarterly*, XXVI (1957), 453–64.

——. *The Sources of John Dryden's Comedies*. Ann Arbor, Mich., 1935.

AVERY, EMMETT L., SCOUTEN, ARTHUR H., VAN LENNEP, WILLIAM, et al. *The London Stage 1660–1800: A Calendar of Plays*. 8 vols. published. Carbondale, Ill., 1960—.

BATESON, F. W. "Comedy of Manners," *Essays in Criticism*, I (1950), 89–93.

BOWERS, FREDSON. "Current Theories of Copy-Text, with an Illustration from Dryden," *Modern Philology*, XLVIII (1950), 12–20.

——. "The Text of This Edition," *The Dramatic Works in the Beaumont and Fletcher Canon*. Cambridge, 1966.

——. *A Supplement to the Woodward and McManaway Check List of English Plays 1641–1700*. Charlottesville, Va., 1949.

BROOKS, HAROLD. "Some Notes on Dryden, Cowley and Shadwell," *Notes and Queries*, CLXVIII (1935), 94–95.

CIBBER, COLLEY. *An Apology for the Life of Mr. Colley Cibber, Comedian*. Edited by Robert W. Lowe. 2 vols. London, 1889.

COTGRAVE, RANDALL. *A Dictionarie of the French and English Tongues*. London, 1611.

COTTON, CHARLES. *The Compleat Gamester*. Reprinted in *Games and Gamesters of the Restoration*. Edited by C. H. Hartmann. London, 1930.

B[EHN], A[PHRA, collector]. *Covent Garden Drollery* (based on the revised edition of 1672). Edited by G. Thorn-Drury. London, 1928.

——. *Covent Garden Drollery* (partly from the unrevised edition of 1672 and partly from the revised edition). Edited by Montague Summers. London, 1927.

DOBELL, P. J. *John Dryden, Bibliographical Memoranda*. London, 1922.

DOBRÉE, BONAMY. *John Dryden* ("Writers and Their Work.") London, 1956.

——. *Restoration Comedy, 1660–1720*. Oxford, 1924.

DOWNES, JOHN. *Roscius Anglicanus; or, An Historical Review of the Stage from 1660–1706*. Edited by Montague Summers. London, [1928].

DRYDEN, JOHN. *Dryden: The Dramatic Works*. Edited by Montague Summers. 6 vols. London, 1931–32.

——. *Marriage à la Mode*. Edited by J. R. Sutherland. London, 1934.

——. *Of Dramatic Poesy and Other Critical Essays*. Edited by George Watson. 2 vols. London, 1962.

——. *The Selected Dramas of John Dryden*. Edited by George R. Noyes. Chicago, 1910.

——. *The Songs of John Dryden*. Edited by Cyrus Lawrence Day. Cambridge, Mass., 1932.

————. *The Works of John Dryden*. Edited by Sir Walter Scott, revised and corrected by George Saintsbury. 18 vols. Edinburgh, 1882–93.

————. *The Works of John Dryden*. Vol. VIII. Edited by John Harrington Smith, Dougald MacMillan, and Vinton A. Dearing. Vol. IX. Edited by John Lofts and Vinton A. Dearing. Berkeley and Los Angeles, 1962, 1966.

EMPSON, WILLIAM. *Some Versions of Pastoral*. London, 1935. (Retitled *English Pastoral Poetry*. New York, 1938.)

EVELYN, JOHN. *Diary*. Edited by E. S. de Beer. 6 vols. Oxford, 1955.

FARMER, JOHN S. and HENLEY, W. E. *Slang and Its Analogues*. 7 vols. London, 1890–1904.

FUJIMURA, THOMAS. *Restoration Comedy of Wit*. Princeton, 1952.

HEINSIUS, DANIEL. *Q. Horati Flacci Opera*. Leyden, 1612.

GREG, W. W. "The Rationale of Copy-Text," *Studies in Bibliography*, III (1950–51), 19–36.

HOLLAND, NORMAN. *The First Modern Comedies, The Significance of Etherege, Wycherley, and Congreve*. Cambridge, Mass., 1959.

HORACE. *Satires, Epistles, and Ars Poetica*. Translated by H. R. Fairclough. London, 1926.

JUVENAL. *Juvenal and Persius*. Translated by G. G. Ramsay. London, 1912.

KING, BRUCE. *Dryden's Major Plays*. Edinburgh, 1966.

————. "Dryden's *Marriage a la Mode*" *Drama Survey*, IV (1965), 28–37.

KNIGHTS, L. C. "Restoration Comedy: The Reality and the Myth," *Scrutiny*, VI (1937), 122–43.

LYNCH, KATHLEEN. *The Social Mode of Restoration Comedy*. New York, 1926.

MACDONALD, HUGH. *John Dryden: A Bibliography of Early Editions and of Drydeniana*. Oxford, 1939.

MARTIAL. *Epigrams*. Translated by W. C. A. Ker. 2 vols. London, 1919–20.

METTLER, CECILIA CHARLOTTE. *History of Medicine, a Correlative Text Arranged according to Subjects*. Philadelphia, 1947.

MONK, SAMUEL. *John Dryden: A List of Critical Studies*. Minneapolis, 1950.

MOORE, FRANK HARPER. *The Nobler Pleasure: Dryden's Comedy in Theory and Practice*. Chapel Hill, N.C., 1963.

NICOLL, ALLARDYCE. *Restoration Drama, 1660–1700*. Fourth edition, revised. Cambridge, 1952.

OSBORN, JAMES. *John Dryden: Some Biographical Facts and Problems*. Revised edition. Gainsville, Fla., 1965.

PENDLEBURY, B. J. *Dryden's Heroic Plays, a Study of the Origins*. London, 1923.

PEPYS, SAMUEL. *The Diary of Samuel Pepys*. Transcribed by Rev. Mynors Bright, edited with additions by Henry B. Wheatley. 10 vols. London, 1893–99.

PINTO, VIVIAN DE SOLA. *Enthusiast of Wit: A Portrait of John Wilmot Earl of Rochester 1647–1680*. Lincoln, Nebr., 1962.

POPE, ALEXANDER *et al. The Art of Sinking in Poetry; Martinus*

Scriblerus' περὶ βάδος. Edited by Edna Leake Steeves. New York, 1952.

QUINTILIAN. *The Instituto Oratoria.* Edited and translated by H. E. Butler. 4 vols. London, 1920.

RICHMOND, HUGH M. *The School of Love; the Evolution of the Stuart Lyric.* Princeton, 1964.

ROSENBERG, HAROLD. "Character Change and the Drama" in *The Tradition of the New.* New York, 1959.

SCUDÉRY, MADELEINE DE. *Artamène, ou le Grand Cyrus.* 10 vols. Paris, 1649–53. English edition, translated by F. G. 5 vols. London, 1653–55.

———. *Ibrahim, ou l'Illustre Bassa.* Paris, 1641. English edition, translated by H. Cogan. London, 1652. Second edition, London, 1674.

SMITH, JOHN HARRINGTON. "Dryden and Buckingham: The Beginnings of the Feud," *Modern Language Notes,* LXIX (1954), 242–45.

———. *The Gay Couple in Restoration Comedy.* Cambridge, Mass., 1948.

SOUTHERN, RICHARD. *Changeable Scenery, Its Origin and Development in the British Theatre.* London, 1952.

TROWBRIDGE, HOYT. "The Place of Rules in Dryden's Criticism," *Modern Philology,* XLIV (1946), 84–96.

VIRGIL. *Virgil.* Translated by H. R. Fairclough. 2 vols. London, 1918.

WARD, CHARLES E. *The Life of John Dryden.* Chapel Hill, N. C., 1961.

WILSON, JOHN HAROLD. *All the King's Ladies; Actresses of the Restoration.* Chicago, 1958.

———. *A Preface to Restoration Drama.* Boston, 1965.

WOODWARD, GERTRUDE L. and MCMANAWAY, JAMES G. *A Check List of English Plays 1641–1700.* Chicago, 1945.